D0205842

The Jewish Century

The Jewish Century

Yuri Slezkine

PRINCETON UNIVERSITY PRESS
PRINCETON AND OXFORD

Copyright © 2004 by Princeton University Press
Published by Princeton University Press, 41 William Street,
Princeton, New Jersey 08540
In the United Kingdom: Princeton University Press,
3 Market Place, Woodstock, Oxfordshire OX20 1SY

Library of Congress Cataloging-in-Publication Data

Slezkine, Yuri, 1956–
The Jewish century / Yuri Slezkine.
p.   cm.
Includes bibliographical references and index.
ISBN 0-691-11995-3 (alk. paper)
1. Jews—Europe—Economic conditions. 2. Jews—Europe—Social conditions.
3. Jews—Russia—Economic conditions—19th century. 4. Jews—Russia—Economic
conditions—20th century. 5. Jews—Russia—Social conditions—19th century. 6. Jews—
Russia—Social conditions—20th century. 7. Russia—Ethnic relations. 8. Russia—
Civilization—Jewish influences. 9. Civilization, Modern—Jewish influences.
10. Social integration—Russia. 11. Capitalism—Social aspects. 12. Entrepreneurship—
Social aspects. I. Title.
DS140.5.S59   2004
940′.04924—dc22   2003069322

British Library Cataloging-in-Publication Data is available

This book has been composed in Galliard text with Bodega Sans Display

Printed on acid-free paper. ∞

pup.princeton.edu

Printed in the United States of America

1   3   5   7   9   10   8   6   4   2

Contents

Preface

Growing up in the Soviet Union, I was close to both my grandmothers. One, Angelina Ivanovna Zhdanovich, was born to a gentry family, attended an institute for noble maidens, graduated from the Maly Theater acting school in Moscow, and was overtaken by the Red Army in Vladikavkaz in 1920. She took great pride in her Cossack ancestors and lost everything she owned in the revolution. At the end of her life, she was a loyal Soviet citizen at peace with her past and at home in her country. The other, Berta (Brokhe) Iosifovna Kostrinskaia, was born in the Pale of Settlement, never graduated from school, went to prison as a Communist, emigrated to Argentina, and returned in 1931 to take part in the building of socialism. In her old age, she took great pride in her Jewish ancestors and considered most of her life to have been a mistake. This book is dedicated to her memory.

Acknowledgments

Various drafts of this book have been read by numerous friends and colleagues: Margaret Lavinia Anderson, Andrew E. Barshay, David Biale, Victoria E. Bonnell, Rogers Brubaker, John M. Efron, Terence Emmons, Sheila Fitzpatrick, Gregory Freidin, Gabriele Freitag, Jon Gjerde, Konstantin Gurevich, Benjamin Harshav, David A. Hollinger, Sergey Ivanov, Joachim Klein, Masha Lipman, Lisa Little, Martin Malia, Tim McDaniel, Elizabeth McGuire, Joel Mokyr, Eric Naiman, Norman M. Naimark, Benjamin Nathans, Irina Paperno, Igor Primakov, Nicholas V. Riasanovsky, Irwin Scheiner, James J. Sheehan, Peter Slezkine, Ronald Grigor Suny, Maria Volkenshtein, Edward W. Walker, Amir Weiner, Wen-hsin Yeh, Victor Zaslavsky, Reginald E. Zelnik, and Viktor M. Zhivov. Most of them disagreed with some of my arguments, some disagreed with most, and none (except for Lisa Little, who vowed to share all, and Peter Slezkine, who has no choice) is responsible for any. Two people deserve special mention: Gabriele Freitag, whose dissertation and conversation gave me the idea to write this book, and Benjamin Harshav, whose book *Language in Time of Revolution* suggested the structure of the last chapter and the concept of the "Jewish Century." Two seminars, at the University of Chicago and Stanford University, resulted in several substantive revisions. Several presentations—at Berkeley, Harvard, Vassar, Yale, and the Center for Advanced Judaic Studies at the University of Pennsylvania—led to useful discussions. A number of colleagues, including Jamsheed K. Choksy, István Deák, David Frick, Donghui He, Andrew C. Janos, Tabitha M. Kanogo, Brian E. Kassof, Peter Kenez, G. V. Kostyrchenko, Matthew Lenoe, Ethan M. Pollock, Frank E. Sysyn, and Frederic E. Wakeman, Jr., helped by responding to specific queries. At Princeton University Press, Brigitta van Rheinberg presided over the project, Lauren Lepow improved the text, and Alison Kalett attended to every detail.

The funding for the research and writing was provided by the National Endowment for the Humanities, the John Simon Guggenheim Memorial Foundation, and the Center for Advanced Study in the Behavioral Sciences (which also supplied good weather and much lively companionship). Eleonor Gilburd was an incomparable research assistant; Jarrod Tanny was a great help in the final stages of writing; Vassar College, Pinar Batur, and John M. Vander-Lippe combined to make the spring semester of 2002 pleasant as well as productive; and the History Department at Berkeley has been, for over a decade, an extremely enjoyable and stimulating place to work.

The Jewish Century

The Modern Age is the Jewish Age, and the twentieth century, in particular, is the Jewish Century. Modernization is about everyone becoming urban, mobile, literate, articulate, intellectually intricate, physically fastidious, and occupationally flexible. It is about learning how to cultivate people and symbols, not fields or herds. It is about pursuing wealth for the sake of learning, learning for the sake of wealth, and both wealth and learning for their own sake. It is about transforming peasants and princes into merchants and priests, replacing inherited privilege with acquired prestige, and dismantling social estates for the benefit of individuals, nuclear families, and book-reading tribes (nations). Modernization, in other words, is about everyone becoming Jewish.

Some peasants and princes have done better than others, but no one is better at being Jewish than the Jews themselves. In the age of capital, they are the most creative entrepreneurs; in the age of alienation, they are the most experienced exiles; and in the age of expertise, they are the most proficient professionals. Some of the oldest Jewish specialties—commerce, law, medicine, textual interpretation, and cultural mediation—have become the most fundamental (and the most Jewish) of all modern pursuits. It is by being exemplary ancients that the Jews have become model moderns.

The principal religion of the Modern Age is nationalism, a faith that represents the new society as the old community and allows newly urbanized princes and peasants to feel at home abroad. Every state must be a tribe; every tribe must have a state. Every land is promised, every language Adamic, every capital Jerusalem, and every people chosen (and ancient). The Age of Nationalism, in other words, is about every nation becoming Jewish.

In nineteenth-century Europe (the birthplace of the Age of Nationalism), the greatest exception was the Jews themselves. The most successful of all modern tribes, they were also the most vulnerable. The greatest beneficiaries of the Age of Capitalism, they would become the greatest victims of the Age of Nationalism. More desperate than any other European nation for state protection, they were the least likely to receive it because no European nation-state could possibly claim to be the embodiment of the Jewish nation. Most European nation-states, in other words, contained citizens who combined spectacular success with irredeemable tribal foreignness. The Jewish Age was also the Age of anti-Semitism.

All the main modern (antimodern) prophecies were also solutions to the Jewish predicament. Freudianism, which was predominantly Jewish, proclaimed the beleaguered loneliness of the newly "emancipated" to be a universal human condition and proposed a course of treatment that applied liberal checks and balances (managed imperfection) to the individual human soul. Zionism, the most eccentric of all nationalisms, argued that the proper way to overcome Jewish vulnerability was not for everyone else to become like the Jews but for the Jews to become like everyone else. Marx's own Marxism began with the proposition that the world's final emancipation from Jewishness was possible only through a complete destruction of capitalism (because capitalism was naked Jewishness). And of course Nazism, the most brutally consistent of all nationalisms, believed that the creation of a seamless national community was possible only through a complete destruction of the Jews (because Jewishness was naked cosmopolitanism).

One reason the twentieth century became the Jewish Century is that Hitler's attempt to put his vision into practice led to the canonization of the Nazis as absolute evil and the reemergence of the Jews as universal victims. The other reasons have to do with the collapse of the Russian Empire's Pale of Settlement and the three messianic pilgrimages that followed: the Jewish migration to the United States, the most consistent version of liberalism; the Jewish migration to Palestine, the Promised Land of secularized Jewishness; and the Jewish migration to the cities of the Soviet Union, a world free of both capitalism and tribalism (or so it seemed).

This book is an attempt to tell the story of the Jewish Age and explain its origins and implications. Chapter 1 discusses diaspora

Jewish life in a comparative perspective; chapter 2 describes the transformation of peasants into Jews and Jews into Frenchmen, Germans, and others; chapter 3 focuses on the Jewish Revolution within the Russian Revolution; and chapter 4 follows the daughters of Tevye the Milkman to the United States, Palestine, and—most particularly—Moscow. The book ends at the end of the Jewish Century—but not at the end of the Jewish Age.

The individual chapters are quite different in genre, style, and size (growing progressively by a factor of two but stopping mercifully at four altogether). The reader who does not like chapter 1 may like chapter 2 (and the other way around). The reader who does not like chapters 1 and 2 may like chapter 3. The reader who does not like chapters 1, 2, and 3 may not benefit from trying to carry on.

Finally, this book is about Jews as much as it is about the Jewish Century. "Jews," for the purposes of this story, are the members of traditional Jewish communities (Jews by birth, faith, name, language, occupation, self-description, and formal ascription) and their children and grandchildren (whatever their faith, name, language, occupation, self-description, or formal ascription). The main purpose of the story is to describe what happened to Tevye's children, no matter what they thought of Tevye and his faith. The central subjects of the story are those of Tevye's children who abandoned him and his faith and were, for a time and for that reason, forgotten by the rest of the family.

Chapter 1

MERCURY'S SANDALS: THE JEWS AND OTHER NOMADS

Let Ares doze, that other war
Is instantly declared once more
'Twixt those who follow
Precocious Hermes all the way
And those who without qualms obey
Pompous Apollo.

—W. H. Auden, "Under Which Lyre"

There was nothing particularly unusual about the social and economic position of the Jews in medieval and early modern Europe. Many agrarian and pastoral societies contained groups of permanent strangers who performed tasks that the natives were unable or unwilling to perform. Death, trade, magic, wilderness, money, disease, and internal violence were often handled by people who claimed—or were assigned to—different gods, tongues, and origins. Such specialized foreigners could be procured sporadically as individual slaves, scribes, merchants, or mercenaries, or they could be permanently available as demographically complete endogamous descent groups. They might have been allowed or forced to specialize in certain jobs because they were ethnic strangers, or they might have become ethnic strangers because they specialized in certain jobs—either way, they combined renewable ethnicity with a dangerous occupation. In India, such self-reproducing but not self-sufficient communities formed a complex symbolic and economic hierarchy; elsewhere, they led a precarious and sometimes ghostly existence as outcasts without a religiously sanctioned caste system.

In medieval Korea, the Koli such'ok and Hwach'ok-chaein peoples were employed as basket weavers, shoemakers, hunters, butchers, sorcerers, torturers, border guards, buffoons, dancers, and puppeteers. In Ashikaga and Tokugawa Japan, the Eta specialized in animal slaughter, public executions, and mortuary services, and the Hinin monopolized begging, prostitution, juggling, dog training, and snake charming. In early twentieth-century Africa, the Yibir practiced magic, surgery, and leatherwork among the Somalis; the Fuga of southern Ethiopia were ritual experts and entertainers as well as wood-carvers and potters; and throughout the Sahel, Sahara, and Sudan, traveling blacksmiths often doubled as cattle dealers, grave diggers, circumcisers, peddlers, jewelers, musicians, and conflict mediators. In Europe, various "Gypsy" and "Traveler" groups specialized in tinsmithing, knife sharpening, chimney sweeping, horse dealing, fortune-telling, jewelry making, itinerant trading, entertainment, and scavenging (including begging, stealing, and the collection of scrap metal and used clothing for resale).

Most itinerant occupations were accompanied by exchange, and some "stranger" minorities became professional merchants. The Sheikh Mohammadi of eastern Afghanistan followed seasonal migration routes to trade manufactured goods for agricultural produce; the Humli-Khyampa of far western Nepal bartered Tibetan salt for Nepalese rice; the Yao from the Lake Malawi area opened up an important segment of the Indian Ocean trade network; and the Kooroko of Wasulu (in present-day Mali) went from being pariah blacksmiths to Wasulu-wide barterers to urban merchants to large-scale commercial kola nut distributors.[1]

Outcast-to-capitalist careers were not uncommon elsewhere in Africa and in much of Eurasia. Jewish, Armenian, and Nestorian (Assyrian) entrepreneurs parlayed their transgressor expertise into successful commercial activities even as the majority of their service-oriented kinsmen continued to ply traditional low-status trades as peddlers, cobblers, barbers, butchers, porters, blacksmiths, and moneylenders. Most of the world's long-distance trade was dominated by politically and militarily sponsored diasporas— Hellene, Phoenician, Muslim, Venetian, Genoese, Portuguese, Dutch, and British, among others—but there was always room for unprotected and presumably neutral strangers. Just as an itinerant Sheikh Mohammadi peddler could sell a bracelet to a secluded Pashtun woman or mediate between two warriors without jeopardizing their honor, the Jewish entrepreneur could cross the Christian-Muslim divide, serve as an army contractor, or engage in tabooed but much-needed "usury." In the sixteenth and seventeenth centuries, Armenian merchants presided over a dense commercial network that connected the competing Ottoman, Safavid, Mughal, Russian, and Dutch empires by making use of professionally trained agents, standardized contracts, and detailed manuals on international weights, measures, tariffs, and prices. In the eighteenth century, the clashing interests of the Russian and Ottoman empires were ably represented by Baltic German and Phanariot Greek diplomats.[2]

Internally, too, strangeness could be an asset. By not intermarrying, fraternizing, or fighting with their hosts, outcast communities were the symbolic equivalents of eunuchs, monks, and celibate or hereditary priests insofar as they remained outside the traditional web of kinship obligations, blood friendships, and family feuds. The strictly endogamous Inadan gunsmiths and jewelers of the Sahara could officiate at Tuareg weddings, sacrifices, child-naming ceremonies, and victory celebrations because they were not subject to the Tuareg avoidance rules, marriage politics, and dignity requirements. Similarly, the Nawar peddlers allowed the Rwala Bedouin households to exchange delicate information with their neighbors; the Armenian "Amira" provided the Ottoman court with trustworthy tax farmers, mint superintendents, and gunpowder manufacturers; and Jewish leaseholders and innkeepers made it possible for Polish landowners to squeeze profits from their serfs without abandoning the rhetoric of patriarchal reciprocity.[3]

The rise of European colonialism created more and better-specialized strangers as mercantile capitalism encroached on previously unmonetized regional exchange systems and peasant economies. In India, the Parsis of Bombay and Gujarat became the principal commercial intermediaries between the Europeans, the Indian hinterland, and the Far East. Descendants of eighth-century Zoroastrian refugees from Muslim-dominated Iran, they formed a closed, endogamous, self-administered community that remained outside the Hindu caste system and allowed for relatively greater mobility. Having started out as peddlers, weavers, carpenters, and liquor purveyors, with the arrival of the Europeans in the sixteenth century they moved into brokering, moneylending, shipbuilding, and international commerce. By the mid–nineteenth century, the Parsis had become Bombay's leading bankers, industrialists, and professionals, as well as India's most proficient English-speakers and most determined practitioners of Western social rituals.

In the second half of the nineteenth century, more than two million Chinese followed European capital to Southeast Asia (where they found numerous earlier colonies), the Indian Ocean, Africa, and the Americas. Some of them went as indentured laborers, but the majority (including many erstwhile "coolies") moved into the service sector, eventually dominating Southeast Asian trade and industry. In East Africa, the "middleman" niche between the European elite and the indigenous nomads and agriculturalists was occupied by the Indians, who were brought in after 1895 to build (or die building) the Uganda Railway but ended up monopolizing retail trade, clerical jobs, and many urban professions. Hindus, Muslims, Sikhs, Jains, and Goan Catholics from a variety of castes, they all became *baniyas* (traders). Similar choices were made by Lebanese and Syrian Christians (and some Muslims) who went to West Africa, the United States, Latin America, and the Caribbean. The majority started out as peddlers (the "coral men" of the African "bush" or *mescates* of the Brazilian interior), then opened permanent shops, and eventually branched out into industry, banking, real estate, transportation, politics, and entertainment. Wherever the Lebanese went, they had a good chance of facing some competition from Armenians, Greeks, Jews, Indians, or Chinese, among others.[4]

All these groups were nonprimary producers specializing in the delivery of goods and services to the surrounding agricultural or pastoral populations. Their principal resource base was human, not natural, and their expertise was in "foreign" affairs. They were the descendants—or predecessors—of Hermes (Mercury), the god of all those who did not herd animals, till the soil, or live by the sword;

the patron of rule breakers, border crossers, and go-betweens; the protector of people who lived by their wit, craft, and art.

Most traditional pantheons had trickster gods analogous to Hermes, and most societies had members (guilds or tribes) who looked to them for sanction and assistance. Their realm was enormous but internally coherent, for it lay entirely on the margins. Hermes' name derives from the Greek word for "stone heap," and his early cult was primarily associated with boundary markers. Hermes' protégés communicated with spirits and strangers as magicians, morticians, merchants, messengers, sacrificers, healers, seers, minstrels, craftsmen, interpreters, and guides—all closely related activities, as sorcerers were heralds, heralds were sorcerers, and artisans were artful artificers, as were traders, who were also sorcerers and heralds. They were admired but also feared and despised by their food-producing and food-plundering (aristocratic) hosts both on and off Mount Olympus. Whatever they brought from abroad could be marvelous, but it was always dangerous: Hermes had the monopoly on round-trips to Hades; Prometheus, another artful patron of artisans, brought the most marvelous and dangerous gift of all; Hephaestus, the divine blacksmith, created Pandora, the first woman and source of all the trouble and temptation in the world; and the two Roman gods of the boundary (besides Mercury) were Janus, the two-faced sponsor of beginnings whose name meant "doorway," and Silvanus, the supervisor of the savage (*silvaticus*) world beyond the threshold.[5]

One could choose to emphasize heroism, dexterity, deviousness, or foreignness, but what all of Hermes' followers had in common was their mercuriality, or impermanence. In the case of nations, it meant that they were all transients and wanderers—from fully nomadic Gypsy groups, to mostly commercial communities divided into fixed brokers and traveling agents, to permanently settled populations who thought of themselves as exiles. Whether they knew no homeland, like the Irish Travelers or the Sheikh Mohammadi, had lost it, like the Armenians and the Jews, or had no political ties to it, like the Overseas Indians or Lebanese, they were perpetual resident aliens and vocational foreigners (the Javanese word for "trader," *wong dagang*, also means "foreigner" and "wanderer," or "tramp"). Their origin myths and symbolic destinations were always different from those of their clients—and so were their dwellings, which were either mobile or temporary. A Jewish house in Ukraine did not resemble the peasant hut next door, not because it was Jewish in architecture (there was no such thing) but because it was never painted, mended, or decorated. It did not belong to the landscape; it was a dry husk that contained the real treasure—the children of Israel and their memory. All nomads defined themselves in genealogical terms; most "service nomads" persisted in doing so in the midst of dominant agrarian societies that sacralized space. They were people wedded to time, not land; people seen as both homeless and historic, rootless and "ancient."[6]

Whatever the sources of difference, it was the fact of difference that mattered the most. Because only strangers could do certain dangerous, marvelous, and distasteful things, the survival of people specializing in such things depended on their success at being strangers. According to Brian L. Foster, for example, in the early 1970s the Mon people of Thailand were divided into rice farmers and river traders. The farmers referred to themselves as Thai, spoke little Mon, and claimed to speak even less; the traders called themselves Mon, spoke mostly Mon, and claimed to speak even more. The farmers were frequently unsure whether they were of Mon ancestry; the traders were quite sure that their farmer clients were not (or they would not have been their clients). Everyone involved agreed that it was impossible to engage in commerce without being crooked; being crooked meant acting in ways that farmers considered unbecoming a fellow villager. "In fact, a trader who was subject to the traditional social obligations and constraints would find it very difficult to run a viable business. . . . It would be difficult for him to refuse credit, and it would not be possible to collect debts. If he followed the ideology strictly, he would not even try to make a profit."[7]

To cite an earlier injunction to the same effect, "Thou shalt not lend upon usury to thy brother; usury of money, usury of victuals, usury of any thing that is lent upon usury: Unto a stranger thou mayest lend upon usury; but unto thy brother thou shalt not lend upon usury: that the Lord thy God may bless thee in all that thou settest thine hand to in the land whither thou goest to possess it" (Deut. 23:19–20). This meant—among other things—that if thou set thine hand to credit operations, thou had to play the trespasser (or submit to domestication through various "clientelization" and "blood brotherhood" techniques).

In the eyes of the rural majority, all craftsmen were crafty, and all merchants, mercenary (both—as was Mercury himself—derived from *merx*, "goods"). And of course Hermes was a thief. Accordingly, European traders and artisans were usually segregated in special urban communities; in some Andean villages in today's Ecuador, store owners are often Protestants; and one Chinese shopkeeper observed by L. A. Peter Gosling in a Malay village "appeared to be considerably acculturated to Malay culture, and was scrupulously sensitive to Malays in every way, including the normal wearing of sarong, quiet and polite Malay speech, and a humble and affable manner. However, at harvest time when he would go to the field to collect crops on which he had advanced credit, he would put on his Chinese costume of shorts and under-shirt, and speak in a much more abrupt fashion, acting, as one Malay farmer put it, 'just like a Chinese.' "[8]

Noblesse oblige, and so most mercurial strangers make a point—and perhaps a virtue—of not doing as the Romans do. The Chinese unsettle the Malays by being *kasar* (crude); the Inadan make a mockery of the Tuareg notions of dignified behavior (*takarakayt*); the Japanese Burakumin claim to be unable to control their emotions; and Jewish shopkeepers in Europe rarely failed to impress the Gentiles with their unseemly urgency and volubility ("the wife, the daughter, the servant, the dog, all howl in your ears," as Sombart quotes approvingly). Gypsies, in particular, seem to offend against business rationality by offending the sensibilities of their customers. They can "pass" when they find it expedient to do so, but much more often they choose to play up their foreignness by preferring bold speech, bold manners, and bold colors—sometimes as part of elaborate public displays of defiant impropriety.[9]

What makes such spectacles especially offensive to host populations is that so many of the offenders are women. In traditional societies, foreigners are dangerous, disgusting, or ridiculous because they break the rules, and no rules are more important in the breach than the ones regulating sexual life and the sexual division of labor. Foreign women, in particular, are either promiscuous or downtrodden, and often "beautiful" (by virtue of being promiscuous or downtrodden and because foreign women are both cause and prize of much warrior activity). But of course some foreigners are more foreign than others, and the internal ones are very foreign indeed because they are full-time, professional, and ideologically committed rule breakers. Traders among sharers, nomads among peasants, or tribes among nations, they frequently appear as mirror images of their hosts—sometimes quite brazenly and deliberately so, as many of them are professional jesters, fortune-tellers, and carnival performers. This means, as far as the hosts are concerned, that their women and men have a tendency to change places—a perception that is partly a variation on the "perversity of strangers" theme but mostly a function of occupational differences. Traders and nomads assign more visible and economically important roles to women than do peasants or warriors, and some trading nomads depend primarily on women's labor (while remaining patriarchal in political organization). The Kanjar of Pakistan, who specialize in toy making, singing, dancing, begging, and prostitution, derive most of their annual income from female work, as do many European Gypsy groups that emphasize begging and fortune-telling. In both of these cases, and in some merchant communities such as the Eastern European Jewish market traders, women are vital links to the outside world (as performers, stall attendants, or negotiators) and are often considered sexually provocative or socially aggressive—a perception they occasionally reinforce by deliberate displays.[10]

The same purpose is served by demonstrative male nonbelligerence, which is both a necessary condition for the pursuit of stranger occupations and an important indication of continued strangeness (a refusal to fight, like a refusal to accept hospitality, is an effective way of setting oneself apart from the usual conventions of cross-cultural interaction). The Burakumin, Inadan, and Gypsies may be seen as "passionate" or "spontaneous" in the way children and pranksters are; what matters is that they are not expected to have warrior honor. To be competitive as functional eunuchs, monks, confessors, or jesters, they cannot be seen as complete men. And so they were not. According to Vasilii Rozanov, one of Russia's most articulate fin de siècle anti-Semites, all Jewish qualities stemmed from "their femininity—their devotion, cleaving, their almost erotic attachment, to the particular person each one of them is dealing with, as well as to the tribe, atmosphere, landscape, and everyday life that they are surrounded by (as witness both the prophets' reproaches and the obvious facts)."[11] Hermes was as physically weak as he was clever (with cleverness serving as compensation for weakness); Hephaestus was lame, ugly, and comically inept at everything except prodigious handicraft; the clairvoyant metalworkers of Germanic myths were hunchbacked dwarves with oversized heads; and all of them—along with the tradesmen they patronized—were associated with dissolute, dangerous, and adulterous sexuality. The three images—bloodless neutrality, female eroticism, and Don Juan rakishness—were combined in various proportions and applied in different degrees, but what they all shared was the glaring absence of dignified manliness.

It is not only images, however, that make strangers—it is also actions; and of all human actions, two are universally seen as defining humanity and community: eating and procreating. Strangers (enemies) are people with whom one does not eat or intermarry; radical strangers (savages) are people who eat filth and fornicate like wild animals. The most common way to convert a foreigner into a friend is to partake of his food and "blood"; the surest way to remain a foreigner is to refuse to do so.[12]

All service nomads are endogamous, and many of them observe dietary restrictions that make fraternizing with their neighbors/clients impossible (and thus service occupations conceivable). Only Phinehas's act of atonement could save the children of Israel from the Lord's wrath when "the people began to commit whoredom with the daughters of Moab," and one man in particular brought "a Midianitish woman in the sight of Moses." For he (Phinehas, the son of Eleazar, the son of Aaron, the priest) "took a javelin in his hand, and he went after the man of Israel into the tent, and thrust both of them through, the man of Israel, and the woman through her belly. So the plague was stayed from the children of Israel" (Num. 25:1–18). Elsewhere, men had a reasonable chance of escaping punishment, but in most traditional Jewish and Gypsy communities, a woman's marriage to an outsider signified irredeemable defilement and resulted in excommunication and symbolic death. There was nothing unusual about Phinehas's act at a time when all gods were jealous; there was something peculiar about a continued commitment to endogamy amid the divinely sanctioned whoredom of religious universalism.

Food taboos are less lethal but more evident as everyday boundary markers. No Jew could accept non-Jewish hospitality or retain his ritual purity in an alien environment; the craftsmen and minstrels living among the Margi of the western Sudan were readily recognizable by the distinctive drinking baskets they carried around to avoid pollution; and the English Travelers, who obtained most of their food from the dominant society, lived in constant fear of contagion (preferring canned, packaged, or bottled food not visibly contaminated by non-Travelers, and eating with their hands to avoid using cafeteria silverware). The Jains, who along with the Parsis became colonial India's most successful entrepreneurs, were, like the Parsis, formally outside the Hindu caste system, but what made them truly "peculiar people" was their strict adherence to *ahimsa*, the doctrine of nonviolence toward all living things. This meant, besides strict vegetarianism, a ban on all food that might be contaminated by small insects or worms, such as potatoes and radishes, and a prohibition on eating after sunset, when the danger of causing injury was especially great. It also meant that most kinds of manual labor, especially agriculture, were potentially polluting. Whatever came first—the change in professional specialization or the ascetic challenge to Hinduism—the fact remains that the Jains, who started out as members of the Kshatriya warrior caste, became mostly Baniyas specializing in moneylending, jewelry making, shopkeeping, and eventually banking and industry. What emigration accomplished in East Africa, the pursuit of ritual purity did back home in India.[13]

The opposition between purity and pollution lies at the heart of all moral order, be it in the form of traditional distinctions (between body parts, parts of the world, natural realms, supernatural forces, species of humanity) or of various quests for salvation, religious or secular. In any case, "dirt" and "foreignness" tend to be synonymous—and dangerous—with regard to both objects and people. Universalist egalitarian religions attempted to banish foreignness by reinterpreting it (even proclaiming, in one case, that it is "not that which goeth into the mouth defileth a man; but that which cometh out of the mouth, this defileth a man" [Matt. 15:11]). They were not totally successful (the world was still full of old-fashioned, filth-eating foreigners, including many converted ones), but they did make filth and foreignness appear less formidable and ultimately conquerable—except in the case of those whose fate and faith seemed inseparable from foreignness and thus unreformable and irredeemable. Most of the time, the Jews, Gypsies, and other service nomads seemed to share this view; largely unpersuaded by universalist rhetoric, they retained the traditional division of the world into two separate entities, one associated with purity (maintained through ritual observance), the other with pollution. Whereas in the Christian and Muslim realms, words representing foreigners, savages, strangers, the heathen, and the infidel competed with each other, did not fully overlap, and could no longer be subsumed under one heading, the Jewish and Gypsy concepts of "Goy" and "Gajo" (among other terms and spellings) allowed one to conceive of all non-Jews or non-Gypsies as one alien tribe, with individual Goyim or Gajos as members. Even the Christians and Muslims who specialized in service nomadism tended to belong to endogamous, nonproselytizing, "national" churches, such as the Gregorian (the Armenian word for non-Armenians, *odar*, is probably a cognate of the English "other"), Nestorian, Maronite, Melchite, Coptic, Ibadi, and Ismaili.

They were all chosen people, in other words, all "tribal" and "traditional" insofar as they worshiped themselves openly and separated themselves as a matter of principle. There were others like them, but few were as consistent. Most agrarian nobilities, for example, routinely (and sometimes convincingly) traced their descent from nomadic warriors, stressed their foreignness as a matter of honor, practiced endogamy, and performed complex distancing rituals. Priests, too, removed themselves from important modes of social exchange by forming self-reproducing castes or refraining from reproduction altogether. Both groups, however, usually shared a name, a place, or a god (and perhaps an occasional meal or a wife) with others, whose labor they appropriated by virtue of controlling access to land or salvation. Besides, many of them subscribed to universalist creeds that set limits to particularism and imposed commitments that might prompt crusades, deportations, and concerted missionary endeavors aiming at the abolition of difference.

The "Mercurians" had no such commitments, and the most uncompromising among them, such as the Gypsies and the Jews, retained radical dualism and strict pollution taboos through many centuries of preaching and persecution. The black silk cord that pious Jews wore around their waists to separate the upper and lower body might be reincarnated as the "fence" (*eyruv*) that converted an entire shtetl into one home for the purpose of Sabbath purity, and, at the outer limits, as the invisible but ritually all-important barrier that demarcated the Jew-Gentile border. Gypsy defenses against impurity were similar, if much more rigid and numerous, because in the absence of a scriptural tradition, they had to bear the full burden of ethnic differentiation. Just being Gypsy involved a desperate struggle against *marime* (contagion)—a task all the more daunting because Gypsies had no choice but to live among the Gajo, who were the principal source and embodiment of that contagion. (Perhaps ironically, they also had no choice but to have Gajos live among them—as slaves or servants employed to do the unclean work.) When religious injunctions appeared to weaken, the "hygienic" ones took their place—or so it might seem when observant Gypsies bleached their dwellings or used paper towels to turn on taps or open bathroom doors. The Jews, considered dirty in a variety of contexts, could also arouse the suspicion or admiration of their neighbors because of their preoccupation with bodily cleanliness. And even on the Indian subcontinent, where all ethnosocial groups surrounded themselves with elaborate pollution taboos, the Parsis were remarkable for the strictness of their constraints on menstruating women and the intensity of their concern for personal hygiene.[14]

Next to purity and pollution, and closely related to them as a sign of difference, is language. "Barbarian" originally meant a "babbler" or "stutterer," and the Slavic word for "foreigner" (later "German") is *nemec*, "the mute one." Most "Mercurian" peoples are barbarians and "Germans" wherever they go, sometimes by dint of considerable effort. If they do not speak a language that is foreign to the surrounding majority (as a result of recent immigration or long-term language maintenance), they create one. Some European Gypsies, for example, speak Romani, an inflected, morphologically productive Indic language probably related to the Dom languages of the Middle East and possibly derived from the idiom of an Indian caste of metalworkers, peddlers, and entertainers. (Romani is, however, unusual in that it cannot be traced to any particular regional variety and seems to have experienced an extraordinary degree of morphosyntactic borrowing—some say "fusion"—leading a minority of scholars to deny its coherence and independence.)[15] Many others speak peculiar "Para-Romani" languages that combine a Romani lexicon with the grammar (phonology, morphology, and syntax) of coterritorial majority languages. There are Romani versions of English, Spanish, Basque, Portuguese, Finnish, Swedish, and Norwegian, among others, all of them unintelligible to host communities and variously described as former Romani dialects transformed by means of "massive grammatical replacement"; creole languages derived from pidgins (simplified contact languages) used by original Roma immigrants to communicate with local outlaws; "mixed dialects" created by speakers who had lost full-fledged inflected Romani but still had access to it (older kinsmen, new immigrants) as an "alienation" resource; "mixed languages" (local grammar, immigrant vocabulary) born of the intertwining of two parent languages, as in the case of frontier languages spoken by the offspring of immigrant fathers and native mothers; and finally ethnolects or cryptolects consciously created by the native speakers of standard languages with the help of widely available Romani and non-Romani items.[16]

Whatever their origin, the "Para-Romani" languages are specific to service nomads, learned in adolescence (although some may have been spoken natively at some point), and retained as markers of group identity and secret codes. According to Asta Olesen's Sheikh Mohammadi informants, their children speak Persian until they are six or seven, when they are taught Adurgari, "which is spoken 'when strangers should not understand what we talk about.' " The same seems to be true of the "secret languages" of the Fuga and Waata service nomads of southern Ethiopia.[17]

When a language foreign to the host society is not available and loan elements are deemed insufficient, various forms of linguistic camouflage are used to ensure unintelligibility: reversal (of whole words or syllables), vowel changes, consonant substitution, prefixation, suffixation, paraphrasing, punning, and so on. The Inadan make themselves incomprehensible by adding the prefix *om-* and suffix *-ak* to certain Tamacheq (Tamajec, Tamashek) nouns; the Halabi (the blacksmiths, healers, and entertainers of the Nile valley) transform Arabic words by adding the suffixes *-eishi* or *-elheid*; the Romani English (Angloromani) words for "about," "bull," and "tobacco smoke" are *aboutas, bullas,* and *fogas*; and the Shelta words for the Irish *do* ("two") and *dorus* ("door") are *od* and *rodus,* and for the English "solder" and "supper," *grawder* and *grupper*.[18] Shelta was spoken by Irish Travelers (reportedly as a native tongue in some cases) and consists of an Irish Gaelic lexicon, much of it disguised, embedded in an English grammatical framework. Its main function is nontransparency to outsiders, and according to the typically prejudiced (in every sense) account of the collector John Sampson, who met two "tinkers" in a Liverpool tavern in 1890, it served its purpose very well. "These men were not encumbered by any prejudices in favor of personal decency or cleanliness, and the language used by them was, in every sense, corrupt. Etymologically it might be described as a Babylonish, model-lodging-house jargon, compounded of Shelta, 'flying Cant,' rhyming slang, and Romani. This they spoke with astonishing fluency, and apparent profit to themselves."[19]

Various postexilic Jewish languages have been disparaged in similar ways and spoken by community members with equal fluency and even greater profit (in the sense of meeting a full range of communicative and cognitive needs as well as reinforcing the ethnic boundary). The Jews lost their original home languages relatively early, but nowhere—for as long as they remained specialized service nomads—did they adopt unaltered host languages as a means of internal communication. Wherever they went, they created, or brought with them, their own unique vernaculars, so that there were Jewish versions (sometimes more than one) of Arabic, Persian, Greek, Spanish, Portuguese, French, and Italian, among many others. Or perhaps they were not just "versions," as some scholars, who prefer "Judezmo" over "Judeo-Spanish" and "Yahudic" over "Judeo-Arabic," have suggested (echoing the "Angloromani" versus "Romani English" debate). Yiddish, for example, is usually classified as a Germanic language or a dialect of German; either way, it is unique in that it contains an extremely large body of non-Germanic grammatical elements; cannot be traced back to any particular dialect (Solomon Birnbaum called it "a synthesis of diverse dialectal material"); and was spoken exclusively by an occupationally specialized and religiously distinct community wherever its members resided.[20] There is no evidence that the early Jewish immigrants to the Rhineland ever shared a dialect with their Christian neighbors; in fact, there is evidence to suggest that the (apparently) Romance languages that they spoke at the time of arrival were themselves uniquely Jewish.[21]

Some scholars have suggested that Yiddish may be a Romance or Slavic language that experienced a massive lexicon replacement ("relexification"), or that it is a particular type of creole born out of a "pidginized" German followed by "expansion in internal use, accompanied by admixture."[22] The two canonical histories of Yiddish reject the Germanic genesis without attempting to fit the language into any conventional nomenclature (other than "Jewish languages"): Birnbaum calls it a "synthesis" of Semitic, Aramaic,

Romance, Germanic, and Slavic "elements," whereas Max Weinreich describes it as a "fusion language" molded out of four "determinants"—Hebrew, Loez (Judeo-French and Judeo-Italian), German, and Slavic. More recently, Joshua A. Fishman has argued that Yiddish is a "multicomponential" language of the "postexilic Jewish" variety that is commonly seen as deficient by its speakers and other detractors but was never a pidgin because it never passed through a stabilized reduction stage or served as a means of intergroup communication.[23] Generally, most creolists mention Yiddish as an exception or not at all; most Yiddish specialists consider it a mixed language without proposing a broader framework to fit it into; a recent advocate of a general "mixed language" category does not consider it mixed enough; and most general linguists assign Yiddish to the Germanic genetic group without discussing its peculiar genesis.[24]

What seems clear is that when service nomads possessed no vernaculars foreign to their hosts, they created new ones in ways that resembled neither genetic change (transmission from generation to generation) nor pidginization (simplification and role restriction). These languages are—like their speakers—mercurial and Promethean. They do not fit into existing "families," however defined. Their raison d'être is the maintenance of difference, the conscious preservation of the self and thus of strangeness. They are special secret languages in the service of Mercury's precarious artistry. For example, the argot of German Jewish cattle traders (like that of the rabbis) contained a much higher proportion of Hebrew words than the speech of their kinsmen whose communication needs were less esoteric. With considerable insight as well as irony, they called it *Loshen-Koudesh*, or "sacred language" / "cow language," and used it, as a kind of Yiddish in miniature, across large territories. (Beyond the Jewish world, Yiddish was, along with Romani, a major source of European underworld vocabularies.)[25] But mostly it was religion, which is to say "culture," which is to say service nomadism writ large, that made Mercurian languages special. As Max Weinreich put it, " 'Ours differs from theirs' reaches much further than mere disgust words or distinction words." Or rather, it was not just the filthy and the sublime that uncleansed "Gentile" words could not be allowed to express; it was charity, family, childbirth, death, and indeed most of life. One Sabbath benediction begins with "He who distinguishes between the sacred and the profane" and ends with "He who distinguishes between the sacred and the sacred." Within the Jewish—and Gypsy—world, "all nooks of life are sacred, some more, some less," and so secret words multiplied and metamorphosed, until the language itself became secret, like the people it served and celebrated.[26]

In addition to more or less secret vernaculars, some service nomads possess formally sacred languages and alphabets that preserve their scriptural connection to their gods, past, home, and salvation (Hebrew and Aramaic for the Jews, Avestan and Pahlavi for the Parsis, Grabar for the Armenians, Syriac for the Nestorians). Indeed, all literate service nomads (including the Overseas Chinese and Eastern European Germans, for example) can be said to possess such languages, for all modern "national" languages are sacred to the extent that they preserve their speakers' connection to their (new) gods, past, home, and salvation. All Mercurians are multilingual, in other words (Hermes was the god of eloquence). As professional internal strangers equally dependent on cultural difference and economic interdependence, they speak at least one internal language (sacred, secret, or both) and at least one external one. They are all trained linguists, negotiators, translators, and mystifiers, and the literate groups among them tend to be much more literate than their hosts—because literacy, like language generally, is a key to both the maintenance of their separate identity and the fulfillment of their commercial (conjoining) function.

Once again, however, difference is primary. The continued fulfillment of their conjoining function (like all acts of mediating, negotiating, and translating) hinges on the perpetuation of difference, and difference makes for strange bedfellows: wherever Mercurians live, their relations with their clients are those of mutual hostility, suspicion, and contempt. Even in India, where the entire society consists of endogamous, economically specialized, pollution-fearing strangers, the Parsis tend to feel, and may be made to feel, stranger and cleaner than most.[27] Elsewhere, there was little doubt about a mutual antipathy based ultimately on the fear of pollution. "They" always eat filth, smell funny, live in squalor, breed like rabbits, and otherwise mix the pure and the impure so as to contaminate themselves beyond redemption (and thus become the object of intense sexual curiosity). All contact with them, especially through food (hospitality) and blood (marriage), is dangerous, and therefore forbidden—and therefore desirable. And therefore forbidden. Such fears are rarely symmetrical: border crossers are always interlopers and outcasts and thus more contagious, more difficult to contain and domesticate. In complex societies with well-established universalist religions the nature of the relationship may change: the border crossers retain their preoccupation with everyday pollution and intermarriage (*shiksa* means "filthy"), and the host majorities profess to fear certain religious practices and political conspiracies. Still, much of the anti-Mercurian rhetoric has to do with contagion/infestation and, in cases of particular resonance, specifically with food and blood: casting spells to destroy the harvest, using the blood of infants to prepare ritual meals, and jeopardizing Christian Spain's *limpieza de sangre* ("blood purity")—in addition to basic untidiness.

The asymmetry goes much further, of course. The host societies have numbers, weapons, and warrior values, and sometimes the state, on their side. Economically, too, they are generally self-sufficient—not as comfortably as Ferdinand and Isabella of Spain may have believed, but incomparably more so than the service nomads, who are fully dependent on their customers for survival. Finally, beyond the basic fear of pollution, the actual views that the two parties hold of each other are very different. In fact, they tend to be complementary, mutually reinforcing opposites making up the totality of the universe: insider-outsider, settled-nomadic, body-mind, masculine-feminine, steady-mercurial. Over time, the relative value of particular elements may change, but the oppositions themselves tend to remain the same (Hermes possessed most of the qualities that the Gypsies, Jews, and Overseas Chinese would be both loathed and admired for).[28]

Most important, many of these views were true. Not in the sense of the reality of certain acts or the applicability of generalizations to particular individuals, but insofar as they described the cultural values and economic behaviors of one community in terms of another. Indeed, very often the two communities agreed on the general terms, if not the specific formulations. The view that service nomads kept aloof, "did not belong," had other loyalties, insisted on their difference, and resisted assimilation was shared by all (and was an accusation only in those relatively few societies where assimilation was occasionally seen as a good thing). Strangeness was their profession; aloofness was their way of remaining strange; and their primary loyalty was to each other and their common fate.

Even the reasons for their strangeness were not, in essence, controversial. European anti-Semitism is often explained in connection with the Jewish origins of Christianity and the subsequent casting of unconverted Jews in the role of deicides (as the mob's cry, "his blood be on us, and on our children," was reinterpreted in "ethnic" terms). This is true in more ways than one (the arrival of the Christian millennium is, in fact, tied to the end of Jewish wanderings), but it is also true that before the rise of commercial capitalism, when Hermes became the supreme deity and certain kinds of service nomadism became fashionable or even compulsory, Mercurian life was universally seen—by the service nomads themselves, as well as by their hosts—as divine punishment for an original transgression.

One "griot" group living among the Malinke was "condemned to eternal wandering" because their ancestor, Sourakhata, had attempted to kill the Prophet Muhammad. The Inadan were cursed for selling a strand of the Prophet Muhammad's hair to some passing Arab caravan traders. The Waata (in East Africa) had to depend on the Boran for food because their ancestor had been late to the first postcreation meeting, at which the Sky-God was distributing livestock. The Sheikh Mohammadi say that their ancestor's sons behaved badly, "so he cursed them all and said, 'May you never be together!' So they scattered and went on scattering in many places.'" And Siaun, the ancestor of the Ghorbat in Afghanistan, "sat atop a hill weaving a sieve and then he grew hungry. A piece of bread appeared, first within reach, but then, since God was angry with our ancestor, the bread rolled down the hill and up the next and Siaun had to run after it for many miles before he could finally catch it. This is why we, his descendants, still have to walk so far and wide to find our *ruzi* (food)." Of the many legends accounting for the Gypsy predicament, one claims that Adam and Eve were so fruitful that they decided to hide some of their children from God, who became angry and condemned the ones he could not see to eternal homelessness. Other explanations include punishment for incest or refusal of hospitality, but the most common one blames the Gypsies for forging the nails used to crucify Jesus. A positive version has them refuse to forge the fourth nail and, as a reward, receive freedom to roam and a dispensation to steal, but it seems to be of more recent vintage (like the explanation of the Jewish exile as a result of Gentile oppression). Before the rise of secularism and industrialism, everyone in agrarian societies seems to have agreed that service nomadism meant homelessness, and that homelessness was a curse. Perhaps the most famous punishments in the European tradition were meted out to Prometheus, the mischievous master craftsman who stole Zeus's fire; Sisyphus, "the craftiest of men," who cheated Death, and of course Odysseus/Ulysses, that most Jewish of Greeks, whose jealous crew let loose the hostile winds that would keep them away from home.[29]

Another common host stereotype of the Mercurians is that they are devious, acquisitive, greedy, crafty, pushy, and crude. This, too, is a statement of fact, in the sense that, for peasants, pastoralists, princes, and priests, any trader, moneylender, or artisan is in perpetual and deliberate violation of most norms of decency and decorum (especially if he happens to be a babbling infidel without a home or reputable ancestors). "For the Rwala [Bedouin], wealth, in terms of camels, goods, and gold, could not be conserved; it had to be converted into reputation (or honor). For the peripatetics [service nomads], most of whom were emissaries from the towns, and all of whom were regarded as such, rightly or wrongly, by the Rwala, wealth is measured by possessions, be these objects or cash. Among the Rwala, to be rich in possessions implied a lack of generosity, which led to a diminution of honor, and in turn, a decrease in influence. Among townsmen—and by extension, peripatetics—possessions implied power and influence."[30] All economic division of labor involves value differentiation; next to the division based on sex, perhaps the deepest is the one separating food producers and predators from service providers. Apollonians and Dionysians are usually the same people: now sober and serene, now drunk and frenzied. The followers of Hermes are neither; they have been seen as artful and shrewd ever since Hermes, on the day of his birth, invented the lyre, made himself some "unspeakable, unthinkable, marvelous" sandals, and stole Apollo's cattle.

Hermes had nothing except his wit; Apollo, his big brother and condescending antipode, possessed most things in the universe because he was the god of both livestock and agriculture. As the patron of food production, Apollo owned much of the land, directed the flow of time, protected sailors and warriors, and inspired true poets. He was both manly and eternally young, athletic and artistic, prophetic and dignified—the most universal of all gods and the most commonly worshiped. The difference between Apollo and Dionysus—made much of by Nietzsche—is relatively minor because wine was but one of the countless fruits of the earth and sea that Apollo presided over. (Dionysians are Apollonians at a festival—peasants after the harvest.) The difference between Apollonians and Mercurians is the all-important difference between those who grow food and those who create concepts and artifacts. The Mercurians are always sober but never dignified.

Whenever the Apollonians turn cosmopolitan, they find the Mercurians to be uncommonly recalcitrant and routinely accuse them of tribalism, nepotism, clannishness, and other sins that used to be virtues (and still are, in a variety of contexts). Such accusations have a lot to do with the old mirror-image principle: if cosmopolitanism is a good thing, strangers do not have it (unless they belong to a noble savage variety preserved as a reproach to the rest of us). But they have even more to do with reality: in complex agrarian societies (no other preindustrial kind has much interest in cosmopolitanism), and certainly in modern ones, service nomads tend to possess a greater degree of kin solidarity and internal cohesion than their settled neighbors. This is true of most nomads, but especially the mercurial kind, who have few other resources and no other enforcement mechanisms. In the words of Pierre van den Berghe, "Groups with a strong network of extended family ties and with a strong patriarchal authority structure to keep extended families together in the family business have a strong competitive advantage in middleman occupations over groups lacking these characteristics."[31]

Whether "corporate kinship" is the cause or consequence of service nomadism, it does appear that most service nomads possess such a system.[32] Various Rom "nations" are composed of restricted cognatic descent groups (*vitsa*), which are further subdivided into highly cohesive extended families that often pool their income under the jurisdiction of the eldest member; in addition, migration units (*tabor*) and territorial associations (*kumpania*) apportion areas to be exploited and organize economic and social life under the leadership of one family head.[33]

The Indians in East Africa escaped some of the occupational restrictions and status-building requirements of the subcontinent ("we are all *baniyas*, even those who do not have *dukas* [shops]") but retained endogamy, pollution taboos, and the extended family as an economic unit.[34] In West Africa, all Lebanese businesses were family affairs. This "meant that outsiders (without really understanding them) could count on the continuity of the business. A son would honor the debts of his father and would expect the repayment of credits extended by his father. The coherence of the family was the social factor which was the backbone of the economic success of the Lebanese traders: the authority of a man over his wife and children meant that the business was run as resolutely [and as cheaply!] as by a single person and yet was as strong as a group." Disaster insurance, expansion opportunities, different forms of credit, and social regulation were provided by larger kinship networks and occasionally by the whole Lebanese community.[35] Similarly, the Overseas Chinese gained access to capital, welfare, and employment by becoming members of ascriptive, endogamous, centralized, and mostly coresidential organizations based on surname (clan), home village, district, and dialect. These organizations formed rotating credit associations, trade guilds, benevolent societies, and chambers of commerce that organized economic life, collected and disseminated information, settled disputes, provided political protection, and financed schools, hospitals, and various social activities. The criminal versions of such entities ("gangster tongs") represented smaller clans or functioned as fictitious families complete with elaborate rites of passage and welfare support.[36] (In fact, all durable "mafias" are either offshoots of service nomadic communities or their successful imitations.)

Clannishness is loyalty to a limited and well-defined circle of kin (real or fictitious). Such loyalty creates the internal trust and external impregnability that allow service nomads to survive and, under certain conditions, succeed spectacularly in an alien environment. "Credit is extended and capital pooled with the expectation that commitments will be met; delegation of authority takes place without fear that agents will pursue their own interests at the expense of the principal's."[37] At the same time, clearly marked aliens are kept securely outside the community: "Unto a stranger thou mayest lend upon usury." Clannishness is loyalty as seen by a stranger.

Economic success, and indeed the very nature of the Mercurians' economic pursuits, are associated with another common and essentially accurate perception of their culture: "They think they are better than everybody, they are so clever." And of course they do, and they are. It is better to be chosen than not chosen, whatever the price one has to pay. "Blessed art thou, O Lord, King of the Universe, who hast not made me a Gentile," says the Jewish prayer. "It is good that I am a descendant of Jacob, and not of Esau," wrote the great Yiddish writer, Sholem Aleichem.[38] "It is the feeling you might have if you went to an elite school, and then you attended a polytechnic," explained a Parsi informant burdened by an apparently inescapable sense of superiority toward other Indians. "You feel proud of your elite school, but you're embarrassed if other people know. You're embarrassed because you think they think you feel superior to them, and you do and know it's wrong."[39]

It has not been wrong for very long. Mercurians owe their survival to their sense of superiority, and when it comes to generalizations based on mutual perceptions, that superiority is seen to reside in the intellect. Jacob was too smart for the hairy Esau, and Hermes outwitted Apollo and amused Zeus when he was a day old (one wonders what he would have done to the drunk Dionysus). Both stories—and many more like them—are told by the tricksters' descendants. The Kanjar despise their gullible hosts; the Irish Travelers believe that what distinguishes them from their clients is agility of mind ("cleverness"); much of Rom folklore is about outsmarting slow, dull-witted non-Gypsies; and on the best of days, a shtetl Jew might concede, in the words of Maurice Samuel, "that at bottom Ivan was not a bad fellow; stupid, perhaps, and earthy, given to drink and occasional wife-beating, but essentially good-natured . . . , as long as the higher-ups did not begin to manipulate him."[40]

In their own eyes, as well as those of others, the Mercurians possess a quality that the Greeks called *metis*, or "cunning intelligence" (with an emphasis on either "cunning" or "intelligence," depending on who does the labeling). Supervised by Hermes and fully embodied on this earth by Odysseus/Ulysses, it is the most potent weapon of the weak, the most ambiguous of virtues, the nemesis of both brute force and mature wisdom. As Marcel Detienne and Jean-Pierre Vernant put it in their study of Homer,

> There are many activities in which man must learn to manipulate hostile forces too powerful to be controlled directly but which can be exploited despite themselves, without ever being confronted head on, to implement the plan in mind by some unexpected, devious means; they include, for example, the stratagems used by the warrior the success of whose attack hinges on surprise, trickery or ambush, the art of the pilot steering his ship against winds and tides, the verbal ploys of the sophist making the adversary's powerful argument recoil against him, the skill of the banker and the merchant who, like conjurors, make a great deal of money out of nothing, the knowing forethought of the politician whose flair enables him to assess the uncertain course of events in advance, and the sleights of hand and trade secrets which give craftsmen their control over material which is always more or less intractable to their designs. It is over all such activities that *metis* presides.[41]

The Mercurians' views of the Apollonians are ultimately as rational as the Apollonians' views of the Mercurians. It wasn't Mother Earth or Apollo's herds that nourished, beguiled, and shaped the service nomads; it was people. Traders, healers, minstrels, or artisans, they always performed for the consumer, who was always right, in his own way. And so they had to pay attention. "The Kanjar know a great deal about the human resources they exploit; whereas members of sedentary communities know almost nothing about Kanjar society and culture—their experience is limited to passive audience roles in contrived performance settings."[42] Singers know people's tastes, fortune-tellers their hopes (and thus their fate), merchants their needs, doctors their bodies, and thieves their habits, dwellings, and hiding places. "When begging, Irish Traveller women wear a shawl or 'rug' (plaid blanket), both symbols of Ireland's past poverty; take a baby or young child with them, even if they must borrow one from another family; and ask for tiny amounts such as a 'sup' of milk or a 'bit' of butter, playing on their client's sympathy and making any refusal seem miserly."[43]

As professional cultivators of people, Mercurians use words, concepts, money, emotions, and other intangibles as tools of their trade (whatever the particular trade may be). They assign value to a much larger portion of the universe than do peasants or pastoralists, and they see value in many more pursuits. Their world is larger and more varied—because they cross conceptual and communal borders as a matter of course, because they speak more tongues, and because they have those "unspeakable, unthinkable, marvelous" sandals that allow them to be in several places at once. Gypsies are always just passing through, and so, in more ways than one, are the Jews. In "ghetto times," according to Jacob Katz, "no community, even the largest, could be said to have been self-contained and self-sufficient. Business transactions brought members of different communities into touch through correspondence or personal contact. It was a typical feature of Jewish economic activity that it could rely on business connections with Jewish communities in even far-flung cities and countries. . . . Jews who made a living by sitting in their shops waiting for clients were the minority rather than the prevalent type."[44] Bankers, peddlers, yeshiva students, and famous rabbis traveled far and wide, well beyond the edges of peasant imagination.

They did not travel just by land or water. Some service nomads were literate, and thus doubly nomads. By a natural extension of his expertise in eloquence and wit, Mercury became a patron of writers (*Mercuriales viri*, "Mercury's men," as Horace called them), so that Mercurians who happened to be literate became the preeminent manipulators of texts. In traditional societies, writing was the monopoly of priests or bureaucrats; among literate Mercurians, every male was a priest. The Jews, Parsis, Armenians, Eastern European Germans, Overseas Indians, and Overseas Chinese were not only more literate (on average) than their clients; they were acutely aware of being more literate—and thus more knowledgeable and more sophisticated. What the Rom, Nawar, and Inadan are to oral culture, the scriptural Mercurians are to the culture of the written word. Businessmen, diplomats, doctors, and psychotherapists are literate peddlers, heralds, healers, and fortune-tellers. Sometimes they are also blood relatives.

Either way, they would all take a justifiably dim view of Ivan. If one values mobility, mental agility, negotiation, wealth, and curiosity, one has little reason to respect either prince or peasant. And if one feels strongly enough that manual labor is sacred, physical violence is honorable, trade is tricky, and strangers should be either fed or fought (or perhaps that there should be no strangers at all), one is unlikely to admire service nomads. And so, for much of human history, they have lived next to each other in mutual scorn and suspicion—not because of ignorant superstition but because they have had the chance to get to know each other.

For much of human history, it seemed quite obvious who had the upper hand. The Mercurians may have known more about the Apollonians than the Apollonians knew about the Mercurians (or about themselves), but that knowledge was a weapon of weakness and dependence. Hermes needed his wit because Apollo and Zeus were so big and strong. He would tease and dissimulate when the opportunity presented itself, but mostly he used his sandals and his lyre to run errands, amuse, and officiate.

Then things began to change: Zeus was beheaded, repeatedly, or made a fool of; Apollo lost his cool; and Hermes bluffed his way to the top—not in the sense of the Inadan lording it over the Tuareg, but to the extent that the Tuareg were now forced to be more like the Inadan. Modernity was about everyone becoming a service nomad: mobile, clever, articulate, occupationally flexible, and good at being a stranger. In fact, the task was even more daunting because both the Tuareg and the Inadan were under pressure to become like the Armenians and the Jews, whose economic and cultural border-crossing was greatly aided by their habit of writing things down (in their own way).

Some predominantly oral Mercurians (such as the Ibo of Nigeria) would embrace the transition; others (such as the Gypsies) would continue to service the ever shrinking world of folk culture and small pariah entrepreneurship. Some Apollonian groups would prove willing and able to convert to Mercurianism; others would balk, fail, or rebel. No one would remain immune, however, and no one was better at being a scriptural Mercurian—and therefore "modern"—than scriptural Mercurians, old and new.[45] The over-representation of the Armenians and Jews in entrepreneurial and professional jobs in Europe and the Middle East (discrimination notwithstanding) was matched or exceeded by the Chinese in Southeast Asia, the Parsis in India, the Indians in Africa, and the Lebanese in Latin America and the Caribbean, among others. Having established themselves as commercial intermediaries with the arrival of the Portuguese, the Parsis became British India's premier financiers, industrialists, and urban professionals—including the most famous and most successful of them all, Jamsetji Nusserwanji Tata. The principal nineteenth-century Indian politician ("the Grand Old Man of India" Dadabhai Naoroji) was also a Parsi, as was the ideologue of violent nationalism Bhikhaiji Rustom Cama; all three Indian members of the British Parliament; the first Indian baronet; the first prime minister of the Bombay Presidency; the "Uncrowned King of Bombay"; the "Potato King of Bombay"; the pioneer of coffee production in the East; the first Indian to fly from Europe to India; the most prominent Indian Freemasons; most Western musicians (including, eventually, Zubin Mehta); and every single member of the first all-India cricket team. In 1931, 79 percent of all Parsis (and 73 percent of the females) were literate, as compared to 51 percent of Indian Christians and 19 percent of Hindus and Muslims.[46] Similar lists could be compiled for all scriptural Mercurians (although in some areas they thought it wise to stay out of public politics).

A small minority wherever they find themselves, the Arabic-speaking immigrants from the Levant (Syrians, Palestinians, and Lebanese, known in Latin America as "turcos") established a virtual monopoly of the Amazon trade during the rubber boom around the turn of the twentieth century and eventually came to dominate the economic life of Jamaica, the Dominican Republic, and Honduras, among other places. Between 1919 and 1936, Arab entrepreneurs controlled 67 percent of the Honduran import and export sector, and by the late 1960s, they employed 36 percent and 45 percent of the manufacturing labor force in the country's industrial centers of Tegucigalpa and San Pedro Sula. Over the past two decades, at least seven of the New World's heads of state have been of Lebanese origin: Julio Cesar Turbay Ayala of Colombia, Abdala Bucaram and Jamil Mahuad of Ecuador, Carlos Roberto Flores Facusse of Honduras, Carlos Menem of Argentina, Said Musa of Belize, and Edward Seaga of Jamaica. In the United States, descendants of Lebanese Christian immigrants are strongly overrepresented in the political, economic, and cultural elite; one of them, Ralph Nader, was a contender for the presidency in the 2000 election. In postindependence Sierra Leone, in West Africa, the Lebanese (less than 1 percent of the population) acquired full control of the most productive sectors of the economy, including the gold and diamond trade, finance, retail, transportation, and real estate. Under President Siaka Stephens, in particular, five Lebanese oligarchs (to borrow a term from post-Soviet Russia) were the country's de facto government.[47]

Various Indian diasporas have outlived the British Empire (which did so much to propel them), and moved farther afield, specializing in traditional Mercurian ("Jewish") occupations such as trading, finance, garments, jewelry, real estate, entertainment, and medicine. Despite continued discrimination, Goans, Jains, Ismailis, and Gujaratis, among others, have continued to dominate the economic and professional life of large parts of East Africa (accounting for between 70 and 80 percent of all manufacturing firms in postindependence Kenya, for example). The Jains, the most "puritanical" and probably the wealthiest of all Indian diaspora communities, are second only to the Jews in the international diamond trade; in the late 1980s, having established themselves in such diamond centers as New York, Antwerp, and Tel Aviv, they accounted for about one-third of all purchases of rough diamonds in the world. In the United States, Indians (mostly Gujaratis) own about 40 percent of all small motels, including about one-fourth of the franchises of the Days Inn chain, and a substantial number of low-cost hotels in large urban centers. In 1989, the combined global real estate investment of Overseas Indians was estimated to be worth about $100 billion. At the same time (in the 1980s), the number of Indian students studying in the United States quadrupled to more than 26,000. By 1990, there were about 5,000 Indian engineers and several hundred Indian millionaires in California's Silicon Valley. Altogether, there were about 20,000 Indian engineers and 28,000 physicians in the United States, including 10 percent of all anesthesiologists. But probably the biggest jewel in the Indian diaspora's crown is the old imperial "mother country." London serves as the headquarters of a large number of Indian commercial clans, and in Great Britain as a whole, Indian and Pakistani males have a 60 percent higher rate of self-employment than "white" Britons and make up a disproportionate share of managerial and professional personnel. In the 1970s, the rate of economic upward mobility among Indians and Pakistanis was three times that of the rest of the British population.[48]

By far the largest and most widely dispersed of all Mercurian communities in today's world are the Overseas Chinese. Most of them live in Southeast Asia, where they have encountered relatively little market competition as they have moved from peddling, moneylending, and small artisanship to banking, garment making, and agricultural processing, to virtually total economic dominance (often concealed behind a variety of local frontmen). At the end of the twentieth century, ethnic Chinese (less than 2 percent of the population) controlled about 60 percent of the private economy of the Philippines, including, according to Amy Chua, "the country's four major airlines and almost all of the country's banks, hotels, shopping malls, and major conglomerates." They dominated "the shipping, textiles, construction, real estate, pharmaceutical, manufacturing, and personal computer industries as well as the country's wholesale distribution networks . . . and six out of the ten English-language newspapers in Manila, including the one with the largest circulation." The situation looked similar in Indonesia (over 70 percent of the private economy, 80 percent of the companies listed on the Jakarta Stock Exchange, and all of the country's billionaires and largest corporations), Malaysia (about 70 percent of market capitalization), and Thailand (all but three of the country's seventy most powerful business groups, the exceptions being the Military Bank, the Crown Property Bureau, and a Thai-Indian corporation). In post-Communist Burma and almost-post-Communist Vietnam, the ethnic Chinese were quickly returning to economic prominence; in Rangoon and Mandalay, they owned most shops, hotels, and real estate, and in Ho Chi Minh City, they controlled roughly 50 percent of the city's market activity and dominated light industry, import-export, shopping malls, and private banking. Postcolonial Southeast Asia had become part of an international Overseas Chinese economy, headquartered in Hong Kong, Taiwan, and California.[49]

There is no consensus on why some recently uprooted Apollonians seem able and willing to transform themselves into Mercurians. Why do Chinese and Japanese farmers tend to become entrepreneurs when they arrive on new shores? Why did most Indians in Africa, whatever their background, become *baniyas*? And why did Lebanese villagers consistently ignore the appeals of the Brazilian government (which needed independent farmers to develop the South, farm laborers to replace the slaves, and factory workers to help with industrialization) in order to take up a nomadic and dangerous life as peddlers in the jungle?

Some writers have responded by trying to find a "Protestant ethic" in Zoroastrianism, Jainism, Judaism, Confucianism, or the Tokugawa religion.[50] The difficulty with this endeavor is that there seem to be more service nomads than there are plausible Protestants. One could search for peculiarly Mercurian traits in the nationalized Christianity of the Armenian Gregorians and Lebanese Maronites (the majority of the original Arab immigrants to the Americas), but one could hardly argue that Orthodox Christianity provided the Ottoman Greeks with much entrepreneurial ammunition, or that Roman Catholicism is responsible for the strong representation of Italian Americans in such typically Mercurian pursuits as entertainment, organized crime, and retail trade in urban ghettos. Max Weber, too, may have discouraged some of his followers by insisting on a rigid distinction between rule-based capitalism and tribal entrepreneurship, as well as by suggesting that some "Calvinist" elements in Judaism were relatively late adaptations to the conditions of exile, not sources of commercial inspiration.

Another approach is to refer to the effects of regional trade practices on local attitudes toward economic gain and broad familiarity, and possibly sympathy, with the Mercurian ethos. According to Thomas Sowell, for example, "the economically strategic location of the Middle East, for centuries a crossroads of trade between Europe and Asia, fostered the development of many trading ports and many trading peoples, of whom the Jews, the Armenians, and the Lebanese have been particularly prominent." The same, Sowell argues, is true of the Overseas Chinese, "who originated in similarly demanding regions of southern China, where trade was part of their survival skills in a geographically unpromising region for industry, but which had trading ports." The same may very well be true of some Indian or East Asian Mercurians—but clearly not of others. The Korean and Japanese diasporas, for example, have tended to be much keener on middleman roles and much better at performing them than most migrants from such trading entrepôts as the Baltic or the Mediterranean. [51]

Perhaps the most popular explanation for successful Mercurianism is "corporate kinship," which is said to promote internal trust and obedience while limiting the number of potential beneficiaries. Nepotism may be good for capitalism, in other words—as long as the duties and entitlements of one's nephews are understood clearly and followed religiously.[52] Indeed, virtually all Armenian, Korean, Lebanese, diaspora Indian, and American Italian businesses are family enterprises. Even the largest Overseas Chinese commercial and manufacturing empires, with offices in London, New York, Los Angeles, and San Francisco, are similar to the Rothschild banking house in that the regional branches are usually run by the sons, brothers, nephews, or sons-in-law of the founder. The one true Mercurian faith, according to this theory, is fervent familism (which may, in a strange land, be extended to larger lineages and ultimately the whole—chosen—people). If the core of Confucianism is "the apotheosis of the family," then the behavior of large numbers of Italian immigrants to the Americas may be attributed to what Francis Fukuyama calls "Italian Confucianism."[53]

The problem with the strictly sociobiological explanation of entrepreneurial nepotism (such as the one advanced by Pierre van den Berghe) is that some of the most successful Mercurian enterprises—the German and Japanese ones, as well as the Sicilian Mafia—have not been kin groups. Instead, they have used family models and metaphors to create durable and cohesive quasi-families—from, in the Japanese case, master-disciple swordsmanship groups to *zaibatsu* ("money clique") business partnerships. The upshot, it would seem, is that the best new candidates for Mercurian roles are those groups that most closely resemble the old Mercurian tribes. The principal trait that all aspirants must possess is the combination of internal cohesion and external strangeness: the greater the cohesion, the greater the strangeness, and the greater the strangeness, the greater the cohesion, whichever comes first. The best guarantee of both is an uncompromising and ideologized familism (tribalism), which may be either biological or adoptive and which can be reinforced—or indeed replaced—by a strong sense of divine election and cultural superiority. The millenarian religious sects that do not insist on celibacy are invariably endogamous—and thus potential tribes; the endogamous tribes that take their fate and their strangeness seriously are also religious sects.[54]

Whatever the sources of its most recent versions, service nomadism—old or new, scriptural or oral—has always been a dangerous proposition. Unarmed internal strangers, the Mercurians are as vulnerable as they are foreign, especially because residential segregation (in forest encampments, merchant quarters, or ethnic compounds) is a necessary condition for their continued existence as service nomads among traditional food producers. In stateless societies, they are protected by their supernatural powers and exclusive specialization; elsewhere, they are safeguarded—or not—by tax-collecting elites that profit from their expertise.

The history of most service nomads is a story of sporadic grassroots pogroms and permanent state ambivalence, as various regimes oscillated between more or less rationalized extortion and periodic confiscations, conversions, expulsions, and executions. The European Gypsies were usually seen as parasitic as well as dangerous (entertainment was the only "Bohemian" activity subject to profitable regulation), and thus hounded relentlessly, if rarely with great conviction. The scriptural Mercurians were often considered indispensable as well as dangerous, and thus allowed to remain both resident (including the granting of state protection and economic monopolies) and alien (including the toleration of physical separation, religious self-rule, and administrative autonomy).

The key to continued usefulness was economic success; visible economic success led to heavier taxation, popular violence, and renewed complaints from native competitors. Either way, considerations of long-term usefulness could become secondary to an urgent need for financial revenue or political scapegoats; occasionally, they might be abandoned entirely in favor of religious universalism or bureaucratic transparency. In the Spanish Philippines, for example, 12,000 Chinese were deported in 1596, approximately 23,000 massacred in 1603, another 23,000 in 1639, and then about 20,000 in 1662; in 1755 all non-Christian Chinese were expelled (and many converted); in 1764, 6,000 were killed; and in 1823, the levying of special taxes resulted in mass flight and imprisonment.[55]

The rise of nationalism and communism seemed to pave the way to a final solution. If all nations were entitled to their own states and all states were to embody nations, all internal strangers were potential traitors. They might, or might not, be allowed to assimilate, but they had ever fewer legitimate arguments for continued difference and specialization. In a nation-state, citizenship and nationality ("culture") became inseparable; nonnationals were aliens and thus not true citizens. And if, on the other hand, proletarians of all countries were supposed to inherit the earth, and if only industrial workers (and possibly their peasant allies) could be true proletarians, then service nomads were to be disinherited as "bourgeois lackeys" or just plain bourgeois. Some Mercurians became communist (in opposition to ethnic nationalism), and some became Mercurian nationalists (in opposition to both), but both nationalism and communism were fundamentally Apollonian, so that many Mercurians who were not murdered became Apollonians of Mercurian descent or citizens of the newly "revived" Israel and Armenia (which tended to be more Apollonian—and much more martial—than Apollo himself).

In the summer of 1903, soon after the anti-Jewish riots in Kishinev, the government of Haiti barred foreigners from retail trade and stood by during the repeated anti-Levantine pogroms that followed. For two years, local newspapers (including *L'Antisyrien*, created expressly for the purpose) inveighed against "Levantine monsters" and "descendants of Judas," occasionally calling for "l'extirpation des Syriens." Only pressure from foreign powers (whose representatives were themselves ambivalent about the Levantines) prevented the expulsion orders of March 1905 from taking full effect. About 900 refugees left the country.[56] On the other side of the Atlantic, the Lebanese population of Freetown, Sierra Leone, spent eight weeks in 1919 under protective custody in the town hall and two other buildings as their property was being looted and destroyed. In the aftermath, the British Colonial Office considered wholesale deportation "in the interests of peace" but opted for continued protection. About twenty years later, the cultural commissar of an incoming prime minister of Thailand delivered a much publicized speech in which he referred to Hitler's anti-Semitic policies and declared that "it was high time Siam considered dealing with their own Jews," meaning ethnic Chinese (of whom he himself was one). As King Vajiravudh had written in a pamphlet entitled *The Jews of the East*, "in matters of money the Chinese are entirely devoid of morals and mercy. They will cheat you with a smile of satisfaction at their own perspicacity."[57]

The nearly universal condemnation of the attempted "extirpation" of the Armenians and Assyrians in Turkey and the Jews and Gypsies in Europe did little to diminish this new anti-Mercurian zeal. In the newly independent African states, "Africanization" meant, among other things, discrimination against Indian and Lebanese entrepreneurs and civil servants. In Kenya, they were squeezed out as "Asians"; in Tanzania, as "capitalists"; and in both places, as "bloodsuckers" and "leeches." In 1972, President Idi Amin of Uganda expelled about 70,000 Indians without their assets, telling them as they went that they had "no interest in this country beyond the aim of making as much profit as possible, and at all costs." In 1982, a coup attempt in Nairobi was followed by a massive Indian pogrom, in which about five hundred shops were looted and at least twenty women were raped.[58]

In postcolonial Southeast Asia, ethnic Chinese became the targets of similar nation-building efforts. In Thailand, they were excluded from twenty-seven occupations (1942), in Cambodia from eighteen (1957), and in the Philippines, relentless anti-"alien" legislation affected their ability to own or inherit certain assets and pursue most professions—while making their "alien" status much harder to escape. In 1959–60, President Sukarno's ban on alien retail trade in Indonesia's rural areas resulted in the hasty departure of about 130,000 Chinese, and in 1965–67, General Suharto's campaign against the Communists was accompanied by massive anti-Chinese violence including large-scale massacres, expulsions, extortion, and legal discrimination. Like several other modern Mercurian communities, the Chinese of Southeast Asia were strongly overrepresented among Communists, as well as capitalists, and were often seen by some indigenous groups as the embodiment of all forms of cosmopolitan modernity. In 1969, anti-Chinese riots in Kuala Lumpur left nearly a thousand people dead; in 1975, Pol Pot's entry into Phnom Penh led to the death of an estimated two hundred thousand Chinese (half the ethnic Chinese population, or about twice as high a death toll as among urban Khmers); and in 1978–79, hundreds of thousands of Vietnamese Chinese fled Vietnam for China as "boat people." The end of the century brought the end of Indonesia's president Suharto, who had closed down

Chinese schools and banned the use of Chinese characters (except by one government-controlled newspaper), while relying on the financial support of Chinese-owned conglomerates. The popular demonstrations that brought down the regime culminated in huge anti-Chinese riots. According to one eyewitness account, " 'Serbu ... serbu ... serbu' [attack], the massa [crowds] shouted. Thus, hundreds of people spontaneously moved to the shops. Windows and blockades were destroyed, and the looting began. The massa suddenly became crazy. After the goods were in their hands, the buildings and the occupants were set on fire. Girls were raped." After two days of violence, about five thousand homes were burned down, more than 150 women gang-raped, and more than two thousand people killed.[59]

There is no word for "anti-Sinicism" in the English language, or indeed in any other language except Chinese (and even in Chinese, the term, *paihua*, is limited in use and not universally accepted). The most common way to describe the role—and the fate—of Indonesia's Chinese is to call them "the Jews of Asia." And probably the most appropriate English (French, Dutch, German, Spanish, Italian) name for what happened in Jakarta in May 1998 is "pogrom," the Russian word for "slaughter," "looting," "urban riot," "violent assault against a particular group," which has been applied primarily to anti-Jewish violence. There was nothing unusual about the social and economic position of the Jews in medieval and early modern Europe, but there is something remarkable about the way they have come to stand for service nomadism wherever it may be found. All Mercurians represented urban arts amid rural labors, and most scriptural Mercurians emerged as the primary beneficiaries and scapegoats of the city's costly triumph, but only the Jews—the scriptural Mercurians of Europe—came to represent Mercurianism and modernity everywhere. The Age of Universal Mercurianism became Jewish because it began in Europe.

Chapter 2

SWANN'S NOSE: THE JEWS AND OTHER MODERNS

> The nose looked at the Major and knitted its
> eyebrows a little. "You are mistaken, my dear sir.
> I am entirely on my own."
>
> —N. V. Gogol, "The Nose"

The postexilic Jews were the Inadan of Europe, the Armenians of the North, the Parsis of the Christian world. They were quintessential, extraordinarily accomplished Mercurians because they practiced service nomadism for a long time and over a large territory, produced an elaborate ideological justification of the Mercurian way of life and its ultimate transcendence, and specialized in an extremely wide range of traditional service occupations from peddling and smithing to medicine and finance. They were internal strangers for all seasons, proven antipodes of all things Apollonian and Dionysian, practiced purveyors of "cleverness" in a great variety of forms and in all walks of life.

But they were not just very good at what they did. They were exceptional Mercurians because, in Christian Europe, they were at least as familiar as they were odd. The local Apollonians' God, forefathers, and Scriptures were all Jewish, and the Jews' greatest alleged crime—the reason for their Mercurian homelessness—was their rejection of a Jewish apostate from Judaism. Such symbiosis was not wholly unparalleled (in parts of Asia, all writing and learning, as well as service nomadism, were of Chinese origin), but probably nowhere were tribal exiles as much at home as Jews were in Europe. The Christian world began with the Jews, and it could not end without them.

Most of all, however, the Jews became the world's strangest strangers because they practiced their vocation on a continent that went almost wholly Mercurian and reshaped much of the world accordingly. In an age of service nomadism, the Jews became the chosen people by becoming the model "moderns."

This meant that more and more Apollonians, first in Europe and then elsewhere, had to become more like the Jews: urban, mobile, literate, mentally nimble, occupationally flexible, and surrounded by aliens (and thus keen on cleanliness, unmanliness, and creative dietary taboos). The new market was different from old markets in that it was anonymous and socially unembedded (relatively speaking): it was exchange among strangers, with everyone trying, with varying degrees of success, to play the Jew.

Among the most successful were Max Weber's Protestants, who discovered a humorless, dignified way to be Jewish. One could remain virtuous while engaging in "usury" and deriving prestige from wealth—as opposed to investing wealth in honor by means of generosity and predation (or simply swallowing it all up). At the same time, the retreat of professional priests and divine miracles forced every seeker of salvation to consult God directly, by reading books, and to pursue righteousness formally, by following rules. Churches became more like synagogues (*shuln*, or "schools"); experts on virtue became more like teachers (rabbis); and every believer became a monk or a priest (i.e., more like a Jew). Moses' prayer—"would God that all the Lord's people were prophets" (Num. 11:29)—had been heard.

The new—modern—world (brave in a new way) was based on the endless pursuit of wealth and learning, with both careers open to talent, as in the shtetl or ghetto, and most talents taking up traditional Mercurian occupations: entrepreneurship, of course, but also medicine, law, journalism, and science. The gradual demise of the soul led to an intense preoccupation with bodily purity, so that diet once again became a key to salvation and doctors began to rival priests as experts on immortality. The replacement of sacred oaths and covenants by written contracts and constitutions transformed lawyers into indispensable guardians and interpreters of the new economic, social, and political order. The obsolescence of inherited wisdom and Apollonian dignity (the greatest enemy of curiosity) elevated erstwhile heralds and town criers to the position of powerful purveyors of knowledge and moral memory (the "fourth" and the "fifth" estates). And the naturalization of the universe turned every scientist into a would-be Prometheus.

Even the refusal to pursue wealth or learning was Mercurian in inspiration. The aptly named "bohemians" occupied the periphery of the new market by engaging in new forms of begging, prophesying, and fortune-telling, as well as more or less seditious singing and dancing. Fully dependent on the society of which they were not full-fledged members, they earned their living by scandalizing their patrons in the manner of most traditional providers of dangerous, unclean, and transcendental services. Their own membership requirements included service nomadism, persistent (if sometimes ironic) defiance of dominant conventions, a strong sense of moral superiority over the host society, and a withdrawal from all outside kinship obligations. To mock, challenge, and possibly redeem a society of would-be Jews and Protestants, one had to become a would-be Gypsy.

"Jews and Protestants" is an appropriate metaphor in more ways than one, because there was more than one way of being successful in the modern economy. Werner Sombart was able to attribute the rise of capitalism to the Jews by dramatically overstating his case (and thus seriously compromising it); Weber established an exclusive connection between the Protestant ethic and the spirit of capitalism by emphasizing historical causation (and thus bypassing contemporary Jews); and scholars puzzling over various Asian miracles have felt compelled to either redefine the Protestant ethic or delineate a peculiarly Asian, "familistic" or "network-based," path to capitalism.[1] It seems, however, that the European route contained both paths—familistic and individualist—at the outset: whereas the Jews, in particular, relied on their expertise as a cohesive tribe of professional strangers, the various Protestants and their imitators built their city on a hill by introducing economic calculation into the moral community while converting countless outsiders into moral subjects (and trustworthy clients)—or, as Benjamin Nelson put it, by turning brothers into others and others into brothers (and thus everyone into a civil stranger).[2]

Since Weber, it has usually been assumed that "modern capitalism rises upon the ruins of the tribalistic communalism of the Hebrew brotherhood."[3] In fact, they have coexisted, not always peacefully, as two fundamental principles of modern economic organization: one that employs kinship as a central structural element, and one that enshrines a rational individual pursuing economic self-interest on the basis of formal legality. Both are learned behaviors, acquired through practice, ideological reinforcement, and painstaking self-denial (and, in the real world, mixed in various proportions). The first requires a combination of tribalism and commercialism rarely found outside traditional Mercurian communities; the second demands a degree of asceticism and adherence to impersonal man-made rules that seems beyond reach (or indeed, comprehension) in societies little affected by Protestantism or reformed Catholicism. The first "harnesses nepotism in the service of capitalism"; the second claims—against all evidence—that the two are incompatible. The first enjoys dubious legitimacy and tends to avoid the limelight; the second loudly abhors "corruption" and pretends to be the only true modern.[4]

The Jews did not have a monopoly on familism, of course, but there is no doubt that their entrepreneurial success was due to a combination of internal solidarity and external strangeness—and that the only way native entrepreneurs could compete (as it turned out) was by battling kin solidarity and legislating strangeness. Majorities (hosts) could emulate Mercurians (guests) only by forcing everyone to be an exile. A Scottish Protestant was not just a pork-eating Jew, as Heine would have it; he was a solitary Jew, a Jew without the people of Israel, the only creature to have been chosen.[5]

But that is not the whole story. Not only was the tribal path—along with the Protestant one—a part of European modernity; the Protestant path itself was, in a crucial sense, tribal. The new market, new rights, and new individuals had to be constituted, circumscribed, sanctified, and protected by a newly nationalized state. Nationalism was a function of modernity, as both a precondition and defensive reaction, and modernity was, among other things, a new version of tribalism. Protestants and liberals did not manage to create a world in which "all men are 'brothers' in being equally 'others.' "[6] Instead, they built a new moral community on the twin pillars of the nuclear family, which posed as an individual, and the nation, which posed as a nuclear family. Adam Smith and most of his readers took it for granted that wealth was, in some sense, "of nations," and so they did not pay much attention to the fact that there were others—and then there were *others*.

To put it differently, the Europeans imitated the Jews not only in being modern, but also in being ancient. Modernity is inseparable from the "tribalistic communalism of the Hebrew brotherhood"—in both the sacredness of the nuclear family and the chosenness of the tribe. As the Age of Mercurianism unfolded, Christians saw the error of their ways and began to go easy on universal brotherhood, on the one hand, and the separation between the sacred and the profane (priesthood and laity), on the other. What started out as a nationalization of the divine ended up as a deification of the national. First, it turned out that the Bible could be written in the vernacular, and that Adam and Eve had spoken French, Flemish, or Swedish in Paradise. And then it became clear that each nation had had its own prelapsarian golden age, its own holy books, and its own illustrious but foolhardy ancestors.[7]

Early Christians had rebelled against Judaism by moving Jerusalem to Heaven; modern Christians reverted to their roots, as it were, by moving it back to earth and cloning it as needed. As William Blake proclaimed,

> I will not cease from Mental Fight,
> Nor shall my Sword sleep in my hand:
> Till we have built Jerusalem
> In Englands green & pleasant Land.[8]

Nationalism meant that every nation was to become Jewish. Every single one of them had been "wounded for our transgressions" and "bruised for our iniquities" (Isa. 53:5). Every people was chosen, every land promised, every capital Jerusalem. Christians could give up trying to love their neighbors as themselves—because they had finally discovered who *they* were (French, Flemish, Swedish). They were like Jews in that they loved themselves as a matter of faith and had no use for miracles—the only true miracle being the continuing unfolding of the national story, to which every member of the nation bore witness through ritual and, increasingly, through reading.

In most of Europe, the sacralization and, eventually, standardization of national languages resulted in the canonization of the authors credited with their creation. Dante in Italy, Cervantes in Spain, Camões in Portugal, Shakespeare in England, and later Goethe (with Schiller) in Germany, Pushkin in Russia, Mickiewicz in Poland, and various others became objects of strikingly successful cults (popular as well as official) because they came to symbolize their nation's golden age—or rather, a modern, newly recovered, articulate, and personalized version of their nation's original unity. They molded and elevated their nations by embodying their spirit (in words as well as in their own lives), transforming history and myth into high culture, and turning the local and the absolute into images of each other. They all "invented the human" and "said it all"; they are the true modern prophets because they transformed their mother tongues into Hebrew, the language spoken in Paradise.[9]

The cultivation of tribalism along with strangeness (modernity as universal Mercurianism) involved an intense preoccupation with bodily purity. Civilization as a struggle against odors, excretions, secretions, and "germs" had as much to do with ritual Mercurian estrangement as it did with the rise of science—a fact duly noted by the Gypsies, for example, who welcomed prepackaged meals and disposable utensils as useful aids in their battle with *marime*, and a number of Jewish physicians, who argued that *kashrut*, circumcision, and other ritual practices were modern hygiene *avant la lettre*.[10]

Mercurian strangeness implies cleanliness and aloofness, and so does Mercurian tribalism. Modern states are as keen on the symmetry, transparency, spotlessness, and boundedness of the body politic as traditional Jews and Gypsies are on the ritual purity and autonomy of their communities. In a sense, good citizenship (including patriotism) is a version of the ever vigilant Jewish endeavor to preserve personal and collective identity in an unclean world. Except that modern states are not usually beleaguered and despised minorities (although many imagine themselves so). In the hands of heavily armed, thoroughly bureaucratized, and imperfectly Judaized Apollonians, Mercurian exclusivity and fastidiousness became relentlessly expansive. In the hands of messianically inclined Apollonians, it turned lethal—especially to the Mercurians. The Holocaust had as much to do with tradition as it did with modernity.[11]

The painful transformation of Europeans into Jews was paralleled by the emergence of the Jews from legal, ritual, and social seclusion. In the new society built on formerly unclean occupations, segregated communities specializing in those occupations lost their raison d'être—for the specialists themselves as well as for their clients. At the same time, the new state was growing indifferent to religion, and thus "tolerant" of religious differences—and thus more inclusive as well as more intrusive. As Jewish communities began to lose their independence, coherence, and self-sufficiency, individual Jews began to acquire new legal protections and new moral legitimacy even as they continued to pursue Mercurian occupations. Some of them became Apollonians or even Christians, but most simply joined the world created in their image, a world in which everyone would wear Hermes' "unspeakable, unthinkable, marvelous" sandals.

But of course most Apollonians untempered by the "Protestant ethic" could not wear those sandals any more than Cinderella's stepsisters could wear her glass slipper—at least not until they had had time to practice and make the proper adjustments. The Jewish journey was equally tumultuous, perhaps, but much shorter. The Jews were already urban (including those who represented urbanity in the shtetls—"little cities"—of rural Eastern Europe) and had, compared to their hosts, virtually no tradition of internal estate distinctions ("the whole ghetto was, as it were, 'Third Estate' "). They tended to base social status on personal achievement, associated achievement with learning and wealth, sought learning by reading and interpreting texts, and pursued wealth by cultivating human strangers rather than land, gods, or beasts. In a society of refugees, permanent exiles could feel at home (or so it seemed for a while).[12]

Over the course of the nineteenth century, most of the Jews of Central and Western Europe moved to large cities to participate in the unbinding of Prometheus (as David Landes, conveniently for our purposes, called the rise of capitalism). They did it in their own way—partly because other avenues remained closed but also because their own way was very effective, as well as well rehearsed (Prometheus had been a trickster and manipulator similar to Hermes before becoming a martyred culture hero). Wherever they went, they had a higher proportion of self-employment than non-Jews, a greater concentration in trade and commerce, and a clear preference for economically independent family firms. Most Jewish wage laborers (a substantial minority in Poland) worked in small Jewish-owned shops, and most great Jewish banking houses, including the Rothschilds, Bleichröders, Todescos, Sterns, Oppenheims, and Seligmans, were family partnerships, with brothers and male cousins—often married to cousins—stationed in different parts of Europe (in-laws and outmarrying females were often excluded from direct involvement in business). In the early nineteenth century, thirty of the fifty-two private banks in Berlin were owned by Jewish families; a hundred years later many of these banks became shareholding companies with Jewish managers, some of them directly related to the original owners as well as to each other. The greatest German joint stock banks, including the Deutsche Bank and Dresdner Bank, were founded with the participation of Jewish financiers, as were the Rothschilds' Creditanstalt in Austria and the Pereires' Crédit Mobilier in France. (Of the remaining private—i.e., non–joint stock—banks in Weimar Germany, almost half were owned by Jewish families).[13]

In fin de siècle Vienna, 40 percent of the directors of public banks were Jews or of Jewish descent, and all banks but one were administered by Jews (some of them members of old banking clans) under the protection of duly titled and landed *Paradegoyim*. Between 1873 and 1910, at the height of political liberalism, the Jewish share of the Vienna stock exchange council (*Börsenrath*) remained steady at about 70 percent, and in 1921 Budapest, 87.8 percent of the members of the stock exchange and 91 percent of the currency brokers association were Jews, many of them ennobled (and thus, in a sense, *Paradegoyim* themselves). In industry, there were some spectacularly successful Jewish magnates (such as the Rathenaus in electrical engineering, the Friedländer-Fulds in coal, the Monds in chemical industries, and the Ballins in shipbuilding), some areas with high proportions of Jewish industrial ownership (such as Hungary), and some strongly "Jewish" industries (such as textiles, food, and publishing), but the principal contribution of Jews to industrial development appears to have consisted in the financing and managerial control by banks. In Austria, of the 112 industrial directors who held more than seven simultaneous directorships in 1917, half were Jews associated with the great banks, and in interwar Hungary, more than half and perhaps as much as 90 percent of all industry was controlled by a few closely related Jewish banking families. In 1912, 20 percent of all millionaires in Britain and Prussia (10 million marks and more in the Prussian case) were Jews. In 1908–11, in Germany as a whole, Jews made up 0.95 percent of the population and 31 percent of the richest families (with a "ratio of economic elite overrepresentation" of 33, the highest anywhere, according to W. D. Rubinstein). In 1930, about 71 percent of the richest Hungarian taxpayers (with incomes exceeding 200,000 pengő) were Jews. And of course the Rothschilds, "the world's bankers" as well as the "Kings of the Jews," were, by a large margin, the wealthiest family of the nineteenth century.[14]

Generally speaking, Jews were a minority among bankers; bankers were a minority among Jews; and Jewish bankers competed too fiercely against each other and associated too much with erratic and mutually hostile regimes to be able to have permanent and easily manageable political influence (Heine called Rothschild and Fuld "two rabbis of finance who were as much opposed to one another as Hillel and Shammai"). Still, it is obvious that European Jews as a group were very successful in the new economic order, that they were, on average, better off than non-Jews, and that some of them managed to translate their Mercurian expertise and Mercurian familism into considerable economic and political power. The pre–

World War I Hungarian state owed its relative stability to the active support of the powerful business elite, which was small, cohesive, bound by marriage, and overwhelmingly Jewish. The new German Empire was built not only on "blood and iron," as Otto von Bismarck claimed, but also on gold and financial expertise, largely provided by Bismarck's—and Germany's—banker, Gerson von Bleichröder. The Rothschilds made their wealth by lending to governments and speculating in government bonds, so that when members of the family had a strong opinion, governments would listen (but not always hear, of course). In one of the most amusing episodes in Alexander Herzen's *My Past and Thoughts*, "His Majesty" James Rothschild blackmails Emperor Nicholas I into releasing the money that the father of Russian socialism has received from his serf-owning German mother.[15]

Money was one means of advancement; education was the other. The two were closely connected, of course, but proportions could vary considerably. Throughout modern Europe, education was expected to lead to money; only among Jews, apparently, was money almost universally expected to lead to education. Jews were consistently overrepresented in educational institutions leading to professional careers, but the overrepresentation of the offspring of Jewish merchants seems particularly striking. In fin de siècle Vienna, Jews made up roughly 10 percent of the general population and about 30 percent of classical *gymnasium* students. Between 1870 and 1910, about 40 percent of all *gymnasium* graduates in central Vienna were Jewish; among those whose fathers engaged in commerce, Jews represented more than 80 percent. In Germany, 51 percent of Jewish scientists had fathers who were businessmen. The Jewish journey from the ghetto seemed to lead to the liberal professions by way of commercial success.[16]

The principal way station on that route was the university. In the 1880s, Jews accounted for only 3–4 percent of the Austrian population, but 17 percent of all university students and fully one-third of the student body at Vienna University. In Hungary, where Jews constituted about 5 percent of the population, they represented one-fourth of all university students and 43 percent at Budapest Technological University. In Prussia in 1910–11, Jews made up less than 1 percent of the population, about 5.4 percent of university students, and 17 percent of the students at the University of Berlin. In 1922, in newly independent Lithuania, Jewish students composed 31.5 percent of the student body at the University of Kaunas (not for long, though, because of the government's nativization policies). In Czechoslovakia, the Jewish share of university students (14.5 percent) was 5.6 times their share in the general population. When Jews are compared to non-Jews in similar social and economic positions, the gap becomes narrower (though still impressive); what remains constant is that in much of Central and Eastern Europe, there were relatively few non-Jews in similar social and economic positions. In large parts of Eastern Europe, virtually the whole "middle class" was Jewish.[17]

Because civil service jobs were mostly closed to Jews (and possibly because of a general Jewish preference for self-employment), most Jewish students went into the professions that were "liberal," congruent with Mercurian upbringing, and, as it happens, absolutely central to the functioning of modern society: medicine, law, journalism, science, higher education, entertainment, and the arts. In turn-of-the-century Vienna, 62 percent of the lawyers, half the doctors and dentists, 45 percent of the medical faculty, and one-fourth of the total faculty were Jews, as were between 51.5 and 63.2 percent of professional journalists. In 1920, 59.9 percent of Hungarian doctors, 50.6 percent of lawyers, 39.25 percent of all privately employed engineers and chemists, 34.3 percent of editors and journalists, and 28.6 percent of musicians identified themselves as Jews by religion. (If one were to add converts to Christianity, the numbers would presumably be much higher.) In Prussia, 16 percent of physicians, 15 percent of dentists, and one-fourth of all lawyers in 1925 were Jews; and in interwar Poland, Jews were about 56 percent of all doctors in private practice, 43.3 percent of all private teachers and educators, 33.5 percent of all lawyers and notaries, and 22 percent of all journalists, publishers, and librarians.[18]

Of all the licensed professionals who served as the priests and oracles of new secular truths, messengers were the most obviously Mercurian, the most visible, the most marginal, the most influential—and very often Jewish. In early twentieth-century Germany,

Austria, and Hungary, most of the national newspapers that were not specifically Christian or anti-Semitic were owned, managed, edited, and staffed by Jews (in fact, in Vienna even the Christian and anti-Semitic ones were sometimes produced by Jews). As Steven Beller put it, "in an age when the press was the only mass medium, cultural or otherwise, the liberal press was largely a Jewish press."[19]

The same was true, to a lesser degree, of publishing houses, as well as the many public places where messages, prophecies, and editorial comments were exchanged orally or nonverbally (through gesture, fashion, and ritual). "Jewish emancipation" was, among other things, a search by individual Jews for a neutral (or at least "semineutral," in Jacob Katz's terms) society where neutral actors could share a neutral secular culture. As the marquis d'Argens wrote to Frederick the Great on behalf of Moses Mendelssohn, "A *philosophe* who is a bad Catholic begs a *philosophe* who is a bad Protestant to grant the privilege [of residence in Berlin] to a *philosophe* who is a bad Jew." To be bad in the eyes of God was a good thing because God either did not exist or could not always tell bad from good. For the Jews, the first such corners of neutrality and equality were Masonic lodges, whose members were to adhere "to that religion in which all men agree, leaving their particular opinions to themselves." When it appeared as if the only religion left was the one on which everyone agreed, some particular opinions became "public opinion," and Jews became important—and very public—opinion makers and opinion traders. In the early nineteenth century, the most prominent salon hostesses in the German-speaking world were Jewish women, and Jews of both sexes became a visible, and sometimes the largest, part of the "public" in theaters, concert halls, art galleries, and literary societies. Most of the patrons in Viennese literary coffeehouses seem to have been Jewish—as were many of the artists whose inventions they judged. Central European modernism, in particular, owed a great deal to the creativity of "emancipated" Jews.[20]

And so did science (from *scientia*, "knowledge"), another transgressive Mercurian specialty closely related to the arts and crafts. For many Jews, the transition from the study of the Law to the study of the laws of nature proved congenial and extremely successful. The new science of the individual (named after Psyche, the Greek for "soul" and the perennial victim of Eros's cruelty) was an almost exclusively Jewish affair; the new science of society seemed to the literary historian Friedrich Gundolph (né Gundelfinger) a "Jewish sect"; and virtually all of the old sciences, perhaps especially physics, mathematics, and chemistry, benefited enormously from the influx of Jews. At least five of the nine Nobel Prizes won by German citizens during the Weimar years went to scientists of Jewish descent, and one of them, Albert Einstein, joined Rothschild in becoming an icon of the Modern Age. Or rather, Rothschild remained a name, a ghostly symbol of the "invisible hand," whereas Einstein became a true icon: an image of the divine, the face of the mind, the prophet of Prometheanism.[21]

At the turn of the twentieth century, the spectacular Jewish success in the central compartments of modern life provoked a vigorous debate about its origins. Some of the arguments and outbursts are routinely included in histories of anti-Semitism, but there was a lot more to the debate than anti-Semitism (however defined). Houston Stewart Chamberlain, the racist ideologue and breathless poet of the "free and loyal" Teuton, offered several tenuously related but influential explanations for the fateful (and altogether "negative") fact that the Jews had become "a disproportionately important and in many spheres actually dominant constituent of our life." First, there was the apparently innate Jewish "possession of an abnormally developed will," which gave rise to their "phenomenal elasticity." Second, there was their historically formed faith, which lacked "abstract inconceivable mysteries," politicized man's relationship to God, equated morality with blind obedience to the law, and spawned the corrosive rationalism that had proved the nemesis of the free and loyal Teuton. Finally—and most fatefully—"Judaism and its product, the Jew," were responsible for "the idea of physical race-unity and race-purity": the very idea that Chamberlain admired in the Teutons and urged them to safeguard in the face of the Jewish onslaught. The future Nazi prophet condemned the

Jews for inventing nationalism and intolerance. "Sin is for them a national thing, whereas the individual is 'just' when he does not transgress the 'law'; redemption is not the moral redemption of the individual, but the redemption of the State; that is difficult for us to understand."[22]

Joseph Jacobs, a prominent Jewish historian and folklorist, agreed with Chamberlain that there was a special relationship between the Jews and the Modern Age, but he had a much higher opinion of both. In his account, Jewish "thinkers and sages with eagle vision took into their thought the destinies of all humanity, and rang out in clarion voice a message of hope to the down-trodden of all races. Claiming for themselves and their people the duty and obligations of a true aristocracy, they held forth to the peoples ideals of a true democracy founded on right and justice." Jacobs's explanations for the Jewish preeminence are similar to Chamberlain's, if much more concise and consistent. Regarding religion as a possibly important but ultimately elusive factor, he attributes Jewish success to heredity, or "germ-plasm." "There is a certain probability," he argues, "that a determinate number of Jews at the present time will produce a larger number of 'geniuses' (whether inventive or not, I will not say) than any equal number of men of other races. It seems highly probable, for example, that German Jews at the present moment are quantitatively (not necessarily qualitatively) at the head of European intellect." The spread of such high intellectual ability over dissimilar environments would seem to confirm the theory of a common ancestry of contemporary Jews, and "if this be so, the desirability of further propagation of the Jewish germ-plasm is a matter not merely of Jewish interest." One proof is the observable success of the "Jewish half-breeds": "their existence, in large number, is sufficient to disprove Chamberlain's contention of the radical superiority of the German over the Jewish germ-plasm."[23]

Werner Sombart had little use for the germ-plasm. "What the race-theorists have produced is a new sort of religion to replace the old Jewish or Christian religion. What else is the theory of an Aryan, or German, 'mission' in the world but a modern form of the 'chosen people' belief?" Instead, he argues that the "Jewish genius" stems from perennial nomadism, first of the pastoral, then of the trading kind. "Only in the shepherd's calling, never in the farmer's, could the idea of gain have taken root, and the conception of unlimited production have become a reality. Only in the shepherd's calling could the view have become dominant that in economic activities the abstract quantity of commodities matters, not whether they are fit or sufficient for use." The Jews are the nomads of Europe. " 'Nomadism' is the progenitor of Capitalism. The relation between Capitalism and Judaism thus becomes more clear."

What does become clear from Sombart's account of the relation between capitalism and Judaism is that nomadism is scarcely more useful to his cause than the germ-plasm. Sombart's book *The Jews and Modern Capitalism* was a response to Max Weber, and most of his argument was entirely—if imperfectly—Weberian. Capitalism is inconceivable without the Protestant ethic; Judaism is much more Protestant (older, tougher, and purer) than Protestantism; Judaism is the progenitor of Capitalism. "The whole religious system is in reality nothing but a contract between Jehovah and his chosen people, a contract with all its consequences and all its duties." Every Jew has an account in Heaven, and every Jew's purpose in life is to balance it by following written rules. To follow the rules, one has to know them; hence "the very study itself is made a means of rendering life holy." Relentless study and obedience impel one "to think about one's actions and to accomplish them in harmony with the dictates of reason." Ultimately, religion as law aims "at the subjugation of the merely animal instincts in man, at the bridling of his desires and inclinations and at the replacing of impulses by thoughtful action; in short, at the 'ethical tempering of man.' " The result is worldly asceticism rewarded by earthly possessions, or Puritanism without pork.[24]

> The rationalization of life accustomed the Jew to a mode of living contrary to (or side by side with) Nature and therefore also to an economic system like the capitalistic, which is likewise contrary to (or side by side with) Nature. What in reality is the idea of making profit, what is economic rationalism, but the application to economic activities of the rules by which the Jewish religion shaped Jewish life? Be-

fore capitalism could develop the natural man had to be changed out of all recognition, and a rationalistically minded mechanism introduced in his stead. There had to be a transvaluation of all economic values. And what was the result? The *homo capitalisticus*, who is closely related to the *homo Judaeus*, both belonging to the same species, *homines rationalistici artificiales*.[25]

This was a reinterpretation of the old contrast, most famously expressed by Matthew Arnold, between the legalism, discipline, and "self-conquest" of Hebraism, on the one hand, and the freedom, spontaneity, and harmony of Hellenism, on the other.[26] Arnold had considered both indispensable to civilized life but lamented a growing modern imbalance, produced by the Reformation, in favor of Hebraism. Nietzsche (who provided Sombart with much of his terminology) rephrased the lament and took it into the realm of good and evil—and beyond:

> The Jews have brought off that miraculous feat of an inversion of values, thanks to which life on earth has acquired a novel and dangerous attraction for a couple of millennia; their prophets have fused "rich," "godless," "evil," "violent," and "sensual" into one and were the first to use the word "world" as an opprobrium. This inversion of values (which includes using the word "poor" as synonymous with "holy" and "friend") constitutes the significance of the Jewish people: they mark the beginning of the slave rebellion in morals.[27]

In Nietzsche's theater of two actors, this inversion of values amounted to a victory of "the hopelessly mediocre and insipid man" over the warrior, and thus over Nature—the very transformation, albeit much older, that Max Weber described as the source of that "middle-class life," of which "it might well be truly said: 'Specialists without spirit, sensualists without heart; this nullity imagines that it has attained a level of civilization never before achieved.' " What Sombart did was reconcile the two chronologies by providing the missing link: the Judaic ethic produced the modern Jew; the modern Jew summoned the spirit of capitalism.[28]

Sombart did not like capitalism (any more than did Weber); Jews excelled under capitalism; so Sombart did not like the Jews (any more than Weber liked the Puritans). Madison C. Peters, a celebrated New York preacher and Protestant theologian, associated the Modern Age with freedom, democracy, prosperity, progress, and clipped fingernails—and liked both the Jews and the Puritans very much. It is true, he argued, that the Puritans were born-again Jews who reverted "to biblical precedents for the regulation of the minutest details of daily life," but the important thing is that "the Hebrew Commonwealth" had been held up by "our patriotic divines" as a "guide to the American people in their mighty struggle for the blessings of civil and religious liberty." According to Peters, "it was Jewish money and Jewish encouragement which backed the genius and daring of the Genoese navigator to brave the terrors of the unknown seas," and it was Jewish energy and Jewish enterprise that helped build "the greatness and the glory, the fame and fortune, the prestige and prosperity of this unapproached and unapproachable land." And if Jewish rationalism, studiousness, and a sense of chosenness are bad traits, then so are "their thrift and industry, their devotion to high ideals, their love for liberty and fairness between man and man, their unquenchable thirst for knowledge, their unswerving devotion to the principles of their race and the tenets of their faith." Finally—and not at all trivially— "the Jew is extremely fond of soap and water under all circumstances; especially has he a fondness for the latter. Whenever he gets an opportunity to take a bath he takes one." All things considered, therefore, the Jews epitomize Western civilization—as its original creators, best practitioners, and rightful beneficiaries. And of the many traits that are essential to both, one of the most fundamental is mental agility, or intellectualism. "The only way to prevent Jewish scholars from winning most of the prizes is to shut them out of the competition."[29]

Virtually all of those who associated Jews with modernity judged them according to the traditional Apollonian-Mercurian oppositions of natural versus artificial, settled versus nomadic, body versus mind. Especially body versus mind: what was sterile rationality to Sombart was intellectual ability to Jacobs, but both agreed on the centrality of the two concepts and the permanence of their attachments. The Jews always represented the mind, which always represented the modern world, whether one liked it or not. In the words of John Foster Fraser (a celebrated British journalist and travel writer who liked both the Jews and the modern world), "in what goes to make what is called 'the man of the world'—alertness and knowledge—the Jew is the superior of the Christian," leaving the latter no choice but to "recognize that in fair contest it is pretty certain that the Jew will outstep the Christian." No wonder, then, that the Americans, who value fair contest above all else, get their ideals (which include democracy, frugality, and love of children, among others) "more from the Jews than from their Saxon forebears," whereas the Germans, who resemble their forebears much more closely, have no choice but to resort to *numerus clausus* because the struggle "between the sons of the North, with their blond hair and sluggish intellects, and these sons of the Orient, with their black eyes and alert minds, is an unequal one."[30]

Sombart agreed (curiously enough), as he lamented the fact that "the more slow-witted, the more thick-skulled, the more ignorant of business a people is, the more effective is Jewish influence on their economic life," and so did the British historian (and committed Zionist) Lewis Bernstein Namier, who attributed the rise of Nazism—in familiar Mercurian terms—to the German inability to compete. "The German is methodical, crude, constructive mainly in a mechanical sense, extremely submissive to authority, a rebel or a fighter only by order from above; he gladly remains all his life a tiny cog in a machine"; whereas "the Jew, of Oriental or Mediterranean race, is creative, pliable, individualistic, restless, and undisciplined," providing much needed but never acknowledged leadership in German cultural life. Similar contrasts were easily observed throughout Europe, especially in the East and most strikingly in the Russian Empire, where the Apollonian-Mercurian gap appeared as wide as the legal restrictions were severe. According to Fraser, "if the Russian dispassionately spoke his mind, I think he would admit that his dislike of the Jew is not so much racial or religious—though these play great parts—as a recognition that the Jew is his superior, and in conflicts of wits get the better of him." Indeed, the Russian may be admirable because of "his simplicity of soul, his reverence, his genuine brotherliness, his wide-eyed wondering outlook on life," which shines through in his music and literature, "but when you reckon the Russian in the field of commerce, where nimbleness of brain has its special function, he does not show well."[31]

Nimbleness could always be denigrated as deviousness, whereas soulfulness was the usual consolation of a thick skull; either way, the fact of the Jewish success, or "ubiquity," remained at the center of the debate, the real puzzle to be explained. Between the supernatural tales of conspiracy and possession on the one hand and the arcana of the germ-plasm on the other, the most common explanations were historical and religious ("cultural"). Sombart, who bemoaned the passing of "those Northern forests . . . where in winter the faint sunlight glistens on the rime and in summer the song of birds is everywhere," provided a particularly influential antirationalist account. On the "Enlightenment" side, one of the most eloquent statements belonged to the prolific publicist and social scientist Anatole Leroy-Beaulieu. "We often marvel at the variety of Jewish aptitudes," he wrote by way of summarizing his argument, "at their singular ability to assimilate, at the speed with which they appropriate our knowledge and our methods."

> We are mistaken. They have been prepared by heredity, by two thousand years of intellectual gymnastics. By taking up our sciences, they do not enter an unknown territory, they return to a country already explored by their ancestors. The centuries have not only equipped Israel for stock-market wars and assaults on fortune, they have armed it for scientific battles and intellectual conquests.[32]

Equally mistaken, according to Leroy-Beaulieu, was the talk of a peculiarly Jewish (and peculiarly harmful) messianism—what Chamberlain would call "their talent for planning impossible socialistic and economic Messianic empires without inquiring whether they thereby destroy the whole of the civilization and culture which we have so slowly acquired." In fact, the Jewish Messiah belonged to us all: "we have a name for him, we await him, too, we call him as loudly as we can." It is called Progress—the same progress that had "slumbered in the [Jewish] books, biding its time, until Diderot and Condorcet revealed it to the nations and spread it around the world. But no sooner had the Revolution proclaimed it and begun to implement it than the Jews recognized it and reclaimed it as the legacy of their ancestors." The Messiah finally arrived when, "at the approach of our tricolor, caste barriers and ghetto walls tumbled down," and the liberated Jew stood atop a barricade, at the head of the universal struggle against prejudice and inequality.[33]

Marianne was as Jewish as Rothschild and Einstein, in other words, and most authors agreed that the reasons for their rise could be found in the Jewish past. Even conspiracy theorists explained the Jewish capacity for intrigue as a result of their long-standing traits, and most racial explanations were Lamarckian in that they assumed the inheritance of historically acquired characteristics. But there was another view, of course—one that preferred rootlessness and homelessness to antiquity and continuity. In a 1919 essay which reshaped that tradition to fit a radically Mercurianized world, Thorstein Veblen argued that "the intellectual preeminence of Jews in modern Europe" was due to a break with the past, not its resurrection. "The cultural heritage of the Jewish people" may be very ancient and very distinguished, "but these achievements of the Jewish ancients neither touch the frontiers of modern science nor do they fall in the lines of modern scholarship." Scientific progress "presupposes a degree of exemption from hard-and-fast preconceptions, a sceptical animus, *Unbefangenheit*, release from the dead hand of conventional finality," and the reason "the intellectually gifted Jew" is everywhere on top is that he is the most unattached, the most marginal, and therefore the most skeptical and unconventional of all scientists. "It is by loss of allegiance, or at the best by force of a divided allegiance to the people of his origin, that he finds himself in the vanguard of modern inquiry. . . . He becomes a disturber of the intellectual peace, but only at the cost of becoming an intellectual wayfaring man, a wanderer in the intellectual no-man's-land, seeking another place to rest, farther along the road, somewhere over the horizon." The eternal Jew meets the new Jewish scientist and likes what he sees. By curing the Jews of their homelessness, Zionism would spell the end of their "intellectual preeminence."[34]

Where Sombart had compared the Jews to Mephistopheles shadowing the Christian Faust, Veblen insisted that it was Faust who was the real Jew. But both agreed—and so did everyone else—that there was a peculiar kinship between Jews and the Modern Age, that the Jews, in some very important sense, *were* the Modern Age. No matter what the standard—rationalism, nationalism, capitalism, professionalism, Faustian Prometheanism, literacy, democracy, hygiene, alienation, or the nuclear family—Jews seemed to have been there first, done it earlier, understood it best. Even Zarathustra, whom Nietzsche chose to speak on his behalf, turned out to be the exclusive God of the "Jews of India." In the words of the Parsi poet Adil Jussawalla, "Nietzsche did not know that Superman Zarathustra was the Jews' first brother."[35]

The identification of the Jews with the forces that were molding the modern world was one of the few things that most European intellectuals, from the Romantics of the "Northern forests" to the prophets of Reason and the tricolor, could occasionally agree on. Perhaps not surprisingly, therefore, the two great apocalyptic revolts against modernity were also the two final solutions to the "Jewish problem." Marx, who began his career by equating capitalism with Judaism, attempted to solve his own Jewish problem (and that of so many of his disciples) by slaying capitalism. Hitler, whose "long soul struggle" as a young man had revealed the Jewish roots of urban "corruption," attempted to tame capitalism by murdering Jews.[36]

The Jewish economic and professional success beyond the ghetto walls was accompanied by the easing of the old "blood" and food taboos and the adoption of new languages, rituals, names, clothes, and kinsmen in a dramatic makeover commonly described as "assimilation." But who were the Jews becoming similar to? Certainly not their peasant neighbors and clients, who were undergoing an agonizing "urbanization," "modernization," and "secularization" of their own. Both were moving, at the same time, into the same semineutral spaces of modern citizenship by paying the required fee of ceasing to be "themselves." The Jews were shedding their names and their tribe in order to keep their Mercurian trades and Mercurian cleverness; the peasants had to forsake their whole world in order to keep their name and their tribe. Both were deluded: whereas the assimilating Jews believed, reasonably but mistakenly, that they were discarding something that had lost all meaning, the urbanizing peasants assumed, absurdly but correctly, that they could change completely while remaining the same. At the dawn of the Modern Age, Henri de Navarre had been able to say that Paris was "worth a mass" because religion no longer mattered much to him. Many nineteenth-century European Jews felt the same way, forgetting that there was a new religion abroad. The mass, it is true, was not worth very much, but Paris was now the capital of a nation, and it was asking a much higher price. All modern states were Mercurias in Apollonian garb; old Mercurians, of all people, should never have underestimated the importance of disguise.

The Modern Age was Jewish not only because everyone was now a stranger but also because strangers were organized—or reassembled—into groups based on common descent and destiny. The Weberian world of "mechanized petrification embellished with a sort of convulsive self-importance" could be sustained—indeed, conceived—only within states that posed as tribes. The ordeal of peasant conversion to city life could be endured only if the city claimed convincingly and sincerely enough that it was but an expanded and improved version of the peasant village, not its demonic slayer. The transformation of peasants into Frenchmen could be accomplished only if France stood for Patrie as well as Progress.[37]

This combination of patriotism and progress, or the worship of the new state as an old tribe (commonly known as nationalism) became the new opium of the people. Total strangers became kinsmen on the basis of common languages, origins, ancestors, and rituals duly standardized and disseminated for the purpose. The nation was family writ large: ascriptive and blood-bound but stretched well beyond human memory or face recognition, as only a metaphor could be. Or perhaps it was Christianity writ small: one was supposed to love certain others as brothers and certain neighbors as oneself. In other words, the Jews were doomed to a new exile as a result of the Judaizing of their Apollonian hosts: no sooner had they become ready to become Germans (for who needed chosenness, *kashrut*, or the *shadkhen* [matchmaker] if everyone was becoming Jewish anyway?) than the Germans themselves became "chosen." It was now as difficult for a Jew to become German as it had always been for a German to become Jewish. Christianity, at least in principle, had been open to all by means of conversion, but back when Christianity was being taken seriously, so was Judaism, which meant that conversions were true acts of apostasy. Only when Judaism became less legitimate among the "enlightened" and the "assimilated," and conversion became a more or less formal oath of allegiance to the bureaucratic state, did the bureaucratic state became national and thus jealously exclusive.

A male convert to Judaism had always cut a lonely and melancholy figure because it was not easy to "imagine" one's way into an alien community bounded by sacralized common descent and a variety of physical and cultural markers that served as both proof of shared parentage and a guarantee of continued endogamy. The would-be Jewish converts to Germanness or Hungarianness found themselves in a similar but much more difficult position, because Germanness and Hungarianness were represented by a powerful state that claimed to be both national and (more or less) liberal while also insisting on being the sole guardian of rights and judge of identity.

The most common early strategy of the newly "emancipated" and "assimilated" Jews was to promote the liberal cause by celebrating "neutral spaces" in public life and cultivating a liberal education and the liberal professions in their own. Jews were not just the embodiment of Reason and Enlightenment—they were among their most vocal and loyal champions. They voted for liberal parties, argued the virtues of individual liberties, and faithfully served those states that allowed them to do so. The Habsburg Empire—as well as France, of course—was the object of much loyalty and admiration because, as the historian Carl Schorske put it, "the emperor and the liberal system offered status to the Jews without demanding nationality; they became the supra-national people of the multinational state, the one folk which, in effect, stepped into the shoes of the earlier aristocracy."[38]

To join the later—liberal—aristocracy, one needed to acquire a new secular education and professional expertise. And that is exactly what the Jews, as a group, did—with an intensity and fervor worthy of a yeshiva and a degree of success that was the cause of much awe and resentment. Gustav Mahler's father read French philosophers when he was not selling liquor; Karl Popper's father translated Horace when he was not practicing law; and Victor Adler's grandfather divided his time between Orthodox Judaism and European Enlightenment. But what mattered most—to them and thousands like them, as well as to History—is whose fathers they were. Liberal education as the new Jewish religion was very similar to the old Jewish religion—except that it was much more liberal. Secularized Jewish fathers—stern or indulgent, bankers (like Lukács's father) or haberdashers (like Kafka's)—did their best to bring up free, cosmopolitan Men: men without fathers. They were remarkably successful: indeed, few generations of patriarchs were as good at raising patricides and grave diggers as first-generation Jewish liberals. And no one understood it better than Sigmund Freud and Karl Marx.[39]

Liberalism did not work because neutral spaces were not very neutral. The universities, "free" professions, salons, coffeehouses, concert halls, and art galleries in Berlin, Vienna, and Budapest became so heavily Jewish that liberalism and Jewishness became almost indistinguishable. The Jews' pursuit of rootlessness ended up being almost as familial as their pursuit of wealth. Success at "assimilation" made assimilation more difficult, because the more successful they were at being modern and secular, the more visible they became as the main representatives of modernity and secularism. And this meant that people who were not very good at modernity and secularism, or who objected to them for a variety of Apollonian (and Dionysian) reasons, were likely to be impressed by political anti-Semitism. As Käthe Leichter remembered her high school days in fin de siècle Vienna, "with my [Jewish] friends I discussed the meaning of life, shared my ideas about books, poetry, nature, and music. With the daughters of government officials I played 'house.'" Käthe Leichter grew up to be a socialist and a sociologist; at least some of those officials' daughters grew up to be anti-Semites.[40]

But mostly liberalism did not work because it never could—not in the sense of interchangeable cosmopolitan individuals and certainly not in the Apollonian Babylon of Central and Eastern Europe. The facts that nobody spoke Liberalese as a native tongue and that the Man who had Rights also had citizenship and family attachments were easy to forget if one lived in a state that was more or less successful at equating itself with both family and the universe. It was much harder to do in a doomed Christian state or a youthful national one. Nobody spoke Austro-Hungarian, on the one hand, and on the other, it took a lot of practice to start thinking of Czech as a language of high secular culture. The Jews who did not wish to speak the language of particularism (Yiddish, for most of them) had to find the language of universalism by shopping around. The main selling points of would-be national universalisms (French, German, Russian, Hungarian) were a claim to a prestigious high-cultural tradition and, most important, a state that would give that claim some muscle and conviction. Esperanto—conceived in Białystok by the Jewish student Ludwik Zamenhof—had no chance of living to maturity. Universalism relied on the nation-state as much as the nation did.

The Jews did not launch the Modern Age. They joined it late, had little to do with some of its most important episodes (such as the Scientific and Industrial Revolutions), and labored arduously to adjust to its many demands. They did adjust better than most—and reshaped the modern world as a consequence—but they were not present at the creation and missed out on some of the early role assignments.

By most accounts, one of the earliest episodes in the history of modern Europe was the Renaissance, or the rebirth of godlike Man. But the Renaissance did not just create the cult of Man—it created cults of particular men whose job it was to write the new Scriptures, to endow an orphaned and deified humanity with a new shape, a new past, and a new tongue fit for a new Paradise. Dante, Camões, and Cervantes knew themselves to be prophets of a new age, knew their work to be divinely inspired and "immortal," knew they were writing a new Bible by rewriting the *Odyssey* and the *Aeneid*. Even as Christianity continued to claim a complete monopoly on the transcendental, the Modern Age turned polytheistic—or rather, reverted to the days of divine oligarchy, with the various gods enjoying universal legitimacy (the "Western canon") but serving as patrons and patriarchs of particular tribes. Dante, Camões, and Cervantes defined and embodied national golden ages, national languages, and national journeys toward salvation. Ethnic nationalism, like Christianity, had a content, and every national Genesis had an author. Cervantes may be the inventor of the modern novel and an object of much reverence and imitation, but only among Spanish-speakers is he worshiped rapturously and tragically, as a true god; only in Spanish high culture must every contender for canonical status take part in the continuing dialogue between Don Quixote and Sancho Panza.[41]

In England, the Age of Shakespeare coincided with, and perhaps ushered in, the Universal Age of Discovery, or the Era of Universal Mercurianism. This was true of all national golden ages, but the English one proved more equal than others because England (along with Holland but much more influentially) became the first Protestant nation, the first nation of strangers, the first nation to replace God with itself—and with its Bard. By being the English national poet, Shakespeare became "the inventor of the human." The Renaissance met the Reformation, or, as Matthew Arnold put it, "Hellenism reentered the world, and again stood in the presence of Hebraism, a Hebraism renewed and purged."[42]

In this context, the French Revolution was an attempt to catch up by taking a shortcut—an attempt to build a nation of strangers by creating a world of brothers. According to Ernest Gellner, "the Enlightenment was not merely a secular prolongation and more thorough replay of the Reformation. In the end it also became an inquest by the unreformed on their own condition, in the light of the successes of the reformed. The *philosophes* were the analysts of the under-development of France."[43] France is the only European nation without a consecrated and uncontested national poet, the only nation for which the rational Man is a national hero. It is "ethnic" as well, of course, with its "ancestors the Gauls" and its jealous worship of the national language, but the seriousness of its civic commitments is unique in Europe. Rabelais, Racine, Molière, and Victor Hugo have failed to unseat Reason and have had to cohabit with it, however uncomfortably.

From then on, England and France presented two models of modern nationhood: build your own tribe of strangers complete with an immortal Bard, or claim, more or less convincingly, to have transcended tribalism once and for all. The English road to nationalism was the virtually universal first choice. The old "Renaissance nations" with established modern pantheons and golden ages (Dante's Italy, Cervantes's Spain, Camões's Portugal) had only the Mercurian ("bourgeois") half of the task ahead of them; the new Protestant nations (Holland, Scotland, Denmark, Sweden, possibly Germany) could take their time searching for an appropriate bard; all the others had to scramble desperately on both fronts and perhaps entertain the French option when in trouble. Romanticism was a rebirth of the Renaissance and a time of frenetic Bible writing (on canvas and music sheets, as well as on paper). Those laboring in the shadow of an already canonized national divinity (Wordsworth and Shelley, for example) had to settle for demigod status, but elsewhere the field was wide open, for better or worse. The new Romantic intelligentsias east of the Rhine were all raised to be "self-hating" because they had been born in the twilight of Christian universalism and had promptly found themselves belonging to inarticulate, undifferentiated, and unchosen tribes (and possibly to illegitimate states, as well). Petr Chaadaev, the founding father of the Russian intelligentsia, was speaking for all of them when he said that Russia lived "in the narrowest of presents, without past or future, amidst dull stagnation. . . . Alone in the world, we have not given the world anything, have not taken anything from the world, have contributed nothing to the advance of human thought, and have distorted whatever traces of that advance we did receive." His words rang out like "a shot in the dark night," according to Herzen, and soon everyone woke up and went to work. Goethe, Pushkin, Mickiewicz, and Petőfi, among many others, were celebrated as national messiahs in their lifetimes and formally deified soon after their deaths. New modern nations were born: certifiably chosen and thus immortal, ready to tackle History in general and the Age of Mercurianism, in particular.[44]

Jews who wanted to join the world of equal and inalienable rights had to do it through one of these traditions. To enter the neutral spaces, one had to convert to a national faith. And that is precisely what many European Jews did—in much greater numbers than those who converted to Christianity, because the acceptance of Goethe as one's savior did not seem to be an apostasy and because it was much more important and meaningful than baptism. After the triumph of cultural nationalism and the establishment of national pantheons, Christianity was reduced to a formal survival or reinterpreted as a part of the national journey. One could be a good German or Hungarian without being a good Christian (and in an ideal liberal Germany or Hungary, religion in the traditional sense would become a private matter "separate from the state"), but one could not be a good German or Hungarian without worshiping the national canon. This was the real new church, the one that could not be separated from the state lest the state lose all meaning, the one that was all the more powerful for being taken for granted, the one that Jews could enter while still believing that they were in a neutral place worshiping Progress and Equality. It was possible to be an American "of Mosaic faith" because the American national religion was not based on tribal descent and the cult of the national soul embodied by a national bard. In turn-of-the-century Central and Eastern Europe, it was impossible because the national faith was itself Mosaic.

Having entered the new church, Jews proceeded to worship. At first the preferred medium was German, but with the establishment of other strong, institutionalized canons, large numbers of Jews became Hungarian, Russian, and Polish believers. Osip Mandelstam's description of his bookcase tells the story of these Jews chronologically, genealogically (his mother's and father's lineages), and, from his vantage point as a Russian poet, hierarchically:

> I remember the lower shelf as being always chaotic: the books were not standing side by side but lay like ruins: the rust-colored Pentateuchs with their tattered bindings, a Russian history of the Jews, written in the clumsy and timid language of a Russian-speaking Talmudist. This was the Judaic chaos abandoned to the dust. . . .
>
> Above these Judaic remnants the books stood in orderly formation; these were the Germans—Schiller, Goethe, Koerner, and Shakespeare in German—the old Leipzig and Tübingen editions, short and stout in their embossed dark-red bindings, with the fine print meant for youthful sharp-sightedness and with delicate engravings hinting at classical antiquity: the women with their hair down and arms outstretched, the lamp depicted as an oil-burning one, the horsemen with their high foreheads, and the grape clusters in the vignettes. That was my father the autodidact fighting his way into the Germanic world through the Talmudic thicket.
>
> Higher still were my mother's Russian books: Pushkin in the 1876 Isakov edition. I still think it was an absolutely marvelous edition and like it better than the Academy one. There is nothing superfluous in it; the type is gracefully arranged; the columns of verse flow freely, like soldiers in flying battalions, and leading them, like generals, are the sensible, distinct year headings all the way through 1837. What color is Pushkin? Every color is accidental—for what color could capture the wizardry of words?[45]

The secular Jews' love of Goethe, Schiller, and other Pushkins—as well as the various northern forests they represented—was sincere and tender. (Germany was peculiar in having twin gods, as Mandelstam called them. They are still together in their Weimar mausoleum.) "At night I think of Germany / And then there is no sleep for me," wrote Heine, with as much longing as irony, in his Parisian exile. "Were we not raised on German legends?" asked Moritz Goldstein more than half a century later, "Does not the Germanic forest live within us?" His own answer was a resounding "yes": virtually all the Jewish households in the German lands—

and far, far beyond—had their own Schiller shelves next to, and increasingly above, the "rust-colored Pentateuchs with their tattered bindings." So strong was the passion and so complete the identification that very soon Jews became conspicuous in the role of priests of various national cults: as poets, painters, performers, readers, interpreters, and guardians. "We Jews administer the spiritual possessions" of Germany, wrote Moritz Goldstein.[46]

The prominence of Jews in the administration of Germany's spiritual possessions posed a problem. First, because there seemed to be more to Germany than spiritual possessions. In the words of Gershom Scholem, "for many Jews the encounter with Friedrich Schiller was more real than their encounter with actual Germans." And who were the actual Germans? According to Franz Rosenzweig, they were "the assessor, the fraternity student, the petty bureaucrat, the thick-skulled peasant, the pedantic school master." If one wished to be German, one had to join them, embrace them, become them—if one knew how.[47] "We meet the Russian people through their culture," wrote Vladimir Jabotinsky in 1903, "mostly their writers—or rather, the best, highest, purest manifestations of the Russian spirit." However, he continued,

> Because we do not know the daily life of Russia—the Russian dreariness and philistinism—we form our impression of the Russian people by looking *only* at their geniuses and leaders, and of course we get a beautiful fairy tale as a result. I do not know if many of us love Russia, but many, too many of us, children of the Jewish intelligentsia, are madly, shamefully in love with Russian culture, and through it with the whole Russian world.[48]

This is a "distorted image," to borrow Sidney Bolkosky's expression. Not only because "stupid Ivan" remained—in the shtetls, at least—the dominant Jewish representation of their non-Jewish neighbors, but also because the assessors, petty bureaucrats, and thick-skulled peasants were themselves trying to learn who their geniuses were and how to love them madly. The meaning of nationalism and the point of state-run mass education systems is to persuade large numbers of vaguely related rural Apollonians that they belong to a chosen tribe that is much bigger than the local community of shared customs and meals, but much smaller than the more or less universal Christianity of shared humanity and devotion. The various assessors, petty bureaucrats, and thick-skulled peasants had to learn—along with Jabotinsky's Jewish children but with much greater difficulty—that "the whole Russian world" was a reflection of Russian culture, and that Russian culture, like any other high culture worthy of the name, had its auspicious folkloric beginnings, its glorious golden age, its very own Shakespeare, its many geniuses who sprouted in his wake, and—if they were lucky—its own mighty state that defended and promoted that culture and its proud bearers. No one was supposed to love the "dreariness" and the "daily life" for their own sake, and no one was seriously expected to become a thick-skulled peasant (except perhaps in the summer, when colleges were not in session).

The non-Jewish "intelligentsia children" had as much trouble trying to embrace "the people" as the Jewish ones did, because both had become accustomed, as a result of intensive training, to viewing "actual Germans" through Friedrich Schiller. The "people," meanwhile, were scratching their heads trying to combine authenticity with education. Like all great religions, nationalism is based on an absurd doctrine, and it so happened that the two high-culture areas where most European Jews lived failed to come to terms with it. In Germany, the assessor, the fraternity student, the petty bureaucrat, the pedantic schoolmaster, and the thick-skulled peasant were able to lash out against the impossible demands of modernity by identifying them with the Jews and staging the world's most brutal and best-organized pogrom; in Russia, the children of the intelligentsia (many of them Jewish) took power and attempted to implement an uncompromising version of the "French model" by waging the world's most brutal and best-organized assault against the assessor, the fraternity student, the petty bureaucrat, the pedantic schoolmaster, and the thick-skulled peasant. Especially the thick-skulled peasant.

In any case, the Jewish problem with national canons was not that the Jews loved Pushkin too much (it is impossible to live in Russia and love Pushkin too much) but that they were too good at it. It was the same problem, in other words, as the one faced by Jewish doctors, lawyers, and journalists—except that the object in question was the "spiritual possessions of a nation." In pre–World War I Odessa, according to Jabotinsky, "assimilated Jews found themselves in the role of the only public bearers and propagandists of Russian culture," with no choice but "to honor Pushkin . . . in total isolation." Something similar—allowing for Goldstein's polemical hyperbole—was happening in Vienna and Budapest. Much to their own surprise and discomfort (as well as pride), Jews became extremely visible in the occupations whose function was to disguise the irreversibility of what was happening to yesterday's Apollonians. To promote liberalism, they took up national canons, and by promoting national canons, they undermined liberalism and their own position—because the point of national canons was to validate therapeutic claims to tribal continuity. Pushkin, Mickiewicz, Goethe-Schiller, Petőfi, and their successors enacted and symbolized the conversion of legendary Slavic, Germanic, and Magyar pasts into modern high cultures, to be used by the putative descendants of those pasts. Jews could not and mostly did not pretend to partake of that tribal connection and thus were seen as interlopers. To complete the quotation from Moritz Goldstein, "We Jews administer the spiritual possessions of a people that denies us the capability of doing so."[49]

The stronger the denial, the greater the perceived Jewishness of the "administrators," many of whom never agreed to become German on German terms in any case. As Eugen Fuchs, the president of the largest German Jewish organization, said in 1919, "We are German and want to remain German, and achieve here, in Germany, on German soil, our equal rights, regardless of our Jewish characteristics. . . . Also, we want inner regeneration, a renaissance of Judaism, not assimilation. And we want proudly to remain true to our characteristics and our historical development."[50] This statement can serve as a useful explication of the paradox contained in the title of Fuchs's organization: Zentralverein für deutsche Staatsbürger jüdischen Glaubens, or Central Association of German Citizens of the Jewish Faith. In the Age of Nationalism, one could not be German without sharing the German "historical development" any more than one could separate "the Jewish faith" from ethnic belonging.

But being unable or unwilling to be German in Germany or Russian in Russia was only half the problem, because most Jews of Central and Eastern Europe did not live among Germans or Russians. At the turn of the twentieth century, most Jews of Central and Eastern Europe were "the bearers and propagandists" of German culture among Czechs, Latvians, and Romanians; Magyar culture among Slovaks, Ukrainians, and Romanians; Russian culture among Ukrainians, Belorussians, Lithuanians, and Poles; and Polish culture among Ukrainians, Lithuanians, and Belorussians (to simplify a dizzyingly diverse picture). The Jews allied themselves with powerful states and cohesive national elites because that was their path to Progress; many of their neighbors strongly objected to those states and those elites—and therefore to the Jews—because they were on a different path to Progress. And so while the Jews worshiped Goethe-Schiller and Pushkin, their old Apollonian clients were learning how to express their love for Shevchenko and perhaps dreaming of a savior-state that would unite them for eternity. To the traditional Apollonian dislike of Mercurians was added a new resentment of the Jewish association, however tenuous, with a foreign nation-state, as well as the Jewish monopoly of the jobs that more and more Apollonians now wanted for themselves. Slovaks moving into towns found Jews occupying many high-status jobs and persisting in speaking German or Hungarian. The old secret language of Mercurian trade had been replaced by the new secret language of alien modernity. What pogroms, persuasion, and competition could not accomplish, perhaps one's "own" state would.

The Jewish Age was also the Age of Anti-Semitism. Because of their Mercurian training, the Jews excelled in the entrepreneurial and professional occupations that were the source of status and power in the modern state; because of their Mercurian past, they were tribal strangers who did not belong in the modern state, let alone in its centers of power. This was a completely new "Jewish problem": in the traditional society, Apollonians and Mercurians had lived in separate worlds defined by their different economic roles; their need and contempt for each other had been based on the continual reproduction of that difference. Now that they were moving into the same spaces without becoming interchangeable, the mutual contempt grew in reverse proportion to mutual need. Except that it was the Apollonians who wanted the Mercurian jobs and the Apollonians who "owned" the nation-state. The better the Jews were at becoming Germans or Hungarians, the more visible they became as an elite and the more resented they were as tribal aliens ("hidden" and therefore much more frightening, to be defined as "contagion" and combated by "cleansing"). Even when the transformation, or disguise, seemed successful, the never-ending influx of immigrants from the East, with their secret language, distinctive appearance, and traditional peddling and tailoring occupations, continually exposed the connection. The Jews were associated with both faces of modernity: capitalism and nationalism. As capitalists and professionals, they seemed to be (secretly) in charge of a hostile world; as the "administrators" of national cultures, they appeared to be impostors.

The "Jewish problem" was not just the problem that various (former) Christians had with the Jews; it was also the problem that various (former) Jews had with their Jewishness. Like other modern intelligentsias that did not have a secular national canon or nation-state to call their own, the "enlightened" Jews had some apocalyptic things to say about their fathers' world. In 1829, Petr Chaadaev, the first prophet of Russian national despair, had written that Russians lived "like illegitimate children: without inheritance, without any connection to those who went before, without any memory of lessons learned, each one of us trying to reconnect the torn family thread."[51] By the turn of the twentieth century, many Jewish writers felt the same way about their own paternity. According to Otto Weininger, the Jew was lacking in a "free intelligible ego," "true knowledge of himself," "the individual sense of ancestry," and ultimately in a "soul."[52] And in 1914 Joseph Hayyim Brenner wrote:

> We have no inheritance. Each generation gives nothing of its own to its successor. And whatever was transmitted—the rabbinical literature—were better never handed down to us. . . . We live now without an environment, utterly outside any environment. . . . Our function

now is to recognize and admit our meanness since the beginning of history to the present day, and the faults in our character, and then to rise and start all over again.[53]

This is "self-hatred" as the lowest and earliest stage of national pride. Chaadaev, Weininger, Brenner, and many more like them, Jews and non-Jews, were prophets reminding their people of their chosenness. "The ox knoweth his owner, and the ass his master's crib: but Israel doth not know, my people doth not consider" (Isa. 1:3). All three were martyrs: Chaadaev was declared insane; Weininger committed suicide; and Brenner was killed in Palestine. All three suffered in the name of national salvation—including Weininger, who appeared uncompromising in his negation: "Christ was a Jew, precisely that He might overcome the Judaism within Him, for he who triumphs over the deepest doubt reaches the highest faith; he who has raised himself above the most desolate negation is most sure in his position of affirmation."[54]

But what would be the salvation of secular Jews? One year after Chaadaev published his "First Philosophical Letter," Pushkin was killed in a duel and Russia acquired its national poet and cultural legitimacy along with an inheritance and a future. To most Jewish intellectuals, meanwhile, the nationalist solution (proposed by the Zionist Brenner) seemed neither likely nor desirable. Were they not already Mercurian? Would they not have to go backward (away from Progress)? Did they really want to transform themselves into thick-skulled peasants now that the actual peasants had, for all practical purposes, admitted the error of their ways? Some did (by posing the questions differently), but the majority continued to battle, tragically, with various ethnic editions of European Enlightenment. The Jewish embrace of Pushkin was not being returned, and the more they loved him, the less fond he seemed to be of them (to paraphrase a line from *Eugene Onegin*).

With all their success—because of all their success—the highly cultivated children of upwardly mobile Jewish businessmen felt lonely indeed. The great modern transformation did not just combine tribalism with "ascetic rationalism." As far as the European Jews, at least, were concerned, it was primarily—and tragically—

about tribalism. By acting in a Weberian (ascetic rational) fashion, many of them found themselves in an impossible, and possibly unique, situation. Deprived of the comforts of their tribe and not allowed into the new ones created by their Apollonian neighbors, they became the only true moderns.

Thus the Jews stood for the discontents of the Modern Age as much as they did for its accomplishments. Jewishness and existential loneliness became synonyms, or at least close intellectual associates. "Modernism" as the autopsy and indictment of modern life was not Jewish any more than it was "degenerate," but there is little doubt that Jewishness became one of its most important themes, symbols, and inspirations.

Modernism was a rebirth of Romanticism and the next great Promethean, prophetic revolution. (Realism did not propose a brand-new universe and thus never left the shadow of Romanticism.) Once again, would-be immortals set out to overcome history and reinvent the human by improving on Homer and the Bible. This time, it was an internal odyssey in search of the lost self: the confession, and perhaps salvation, of the Eternal Jew as the Underground Man. Modernism was a rebellion against the two bodies of modernity, and no one expressed or experienced it more fully than the chosen Jewish son who had rejected the capitalism and tribalism of his father and found himself all alone. It was a culture of solitude and self-absorption, a personification of Mercurian exile and reflexivity, a manifesto of the newly invented rebellious adolescence as a parable for the human condition.

Of the three most canonical voices of this revolution, one belonged to Franz Kafka, who classified—and damned—his businessman father as belonging to that "transitional generation of Jews which had migrated from the still comparatively devout countryside to the cities" and failed to retain, much less pass on, any meaningful Judaism beyond "a few flimsy gestures." According to his filial denunciation (a genre that another modern Jewish prophet would make compulsory), "this sense of nothingness that often dominates me (a feeling that is in another respect, admittedly, also a noble and fruitful one) comes largely from your influence." Brutally but "guiltlessly," his father had created a perfect witness to the continual Fall of Man (as the junior Kafka described it). "What have I in common with Jews?" he wrote in his diary on January 8, 1914, at the age of thirty. "I have hardly anything in common with myself and should stand very quietly in the corner, content that I can breathe." But of course he did no such thing, because it was precisely his "sense of nothingness"—which is to say, his Jewishness—that enabled him to "raise the world into the pure, the true, and the immutable."[55]

Another great poet of sublime loneliness and narcissism was Marcel Proust, the grandson of a successful Jewish foreign-exchange speculator and the baptized son of a woman who bore her liberal education and lost religion with an irony that Marcel seems to have found seductive. Seductive but not irresistible: elusive and protean as Proust's characters appear to be, there existed, in his memory-induced world, two marginal "races" that circumscribed human fluidity even as they embodied it. Endowed with irreducible qualities that, once perceived, make persons and lives "intelligible" and "self-evident," Jews and "inverts" are more proficient at wearing masks because they have more recognizable faces:

> Shunning one another, seeking out those who are most directly their opposite, who do not want their company, forgiving their rebuffs, enraptured by their condescensions; but also brought into the company of their own kind by the ostracism to which they are subjected, the opprobrium into which they have fallen, having finally been invested . . . with the physical and moral characteristics of a race, sometimes beautiful, often hideous, finding (in spite of all the mockery with which one who, more closely integrated with, better assimilated to the opposing race, is in appearance relatively less inverted, heaps upon one who has remained more so) a relief in frequenting the society of their kind, and even some support in their existence, so much so that, while steadfastly denying that they are a race (the name of which is the vilest of insults), they readily unmask those who succeed in concealing the fact that they belong to it.[56]

Accordingly, when Swann approached death, his "sense of moral solidarity with the rest of the Jews, a solidarity which Swann seemed to have forgotten throughout his life," became wholly intelligible and self-evident. "Swann's punchinello nose, absorbed for long years into an agreeable face, seemed now enormous, tumid, crimson, the nose of an old Hebrew rather than of a dilettante Valois." Swann's nose was both his curse and his strength. As Hannah Arendt summed up her discussion of Proust's pursuit of things lost and recovered, "Jewishness was for the individual Jew at once a physical stain and a mysterious personal privilege, both inherent in a 'racial predestination.' "[57]

But it is the defiantly European disciple of Irish Jesuits who is most frequently credited with the creation of modernism's most sacred text. An odyssey of "silence, exile, and cunning," *Ulysses* does battle with the Bible, *Hamlet,* and every other certifiably divine comedy from *Don Quixote* to *Faust* as it follows the wanderings of the "half-and-half" Jew Leopold Bloom, whose son is dead, whose wife is unfaithful, and whose peripatetic father (a peddler, innkeeper, and alleged "perpetrator of frauds" from Szombathely ["Sabbathville"], Hungary) has changed his name, converted to Protestantism, and—in case more proof were needed—committed suicide. Bloom is a modern Everyman because he is the modern Ulysses, and the modern Ulysses has got to be a Jew: "Jewgreek is greekjew." Or rather, the modern Ulysses is a *modern* Jew, who is remorseful but unapologetic about preferring Reason to Jerusalem and "treating with disrespect" such "beliefs and practices . . . as the prohibition of the use of fleshmeat and milk at one meal: the hebdomadary symposium of incoordinately abstract, perfervidly concrete mercantile coexreligionist excompatriots: the circumcision of male infants: the supernatural character of Judaic scripture: the ineffability of the tetragrammaton: the sanctity of the sabbath" (*U*17:1894–1901).[58]

Thrice converted, Bloom remains a Mercurian among Apollonians (Odysseus among monsters and lesser gods). He "hates dirty eaters," disapproves of drunkenness, "slips off when the fun gets too hot," decries the death penalty, "resents violence and intolerance in any shape or form," abominates the "patriotism of barspongers," and believes that "if a fellow had a rower's heart violent exercise was bad." He is "a new womanly man": a man of insatiable loquacity and curiosity who journeys ceaselessly in search of lost time, scientific knowledge, personal enrichment, and a social improvement "provocative of friendlier intercourse between man and man." He is both Homer's cunning Odysseus and Dante's tragic Ulysses, both Don Quixote and Faust. He is "a perverted Jew," as one of his friends and tormentors puts it (*U*8:696, 979; *U*16:1099–1100; *U*15:1692; *U*12:891–93; *U*15:1798; *U*16:1136–37; *U*12:1635).

But Bloom is not the only Mercurian in the Inferno of modern Dublin. Having buried his son and betrayed his father, he gains immortality by playing Virgil to an Apollonian bard who would redeem and transcend his birthplace by composing the Irish "national epic." A modern prophet as a young artist, Stephen Dedalus knows that the Word comes before the chosen people: "You suspect . . . that I may be important because I belong to the *faubourg Saint-Patrice* called Ireland for short. . . . But I suspect . . . that Ireland must be important because it belongs to me" (*U*16:1160–65). Both Stephen and Ireland (as well as Bloom) will attain immortality when he has written his *Ulysses*.

Before he can accomplish his mission, however, he must renounce his mother, defy his God, leave his home, and accept Bloom as his father and savior. They need each other, and Ireland needs both of them: "Stephen dissented openly from Bloom's views on the importance of dietary and civic selfhelp while Bloom dissented tacitly from Stephen's views on the eternal affirmation of the spirit of man in literature" (*U*17:28–30). Both were wrong and both knew it. At the end of their Odyssey, Bloom will have become reconciled to his Catholic Penelope, and Stephen will have become anointed as Odysseus ("a perverted Jew").

> What, reduced to their simplest reciprocal form, were Bloom's thoughts about Stephen's thoughts about Bloom and about Stephen's thoughts about Bloom's thoughts about Stephen?
> He thought that he thought that he was a jew whereas he knew that he knew that he knew that he was not. (*U*17:527–32)

Or maybe he knew that he knew that they were. Stephen was adopted (and symbolically conceived) by Bloom, and Bloom had

Swann's nose as his "endemic characteristic"—and knew that Stephen knew that he knew it. His "nasal and frontal formation was derived in a direct line of lineage which, though interrupted, would continue at distant intervals to more distant intervals to its most distant intervals" (*U*17:872–74).

But will Stephen the son of Bloom be able to produce the Irish national epic? *Ulysses*—his creature as well as creator and thus a kind of Bloom in its own right—seems perfectly equivocal on this question. Joyce's modernist Bible is recognized as such, of course (witness the manner of notation and textual exegesis), but who are its chosen people besides the two Supermen "sensitive to artistic impressions" and skeptical of "many orthodox religious, national, social, and ethical doctrines"? (*U*17:20–25). It was obviously foolish of Bloom to attempt an earnest conversation with the "truculent troglodytes" of popular nationalism in Barney Kiernan's public house, and neither Stephen Dedalus nor James Joyce was going to repeat Bloom's mistake. *Ulysses* is written by an Odysseus, not by a Homer.

And then there is the question of the *lingua Adamica*. *Ulysses* (much of it untranslatable) is as much about the English language as it is about Ulysses. The chapter devoted to Stephen's conception and subsequent gestation is also a history of English literature, while Bloom the father is also Shakespeare, or perhaps the ghost of Hamlet's father. The Bible of universal homelessness is an ardent, ambivalent, and mostly unheeded tribute to a bounded speech community. "Our young Irish bards, John Eglinton censured, have yet to create a figure which the world will set beside Saxon Shakespeare's Hamlet, though I admire him, as old Ben did, on this side of idolatry" (*U*9:43). Perhaps they have created them by now, and have become such figures themselves, but there is little doubt that they have no choice but to inhabit the world fathered and measured by Shakespeare. Hamlet may have had to make some room, but the idolaters of Pushkin and Cervantes only shrugged.

———

Nationalism—the great reward of the Apollonian odyssey and the nemesis of Jewish emancipation—was not the only modern religion. There were two more, both largely Jewish in their origins:

Marxism and Freudianism. Both competed with nationalism on its own turf by offering to overcome the loneliness of the new Mercurian world (and by extension human unhappiness); both countered nationalism's quaint tribalism with a modern (scientific) path to wholeness; both equaled nationalism in being capable of legitimizing modern states (socialism in one case and welfare capitalism in the other); and both seemed to eclipse nationalism by being able to determine the precise source of evil in the world and guarantee a redemption that was both specific and universal.

In Marxism, the original sin is in the historical division of labor, which leads to the alienation of labor, the enslavement of human beings by their own creations, and the fall of man into false consciousness, injustice, and degradation. The fall itself ensures salvation, however, for History, in its inexorable unfolding, creates a social class that, by virtue of its utter dehumanization and existential loneliness, is destined to redeem humanity by arriving at full self-realization. Proletarian free will and historical predestination (liberty and necessity) will merge in the act of an apocalyptic revolt against History in order to produce communism, a state in which there is no alienation of labor and thus no "contradictions," no injustice, and no Time. This is collective salvation, in that the reconciliation with the world is achieved by the whole of humanity on Judgment Day, but it is also strikingly modern because it results from technological progress and has been prophesied scientifically. The omnivorous monster of modernity releases its victims by devouring itself.

Freudianism locates the original sin within the individual by postulating a demonic, elusive, self-generating, and inextinguishable "unconscious." Salvation, or making the world whole again, amounts to individual self-knowledge, or the overcoming of the alienation between ego and libido and the achievement of inner peace ("mental unity"). This cannot be accomplished by "maladjusted" people themselves, because they are, by definition, possessed by the demon of the unconscious. Only professionally trained experts in touch with their own selves can tame (not exorcise!) the unruly unconscious, and only willing patients ready to open their hearts to their analysts can be healed. The séance itself combines features of both Christian confession and medical intervention but differs from them radically (possibly in the direction of greater efficacy) in that the sinner/patient is assumed to possess neither free will nor reason. "The modern malaise" is just that— a sickness that can be treated. Indeed, both the sickness and the treatment are perfect icons of the modern condition: the afflicted party is a lone individual, and the healer is a licensed professional hired by the sufferer (in what is the only certifiably rational act on his part). The result is individual, market-regulated, this-worldly redemption.[59]

Both Marxism and Freudianism were organized religions, with their own churches and sacred texts, and both Marx and Freud were true messiahs insofar as they stood outside time and could not be justified in terms of their own teachings. Marx knew History before History could know itself, and Freud—Buddha-like—was the only human to have achieved spontaneous self-knowledge (through a heroic act of self-healing that made all future healing possible). Both Marxism and Freudianism addressed the modern predicament by dealing with eternity; both combined the language of science with a promise of deliverance; and both spawned coherent all-purpose ideologies that claimed access to the hidden springs of human behavior. One foresaw and welcomed the violent suicide of universal Mercurianism; the other taught how to adjust to it (because there was nothing else one could do). Neither one survived in Central Europe, where they were born: one went east to become the official religion of a cosmopolitan state that replaced the most obstinate ancien régime in Europe; the other moved to the United States to reinforce democratic citizenship with a much-needed new prop. Liberalism had always made use of nationalism to give some life, color, and communal legitimacy to its Enlightenment premise; in America, where nationwide tribal metaphors could not rely on theories of biological descent, Freudianism came in very handy indeed. Besides trying to reconcile individual egoisms with a common interest by means of formal checks and balances, the state undertook, increasingly, to cure individual souls. This was not a new development (as Foucault tried to show, in too many words), but it gained a great deal of support from the psychoanalytic revolution. The Explicitly Therapeutic State—one that dispensed spiritual welfare along with material entitlements—was born at about the same time as its two ugly cousins: Hitler's *Volksgemeinschaft* and Stalin's "fundamentally" socialist state free from "class antagonism."

One of the main reasons why Marxism and Freudianism could compete with nationalism was that they, too, endorsed universal Mercurianism even as they condemned it. Freud stood Nietzsche on his head by suggesting the possibility of a well-functioning society of well-adjusted supermen: individuals who, with some help from Freud and friends, could defeat their own strangeness by taking charge of it. It was not a society of slaves or even of Weber's "specialists without spirit": it was a world of "freedom as perceived necessity." As for Marx, not only was communism the only natural offspring, conceived in sin and born in suffering, of capitalism's Prometheus Unbound; it was the ultimate bourgeois wish fulfillment—Nietzsche's and Weber's worst nightmare, the spirit of capitalism without capitalism. It was industriousness as a way of life, eternal work for its own sake. What Marx stood on its head was the traditional Apollonian concept of punishment and reward. Paradise became a place of ceaseless, spontaneous, unforced labor.[60]

Like nationalism (and, indeed, Christianity, which combined the Old and New Testaments), Marxism and Freudianism were greatly strengthened by the creative power of a moral and aesthetic dualism. Marxist regimes could speak the language of prelapsarian nostalgia, romantic rebellion, and eternal life, while also insisting on rigid materialism and economic determinism. In the same way, the Western postindustrial states could draw on Freudian concepts to prescribe—in varying proportions—both civilization and its discontents. On the one hand, instincts were all-powerful and unrelenting (a bad thing because we are their prisoners, or a good thing because to know them is to master them and perhaps to enjoy the consequences). On the other hand, the possibility of treatment suggested the hope for a cure (a good thing because a rational individual could talk his way out of unhappiness, or a bad thing because licensed bureaucrats might mold our souls to fit a soulless civilization). Freudianism never became the official religion of any state, but Freud's revelation of the true causes of human wretchedness did much to help the actually existing "welfare state" defeat its transcendentally inclined socialist nemesis.

Both Freud and Marx came from middle-class Jewish families. Freud's was a bit more Jewish (his parents were *Ostjude* immigrants from Galicia to Moravia), Marx's a bit more middle-class (his father, Herschel Levi, had become Heinrich Marx, a lawyer, a convinced *Aufklärer*, and a nominal Christian before Karl was born). Accordingly, each is probably best understood in the light of the other man's doctrine: Freud became the great savior of the middle class, Marx assailed the world in order to slay his Jewish father (and insisted that capitalism would be buried by its own progeny). "What is the secular basis of Judaism?" he wrote when he was twenty-five years old. "*Practical* need, self-interest. What is the secular cult of the Jew? *Haggling*. What is his secular God? *Money*. Well then! Emancipation from *haggling* and from *money*, i.e. from practical, real Judaism, would be the same as the self-emancipation of our age." To be more specific,

> The Jew has emancipated himself in a Jewish way not only by acquiring financial power but also because through him and apart from him *money* has become a world power and the practical Jewish spirit has become the practical spirit of the Christian peoples. The Jews have emancipated themselves in so far as the Christians have become Jews.

Hence,

> As soon as society succeeds in abolishing the *empirical* essence of Judaism—the market and the conditions which give rise to it—the Jew will have become *impossible*, for his consciousness will no longer have an object, the subjective basis of Judaism—practical need—will have become humanized and the conflict between man's individual sensuous existence and his species-existence will have been superseded.[61]

Any exploration of the national origins of the two doctrines is necessarily speculative—as are the many theories that try to explain their particular qualities and fortunes by relating them to the Judaic tradition. But it is undeniable that both appealed greatly to more or less middle-class Jewish audiences: Freudianism to the more middle-class, Marxism to the more Jewish (i.e., Yiddish). The two promises of nonnationalist salvation from modern loneliness were heeded by those lonely moderns who could not or would not be helped by nationalism.

No wonder, then, that the wandering Jewish apostate Leopold Bloom, who usually combated nationalism with pedestrian liberalism ("I want to see everyone, . . . all creeds and classes *pro rata* having a comfortable tidysized income" [*U*16:1133–34]), could also envision a "new Bloomusalem in the Nova Hibernia of the Future":

> I stand for the reform of municipal morals and the plain ten commandments. New worlds for old. Union for all, Jew, Moslem and gentile. Three acres and a cow for all children of nature. Saloon motor hearses. Compulsory manual labor for all. All parks open to the public day and night. Electric dishscrubbers. Tuberculosis, lunacy, war and mendicancy must now cease. General amnesty, weekly carnival with masked licence, bonuses for all, Esperanto the universal language with universal brotherhood. No more patriotism of barspongers and dropsical impostors. Free money, free rent, free love and a free lay church in a free lay state. (*U*15:1685–93)

On cooler reflection—and in the overall design of *Ulysses*— Bloom forswore revolution and sought deliverance through reconciliation with his Penelope and his self, for

> There remained the generic conditions imposed by natural as distinct from human law as integral parts of the human whole: the necessity of destruction to procure alimentary sustenance: the painful character of the ultimate functions of separate existence, the agonies of birth and death; the monotonous menstruation of simian and (particularly) human females extending from the age of puberty to the menopause. (*U*17:995–1000)

Freud's science was largely "a Jewish national affair," as he put it, with the non-Jewish Jung perceived as a stranger and cultivated as a *Paradegoy*.[62] Marxism was much more cosmopolitan, but Jewish participation in socialist and communist movements (especially in elite positions) was impressive indeed. Some of the most important theorists of German Social Democracy were Jews (Ferdinand Lassalle, Eduard Bernstein, Hugo Haase, Otto Landsberg), as were virtually all "Austro-Marxists" with the exception of Karl Renner (Rudolf Hilferding, Otto Bauer, Max Adler, Gustav Eckstein, Friedrich Adler). Socialists of Jewish descent—among them the creator of the Weimar constitution, Hugo Preuss, and the prime ministers of Bavaria (Kurt Eisner, 1918–19), Prussia (Paul Hirsch, 1918–20), and Saxony (Georg Gradnauer, 1919–21)—were well represented in various governments established in Germany in the wake of the imperial defeat in World War I. The same was true of the Communist uprisings of 1919: Spartacist leaders in Berlin included Rosa Luxemburg, Leo Jogisches, and Paul Levi; the Bavarian "Soviet republic" was headed (after April 13) by Eugen Leviné and at least seven other Jewish commissars (including the exuberant Ernst Toller and Gustav Landauer); and Béla Kun's revolutionary regime in Hungary consisted almost entirely of young Jews (20 out of 26 commissars, or, if one believes R. W. Seton-Watson, who was in Budapest at the time, "the whole government, save 2, and 28 out of the 36 ministerial commissioners").[63]

Between the wars, Jews remained prominent in the Weimar Republic's Social Democratic Party, especially as journalists, theorists, teachers, propagandists, and parliamentarians. Indeed, most professional socialist intellectuals in Germany and Austria were of Jewish descent (mostly children of upwardly mobile professionals and entrepreneurs). The circle around *Die Weltbühne*, a radical journal that inveighed tirelessly against Weimar philistinism, nationalism, militarism, and overall thickheadedness was about 70 percent Jewish. As István Deák put it,

> Apart from orthodox Communist literature where there were a majority of non-Jews, Jews were responsible for a great part of leftist literature in Germany. *Die Weltbühne* was in this respect not unique; Jews published, edited, and to a great part wrote the other left-wing intellectual magazines. Jews played a decisive role in the pacifist and feminist movements, and in the campaigns for sexual enlightenment.

The left-wing intellectuals did not simply 'happen to be mostly Jews' as some pious historiography would have us believe, but Jews created the left-wing intellectual movement in Germany.[64]

Probably the most influential (in the long run) left-wing intellectuals in Weimar Germany belonged to the so-called Frankfurt School, all of whose principal members (Theodor W. Adorno, Walter Benjamin, Erich Fromm, Max Horkheimer, Leo Löwenthal, and Herbert Marcuse, among others) came from middle-class Jewish homes. Determined to retain the promise of salvation but disheartened by the unwillingness of the German proletariat to bury capitalism (or rather, its apparent willingness to read Marx backward and attack Jews directly), they attempted to combine Marxism and Freudianism by means of psychoanalyzing deviant classes and collectivizing psychoanalytic practice. "Critical theory" was akin to religion insofar as it postulated a fateful chasm between the contingency of human existence and a state of complete self-knowledge and universal perfection; identified the ultimate source of evil in the world ("reification," or the enslavement of man by quasi-natural forces); foretold a final overcoming of history by way of merging necessity and freedom; and originated as a fully transcendental prophecy (because critical theorists were not subject to reification, for reasons that could not be supported by the critical theory itself). It was a feeble prophecy, however—elitist, skeptical, and totally lacking in the grandeur, certainty, and intensity of its heroic parents: a prophecy without an audience, Freudianism without the cure, Marxism without either scientism or imminent redemption. The critical theorists did not promise to change the world instead of explaining it; they suggested that the world might be changed by virtue of being explained (provided the blindfold of reified consciousness could be magically removed). They were not true prophets, in other words—resembling as they did therapists who had found their patients' condition to be serious, expressed full confidence in their eventual recovery (as a group), but were unable to either prescribe a course of treatment or present credible credentials. This stance proved productive on college campuses in the postwar United States, but it could hardly sustain the embattled opponents of nationalism in interwar Europe.

Members of the Frankfurt School did not wish to discuss their Jewish roots and did not consider their strikingly similar backgrounds relevant to the history of their doctrines (a perfectly understandable position because would-be prophets cannot be expected to be seriously self-reflective, and critical theorists, in particular, cannot be expected to relativize their unique claim to a nonreified consciousness). If their analysis of anti-Semitism is any indication, the proper procedure is either Marxist or Freudian, with the Marxist strain ("bourgeois anti-Semitism has a specific economic reason: the concealment of domination in production") fading inexorably into the background. According to Horkheimer and Adorno, anti-Semitism is primarily a "symptom," "delusion," and "false projection" that is "relatively independent of its object" and ultimately "irreconcilable with reality" (however defined). It is "a device for effortless 'orientation' in a cold, alienated, and largely ununderstandable world" used by the bourgeois self to project its own unhappiness—"from the very basis of which it is cut off by reason of its lack of reflective thought." One of the reasons for this unhappiness is envy, more specifically the envy of the Jewish nose—that "physiognomic *principium individuationis*, symbol of the specific character of the individual, described between the lines of his countenance. The multifarious nuances of the sense of smell embody the archetypal longing for the lower forms of existence, for direct unification with circumambient nature, with the earth and mud. Of all the senses, that of smell—which is attracted without objectifying—bears closest witness to the urge to lose oneself in and become 'the other.' " Marcel Proust could not have said it better.[65]

If one were to use a similar procedure in an attempt to examine Adorno's and Horkheimer's struggle with their own Jewishness, the most appropriate symptom would probably be their analysis of Homer's *Odyssey*, which they, revealingly (and apparently without the benefit of reading *Ulysses*), considered to be the foundational story of the modern self, "the schema of modern mathematics," the

Genesis of the all-enslaving Enlightenment. Odysseus, they claim, is "the prototype of the bourgeois individual" who forever betrays himself by tricking others. Physically weaker than the world he confronts, he "calculates his own sacrifice" and comes to embody deception "elevated to self-consciousness." The hero of "sobriety and common sense" as the highest and final stage of mythological cunning, he restrains himself "merely to confirm that the title of hero is only gained at the price of the abasement and mortification of the instinct for complete, universal, and undivided happiness." "Mutilated" by his own artifice, he pursues his "atomistic interest" in "absolute solitude" and "radical alienation," with nothing but the myth of exile and family warmth to keep him afloat. In other words, he has a pronounced "Semitic element"—especially because "the behavior of Odysseus the wanderer is reminiscent of that of the casual barterer" who relies on *ratio* in order to vanquish "the hitherto dominant traditional form of economy."[66]

> The wily solitary is already *homo oeconomicus*, for whom all reasonable things are alike; hence the Odyssey is already a *Robinsonade*. Both Odysseus and Crusoe, the two shipwrecked mariners, make their weakness (that of the individual who parts from the collectivity) their social strength. . . . Their impotence in regard to nature already acts as an ideology to advance their social hegemony. Odysseus' defenselessness against the breakers is of the same stamp as the traveler's justification of his enrichment at the expense of the aboriginal savage.[67]

Odysseus the clever barterer is thus the prototype of "the irrationalism of totalitarian capitalism, whose way of satisfying needs has an objectified form determined by domination which makes the satisfaction of needs impossible and tends toward the extermination of mankind." Marx and Freud meet Sombart (again). The theorists of "bourgeois self-hatred" and capitalist domination appear to be the grave diggers of their fathers' weakness and cunning.[68]

But that is not all. Enter the Nazis as man-eating Cyclopes, and Odysseus, "who calls himself Nobody for his own sake and manipulates approximation to the state of nature as a means of mastering nature, falls victim to *hubris*." Unable to stop talking, he invites death by tauntingly revealing his true identity to the blind monster and his wrathful divine protector.

> That is the dialectic of eloquence. From antiquity to fascism, Homer has been accused of prating both through his heroes' mouths and in the narrative interpolations. Prophetically, however, Ionian Homer showed his superiority to the Spartans of past and present by picturing the fate which the cunning man—the middleman—calls down upon himself by his words. Speech, though it deludes physical force, is incapable of restraint. . . . Too much talking allows force and injustice to prevail as the actual principle, and therefore prompts those who are to be feared always to commit the very action that is feared. The mythic compulsiveness of the word in prehistory is perpetuated in the disaster which the enlightened world draws down upon itself. Udeis [Nobody], who compulsively acknowledges himself to be Odysseus, already bears the characteristics of the Jew who, fearing death, still presumes on the superiority which originates in the fear of death; revenge on the middleman occurs not only at the end of bourgeois society, but—as the negative utopia to which every form of coercive power always tends—at its beginning.[69]

It may not be entirely clear how the loquacious progenitors of "totalitarian capitalism" bring about their own destruction; how deserved—considering their tendency "toward the extermination of mankind"—that destruction may be; or where the modern Cyclopes not blinded by Odyssean reason can possibly come from. But perhaps this was never meant to be history, anthropology, or even moral philosophy. Perhaps this was self-critical theory. Perhaps this was their way of saying, with Brenner, that their function was "to recognize and admit," through speech incapable of restraint, the "meanness" of their ancestors "since the beginning of history to the present day, and the faults in [their] character, and then to rise and start all over again." They did claim to hope, after all, that "the Jewish question would prove in fact to be the turning point of history. By overcoming that sickness of the mind which thrives on the ground of self-assertion untainted by reflective thought, mankind would develop from a set of opposing races to the species which, even as nature, is more than mere nature."[70] Leopold Bloom agreed: "All those wretched quarrels, in his humble opinion, stirring up bad blood, from some bump of combativeness or gland of some kind, erroneously supposed to be about a punctilio of honour and a flag, were very largely a question of the money question which was at the back of everything greed and jealousy, people never knowing when to stop" (*U*16:1111–15).

———

Whether such statements are examples of self-assertion or reflective thought, the statistical connection between "the Jewish question" and the hope for a new species of mankind seems fairly strong. In Hungary, first- or second-generation Magyars of Jewish descent were overrepresented not only among socialist intellectuals but also among communist militants. In Poland, "ethnic" Jews composed the majority of the original Communist leadership (7 out of about 10). In the 1930s, they made up from 22 to 26 percent of the overall Party membership, 51 percent of the Communist youth organization (1930), approximately 65 percent of all Warsaw Communists (1937), 75 percent of the Party's propaganda apparatus, 90 percent of MOPR (the International Relief Organization for Revolutionaries), and most of the members of the Central Committee. In the United States in the same period, Jews (most of them immigrants from Eastern Europe) accounted for about 40 to 50 percent of Communist Party membership and at least a comparable proportion of the Party's leaders, journalists, theorists, and organizers.[71]

Jewish participation in radical movements of the early twentieth century is similar to their participation in business and the professions: most radicals were not Jews and most Jews were not radicals, but the proportion of radicals among Jews was, on average, much higher than among their non-Jewish neighbors. One explanation is that there is no need for a special explanation: in the age of universal Mercurianism, Mercurians have a built-in advantage over Apollonians; intellectualism ("cleverness" and "reflective thought") is as central to traditional Mercurianism as craftsmanship and moneylending; and in nineteenth- and early twentieth-century Central and Eastern Europe, most intellectuals were radicals (intelligentsia members) because neither the economy nor the state allowed for their incorporation as professionals. According to Stephen J. Whitfield, "if Jews have been disproportionately radicals, it may be because they have been disproportionately intellectuals"—the reason being either traditional strangeness or a newfound marginality. Whitfield himself preferred the "Veblen thesis" as formulated by Nikos Kazantzakis (the author of new versions of the Bible and the *Odyssey*, among other things): the "Age of Revolution" is a "Jewish Age" because "the Jews have this supreme quality: to be restless, not to fit into realities of the time; to struggle to escape; to consider every status quo and every idea a stifling prison." Or rather, Marx and Trotsky are to politics what Schoenberg and Einstein are to the arts and sciences ("disturbers of the peace," in Veblen's terminology). As Freud put it, "to profess belief in a new theory called for a certain degree of readiness to accept a position of solitary opposition—a position with which no one is more familiar than a Jew."[72]

The "marginality" argument was not the only one that fit revolution as nicely as it did entrepreneurship and science. Most explanations of the Jewish affinity for socialism mirrored the explanations of the Jewish proclivity for capitalism. The Nietzsche-Sombart line (with an extra emphasis on "ressentiment") was ably represented by Sombart himself, whereas the various theories involving Judaic tribalism and messianism were adapted with particular eloquence by Nikolai Berdiaev. Socialism, according to Berdiaev, is a form of "Jewish religious chiliasm, which faces the future with a passionate demand for, and anticipation of, the realization of the millennial Kingdom of God on earth and the coming of Judgment Day, when evil is finally vanquished by good, and injustice and suffering in human life cease once and for all." No other nation, according to Berdiaev, could ever create, let alone take seriously as a worldly guide, a vision like Isaiah's:

> The wolf also shall dwell with the lamb, and the leopard shall lie down with the kid; and the calf and the young lion and the fatling together; and a little child shall lead them. And the cow and the bear shall feed; their young ones shall lie down together: and the lion shall eat straw

like an ox. And the suckling child shall play on the hole of the asp, and the weaned child shall put his hand on the cockatrice's den. (Isa. 11:6–8)

Add to this the fact that Jewish liberty and immortality are collective, not individual, and that this collective redemption is to occur in this world, as a result of both daily struggle and predestination, and you have Marxism.

> Karl Marx, who was a typical Jew, solved, at history's eleventh hour, the old biblical theme: in the sweat of thy brow shalt thou eat bread. . . . The teaching of Marx appears to break with the Jewish religious tradition and rebel against all things sacred. In fact, what it does is transfer the messianic idea associated with the Jews as God's chosen people to a class, the proletariat.[73]

Or maybe it was the other way around, as Sonja Margolina has argued recently (echoing Isaac Deutscher's genealogy of the "non-Jewish Jews"). Maybe Marx appeared to preserve Judaism in a new guise while in fact breaking with the Jewish religious tradition—in the same way as the most famous, and perhaps the most Jewish, Jew of all.

> His name is Jesus Christ. Estranged from orthodox Jews and dangerous to the rulers, he dispossessed the Jewish God and handed him over to all the people, irrespective of race and blood. In the modern age, this internationalization of God was reenacted in secular form by Jewish apostates. In this sense, Marx was the modern Christ, and Trotsky, his most faithful apostle. Both—Christ and Marx—tried to expel moneylenders from the temple, and both failed.[74]

Whatever their thoughts on Christianity as a Jewish revolution, some Jewish revolutionaries agreed that they were revolutionaries because they were Jewish (in Berdiaev's sense). Gustav Landauer, the anarchist, philosopher, and martyred commissar of culture of the Bavarian Soviet Republic, believed that the Jewish god was a rebel and a rouser (*Aufrührer* and *Aufrüttler*); that the Jewish religion was an expression of the "people's holy dissatisfaction with itself"; and that it was "one and the same to await the Messiah while in exile and dispersed, and to be the Messiah of the nations." Franz Rosenzweig, who considered "a relinquishing of the free and unrestricted market" a precondition to the coming of the Kingdom of God, rejoiced that "liberty, equality, and fraternity, the canons of the faith, have now become the slogans of the age." And Lev Shternberg, a onetime revolutionary terrorist, a longtime Siberian exile, and the dean of Soviet anthropologists until his death in 1927, came to see modern socialism as a specifically Jewish achievement. "It is as though thousands of the prophets of Israel have risen from their forgotten graves to proclaim, once again, their fiery damnation of those 'that join house to house, field to field'; their urgent call for social justice; and their ideals of a unified humanity, eternal peace, fraternity of peoples, and Kingdom of God on earth!" Let anti-Semites use this in their arguments: "anti-Semites will always find arguments" because all they need are excuses. The important thing is to nurture and celebrate "what is best in us: our ideals of social justice and our social activism. We cannot be untrue to ourselves so as to please the anti-Semites—we could not do it even if we wanted to. And let us remember that the future is on our side, not on the side of the dying hydra of the old barbarism."[75]

Chamberlain and Sombart seemed to be right, according to Shternberg, in describing Judaism as a peculiar combination of relentless rationalism and exuberant messianism, for it was this very combination that had assured the final liberation of humanity.

> The first heralds of socialism in the nineteenth century were non-Jews, the Frenchmen Saint-Simon and Fourier. But that was utopian socialism. . . . Finally, the time was ripe for the emergence of *scientific* socialism. It was then that the *rationalist* Jewish genius arrived on the scene in the shape of Karl Marx, who alone was capable of erecting the whole structure of the new teaching, from the foundation to the top, crowned by the grandiose *monistic* system of historical materialism. But what is particularly striking about the Jewish socialists is a remarkable combination of rationalist thinking with social emotionalism and activism—the very psychic peculiarities of the Jewish type that we see so clearly in all the previous periods of Jewish history, especially in the prophets. Nowhere is it more evident than in the

cases of Marx and Lassalle. Marx combined the genius of theoretical, almost mathematical, thinking with the fiery temperament of a fanatical fighter and the historical sense of a true prophet. The works of Marx are not only the new Bible of our time, but also a new kind of book of social predictions! Even now, the exegetics of Marx's teachings and social predictions exceeds all the volumes of the Talmud. Lassalle, though of a different caliber, belonged to the same psychological type, with the addition of a great talent as a popular tribune and political organizer.[76]

Another political organizer, perhaps the most efficient of them all, was Stalin's "iron commissar," Lazar Kaganovich, who remembers having to divide his early education between the Russian poets and Jewish prophets. According to his *Reminiscences of a Worker, Communist-Bolshevik, and a Trade Union, Party, and Soviet-State Official,*

> We used to study the Bible when we were children. We sensed that Amos was denouncing the tsars and the rich people, and we liked it very much. But, of course, we had an uncritical attitude toward the prophets who, while expressing the dissatisfaction of the popular masses and criticizing their oppressors, urged patience and expected salvation from God and his Messiah instead of calling for struggle against the oppressors of the poor people. Naturally, when I was a child, I did not understand the correctness of this conclusion, but I remember how in 1912 in Kiev, when I had to speak against the Zionists, I used Amos's words well and with great success, this time drawing appropriate Bolshevik conclusions.[77]

Possible Jewish origins of important Communist rituals and styles (as well as words) were widely alleged by contemporaries, many of them Jewish, Communist, or both. Ilya Ehrenburg, who was a certified fellow traveler when he published *The Stormy Life of Lazik Roitshvanetz,* caricatured early Soviet orthodoxy by making it seem indistinguishable from Talmudic exegesis. Both were built around the division of the world into "clean" and "unclean" spheres, and—as Lazik the Wandering Jew was meant to discover— both pursued purity by multiplying meaningless rules and by pretending to reconcile them to each other and to the unruly reality of human existence.

> Now I see that the Talmudists were the most ridiculous of pups [says Lazik on being asked to purge the library in the manner of the "spring cleaning before Passover"]. For what did they think of? That Jews shouldn't eat sturgeon, for example. Is it because sturgeon is expensive? No. Is it because it doesn't taste good? Not at all. It's because sturgeon swims around without the appropriate scales. Which means that it's hopelessly unclean and that the Jew who eats it will desecrate his chosen stomach. Let other, lowly people eat sturgeon. But, Comrade Minchik, those pups were talking about meals. Now, at last, the real twentieth century has arrived, men have become smarter, and so instead of some stupid sturgeon we have a man like Kant and his 1,071 crimes. Let the French on their volcano read all those unclean things. We have the chosen brains and we cannot soil them with insolent delusions.[78]

Jaff Schatz, in his study of the generation of Polish Jewish Communists born around 1910, reports that some of them (with the retrospective perspicacity of political disgrace and ethnic exile) considered their Marxist education to have been primarily Jewish in style. "The basic method was self-study, supplemented by tutoring by those more advanced. Thus, they read and discussed, and if they could not agree on the meaning of a text, or when issues proved too complicated, they asked for the help of an expert whose authoritative interpretation was, as a rule, accepted." The mentors were more experienced, erudite, and inventive interpreters of texts. "Those who enjoyed the highest respect knew large portions of the classical texts almost by heart. In addition, those more advanced would frequently be able to quote from memory statistical data, for example, on the production of bread, sugar, or steel before and after the October Revolution, to support their analyses and generalizations. . . . 'We behaved like *yeshiva bokhers* and they like rabbis,' one respondent summed up."[79] True knowledge was to be found in sacred texts, and "consciousness" depended, in part, on one's ability to reconcile their many prescriptions, predictions, and prohibitions. "The texts of the classics were regarded with utmost veneration, as the highest authority in which all the questions that could possibly be asked were answered. The practical difficulty was to find the most suitable fragment of the texts and to interpret it correctly, so that the hidden answer would appear. In discussing such texts, as well as in debating social or political questions, there was the characteristic, hair-splitting quality of analysis that many respondents themselves today call 'Talmudic.' "[80]

"Talmudic" was a label widely used by Eastern European Communists to refer to sterile theorizers of all backgrounds (and of course there were more than enough non-Jewish hairsplitters to make the connection dubious), but it does seem possible that Jews were overrepresented among Communist writers and ideologues because they were, on average, better prepared than their non-Mercurian comrades for the work of scriptural interpretation (the non-Jewish workers' circles were similar in style to the Jewish ones but much less successful at producing professional intellectuals). It is also quite possible that the beneficiaries of a "Jewish education," religious or secular, were likely to introduce some elements of that education into the socialism they were building (or journalism they were practicing). What seems striking, however, is that many Jewish radicals associated their revolutionary "awakening" with their youthful revolts against their families. Whatever the nature of their radicalism, their degree of assimilation, or their views on the connection between Judaism and socialism, the overwhelming majority remember rejecting the world of their fathers because it seemed to embody the connection between Judaism and antisocialism (understood as commercialism, tribalism, and patriarchy).[81]

All revolutionaries are patricides, one way or another, but few seem to have been as consistent and explicit on this score as the Jewish radicals of the late nineteenth and early twentieth centuries. Georg Lukács, the son of one of Hungary's most prominent bankers, József Lőwinger, was probably as typical of the wealthier rebels as he was influential among them.

I come from a capitalist, *Lipótváros* [a wealthy district of Pest] family. . . . From my childhood I was profoundly discontented with the *Lipótváros* way of life. Since my father, in the course of his business, was regularly in contact with the representatives of the city patriciate and of the bureaucratic gentry, my rejection tended to extend to them, too. Thus at a very early age violently oppositional feelings ruled in me against the whole of official Hungary. . . . Of course nowadays I regard it as childishly naïve that I uncritically generalized my feelings of revulsion, and extended them to cover the whole of Magyar life, Magyar history, and Magyar literature indiscriminately (save for Petőfi). Nonetheless it is a matter of fact that this attitude dominated my spirit and ideas in those days. And the solid counterweight—the only hard ground on which I then felt I could rest my feet—was the modernist foreign literature of the day, with which I became acquainted at the age of about fourteen and fifteen.[82]

Lukács would eventually move from modernism to socialist realism and from a formless "revulsion" to membership in the Communist Party; only his love for Petőfi would prove lifelong. This, too, is typical: national gods, even those most jealously guarded, were by far the most potent of the age. So potent, in fact, that their cults were taken for granted and barely noticed as various universalist creeds asserted their transcendental claims. Communists, among others, did not associate Petőfi with the "bourgeois nationalism" they were fighting and saw no serious contradiction between the veneration of his poetry and proletarian internationalism. Petőfi—like Goethe-Schiller, Mickiewicz, and others—stood for "culture" in his own domain, and culture (the "high" kind—i.e., the kind defined by Petőfi et al.) was a good thing. All communism started out as national communism (and ended up as nationalism pure and simple). Béla Kun, the leader of the 1919 Communist government in Hungary, the organizer of the Red Terror in the Crimea, and a top official of the Communist International, began his writing career with a prizewinning high school essay titled "The Patriotic Poetry of Sándor Petőfi and János Arany," and ended it, while waiting to be arrested by the Soviet secret police, with an introduction to a Russian translation of Petőfi's poems. And Lazar Kaganovich, who probably signed Kun's death sentence (among thousands of others), reminisced at the end of his life about beginning to acquire culture "through the independent reading of whatever works we had by Pushkin, Lermontov, Nekrasov, L. Tolstoy, and Turgenev."[83]

Whereas national pantheons derived their power from their apparent transparency, family rebellions were significant because they were experienced and represented as epiphanies. Franz Boas remembered the "unforgettable moment" when he first questioned the authority of tradition. "In fact, my whole outlook upon social life is determined by the question: How can we recognize the shackles that tradition has laid upon us? For when we recognize them we are also able to break them." Almost invariably, that first recognition occurred at home. As Leo Löwenthal, the son of a Frankfurt doctor, put it, "My family household, as it were, was the symbol of everything I did not want—shoddy liberalism, shoddy *Aufklärung*, and double standards."[84] The same was true of Schatz's Polish Communists, most of whom were native speakers of Yiddish who knew very little about liberalism or *Aufklärung*: "Whether they came from poor, more prosperous, assimilated, or traditional families, an important common element in their situation was an intense perception of the differences separating them from their parents. Increasingly experienced as unbridgeable, expressed on the everyday level as an inability to communicate and a refusal to conform, these differences led them increasingly to distance themselves from the world, ways, and values of their parents."[85]

The wealthier ones bemoaned their fathers' capitalism, the poorer ones, their fathers' Jewishness, but the real reason for their common revulsion was the feeling that capitalism and Jewishness were one and the same thing. Whatever the relationship between Judaism and Marxism, large numbers of Jews seemed to agree with Marx before they ever read anything he wrote. "Emancipation from *haggling* and from *money*, i.e. from practical, real Judaism, would be the same as the self-emancipation of our age." Revolution began at home—or rather, world revolution began in the Jewish home. According to the historian Andrew Janos, Béla Kun's young commissars "sought out traditionalist Jews with special ferocity as targets of their campaigns of terror." According to the biographer Marjorie Boulton, Ludwik Zamenhof was not free to devote himself to the creation of Esperanto until he broke with his "treacherous" father. And on December 1, 1889, Alexander Helphand (Parvus), a Russian Jew, world revolutionary, international financier, and future German government agent, placed the following notice in the *Sächsische Arbeiterzeitung*: "We announce the birth of a healthy, cheerful enemy of the state. Our son was born in Dresden on the morning of November 29th. . . . And although he was born on the German land, he has no Motherland."[86]

The tragedy of Parvus's son, and the children of so many other Jewish scholars, financiers, and revolutionaries, was that most other Europeans did have a Motherland. Even capitalism, which Parvus milked and sabotaged with equal success, was packaged, distributed, and delivered by nationalism. Even liberalism, which regarded universal strangeness to be a natural human condition, organized individuals into nations and promised to assemble them *de pluribus unum*. Even "La Marseillaise" became a national anthem.

When the uprooted Apollonians arrived on new Mercurian shores, they were told they were at home. Some had to wait, perhaps, or move next door, or slaughter false suitors first, but one way or another, every new Ulysses was to end up on his very own Ithaca—except the original one, who, as Dante alone had divined, could never go home. Jews were no longer allowed to be a global tribe (that was "disloyalty" now, not normal Mercurian behavior), but they still were not welcome in the local ones. According to Hannah Arendt, "the Jews were very clearly the only inter-European element in a nationalized Europe." They were also the only true moderns in Europe, or at any rate spectacularly good at being modern. But modernity without nationalism is cold capitalism. And cold capitalism by itself is, according to so many Europeans, a bad thing. As Karl Marx put it, "The *chimerical* nationality of the Jew is the nationality of the merchant, of the man of money in general. . . . The *social* emancipation of the Jew is the *emancipation of society from Judaism.*"[87]

As Jews emerged from the ghetto and the shtetl, they entered a new world that seemed like the old one in that their skills were seen as highly valuable but morally dubious. There was one crucial difference, however: the Jews were no longer legally recognized professional strangers and thus no longer possessed a special mandate to engage in morally dubious occupations. The new license for immorality was nationalism, and Jews were not eligible. Every Jew's father became immoral—either because he was still a professional stranger or because he was a modern without a legitimate tribe. Both were capitalists and both belonged to a chimerical nationality.

The two great modern prophecies offered two different answers to the question of Jewish patricide. Freudianism claimed that it was a universal human affliction and that the only way to save civilization-as-liberalism was to control the urge therapeutically (and grow up gracefully). Marxism attributed it to the proletariat and urged the killing (more or less metaphorical) of the bad fathers, so as to emancipate the world from Judaism and make sure that no sons would have to kill their fathers ever again.

But there was a third prophecy, of course—as patricidal as the other two but much more discriminating: modern Jewish nationalism. Could not the Jews be transformed from a chimerical nationality into a "normal" one? Could they not have a Motherland of their own? Could they not be protected from capitalism in their own make-believe Apollonia? Could they not be redeemed like everyone else—as a nation? Perhaps they could. A lot of Jews thought it an eccentric idea (the Chosen People without a God? A Yiddish Blood and Soil?), but many were willing to try.[88]

"Normal" nationalisms began with the sanctification of vernaculars and the canonization of national bards. Accordingly, in the second half of the nineteenth century and the first quarter of the twentieth, Yiddish acquired the status of a literary language (as opposed to a shtetl jargon or Mercurian secret code); incorporated, through translation, the "treasury of world culture" (i.e., other modern nations' secular pantheons); accommodated a great variety of genres (so as to become a universal, all-purpose vehicle); and produced its own Shakespeare. It went through the same pangs of rebirth, in other words, as Russian a hundred years earlier or Norwegian at about the same time. Homer, Goethe, and Anatole France were being translated simultaneously, as if they were contemporaries; the beauty and suppleness of Yiddish were found to be remarkable; and Mendele Mokher Sforim (Sholem Yakov Abramovich, 1835–1917) was discovered to have been "the grandfather of Yiddish literature." And then there was Sholem Aleichem. As Maurice Samuel put it, on behalf of most readers of Yiddish, "It is hard to think of him as a 'writer.' He was the common people in utterance. He was in a way the 'anonymous' of Jewish self-expression."[89]

All the elements of "normal" nationalism were there, in other words—except the main one. The point of nationalism is to attach the newly created national high culture to the local Apollonian mythology, genealogy, and landscape; to attribute that high culture to the "spirit of the people"; to modernize folk culture by folklorizing the modern state. Very little of this enterprise made sense in the case of the Jews. They had no attachment or serious claim to any part of the local landscape; their symbolically meaningful past lay elsewhere; and their religion (which stigmatized Yiddish) seemed inseparable from their Jewishness. No European state, however designed, could possibly become a Jewish Promised Land.

Perhaps most important, Yiddish-based nationalism did little to alleviate the problem of unheroic fathers. One could sentimentalize them, or craft a powerful story of their unrelieved martyrdom, but one could not pretend that they had not been service nomads (i.e., cobblers, peddlers, innkeepers, and moneylenders dependent on their "Gentile" customers). One could not, in other words, help Jewish sons and daughters in their quest for Apollonian dignity by arguing that the Yiddish past had not been an exile. Why should one, in fact, if unimpeachably proud and universally recognized biblical heroes were easily available in the dominant and still vibrant Jewish tradition? Having started out as normal, Yiddish nationalism proved too odd to succeed as a movement. In the all-important realms of politics and mythmaking, it could not compete with Hebrew nationalism and global socialism. Most Jews who were ideologically attached to Yiddish (the "language of the Jewish masses") were socialists, and the languages of socialism in Europe—the Bund's efforts notwithstanding—were German and Russian.

In the end, it was the Hebrew-based nationalism that triumphed and, in alliance with Zionism, became the third great Jewish prophecy. Strikingly and defiantly "abnormal" in its premises, it looked forward to a full and final normality complete with a nation-state and warrior dignity. It was nationalism in reverse: the idea was not to sanctify popular speech but to profane the language of God, not to convert your home into a Promised Land but to convert the Promised Land into a home. The effort to turn the Jews into a normal nation looked like no other nationalism in the world. It was a Mercurian nationalism that proposed a literal and ostensibly secular reading of the myth of exile; a nationalism that punished God for having punished his people. Eternal urbanites were to turn themselves into peasants, and local peasants were to be seen as foreign invaders. Zionism was the most radical and revolutionary of all nationalisms. It was more religious in its secularism than any other movement—except for socialism, which was its main ally and competitor.

———————

But Jews were not only the heroes of the most eccentric of nationalisms; they were also the villains of the most brutally consistent of them all. Nazism was a messianic movement that endowed nationalism with an elaborate terrestrial eschatology. To put it differently, Nazism challenged modern salvation religions by using nationhood as the agent of perdition and redemption. It did what none of the other modern (i.e., antimodern) salvation religions had been able to do: it defined evil clearly, consistently, and scientifically. It shaped a perfect theodicy for the Age of Nationalism. It created the devil in its own image.

The question of the origins of evil is fundamental to any promise of redemption. Yet all modern religions except Nazism resembled Christianity in being either silent or confused on the subject. Marxism offered an obscure story of original sin through the alienation of labor and made it difficult to understand what role individual believers could play in the scheme of revolutionary predestination. Moreover, the Soviet experience seemed to show that Marxism was a poor guide in purging the body politic. Given the assumption of Party infallibility, society's continued imperfection had to be attributed to machinations by ill-intentioned humans, but who were they and where did they come from? How were "class aliens" in a more or less classless society to be categorized, unmasked, and eliminated? Marxism gave no clear answer; Leninism did not foresee a massive regeneration of the exterminated enemies; and Stalin's willing executioners were never quite sure why they were executing some people and not others.

Freudianism located evil in the individual human soul and provided a prescription for combating it, but it offered no hope for social perfection, no civilization without discontents. Evil could be managed but not fully eradicated. A collection of cured individuals was not a guarantee of a healthy society.

Zionism did foresee a perfectly healthy society, but its promise was not universal and its concept of evil was too historical to be of lasting utility. The evil of exile was to be overcome by a physical return home. The "diaspora mentality," like Soviet bourgeois consciousness, would be defeated by honest toil for one's own healthy state. Its persistence in Eretz Israel would not be easy to explain.

Nazism was unique in the consistency and simplicity of its theodicy. All the corruption and alienation of the modern world was caused by one race, the Jews. The Jews were inherently evil. Capitalism, liberalism, modernism, and communism were essentially Jewish. The elimination of the Jews would redeem the world and usher in the millennium. Like Marxism and Freudianism, Nazism derived its power from a combination of transcendental revelation and the language of science. Social science could draw any number of conclusions from the statistical data on Jewish overrepresentation in the critical spheres of modern life; racial science undertook to uncover the secrets of personal ethnicity as well as universal history; and various branches of medicine could be used to provide both the vocabulary for describing evil and the means of its "final solution." Nazism rivaled Zionism (and ultimately Judaism) by casting redemptive messianism in national terms; compared favorably to Marxism (and ultimately to Christianity) in its promise of cathartic apocalyptic violence as a prologue to the Millennium; and equaled

Freudianism in its use of modern medicine as the instrument of salvation. Ultimately, it surpassed them all in being able to offer a simple secular solution to the problem of the origins of evil in the modern world. A universe presided over by Man received an identifiable and historically distinct group of human beings as its first flesh-and-blood devil. The identity of the group might change, but the humanization and nationalization of evil proved durable. When the Nazi prophets were exposed as impostors and slain in the apocalypse they had unleashed, it was they who emerged as the new devil in a world without God—the only absolute in the Post-Prophetic Age.

Thus, in the wake of World War I, Jews had found themselves at the center of both the crisis of modern Europe and the most far-reaching attempts to overcome it. Strikingly successful at the pursuits that made up the foundations of modern states—entrepreneurship (especially banking) and the professions (especially law, medicine, journalism, and science)—they were excluded from the modern nations that those states were supposed to embody and represent. In a Europe that draped the economy of capitalism and professional expertise in the legitimacy of nationalism, Jews stood abandoned and unprotected as a ghostly tribe of powerful strangers. In one nation-state, their exclusion would turn into the main article of nationalist faith and a methodical extermination campaign. But exclusion could also become a form of escape and liberation. For most European Jews, this meant three pilgrimages to three ideological destinations. Freudianism became associated with a nonethnic (or multiethnic) liberalism in the United States; Zionism represented a secular Jewish nationalism in Palestine; and Communism stood for the creation of a nation-free world centered in Moscow. The story of twentieth-century Jews is a story of one Hell and three Promised Lands.

Chapter 3

BABEL'S FIRST LOVE: THE JEWS AND THE RUSSIAN REVOLUTION

> Suddenly I heard a voice beside me saying: "Excuse
> me, young man, do you think it is proper to stare
> at strange young ladies in that way?"
> —I. S. Turgenev, "First Love"

At the turn of the twentieth century, most of Europe's Jews (5.2 out of about 8.7 million) lived in the Russian Empire, where they constituted about 4 percent of the total population. Most of Russia's Jews (about 90 percent) resided in the Pale of Settlement, to which they were legally restricted. Most of the Jews in the Pale of Settlement (all but about 4 percent, who were farmers and factory workers) continued to pursue traditional service occupations as middlemen between the overwhelmingly agricultural Christian population and various urban markets. Most of the Jewish middlemen bought, shipped, and resold local produce; provided credit on the security of standing crops and other items; leased and managed estates and various processing facilities (such as tanneries, distilleries, and sugar mills); kept taverns and inns; supplied manufactured goods (as peddlers, shopkeepers, or wholesale importers); provided professional services (most commonly as doctors and pharmacists), and served as artisans (from rural blacksmiths, tailors, and shoemakers to highly specialized jewelers and watchmakers). The proportion of various pursuits could vary, but the association of Jews with the service sector (including small-scale craftsmanship) remained very strong.[1]

As traditional Mercurians dependent on external strangeness and internal cohesion, the majority of Russian Jews continued to live in segregated quarters, speak Yiddish, wear distinctive clothing, observe complex dietary taboos, practice endogamy, and follow a variety of other customs that ensured the preservation of collective memory, autonomy, purity, unity, and a hope of redemption. The synagogue, bathhouse, heder, and the home helped structure space as well as social rituals, and numerous self-governing institutions assisted the rabbi and the family in regulating communal life, education, and charity. Both social status and religious virtue depended on wealth and learning; wealth and learning ultimately depended on each other.

The relations between the majority of Pale Jews and their mostly rural customers followed the usual pattern of Mercurian-Apollonian coexistence. Each side saw the other as unclean, opaque, dangerous, contemptible, and ultimately irrelevant to the communal past and future salvation. Social contact was limited to commercial and bureaucratic encounters. Non-Jews almost never spoke Yiddish, and very few Jews spoke the languages of their Ukrainian, Lithuanian, Latvian, Moldovan, or Belorussian neighbors beyond "the minimum of words which were absolutely necessary in order to transact business."[2] Everyone (and most particularly the Jews themselves) assumed that the Jews were nonnative, temporary exiles; that they depended on their customers for survival; and that the country—however conceived—belonged to the local Apollonians. The history of the people of Israel relived by every Jew on every Sabbath had nothing to do with his native shtetl or the city of Kiev; his sea was Red, not Black, and the rivers of his imagination did not include the Dnieper or the Dvina. "[Sholem Aleichem's] Itzik Meyer of Kasrilevke was told to feel that he himself, with wife and children, had marched out of Egypt, and he did as he was told. He felt that he himself had witnessed the infliction of the ten plagues on the Egyptians, he himself had stood on the farther shore of the Red Sea and seen the walls of water collapse on the pursuers, drowning them all to the last man—with the exception of Pharaoh, who was preserved as an eternal witness for the benefit of the Torquemadas and the Romanovs."[3]

The most prominent—and perhaps the only—local Apollonians retained by the Jewish memory were the Cossack looters and murderers of the seventeenth and eighteenth centuries, and the most frequently invoked of them all (as the modern equivalent of the biblical Haman) was Bohdan Khmelnytsky—the same Bohdan Khmelnytsky whom most Ukrainian-speakers remembered as their deliverer from Catholic captivity and (for a short time) Jewish scheming and spying. Overall, however, the Jews were as marginal to the Eastern European peasant imagination as the Eastern European peasants were to the Jewish one. Apollonians tend to remember battles with other Apollonians, not bargaining with Mercurians (while the Mercurians themselves tend to remember the days when they were Apollonians). The villains of Cossack mythology are mostly Tatars and Poles, with Jews featured episodically as Polish agents (which, in the economic sense, they were—especially as estate leaseholders and liquor-tax farmers).[4]

Most Jewish and non-Jewish inhabitants of the Pale of Settlement shared the same fundamental view of what separated them. Like all Mercurians and Apollonians, they tended to think of each other as universal and mutually complementary opposites: mind versus body, head versus heart, outsider versus insider, nomadic versus settled. In the words of Mark Zborowski and Elizabeth Herzog (whose account is based on interviews with former shtetl residents),

> A series of contrasts is set up in the mind of the shtetl child, who grows up to regard certain behavior as characteristic of Jews, and its opposite, as characteristic of Gentiles. Among Jews he expects to find emphasis on intellect, a sense of moderation, cherishing of spiritual values, cultivation of rational, goal-directed activities, a "beautiful" family life. Among gentiles he looks for the opposite of each item: emphasis on the body, excess, blind instinct, sexual license, and ruthless force. The first list is ticketed in his mind as Jewish, the second as goyish.[5]

Seen from the other side, the lists looked essentially the same, with the values reversed. Intelligence, moderation, learning, rationalism, and family devotion (along with entrepreneurial success) could be represented as cunning, cowardice, casuistry, unmanliness, clannishness, and greed, whereas the apparent emphasis on the body, excess, instinct, license, and force might be interpreted as earthiness, spontaneity, soulfulness, generosity, and warrior strength (honor). These oppositions were informed by actual differences in economic roles and values; sanctified by communal traditions and prohibitions; reinforced by new quasi-secular mythologies (as Marxists and various nationalists employed them more or less creatively but without substantive revisions); and reenacted daily, ritually, and sometimes consciously in personal encounters as well as in prayers, jokes, and gestures.

The non-Jewish words for "Jew" were all more or less pejorative, often diminutive, permanently associated with particular modifiers ("cunning," "mangy"), and used productively to coin new forms (such as the Russian *zhidit'sia*, "to be greedy"). The Jews were equally disparaging but, like all Mercurians, more intensely concerned with pollution, linguistic as well as sexual and dietary. Not only were *goy* ("Gentile"), *sheigets* ("a Gentile young man"), and *shiksa* (a Gentile [i.e., "impure"] woman) generally pejorative terms that could be used metaphorically to refer to stupid or loutish Jews; much of the colloquial Yiddish vocabulary dealing with *goyim* was cryptic and circumlocutory. According to Hirsz Abramowicz, Lithuanian Jews used a special code when talking about their non-Jewish neighbors: "They might be called *sherets* and *shrotse* (reptiles); the word *shvester* (sister) became *shvesterlo*; *foter* (father) *foterlo*; *muter* (mother), *muterlo*, and so on. *Khasene* (wedding) became *khaserlo*; *geshtorbn* (died) became *gefaln* (fell), *geboyrn* (born) became *geflamt* (flamed)." Similarly, according to M. S. Altman, when Jews of his shtetl referred to Gentiles' eating, drinking, or sleeping, they used words normally reserved for animals. The Yiddish for the town of Bila Tserkva ("White Church") was *Shvartse tume* ("Black filth," the word *tume* generally denoting a non-Jewish place of worship).[6]

The reason for this was ritual avoidance (as well as, possibly, secrecy): words relating to the goyim and their religion were as unclean and potentially dangerous as the goyim themselves. (The same devices, including cryptic calques for place-names, are commonly used in "Para-Romani" languages.)[7] M. S. Altman's grandmother "never called Christ anything other than *mamser*, or 'the illegitimate one.' Once, when there was a Christian procession in the streets of Ulla [Belorussia], with people carrying crosses and icons, Grandma hurriedly covered me with her shawl, saying: 'May your clear eyes never see this filth.' "[8]

There were, of course, other reasons to avoid Christian processions. In Joachim Schoenfeld's native shtetl of Sniatyn, in eastern Galicia,

> When a priest was on his way to administer extreme unction to a dying Christian soul, the Jews, as soon as they heard the ringing of the bell by the deacon accompanying the priest, left the streets quickly and locked the doors of their homes and stores lest the Christians, who knelt in the streets in front of the passing priest, would accuse them of not having behaved with dignity at such a moment by remaining standing when everybody else was kneeling. This would have been enough to set anti-Jewish disturbances in motion. The same thing happened when a procession was marching through the streets bearing holy images and banners, for example, on the Corpus Christi holiday. No Jew would dare remain on the streets because he might be accused of host desecration.[9]

Traditional Jews warded off the impurity of strangers by using supernatural protection (as well as their much praised "Jewish heads"); their Apollonian neighbors tended to resort to physical aggression. Violence was an essential part of the relationship— rarely lethal but always there as a possibility, a memory, an essential part of peasant manhood and Jewish victimhood. In Sniatyn, "A Jewish boy would never venture into the streets inhabited by Christians, even when accompanied by an adult. Christian boys would make fun of them, call them names, throw stones at them, and set their dogs upon them. Also, for simple fun, Christian boys would drive pigs into the Jewish streets and throw manure through the open windows of Jewish homes."[10]

In Uzliany, not far from Minsk, "the most innocent threats Jews faced were boys' pranks: during Easter they would crack painted eggs against the teeth of the Jewish boys and girls who happened to be outside." Religious holidays, market days, weddings, departure of army recruits were all legitimate occasions for drinking, fighting, and, if Jews were close by, assaults on the Jews and their property. The superiority of the "big soul" over the "little Jew" was most effectively expressed through violence—just as the superiority of the "Jewish head" over "stupid Ivan" was best achieved and demonstrated through negotiation and competition. Like all Mercurians and Apollonians, the Pale of Settlement Jews and their peasant neighbors needed each other, lived close to each other, feared and despised each other, and never stopped claiming their own preeminence: the Jews by beating the peasants in the battle of wits and boasting about it among themselves, the peasants by beating the Jews for being Jews and bragging about it to the "whole world." But mostly—for as long as the traditional division of labor persisted and they remained specialized Mercurians and Apollonians—the Jews and their neighbors continued to live as "two solitudes." Ivan rarely thought about Itzik Meyer unless he was drunk and feeling sorry for himself. For Itzik Meyer, thinking about Ivan was work, an inevitable part of the profane portion of the week.[11]

There was no meaningful way of measuring legal discrimination in the Russian Empire because there was no common measure that applied to all the tsar's subjects. Everyone, except for the tsar himself, belonged to a group that was, one way or another, discriminated against. There were no interchangeable citizens, no indiscriminate laws, no legal rights, and few temporary regulations that did not become permanent. There were, instead, several social estates with unique privileges, duties, and local variations; numerous religions (including Islam, Lamaism, and a wide assortment of "animisms") under different sets of regulations; countless territorial units (from Finland to Turkestan) administered in diverse ways; and variously described nationalities ("steppe nomads," "wandering aliens," Poles) with special restrictions and exemptions. Everyone being unequal, some groups were—in some sense and in some places—much more unequal than others, but in the absence of a single legal gauge, discriminating among them in any general sense is usually more painstaking than rewarding. Jews had more disabilities than most Orthodox Christian members of their estates (merchants and townsmen, in the vast majority of cases), but a comparison of their status with that of Tatar traders, Kirgiz pastoralists, "priestless" sectarians, or indeed the empire's Russian peasant majority (even after the abolition of serfdom) is possible only with regard to specific privileges and disabilities. The "prisonhouse of nations" was as large as the tsar's domain.

Among the tsar's subjects were several groups that were predominantly or exclusively Mercurian: from various Gypsy communities (extremely visible in "bohemian" entertainment, as well as the traditional smithing and scavenging trades); to small and narrowly specialized literate Mercurians (Nestorians/Assyrians, Karaites, Bukharans); to Russia's very own Puritans, the Old Believers (prominent among the wealthiest industrialists and bankers); to such giants of Levantine commerce as the Greeks (active in the Black Sea trade, especially in wheat export) and the Armenians (who dominated the economy of the Caucasus and parts of southern Russia).

But of course the most prominent Mercurians of the Russian Empire were the Germans, who, following Peter the Great's reforms, had come to occupy central roles in the imperial bureaucracy, economic life, and the professions (very much like Phanariot Greeks and Armenians in the Ottoman Empire). Relying on ethnic and religious autonomy, high literacy rates, strong communal institutions, a sense of cultural superiority, international familial networks, and a variety of consistently cultivated technical and linguistic skills, the Germans had become the face (the real flesh-and-blood kind) of Russia's never-ending Westernization. Not only was the university matriculation rate among Russia's Baltic Germans the highest in Europe (about 300 per 100,000 total population in the 1830s at Dorpat University alone); Germans composed approximately 38 percent of the graduates of Russia's most exclusive educational institution, the Tsarskoe Selo Lycée, and a comparable proportion of the graduates from the Imperial School of Jurisprudence. From the late eighteenth to the twentieth century, Germans constituted from 18 to more than 33 percent of the top tsarist officials, especially at the royal court, in the officer corps, diplomatic service, police, and provincial administration (including many newly colonized areas). According to John A. Armstrong, all through the nineteenth century the Russian Germans "carried about half the burden of imperial foreign relations. Equally indicative is the fact that even in 1915 (during the World War I anti-Germanism), 16 of the 53 top officials in the Minindel [Ministry of Foreign Affairs] had German names." As one of them wrote in 1870, "we watched the success of Russia's European policy attentively, for nearly all our emissaries in all the principal countries were diplomats whom we knew on a first-name basis." In 1869 in St. Petersburg, 20 percent of all the officials in the Police Department of the Ministry of the Interior were listed as Germans. In the 1880s, the Russian Germans (1.4 percent of the population) made up 62 percent of the high officials in the Ministry of Posts and Commerce and 46 percent in the War Ministry. And when they were not elite members themselves, they served the native landowning elite as tutors, housekeepers, and accountants. The German estate manager was the central Russian version of the Pale of Settlement's Jewish leaseholder.[12]

Not all praetorian guards—or "imperial Mamelukes," as one Slavophile called the Russian Germans—are Mercurians (as opposed to foreign mercenaries), and of course not all Mercurians serve as Mamelukes (even though most are qualified because the main eligibility requirement is demonstrable strangeness and internal coherence). The German barons in the Baltic provinces were not Mercurians, and neither were the German merchants in the German city of Riga or the many German farmers imported into the Russian interior. There is no doubt, however, that "the Germans" most urban Russians knew were quintessential Mercurian middlemen and service providers: artisans, entrepreneurs, and professionals. In 1869, 21 percent of all St. Petersburg Germans were involved in metalwork; 14 percent were watchmakers, jewelers, and other skilled craftsmen; and another 10–11 percent were bakers, tailors, and shoemakers. In the same year, Germans (who made up about 6.8 percent of the city's population) accounted for 37 percent of St. Petersburg's watchmakers, 25 percent of bakers, 24 percent of the owners of textile mills, 23 percent of the owners of metal shops and factories, 37.8 percent of industrial managers, 30.8 percent of engineers, 34.3 percent of doctors, 24.5 percent of school-teachers, and 29 percent of tutors. German women made up 20.3 percent of "midlevel" medical personnel (doctor's assistants, pharmacists, nurses), 26.5 percent of schoolteachers, 23.8 percent of matrons and governesses, and 38.7 percent of music teachers. In 1905, German subjects of the Russian tsar accounted for 15.4 percent of corporate managers in Moscow, 16.1 percent in Warsaw, 21.9 percent in Odessa, 47.1 percent in Lodz, and 61.9 percent in Riga. In 1900, in the empire as a whole, the Russian Germans (1.4 percent of the population) made up 20.1 percent of all corporate founders and 19.3 percent of corporate managers (by far the greatest rate of overrepresentation among all ethnic groups). Many of Russia's most important academic institutions (including the Academy of Sciences) and professional associations (from doctors to geographers) were originally staffed by Germans and functioned primarily in German until about the middle of the nineteenth century and in some cases much later.[13]

Employed as Mercurians, they were, predictably enough, represented as such. Whereas much of Russian folklore recalled the battles against various steppe nomads (usually known as "Tatars"), the most important strangers of nineteenth-century high culture were, by a large margin, German: not those residing in Germany and producing books, goods, and songs to be imitated and surpassed, but the internal foreigners who served Russia and the Russians as teachers, tailors, doctors, scholars, governors, and coffin makers. And so they were, mutatis mutandis, head to the Russian heart, mind to the Russian soul, consciousness to Russian spontaneity. They stood for calculation, efficiency, and discipline; cleanliness, fastidiousness, and sobriety; pushiness, tactlessness, and energy; sentimentality, love of family, and unmanliness (or absurdly exaggerated manliness). They were the plenipotentiary ambassadors from the Modern Age, the *homines rationalistici artificiales* to be dreaded, admired, or ridiculed as the occasion demanded. In two of the most productive juxtapositions of Russian high culture, Tolstoy's somnolent Kutuzov restores true peace by ignoring the deadly expertise of his German war counselors, while Goncharov's bedridden Oblomov preserves a false peace by surrendering his life's love (and ultimately life itself) to the cheerfully industrious Stolz. Kutuzov and Oblomov are one and the same person, of course—as are Stolz and the German generals. Neither set is complete, indeed conceivable, without its mirror image. The modern Russian state and the Russian national mythology of the nineteenth century were built around this opposition and forever discussed in its terms. Perhaps paradoxically in light of what would happen in the twentieth century, Germans were, occupationally and conceptually, the Jews of ethnic Russia (as well as much of Eastern Europe). Or rather, the Russian Germans were to Russia what the German Jews were to Germany—only much more so. So fundamental were the German Mercurians to Russia's view of itself that both their existence and their complete and abrupt disappearance have been routinely taken for granted. The absence of Mercurians seems as natural and permanent as their presence seems artificial and temporary.[14]

Until the 1880s, actual Jews were a marginal presence in the Russian state, thought, and street. The official policy was essentially the same as that toward other "aliens," oscillating as it did between legal separation and various forms of "fusion." The most radical means to those ends—punitive raids and cross-border deportations (such as the ones used against insurgents in Turkestan and the Caucasus) or forced conversions and linguistic Russification (such as those used against Aleuts and Poles, among others) were not applied to the Jews. Otherwise, the administrative repertoire was largely familiar: from separation by means of residential segregation, economic specialization, religious and judicial autonomy, administrative self-government, and institutional quotas, to incorporation by means of army conscription, religious conversion, government-run education, agricultural settlement, and the adoption of "European dress and customs." As was the case with Russia's many nomads, who were subject to most of the same policies, conscription was the most resented of all imperial obligations (although the Jewish complaints seemed to suggest a different—and characteristically Mercurian—reason by arguing that the draft was incompatible with their economic role and traditional way of life). The official justifications for these policies were no less familiar: benefit to the treasury, protection of Orthodox Russians, and protection from Orthodox Russians in the case of separation; and benefit to the treasury, legal and administrative consistency, and the civilizing mission, in the case of incorporation. Jews were one of Russia's many "alien" groups: more "cunning" than most, perhaps, but not as "rebellious" as the Chechens, as "backward" as the Samoed, as "fanatical" as the Sart, or as ubiquitous or relentlessly *rationalistici artificiales* as the Germans. Anti-Semitism was common, but probably no more common than anti-Islamism, antinomadism, and anti-Germanism, which may have been more pervasive for being unself-conscious and unapologetic.

And yet there is clearly good reason to argue that the Jews were, in some sense, first among nonequals. They were by far the largest community among those that had no claim to a national home in the Russian Empire; by far the most urbanized of all Russian nationalities (49 percent urban in 1897, as compared to 23 percent for Germans and Armenians); and by far the fastest growing of all national or religious groups anywhere in Europe (having grown fivefold over the course of the nineteenth century). Most important, they were affected by Russia's late-nineteenth-century modernization in ways that were more direct, profound, and fundamental than most other Russian communities, because their very existence as a specialized caste was at stake. The emancipation of the serfs, the demise of the manorial economy, and the expansion of the economic role of the state rendered the role of the traditional Mercurian mediator between the countryside and the town economically irrelevant, legally precarious, and increasingly dangerous. The state took over tax collection, liquor sales, and some parts of foreign trade; the landlord had less land to lease or turned into a favored competitor; the peasant had more produce to sell and turned into a favored competitor (by doing much of the selling himself); the Christian industrialist turned into an even more favored—and more competent—competitor; the train ruined the peddler and the wagon driver; the bank bankrupted the moneylender; and all of these things taken together forced more and more Jews into artisanal work (near the bottom of the Jewish social prestige hierarchy), and more and more Jewish artisans into cottage-industry production or wage labor (in craft shops and increasingly factories). And the more Jews migrated to new urban areas, the more frequent and massive was violence against them.[15]

The imperial state, which presided over Russia's industrialization and thus the demise of the traditional Jewish economy as well as the killing and robbing of individual Jews, did its best to prevent the former middlemen from finding new opportunities. Jews were barred from government employment (including most railway jobs), all but fifteen of Russia's provinces, more than one-half of the Pale's rural districts, and a variety of occupations and institutions. Their access to education was limited by quotas, and their membership in professional organizations was subject to arbitrary regulation. The ostensible—and, apparently, true—reason for these policies was to protect Christian merchants, students, and professionals from Jewish competition, and Christian peasants from Jewish "exploitation." The state that had used the Jews to extract revenue from the peasants was trying to protect the peasants it still depended on from the Jews it no longer needed. The more it protected the peasants, the graver the "Jewish problem" became. The imperial government did not instigate Jewish pogroms; it did, however, help bring them about by concentrating the Jewish population in selected places and occupations and by insisting on separation even as it fostered industrial growth. Fin de siècle Hungary and Germany (and later most of Russia's western neighbors) contributed to the growth of political anti-Semitism by combining vigorous ethnic nationalism with a cautiously liberal stance toward Jewish social and economic mobility; late imperial Russia achieved a comparable result by combining a cautious ethnic nationalism with a vigorous policy of multiplying Jewish disabilities.[16]

The most dramatic and easily observable Jewish response to this double squeeze was emigration. Between 1897 and 1915, about 1,288,000 Jews left the Russian Empire, most of them (more than 80 percent) to the United States. More than 70 percent of all Jewish immigrants to the United States came from the Russian Empire; almost one-half of all immigrants from the Russian Empire to the

United States were Jews (with Poles a distant second with 27 percent, and Finns third with 8.5 percent). The Russian Jews had the highest gross emigration rate (proportion of emigrants to the overall home population) of all immigrants to the United States; during the peak period of 1900–1914, almost 2 percent of all Jewish residents of the Pale of Settlement were leaving every year. The overwhelming majority of them never came back: the Russian Jewish rate of return was the lowest of all immigrant groups in the United States. They left with family members and joined other family members when they arrived. Between 1908 and 1914, according to official statistics, "62% of the Jewish immigrants to the United States had their passage paid by a relative and 94% were on their way to join a relative." As Andrew Godley put it, "Because the costs of moving and settling were reduced by the existence of the informal networks of kith and kin, chain migrants generally arrived with less in their pockets. The Jews arrived with least because of all the immigrants they could count most on a welcome reception. The density of social relations among the East European Jews subsidized both passage and settlement. Such extensive chain migration allowed even the poorest to leave."[17]

Not all—not even most—migrants went abroad. Throughout the Pale of Settlement, Jews were moving from rural areas into small towns, and from small towns to big cities. Between 1897 and 1910, the Jewish urban population grew by almost 1 million, or 38.5 percent (from 2,559,544 to 3,545,418). The number of Jewish communities with more than 5,000 people increased from 130 in 1897 to 180 in 1910, and those over 10,000, from 43 to 76. In 1897, Jews made up 52 percent of the entire urban population of Belorussia-Lithuania (followed by Russians at 18.2 percent), while in the fast-growing New Russian provinces of Kherson and Ekaterinoslav, 85 to 90 percent of all Jews lived in cities. Between 1869 and 1910, the officially registered Jewish population of the imperial capital of St. Petersburg grew from 6,700 to 35,100. The actual number may have been considerably higher.[18]

But the extraordinary thing about the social and economic transformation of the Russian Jews was not the rate of migration, which was also high in Austria, Hungary, and Germany, or even "proletarianization," which was also taking place in New York. The extraordinary thing about the social and economic transformation of the Russian Jews was how ordinary it was by Western standards. Pogroms, quotas, and deportations notwithstanding, the Russian Jews were generally as keen on, and as successful at, becoming urban and modern as their German, Hungarian, British, or American counterparts—which is to say, much keener and much more successful at being capitalists, professionals, myth keepers, and revolutionary intellectuals than most people around them.

The Jews had dominated the commercial life of the Pale for most of the nineteenth century. Jewish banks based in Warsaw, Vilna, and Odessa had been among the first commercial lending institutions in the Russian Empire (in the 1850s, Berdichev had eight active and well-connected banking houses). In 1851, Jews had accounted for 70 percent of all merchants in Kurland, 75 percent in Kovno, 76 percent in Mogilev, 81 percent in Chernigov, 86 percent in Kiev, 87 percent in Minsk, and 96 percent each in Volynia, Grodno, and Podolia. Their representation in the wealthiest commercial elite was particularly strong: in Minsk and Chernigov provinces and in Podolia, all "first guild" merchants without exception (55, 59, and 7, respectively) were Jews. Most were involved in tax-farming, moneylending, and trade (especially foreign trade, with a virtual monopoly on overland cross-border traffic), but the importance of industrial investment had been rising steadily throughout the century. Before the Great Reforms, most of the industry in western Russia had been based on the use of serf labor for the extraction and processing of raw materials found on noble estates. Originally, Jews had been involved as bankers, leaseholders, administrators, and retailers, but already in 1828–32, 93.3 percent of the nonnoble industrial enterprises in Volynia (primarily wool and sugar mills) were owned by Jews. Their reliance on free labor made them more flexible with regard to location, more open to innovation, and ultimately much more efficient. In the sugar industry, Jewish entrepreneurs had pioneered a system of forward contracts, the use of extended warehouse networks, and the employment of traveling salesmen working on commission. By the late 1850s, all serf-based wool mills in the Pale of Settlement had gone out of business. Meanwhile, Jewish entrepreneurs had been able to win lucrative government contracts by speeding up their operations, relying on international connections for credit, and organizing complex networks of trustworthy subcontractors.[19]

The Russian industrialization of the late nineteenth century opened up new opportunities for Jewish businessmen and benefited tremendously from their financial backing. Among Russia's greatest financiers were Evzel (Iossel) Gabrielovich Gintsburg, who had grown rich as a liquor-tax farmer during the Crimean War; Abram Isaakovich Zak, who had begun his career as Gintsburg's chief accountant; Anton Moiseevich Varshavsky, who had supplied the Russian army with food; and the Poliakov brothers, who had started out as small-time contractors and tax farmers in Orsha, Mogilev province.

Several Jewish financiers from Warsaw and Lodz formed the first Russian joint-stock banks; Evzel and Horace Gintsburg founded the St. Petersburg Discount and Loan Bank, the Kiev Commercial Bank, and the Odessa Discount Bank; Iakov Solomonovich Poliakov launched the Don Land Bank, the Petersburg-Azov Bank, and the influential Azov Don Commercial Bank; and his brother Lazar was the main shareholder of the Moscow International Merchant Bank, the South Russia Industrial Bank, the Orel Commercial Bank, and the Moscow and Yaroslavl-Kostroma Land Banks. The father and son Soloveichiks' Siberian Commercial Bank was one of Russia's most important and innovative financial institutions. Other prominent Russian financiers included the Rafalovichs, the Vavelbergs, and the Fridlands. In 1915–16, when the imperial capital was still formally closed to all but specially licensed Jews, at least 7 of the 17 members of the St. Petersburg Stock Exchange Council and 28 of the 70 joint-stock bank managers were Jews or Jewish converts to Christianity. When the merchant of the first guild Grigorii (Gersha Zelik) Davidovich Lesin arrived in St. Petersburg from Zhitomir in October 1907 to open a banking house, it took a special secret police investigation by two different agencies to persuade the municipal authorities, who had never heard of him, to issue the licence. By 1914, Lesin's bank had become one of the most important in Russia.[20]

Nor was finance the only sphere of Jewish business expertise. According to the premier economic historian of Russian Jewry (and first cousin to Israeli prime minister Yitzhak Rabin), Arcadius Kahan, "There was hardly an area of entrepreneurial activity from which Jewish entrepreneurs were successfully excluded. Apart from the manufacturing industries in the Pale of Settlement, one could have encountered them at the oil wells of Baku, in the gold mines of Siberia, on the fisheries of the Volga or Amur, in the shipping lines on the Dnepr, in the forests of Briansk, on railroad construction sites anywhere in European or Asiatic Russia, on cotton plantations in Central Asia, and so forth."[21]

The earliest, safest, most profitable, and ultimately the most productive investment was directed toward railroad construction. Benefiting from the example and direct financial backing of the Rothschilds, Pereires, Bleichröders, and Gomperzes (as well as the budgetary munificence of the imperial government, especially the War Ministry), some Russian-based Jewish bankers built large fortunes while connecting disparate Russian markets to each other and to the outside world. Consortia of Jewish financiers and contractors built the Warsaw-Vienna, Moscow-Smolensk, Kiev-Brest, and Moscow-Brest lines (among many others), while the "railroad king" Samuil Poliakov founded, constructed, and eventually owned a number of private railroads, including the Kursk-Kharkov-Rostov and the Kozlov-Voronezh-Rostov lines. According to H. Sachar, "it was the initiative of Jewish contractors that accounted for the construction of fully three-fourths of the Russian railroad system."[22]

Other important areas of massive Jewish investment included gold mining, commercial fishing, river transportation, and oil production. At the turn of the twentieth century, the Gintsburgs controlled a large portion of the Siberian gold industry, including the Innokentiev mines in Yakutia, Berezovka mines in the Urals, the South Altai and Upper Amur concerns, and largest of them all, the Lena goldfields (which they abandoned in 1912 after a scandal following the massacre of striking miners). The Gessen brothers pioneered new insurance schemes to expand their shipping business connecting the Baltic and the Caspian seas. The Margolins reorganized the transportation system on the Dnieper. And in the Caucasus oil industry, Jewish entrepreneurs were central participants in the Mazut Company and the Batum Oil Association. The Rothschilds, who backed both enterprises, went on to absorb them into their Shell Corporation.[23]

Many of these people competed fiercely with each other, dealt extensively with non-Jewish businessmen and officials, and had varying attitudes toward Judaism and the Russian state, but they obviously constituted a business community that both insiders and outsiders recognized as such, more or less the way Swann would. There was no Jewish master plan, of course, but there was, in the Russian Empire and beyond, a network of people with similar backgrounds and similar challenges who could, under certain circumstances, count on mutual acknowledgment and cooperation. Like all Mercurians, the Jews owed their economic success to strangeness, specialized training, and the kind of intragroup trust that assured the relative reliability of business partners, loan clients, and subcontractors. And like all Mercurians, they tended to think of themselves as a chosen tribe consisting of chosen clans—and to act accordingly. Most Jewish businesses (like the Armenian and Old Believer ones, among others) were family businesses; the larger the business, the larger the family. The Poliakovs were related to each other as well as to the Varshavskys and the Hirsches. The Gintsburgs were related to the Hirsches, Warburgs, Rothschilds, Fulds, the Budapest Herzfelds, the Odessa Ashkenazis, and the Kiev sugar king Lazar Izrailevich Brodsky ("Brodsky himself," as Sholem Aleichem's Tevye used to call him).[24]

Indeed, even Tevye, as a member of the tribe, might be able to partake of Brodsky's wealth and fame—the way he might benefit from the largesse of his Yehupetz customers or the advice of his Russian-educated writer friend (Sholem Aleichem's narrator). To quote Kahan again, Russia's industrialization

actually widened the areas of choice for Jewish entrepreneurs. If few of them actually built railroads, many established subcontracting enterprises that supplied the railroad industry. If very few could enter oil production, many could establish themselves in oil processing, transportation, and marketing. If the basic chemicals required large capital outlays, smaller-size operations and more specialized enterprises using basic chemicals were open for Jewish entrepreneurship. Thus a large area for Jewish entrepreneurial activity was made available and was stimulated by Russian industrialization.[25]

For most Jews, especially the artisans, the collapse of the Jewish economic niche in Eastern Europe meant emigration and proletarianization. For an important minority—a much larger one than among most other groups—it stood for new social and economic opportunities. In 1887 in Odessa, Jews owned 35 percent of factories, which accounted for 57 percent of all factory output; in 1900, half of the city's guild merchants were Jews; and in 1910, 90 percent of all grain exports were handled by Jewish firms (compared to 70 percent in the 1880s). Most Odessa banks were run by Jews, as was much of Russia's timber export industry. On the eve of World War I, Jewish entrepreneurs owned about one-third of all Ukrainian sugar mills (which accounted for 52 percent of all refined sugar), and constituted 42.7 percent of the corporate board members and 36.5 percent of board chairmen. In all the sugar mills in Ukraine, 28 percent of chemists, 26 percent of beet plantation overseers, and 23.5 percent of bookkeepers were Jews. In the city of Kiev, 36.8 percent of all corporate managers were Jews (followed by Russians at 28.9 percent). And in 1881 in St. Petersburg (outside the Pale), Jews made up about 2 percent of the total population and 43 percent of all brokers, 41 percent of all pawnbrokers, 16 percent of all brothel owners, and 12 percent of all trading house employees. Between 1869 and 1890, the proportion of business owners among St. Petersburg Jews grew from 17 percent to 37 percent.[26]

The "Jewish economy" was remarkable for its high rate of innovation, standardization, specialization, and product differentiation. Jewish enterprises tended to find more uses for by-products, produce a greater assortment of goods, and reach wider markets at lower prices than their competitors. Building on previous experience and superior training, utilizing preexisting "ethnic" connections and cheap family labor, accustomed to operating on low profit margins, and spurred on by (sometimes negotiable) legal restrictions, they were—as elsewhere—better at being "Jewish" than most of their new-minted and still somewhat reluctant competitors. In purely economic terms, their most effective strategy was "vertical integration," whereby Jewish firms "fed" each other within a particular line, sometimes covering the entire spectrum from the manufacturer to the consumer. Jewish craftsmen produced for Jewish industrialists, who sold to Jewish purchasing agents, who worked for Jewish wholesalers, who distributed to Jewish retail outlets, who employed Jewish traveling salesmen (the latter practice was introduced in the sugar industry by "Brodsky himself"). In many cases, including such Jewish specialties as the marketing of sugar, timber, grain, and fish, the integrated cycle did not include production and often ended with export, but the principle was the same.[27]

Vertical integration is a very common Mercurian practice, used to great effect by many "middleman minorities" in a variety of locations. In late imperial Russia, where state-run industrialization did battle with a largely unreformed rural economy, experienced Mercurians were in a particularly strong position to benefit from the coming of capitalism. The official view was doubtless correct even though it was official: in a world of universal mobility, urbanity, and marginality, most Russian peasants and their descendants (who embodied the "Orthodoxy" and "nationality" parts of the autocracy's doctrine as well as the "nation" of intelligentsia nationalism) were at an obvious disadvantage compared to all literate service nomads and especially the Jews, who were by far the most numerous, cohesive, exclusive, and urban of Russia's Mercurians. By the outbreak of the Great War, the tsar's Jewish subjects were well on their way to replacing the Germans as Russia's model moderns (the way they had done in much of East-Central Europe). If not for the relentless official restrictions (and the fierce competitiveness and cultural prominence of the Old Believer dissenters), early twentieth-century Russia would probably have resembled Hungary, where the business elite was almost entirely Jewish.

The same was true of the other pillar of the modern state, the professionals. Between 1853 and 1886, the number of all *gymnasium* students in the Russian Empire grew sixfold. During the same period, the number of Jewish *gymnasium* students increased by a factor of almost 50 (from 159, or 1.3 percent of the total, to 7,562, or 10.9 percent). By the late 1870s, they made up 19 percent of the total *gymnasium* population in the Pale of Settlement, and about one-third in the Odessa school district. As the Odessa writer Perets Smolenskin wrote in the early 1870s, "All the schools are filled with Jewish students from end to end, and, to be honest, the Jews are always at the head of the class." When the first classical *gymnasium* opened in 1879 in Nikolaev (also in New Russia), 105 Jews and 38 Christians enrolled.[28] And when the narrator of Babel's "The Story of My Dovecot" passed his entrance exam to that *gymnasium* in 1905, old "Monsieur Lieberman," his Torah teacher,

> gave a toast in my honor in the Hebrew language. The old man congratulated my parents in this toast and said that I had vanquished all my enemies at the exam, had vanquished the Russian boys with fat cheeks and the sons of our coarse men of wealth. Thus in ancient times had David, King of Judah, vanquished Goliath, and just as I had triumphed over Goliath, so would our people by the strength of their intellect vanquish the enemies who had encircled us and were thirsting for our blood. Having said this, Monsieur Lieberman began to weep and, while weeping, took another sip of wine and shouted "Vivat!"[29]

The higher one moved within the expanding Russian education system, the higher the proportion of Jews and the more spectacular their triumph over the imperial Goliath and the Russian boys with fat cheeks. The share of Jewish students in the *gymnasia* was greater than in the *Realschulen*, and their share in the universities was higher than in the *gymnasia* (partly because many Jewish children began their education in heders, yeshivas, or at home—with or without the help of a Monsieur Lieberman). Between 1840 and 1886, the number of university students in Russia increased sixfold (from 2,594 to 12,793). The number of Jews among them grew over a hundred times: from 15 (0.5 percent of the total) to 1,856 (14.5 percent). At Odessa University, every third student in 1886 was Jewish. Jewish women represented 16 percent of the students at the Kiev Institute for Women and at Moscow's Liubianskie Courses, 17 percent at the prestigious Bestuzhev Institute, and 34 percent at the Women's Medical Courses in St. Petersburg.[30]

As elsewhere, the most popular careers were those in law and medicine. In 1886, more than 40 percent of the law and medical students at the universities of Kharkov and Odessa were Jewish. In the empire as a whole, in 1889 Jews accounted for 14 percent of all certified lawyers and 43 percent of all apprentice lawyers (the next generation of professionals). According to Benjamin Nathans, "during the preceding five years, 22% of those admitted to the bar and an astounding 89% of those who became apprentice lawyers were Jews." Jews constituted 49 percent of all lawyers in the city of Odessa (1886), and 68 percent of all apprentice lawyers in the Odessa judicial circuit (1890). In the imperial capital, the proportion of Jewish lawyers was variously estimated at 22 to 42 percent, and of apprentice lawyers, at 43 to 55 percent. At the very top, 6 out of 12 senior lawyers chosen in the mid-1880s to lead seminars for apprentice lawyers in St. Petersburg were Jews. The wave of quotas in the 1880s succeeded in slowing down the Jewish advance in the professions but failed to halt it, partly because a growing number of Jews went to German and Swiss universities, and because some of them practiced illegally. Between 1881 and 1913, the share of Jewish doctors and dentists in St. Petersburg grew from 11 and 9 percent to 17 and 52 percent.[31]

Equally impressive and, in the European context, familiar, was the entry of Jews into Russian high culture. The commercialization of the entertainment market and the creation of national cultural institutions transformed a traditional Mercurian specialty into an elite profession and a powerful tool of modern mythmaking. The Rubinstein brothers founded the Russian Music Society and both the Moscow and St. Petersburg conservatories; the Gnesin sisters created the first Russian music school for children, and Odessa's violin teacher, P. S. Stoliarsky, or "Zagursky," as Babel called him, "supplied prodigies for the concert stages of the world. From Odessa came Mischa Elman, Zimbalist, and Gabrilowich. Jascha Heifetz also began among us." As did David Oistrakh, Elizaveta

Gilels, Boris Goldstein, and Mikhail Fikhtengolts, after Babel's departure from the city.[32] "Zagursky ran a factory of child prodigies, a factory of Jewish dwarves in lace collars and patent-leather shoes. He sought them out in the slums of the Moldavanka and in the evil-smelling courtyards of the Old Market. Zagursky would provide early instruction, after which children would be sent to Professor Auer's in St. Petersburg. In the souls of these tiny runts with swollen blue heads there dwelt a powerful harmony. They became celebrated virtuosi."[33]

Even more remarkable was the success of some scions of the Pale in the world of visual arts (for which there was no Jewish tradition). Because Jewish bankers became prominent as art patrons, Jewish faces became prominent on Russian portraits (including some of the most canonical ones by Valentin Serov, himself the son of a Jewish mother). But much more prominent in every way were Jewish artists, or rather Russian artists of Jewish origin. Leonid Pasternak from Odessa ranked with Serov as one of Russia's most admired portraitists; Léon Bakst (Lev Rozenberg, from Grodno) was the premier Russian stage designer; Mark Antokolsky from Vilna was acclaimed as the greatest Russian sculptor of the nineteenth century; and Isaak Levitan from Kibartai in Lithuania became the most beloved of all Russian landscape painters (and still is). The Kiev and Vitebsk prerevolutionary art schools produced at least as many celebrated artists as Odessa did musicians (Marc Chagall, Iosif Chaikov, Ilya Chashnik, El Lissitzky, Abraham Manievich, Solomon Nikritin, Isaak Rabinovich, Issachar Rybak, Nisson Shifrin, Alexander Tyshler, Solomon Yudovin). Meanwhile, Odessa produced almost as many artists (including Boris Anisfeld, Isaak Brodsky, Osip Braz, and Savely Sorin, in addition to Pasternak) as it did musicians (or poets). And this not counting Natan Altman from Vinnitsa, Chaim Soutine from Minsk, or David Shterenberg from Zhitomir. All of these artists and musicians had to deal with anti-Jewish laws and sentiments, and some of them left the Russian Empire for good. But probably most of them would have agreed with the critic Abram Efros, who said, referring to Shterenberg, that the best thing to do was "to be born in Zhitomir, study in Paris, and become an artist in Moscow." The Russian fin de siècle—

literary as well as artistic—is as difficult to imagine without the refugees from the "ghetto" as are its German, Polish, or Hungarian counterparts.[34]

Before one could become a Russian artist, however, one had to become Russian. As elsewhere in Europe, the Jewish success in Russian business, the professions, and the arts (often in that order within one family) was accompanied by a mastery of the national high culture and an eager conversion to the Pushkin faith. In St. Petersburg, the proportion of Jews who spoke Russian as their native language increased from 2 percent in 1869 to 13 percent in 1881, to 29 percent in 1890, to 37 percent in 1900, to 42 percent in 1910 (during the same period, the share of Estonian-speaking Estonians grew from 75 to 86 percent, and Polish-speaking Poles, from 78 to 94 percent). Jewish youths learned Russian by themselves, in schools, from tutors hired by their parents, from mentors they met in youth circles, and, in wealthy families, from their Russian nannies, who would, in later recollections, become copies of Pushkin's Arina Rodionovna. Lev Deich's father, for example, was a military contractor who made his fortune during the Crimean War, performed Jewish rituals "for business purposes," had learned Russian by himself, spoke it "without an accent, and in appearance—a broad flat beard, a suit, etc.—looked like a perfectly cultured person, a Great-Russian or even a European entrepreneur." His son, the famous revolutionary, had a Polish governess, a "tutor in general subjects," and, as a small child, a Russian nanny "with pleasant features" whom "we children loved very much, both for her kind, friendly nature and especially for the wonderful folktales she told us." Having graduated from a Russian *gymnasium* in Kiev, he became a populist (a socialist millenarian by way of Russian nationalism) who believed that "as soon as Jews began to speak Russian, they would, just as we had, become 'people in general,' 'cosmopolites.' " Many of them did.[35]

Meanwhile, the students at the Vilna and Zhitomir rabbinical seminaries (after 1873, teacher training colleges) were being converted to the religion of the Russian language even as they were being taught to be experts on things Jewish. Joshua Steinberg, the renowned Hebrew scholar who taught at Vilna to a mostly skeptical audience, had learned Russian, according to Hirsz Abramowicz, "from the Synodical translation of the Bible, and throughout his life he used its archaic sentence structure and distinctive biblical expressions when he spoke." He spoke it with "traces of a Jewish accent," but he spoke it (and apparently nothing else) with his family and in his classes, where students spent the bulk of their time translating the texts of Isaiah and Jeremiah into Russian and then back into Hebrew. The idea was to teach Hebrew, but the main result was to make Russian available to countless heder-educated youngsters, the majority of whom never enrolled in the seminary (while the majority of those who did never meant to become rabbis). In the words of Abramowicz, "many of these impoverished young autodidacts learned Russian from his Hebrew-Russian and Russian-Hebrew dictionaries and from his grammar of the Hebrew language, written in Russian, of which they often memorized entire pages."[36]

Young Jews were not just learning Russian the same way they were learning Hebrew: they were learning Russian in order to replace Hebrew, as well as Yiddish, for good. Like German, Polish, or Hungarian in other high-culture areas, Russian had become the Hebrew of the secular world. As Abram Mutnikovich, a Bund theorist, put it: "Russia, the wonderful country. . . . Russia, which gave mankind such a poet of genius as Pushkin. The land of Tolstoy. . . ." Jabotinsky did not approve of the confusion of "Russian culture" with "the Russian world" (including its "dreariness and philistinism"), but then Jabotinsky, unlike Mutnikovich, spoke Russian as a native language, and the particular confusion he was proposing (of Jewish biblical culture with the Jewish world) was different from the Russian kind only to the extent that it was not pret-a-porter and went more naturally with Swann's nose, or the Jewish "hump," as he called it. It was Abraham Cahan, the future New York journalist, who seemed to speak for most Jewish youngsters in the Pale when he described his most fateful experience growing up in Vilna in the 1870s: "My interest in Hebrew evaporated. My burning ambition became to learn Russian and thus to become an educated person." At about the same time, in the Białystok *Realschule*, the future "Dr. Esperanto" was writing a Russian tragedy in five acts.[37]

Russian was the language of true knowledge and of "the striving for freedom" (as the populist terrorist and Siberian ethnographer Vladmir Iokheleson put it). It was a language, as opposed to the "words composed of unknown noises"—"a language, and thus something rooted and self-assured." Osip Mandelstam's mother had been saved by Pushkin: she "loved to speak and rejoiced in the rootedness and the sound of Great-Russian speech, slightly impoverished by intelligentsia conventions. Was she not the first in her family to master the clear and pure Russian sounds?" His father, on the other hand, had barely emerged from "the Talmudic thicket" and thus "had no language at all: just a kind of tongue-tiedness and tonguelessness. It was a completely abstract, invented language; the ornate and convoluted speech of an autodidact, in which ordinary words are intertwined with the ancient philosophical terms from Herder, Leibniz, and Spinoza; the overwrought syntax of a Talmudist; the artificial sentence not always spoken to the end—whatever it was, it was not a language, either Russian or German." Learning how to speak proper Russian (or, for the previous generation, German) meant learning how to speak. Abraham Cahan, who was about the same age as Mandelstam's father, remembered the thrill of becoming articulate: "I felt the Russian language was becoming my own, that I was speaking it fluently. I loved it."[38]

A true conversion to a modern nationalism—and thus world citizenship—could be accomplished only through reading. Speaking was a key to reading; reading was a key to everything else. When F. A. Moreinis-Muratova, the future regicide raised in a very wealthy traditional household, read her first Russian book, she "felt like somebody who lived underground and suddenly saw a beam of bright light." All early Soviet memoirs (Moreinis-Muratova's was written in 1926) travel from darkness to light, and most describe revelation through reading. The Jewish ones (Soviet as well as non-Soviet and native as well as nonnative speakers of Russian) are remarkable for their explicit emphasis on language, on learning new words as a fundamental way of "striving for freedom." The Jewish tradition of emancipation through reading had been extended to the emancipation from the Jewish tradition.[39]

In Babel's "Childhood. At Grandmother's," the little narrator did his studying under his grandmother's watchful eye.

> Grandmother would not interrupt me, God forbid. Her tension, her reverence for my work would make her face look foolish. Her eyes—round, yellow, transparent—would never leave me. Whenever I turned a page, they would slowly follow my hand. Anyone else would have found her relentlessly observant, unblinking gaze very hard to take, but I was used to it.
>
> Then Grandmother would listen to me recite my lessons. It must be said that she spoke Russian poorly, mangling words in her own peculiar way, mixing Russian with Polish and Yiddish ones. She was not literate in Russian, of course, and would hold the book upside down. But this did not prevent me from reciting the lesson to her from beginning to end. Grandmother would listen, understanding none of it, but the music of the words was sweet to her, she was in awe of learning, believed me, believed in me, and wanted me to become a "big man"—that was her name for a rich man.[40]

The boy in the story was reading Turgenev's "First Love." And because Turgenev's "First Love" was the boy's first love, Babel's "First Love" was a version of Turgenev's, except that the boy was even younger. The woman he loved was named Galina Apollonovna (daughter of Apollo), and she was happily married to a young officer who had just returned from the Russo-Japanese war.

> She could not take her eyes off her husband because she had not seen him for a year and a half, but I dreaded that look and kept turning away and trembling. In the two of them, I saw the wonderful and shameful life of all the people in the world. I wanted to fall into a magic sleep so that I could forget about this life that exceeded all my dreams. Galina Apollonovna used to walk around the room with her hair down, wearing red slippers and a Chinese robe. Beneath the lace of her low-cut gown one could see the hollow between the top parts of her white, heavy, swollen breasts. Her robe was embroidered with pink silk dragons, birds, and trees with gnarled trunks.[41]

Before he could partake of the "wonderful and shameful life of all the people in the world," however, he had to overcome his tonguelessness: the violent, throat-stopping hiccups that came upon him the day his grandfather was murdered, his father humiliated, and his doves smashed against his temple—the day he felt such "bitter, ardent, and hopeless" love for Galina Apollonovna.

That first victory—over the "tongue-tiedness and tonguelessness," Turgenev's "First Love," and the "Russian boys with fat cheeks"—always came in due course, usually at a *gymnasium* exam. In a kind of ecstatic Russian bar mitzvah, Jewish adolescents recited specially selected sacred texts to mark their initiation into the wonderful and shameful life of all the people in the world. Babel's narrator was examined by the teachers Karavaev and Piatnitsky. They asked him about Peter the Great.

> Everything I knew about Peter the Great I had memorized from Putsykovich's textbook and Pushkin's verses. I was reciting those verses in a violent sob, when suddenly human faces came rolling into my eyes and mixed themselves up like cards from a new deck. As they were shuffling themselves in the back of my eyes, I shouted out Pushkin's stanzas with all my might, trembling, straightening up, hurrying. I kept shouting them for a long time, and no one interrupted my demented muttering. Through a crimson blindness, through the sense of freedom that had taken possession of me, all I could see was Piatnitsky's bent-down, old face, with its silver-streaked beard. He did not interrupt me but merely said to Karavaev, who was rejoicing for my sake and for Pushkin's,
>
> "What a people," whispered the old man, "these little Jews of yours. There's a devil in them."[42]

Perhaps by coincidence, Samuil Marshak, the famous Soviet children's writer, drew the same question at his exam. He, too, chose to recite Pushkin's verses, possibly the same ones from "Poltava."

> I inhaled as deeply as I could and began not too loudly, saving my breath for the heat of battle. It seemed to me that I had never heard my own voice before.

> In flares of dawn the east is burning
> Along the ridges, down the dales
> The cannon growl. With purple churning
> The smoke of salvos skyward sails
> And drapes the slanting sun in veils.

I had read these verses and recited them by heart over and over again at home, although no one had ever assigned them to me. But here, in this large room, they sounded clearer and more joyous than ever.

I was looking at the people seated at the table, and it seemed to me that, just as I did, they saw before them the smoke-covered battlefield, the flames from the salvos, and Peter on his steed.

> A war-steed presently is brought;
> High-bred, but docile to his weight,
> As if it sensed the touch of fate,
> The charger shudders; eyes athwart,
> It struts amid the dust of battle,
> Proud of the hero in its saddle.

No one interrupted me; no one asked me to stop. Triumphant, I recited the victorious lines:

> He bids the lords beneath his scepters,
> Both Swede and Russian, to his tent;
> And gaily mingling prey and captors
> Lifts high his cup in compliment
> To the good health of his "preceptors."

I stopped. With Pushkin's powerful help, I had defeated my indifferent examiners.[43]

Admitted to the life of all the people in the world, they had a whole world to discover. And the world, as Galina Apollonovna's robe suggested, contained dragons, birds, gnarled trees, and countless other things that Apollonians called "nature." "What is it that you lack?" asked the copper-shouldered and bronze-legged Efim Nikitich Smolich of Babel's bewildered little boy, who wrote tragedies and played the violin but did not know how to swim.

"Your youth is not the problem, it will pass with the years . . . What you lack is a feeling for nature."

He pointed with his stick at a tree with a reddish trunk and a low crown.

"What kind of tree is that?"

I did not know.

"What's growing on that bush?"

I did not know that, either. We were walking through the little park next to Aleksandrovsky Avenue. The old man poked his stick at every tree; he clutched my shoulder every time a bird flew by and made me listen to the different calls.

"What kind of bird is that singing?"

I was unable to reply. The names of trees and birds, their division into species, the places birds fly to, where the sun rises, when the dew is heaviest—all these things were unknown to me.[44]

Babel was a city boy. Abraham Cahan's autobiographical narrator, who was born in a small shtetl in rural Lithuania, did not know the names for daisies or dandelions.

I knew three flowers but not by their names. There was the round, yellow, brushlike blossom that turned into a ball of fuzz that could be blown into the wind. Its stem had a bitter taste. There was the flower that had white petals around a yellow button center. And the flower that looks like a dark red knob. When I grew older I learned their Russian names and, in America, their English names. But in that early time we didn't even know their Yiddish names. We called all of them "tchatchkalech," playthings.[45]

This was not something Zagursky could fix. This called for Efim Nikitich Smolich, the Russian man who had a "feeling for nature" and could not stand the sight of splashing little boys being pulled to the bottom of the sea by "the hydrophobia of their ancestors—Spanish rabbis and Frankfurt money changers."

In the athletic breast of this man there dwelt compassion for Jewish boys. He presided over throngs of rickety runts. Nikitich would gather them in the bug-filled hovels of the Moldavanka, take them to the sea, bury them in the sand, do exercises with them, dive with them, teach them songs and, roasting in the direct rays of the sun, tell them stories about fishermen and animals. Nikitich used to tell the grown-ups that he was a natural philosopher. The Jewish children would roll with laughter at his tales, squealing and snuggling up to him like puppies. . . . I came to love that man with the love that only a boy who suffers from hysteria and migraines can feel for an athlete.[46]

Most Pale of Settlement Jews who entered Russian life had their own mentors of things Apollonian, guides into neutral spaces, and discoverers of "divine sparks." Babel the narrator had Efim Nikitich Smolich; Babel the writer had Maxim Gorky (to whom "The Story of My Dovecot" is dedicated). Abraham Cahan had Vladimr Soko-lov, "the model of what man would be like when the world would turn socialist" and the person who introduced him, "on the basis of equality," to "officers, students, several older persons and even a few ladies, most of them gentiles." Moreinis-Muratova had her parents' tenant, a naval officer who gave her Russian books and once took her to the theater to see an Ostrovsky play (which impressed her so much she "thought of nothing else for several months"). And the Yiddish poet Aron Kushnirov, along with so many others, had World War I.

> It was so hard, but now it's very easy,
> It's been so long, but I have not forgotten
> The lessons I have learned from you, my tough old rabbi:
> My sergeant major, Nikanor Ilyich!

Levitan had Chekhov; Bakst had Diaghilev; Leonid Pasternak had Tolstoy; and Antokolsky and Marshak, among many others, had Vladimr Stasov. Russian high culture was discovering the "powerful harmony" in the souls of Jewish "runts" even as they were discovering Russian high culture—as their first love. For Leo-nid Pasternak, Tolstoy embodied "the principle of love for one's neighbor"; for the sculptor Naum Aronson, the commission to make a bust of Tolstoy was tantamount to joining the elect. "I had great hopes and ambitions but would never have aspired to sculpt the gods—for that is what Tolstoy was for me. Even to approach him seemed blasphemous."[47]

He did sculpt him, however, carving out his own place in eternity as he did so. Osip Braz painted the likeness of Chekhov that became the icon that every Russian grows up with. Marshak was to his *gymnasium* teachers what Peter the Great had been to his haughty Swedish "preceptors." And Isaak Levitan became the official interpreter of the Russian national landscape—and thus a true national divinity in his own right.

Tolstoy was prepared to do his part. When Stasov told him about the young Marshak's great promise (of "something good, pure, bright, and creative"), Tolstoy seemed doubtful: "Oh, these Wunderkinder!" As Stasov wrote to Marshak:

> I feel the same way; I, too, have been disappointed before. But this time I defended and shielded my new arrival, my new joy and consolation! I told him that, to my way of thinking, there was a real golden kernel here. And my LEO seemed to incline his powerful mane and his regal eyes in my direction. And then I told him: "Do this for me, for the sake of everything that is sacred, great, and precious; here, take a look at this little portrait, which I have just received, and let your gaze, by fixing on this young, vibrant little face, be a long-distance blessing for him!" And he did as I asked, and looked for a long time at the tender face of a child / young man who is only beginning to live.[48]

Not everyone could be anointed by a god, but there was no lack of would-be godfathers and priests, as young Jewish men and women continued to join the faith that most of them (including Abraham Cahan in New York) would profess for the rest of their lives. Babel's life, like everybody else's, began on Pushkin Street.

> I stood there alone, clutching my watch, and suddenly, with a clarity such as I had never experienced before, I saw the soaring columns of the Duma, the illuminated foliage on the boulevard, and Pushkin's bronze head touched by a dim reflection of the moon. For the first time in my life, I saw the world around me the way it really was: serene and inexpressibly beautiful.[49]

Raisa Orlova's mother, Susanna Averbukh, died in 1975, at the age of eighty-five. As she lay dying, she asked her daughter to read some Pushkin to her. "I read Pushkin. She started reciting along: line by line, stanza by stanza. She knew these poems from her childhood, from her father. . . . Perhaps she had read Pushkin to my father on their honeymoon?"[50]

Converting to the Pushkin faith meant leaving the parental home. If the Russian world stood for speech, knowledge, freedom, and light, then the Jewish world represented silence, ignorance, bondage, and darkness. In the 1870s and 1880s, the revolution of young Jews against their parents reached Russia—eventually in the form of Marxism but most immediately as Freud's family romance. The Jews who shared Mandelstam's reverence for the "clear and pure Russian sounds" tended to share his horror of the "Judean chaos" of their grandmother's household.

> She kept asking: "Have you eaten? Have you eaten?"—the only Russian words she knew. But I did not like the old people's well-spiced delicacies, with their bitter almond taste. My parents had gone into the city. Every now and then, my mournful grandfather and my sad, fussy grandmother would try speaking with me, only to give up and ruffle their feathers like little old birds in a huff. I kept trying to explain to them that I wanted to be with my mother, but they did not understand. Then I attempted to represent visually my desire to leave by using my middle and index fingers to imitate walking across the table.
>
> Suddenly, Grandfather opened a chest drawer and pulled out a black-and-yellow shawl. He threw it over my shoulders, and made me repeat after him words composed of unfamiliar noises. But then, annoyed by my babble, he became angry and shook his head in disapproval. I felt frightened and suffocated. I do not remember how my mother rescued me.[51]

Modernity meant universal Mercurianism under the nationalist banner of a return to local Apollonianism. The Jews marched under the same (i.e., somebody else's) banner; for them, the joyous return to Russian togetherness meant a permanent escape from the Jewish home. It meant becoming Apollonian—even as they triumphed over the Russian boys with fat cheeks in the marketplace of universal Mercurianism. Their image of home abandoned (regardless of whether they ended up as socialists, nationalists, or trained specialists) was an abridged version of the traditional Apollonian view of Jewish life as babbling, clannish, bad-smelling, pointlessly intricate, lifelessly rational, relentlessly acquisitive, and devoid of color. Babel's grandmother in Odessa was far from Mandelstam's in Riga, but the staging is painfully familiar: "the darkening room, Grandmother's yellow eyes, her small figure wrapped in a shawl, bent and silent in the corner, the hot air, the closed door . . ." And the dream of conquering the world while remaining locked up: " 'Study,' she says with sudden vehemence. 'Study, and you will achieve everything—wealth and fame. You must know everything. All will prostrate and abase themselves before you. Everyone should envy you. Don't trust people. Don't have any friends. Don't give them any money. Don't give them your heart.' "[52]

What matters is not whether Babel's grandmother really said anything of the sort; what matters is how Babel, Mandelstam, and so many others remembered their grandmothers. Lev Deich believed that Jews provided "sufficient reasons for the hostility against them" because of their "preference for unproductive, light, and more profitable occupations." Vladmir Yokhelson, as a student at the Vilna Rabbinical Seminary, considered Yiddish artificial, Hebrew dead, Jewish traditions valueless, and Jews in general a "parasitical class." I. J. Singer, in *The Brothers Ashkenazi*, represented Jewish religion and Jewish business as equally "devious," built on "snares, loaded questions, contradictions," and mostly concerned with "promissory notes, reparations, contamination, and purity." And Lev Trotsky was probably at his most orthodox as a Marxist when he said about his father, David Bronstein: "The instinct of acquisitiveness, the petit-bourgeois outlook and way of life—from these I sailed away with a mighty push, never to return." The life of all the people in the world did not include Jewish parents. Babel's "Awakening" ends in the same way as Trotsky's: "Aunt Bobka held me tightly by the hand, to make sure I did not run away. She was right. I was plotting an escape."[53]

Most such plots were successful because the jailers' only weapon consisted of monologues "composed of unfamiliar noises." Their language was either artificial or dead, and their children could not bring themselves to speak it, even if they knew how. When Abraham Cahan was packing for his "historic trip to Petersburg," his father, with whom he was not on speaking terms, came to help. "I wanted to make peace with my father. But somehow I couldn't. My aunt and my mother pushed me toward him; my uncle pleaded with me. It was no good; I couldn't move from the spot." Moreinis-Muratova's father, an Odessa grain exporter, was much more learned but equally impotent. "Leaving my blind father so soon after he lost our mother was extraordinarily difficult, especially because I loved and respected him very much. I knew that for him my departure would be worse than my death, because it meant disgrace for the family. But I felt it was my duty to leave home and earn my own living."[54]

Every Jewish parent was a King Lear. Jacob Gordin's most famous New York play was his 1898 *The Jewish Queen Lear*, based on his 1892 *The Jewish King Lear*. By far the most successful production of Mikhoels's State Jewish Theater in Moscow was Shakespeare's *King Lear* (1935). And of course the central text of Yiddish literature, Sholem Aleichem's *Tevye the Milkman*, is itself a version of *King Lear*—as are countless family chronicles written in Tevye's shadow.[55]

Bound by the Bard, Jewish fathers were prey to their own foolishness. According to Cahan, all Jewish families were unhappy in two different ways: "There were the families in which children addressed their parents as 'tate' and 'mama.' In the other group, parents were called 'papasha' and 'mamasha,' and it was these families that sent their boys to receive the new, daring, gentile education." As G. A. Landau put it,

> How many Jewish parents of the bourgeois or townsman classes did not watch with sympathy, often pride, or at least indifference how their children were being branded with one of the assorted brands of

one of the assorted revolutionary-socialist ideologies? . . . In fact, they themselves were products of the grandiose cultural and domestic revolution that had brought them, within one or two generations, from an Orthodox shtetl in Lithuania or a Hasidic one in Poland to a Petersburg bank or district court, a Kharkov shop or dental office, the stock exchange or a factory.

They did not even have to travel very far. Cahan's pious and penniless father was no "papasha," and all he had done was move twenty miles from Podberezy to Vilna, and yet he, too, made in 1871 the "astounding decision" to send his son to the state-run rabbinical school, knowing full well "that in that school all teaching was in Russian, that all the students were bareheaded and that along with the teachers they were clean-shaven and wrote and smoked on the Holy Sabbath. To send a youngster to the Rabiner school could only mean 'to turn him into a goy.' " Had he known what he was doing? Cahan did not know. " 'Tis the time's plague that madmen lead the blind"—or so Landau would imply, writing in postrevolutionary exile as an anti-Bolshevik Russian "intelligent" of Jewish extraction. Cahan himself, however, never regretted either his father's decision or his own departure from home (even as he bemoaned, time and again, his emigration from Russia to America). Neither did Deich, Babel, Yokhelson, Moreinis-Muratova, or her brother, M. A. Moreinis, who had left their blind father one day before she did. To say nothing of Trotsky, and perhaps even Trotsky's parents, who felt "ambivalent" as they sat at his trial in 1906. "I was an editor of newspapers, the chairman of the soviet, and I had a name as a writer. The old couple were impressed by all this. Over and over again, my mother tried to talk to the defense lawyers, hoping to hear more flattering things about me."[56]

Even Tevye the Milkman, in his darkest hour, was not sure. His daughter Chava had married a "gentile," and he had done the right thing by mourning her death and pretending "there had never been any Chava to begin with." But then again,

"What are you doing, you crazy old loon?" I asked myself. "Why are you making such a production of this? Stop playing the tyrant, turn your wagon around, and make up with her! She is your own child, after all, not some street waif. . ."

I tell you, I had even weirder thoughts than that in the forest. What did being a Jew or not a Jew matter? Why did God have to create both? And if He did, why put such walls between them, so that neither would look at the other even though both were his creatures? It grieved me that I wasn't a more learned man, because surely there were answers to be found in the holy books . . .[57]

The answers were, indeed, found in the holy books, but not the ones Tevye had in mind. The Jewish refugees from home were not just becoming students, artists, and professionals; they—including most students, artists, and professionals—were becoming members of the "intelligentsia."

The Russian intelligentsia was a community of more or less unattached intellectuals trained to be urban moderns in a rural empire; raised to be "foreigners at home" (as Herzen put it); suspended between the state and the peasants (whom they called "the people"); sustained by transcendental values revealed in sacred texts; devoted to book learning as a key to virtuous living; committed to personal righteousness as a condition for universal redemption; imbued with a sense of chosenness and martyrdom; and bound together by common rites and readings into fraternal "circles." They were, in other words, Puritans possessed by the spirit of socialism, Mercurians of recent Apollonian descent, the wandering Jews of Russian society. Homeless and disembodied, they were the People of the Book prophesying the end of history, chosen to bring it about, and martyred for both the prophesy and the chosenness. In this "ghetto of divine election," as the poetess Marina Tsvetaeva put it, "every poet is a Yid."

Never more so than in the 1870s and 1880s, when the actual Pale of Settlement Jews were beginning to migrate from one chosen people to another. Growing rapidly as a result of the democratization of the education system, underemployed by an economy that was growing much less rapidly, thwarted by an ancien régime that remained unrelentingly autocratic, outraged by the incompleteness of the Great Reforms and at the same time terrified at the prospect of their success (which would result in a prosaic and retarded embourgeoisement), the intelligentsia was in the grips of an intense messianic expectation of a popular revolution.

Populism was a poor man's socialism, a violent response to a modernity that had not yet arrived. The universal brotherhood that was supposed to supplant capitalism was to be realized by the Russian peasant, whose very unfamiliarity with capitalism was a mark of election. The intellectuals, "spoilt for Russia by Western prejudices and for the West by Russian habit," would vindicate themselves and save the world by fusing their Western prejudices with Russian popular habit. Socialism was the reward for Russian nationalism. And Russian nationalism, in the case of the Russian intelligentsia, stood for a "bitter, ardent, and hopeless" devotion to the Russian peasants.[58]

Few passions are as bitter, ardent, and hopeless as the love of repentant Mercurians for their Apollonian neighbors. The members of the intelligentsia—like the Jews—saw the "people" as their opposites: heart to their head, body (and soul) to their mind, simplicity to their complexity, spontaneity to their consciousness, rootedness to their rootlessness. This relationship—often expressed in erotic terms—could be represented as mutual repulsion or perfect complementarity. The era of Populism, for both Russian and Jewish secular intellectuals, was a time of longing for an ecstatic and redemptive union with the "people." Tolstoy's self-reflexive Olenin, in *The Cossacks*, loves his "statuesque beauty" Maryanka, with her "powerful breasts and shoulders," as ardently and as hopelessly as Babel's hiccuping boy loves Galina Apollonovna. Or is it Babel's boy who loves Maryanka? By the time the civil war came, Babel was admiring the beauty of the Cossacks' "gigantic bodies" as ardently as Tolstoy had admired his "tall, handsome" Lukashka's "warlike and proud bearing." But perhaps not as hopelessly . . .[59]

There was one more thing the Russian radicals and Jewish fugitives had in common: they were at war with their parents. Starting in the 1860s, the inability of "fathers and sons" ("fathers and children," in Turgenev's original Russian title) to talk to each other became one of the central themes in intelligentsia culture. Nowhere else did the rebellious Jewish youngsters meet as many like-minded peers as they did in Russia. Having abandoned their own blind fathers and "sad, fussy" mothers, they were adopted by the large fraternities of those who had left behind their gentry, priestly, peasant, and merchant parents. Hierarchical, patriarchal, circumscribed families were being replaced by egalitarian, fraternal, and open-ended ones. The rest of the world was to follow suit.

All modern societies produce "youth cultures" that mediate between the biological family, which is based on rigidly hierarchical role ascription within the kinship nomenclature, and the professional domain, which consists, at least in aspiration, of equal interchangeable citizens judged by universalistic meritocratic standards. The transition from son to citizen involves a much greater adjustment than the transition from son to father. Whereas in traditional societies one is socialized into the "real world" and proceeds to move, through a succession of rites of passage, from one ascriptive role to another, every modern individual is raised on values inimical to the ones that prevail outside. Whatever the rhetoric within the family and whatever the division of labor between husbands and wives, the parent-child relationship is always asymmetrical, with the meaning of each action determined according to the actor's status. Becoming a modern adult is always a revolution.[60]

There are two common remedies for this predicament. One is nationalism, with the modern state posing as a family complete with founding fathers, patriotism, a motherland, brothers-in-arms, sons of the nation, daughters of the revolution, and so on. The other is membership in a variety of voluntary associations, of which youth groups are probably the most common and effective precisely because they combine the ascription, solidarity, and intense intimacy of the family with the choice, flexibility, and open-endedness of the marketplace. What happened in late imperial Russia was that large numbers of young people who had been raised in patriarchal families and introduced to Western socialism rebelled against Russia's backwardness and Western modernity at the same time. They saw both evils as their own ("spoilt" as they were "for Russia by Western prejudices and for the West by Russian habit"), and they saw both of them as strengths, for that very reason. They were going to save the world by saving themselves because Russia's backwardness was the most direct route to Western socialism—either because it was so communal or because, as Lenin would later discover, it was "the weakest link in the chain of imperialism." Suspended between the illegitimate patriarchies of the family and autocracy, they created a durable youth culture imbued with intense millenarian expectation, powerful internal cohesion, and a self-worship so passionate it could be consummated only through self-immolation. For Russia's young intellectuals, the halfway house of a generation had become a temple dedicated to eternal youth and human sacrifice.[61]

These were the neutral spaces—or the "little islands of freedom," as one participant called them—that most Jews entered as they made their way down Pushkin Street. Russia had fewer salons, museums, stock exchanges, professional associations, dental offices, and coffeehouses than the West; their social significance was limited, and Jewish access to them was made difficult by legal handicaps. The temple of youth, on the other hand, was both very large and genuinely welcoming. Jews were appreciated as Jews: a few revolutionaries interpreted the pogroms of the early 1880s as the expression of legitimate popular resentment against exploitation, but the dominant intelligentsia view was that most Jews belonged among the insulted and the injured—and thus among the virtuous. S. Ia. Nadson, the most commercially successful Russian poet of the nineteenth century, "grew up apart from that disparaged nation," to which, he thought, his ancestors had belonged,

> But when your foes, like packs of vicious hounds,
> Are tearing you apart, consumed by greed and hate,
> I'll humbly join the ranks of your determined fighters,
> A nation scorned by fate!

Nadson died of consumption when he was twenty-five years old—for "beautiful are the thorns of suffering for humanity." His fame lasted into the early twentieth century, and so did his image of a Jew weighed down by "the burden of woes" and the "futile expectation of deliverance." The more visible the Jews became as bankers, brokers, doctors, lawyers, students, artists, journalists, and revolutionaries, the more focused Russian highbrow literature became on Jews as victims of abuse. For Chekhov, Uspensky, Garin-Mikhilovsky, Gorky, Andreev, Sologub, Korolenko, Kuprin, Staniukovich, Artsybashev, Briusov, Balmont, Bunin, and countless others (whatever their private ambivalence), the members of the "disparaged nation" had come out of Gogol's "Overcoat," not Gogol's *Taras Bulba* (which had attempted to transfer to high culture the rhetoric of Cossack resentment). There were some dignified old men with silver beards and some beautiful Rebeccas with fiery eyes, but the overwhelming majority were pathetic but irrepressible victims of insult and injury. Jews were not "the people," but they were good people.[62]

Overall, however, Jews were as marginal to the Russian literary imagination as "the Jewish question" was to the ambitions of most Jewish converts to Pushkin and/or the revolution. Most Jews joining reading circles, Russian schools, secret societies, and friendship networks sought admission—and were welcomed—not as Jews but as fellow believers in Pushkin and the revolution, fellow Mercurians longing for Apollonian harmony, fellow rebels against patriarchy, and fellow sufferers for humanity.

In the small towns of the Pale of Settlement, secular education often began at home or in all-Jewish reading circles, sometimes led by a student in the role of the yeshiva rabbi. "I remember as if it were today," wrote one circle participant, "with what remarkable feeling of fear and awe I and other students sat on a wooden bench near a large brick oven that was hardly warm. Opposite us, at a table, sat a young man of twenty-seven or twenty-eight." As another memoirist said of her circle leader, "his knowledge was unlimited. I believed that, were there only a few more like him, one could already begin the revolution." The main subjects were the Russian language, Russian classical literature, and a variety of socialist texts, mostly Russian but also translations from English and German. Better Russian led to more and more reading, and reading usually led to an epiphany similar to the one the future revolutionary M. I. Drei experienced upon reading D. I. Pisarev's "Progress in the World of Plants and Animals":

> All the old, traditional views that I had uncritically accepted as a child evaporated like smoke. The world lay before me, simple and clear, and I was standing in the midst of that world, serene and self-confident. There was nothing mysterious, frightening, incomprehensible left in the world for me, and I thought, like Goethe's Wagner, that I knew a great deal already and would in due course know everything . . . It seemed to me that there were no gaps in my worldview, that doubts and hesitations were no longer possible, and I had found, once and for all, firm ground to stand on . . .
>
> Now, looking back [in 1926 in Moscow], I realize that that was the best time of my life. Never again would I experience the kind of intense exhilaration that is produced by the first awakening of the mind and the first revelation of truth.[63]

With the help of an awakened mind, European dress, fluency in Russian, and another, often non-Jewish, mentor, large numbers of Jewish autodidacts and circle veterans moved into one of the "little islands of freedom" within the Russian radical youth culture (where they met, among others, the Russian-speaking children of previous migrants). "They talked to me as to an equal!" wrote Abraham Cahan. "As if I were one of their own! No distinction between Jew and gentile! In the spirit of true equality and brotherhood!" The circles' cause, whatever their particular brand of socialism, was to remake the world in their own image, to topple all fathers and usher in the kingdom of eternal youth.

> Life took on new meaning. Our society was built on injustices that could be erased. All could be equal. All could be brothers! Just as all were equal and brothers in Volodka's home. It could be done! It must be done! All must be ready to sacrifice even life itself for this new kind of world.
>
> I divided the world into two groups: "they" and "we." I looked on "them" with pity and scorn. I thought of any friend of mine who was one of "them" as an unfortunate being. At the same time my

new belief brought out my better nature, made me more tolerant, led me to speak gently even when mixing scorn with sympathy. A kind of religious ecstasy took hold of me. I did not recognize my former self.[64]

Mandelstam's mother, "the first in her family to master the clear and pure Russian sounds," was in Vilna at about the same time: a bit more literary and less revolutionary, perhaps, but could one really tell the difference?

> The never-ending literary toil, the candles, the applause, the lit-up faces; the circle of a generation and, at the center, the altar—the lecturer's desk with its glass of water. Like summer insects over an incandescent lamp, the whole generation shriveled and burned in the flame of literary celebrations festooned with allegorical roses, each gathering having the feel of a cult performance and an expiatory sacrifice for the generation. . . .
>
> The eighties in Vilna as my mother remembered them. It was the same everywhere: sixteen-year-old girls trying to read John Stuart Mill, while at public recitals luminous personalities with bland features were playing the latest pieces by the leonine Anton, leaning heavily on the pedal and dying out on the arpeggios. But what actually happened was that the intelligentsia, with its Buckle and Rubinstein, led by luminous personalities and moved by a holy fool's recklessness, turned resolutely toward self-immolation. The People's Will martyrs, with Sofia Perovskaia and Zheliabov, burned in full view, like tall tar-coated torches, and the whole of provincial Russia with its "student youth" smouldered in sympathy. Not a single green leaf was to be left untouched.[65]

In the 1870s and 1880s, some of the rhetoric of self-sacrifice and equality was overtly Christian. O. V. Aptekman, whose father was "one of the pioneers of Russian education among the Jews of Pavlodar," found both the Gospel and the "people," in the shape of Parasha Bukharitsyna, "the radiant image of a peasant girl," in the Pskov province in 1874. "I was a socialist, and Parasha a Christian, but emotionally we were alike; I was ready for all kinds of sacrifices, and she was all about self-sacrifice. . . . And so my first pupil, Parasha, accepted my interpretation of the Gospel and became a socialist too. I was in a state of exaltation, which was to some extent religious; it was a complex and rather confused mental state, in which a genuine socialist worldview coexisted with the Christian one."[66]

Solomon Vittenberg, according to his disciple M. A. Moreinis, was a promising Talmudist when, at the age of nine, he learned Russian and persuaded his parents to let him attend the Nikolaev *gymnasium*. In August 1879, on the night before his execution for an attempt on the life of Alexander II and one day after his refusal to convert to Christianity, he wrote to his friends (most of whom were young Jewish rebels):

> Dear friends! Naturally, I do not want to die. To say that I am dying willingly would be a lie on my part. But let this circumstance not cast a shadow on my faith or on the certainty of my convictions. Remember that the highest example of the love of humanity and self-sacrifice was, undoubtedly, the Savior. Yet even he prayed, "Take this cup away from me." Consequently, how can I not pray for the same thing? Like him, I tell myself: If no other way is possible, if for the triumph of socialism it is necessary that my blood be shed, if others can make the transition from the present order to a better one only by trampling over our dead bodies, then let our blood be shed, let it redeem humanity—for I do not doubt that our blood will fertilize the soil from which the seed of socialism will sprout and that socialism will triumph, and triumph soon. This is my faith. Here again I recall the words of the Savior: "Truly, I say unto you, not many of those present here relish death as the coming of the heavenly kingdom"—of this I am convinced as much as I am convinced that the earth moves. And when I climb the scaffold and the rope tightens around my neck, my last thought will be: "And still it moves and nothing in the world can stop its movement."[67]

Over the next four decades, direct references to religion among revolutionaries became less frequent, the image of the peasant girl became less radiant, and even the Nadson cult had trouble outliving Mandelstam's mother's youth, but the fire of self-sacrifice kept burning, and the combination of universal salvation, violence, and Galileo remained meaningful—until it hardened into Marxism.

The switch of allegiance in some (not all!) intelligentsia quarters from Populism to Marxism (beginning in the 1890s) involved a reallocation of redeemer status from the Russian peasant to the international proletariat. Urban collectivism and vertical cityscape replaced rural communalism and horizontal pastoral as the reflection of future perfection, and the angular male worker replaced the peasant girl (or the often feminized—"rotund"—peasant man) as the intellectual's corporal better half. Universal Mercurianism was going to be defeated not by traditional Apollonianism but by Mercurianism itself—or rather, by its quasi-Apollonian bastard child. The proletariat of the Marxist iconography was peculiar in that it was undeniably Apollonian and thus desirable (heart to the intelligentsia's head, body to its soul, spontaneity to its consciousness), while being just as undeniably Mercurian and thus modern (rootless, homeless, global). Eventually, Lenin would transform Marxism into a real social force by taking it halfway back to Populism: modern socialism was possible in backward Russia both in spite and because of its backwardness.

For the Jewish rebels, the fall from grace of the Russian peasant opened up new opportunities. Marxism (especially of the Menshevik variety) proved popular because it was consistent with the world of equality and brotherhood most young Jews wished to join, and possibly because it seemed to allow for the inclusion of the "Jewish masses" (none of whom qualified as peasants) among the saviors and the saved. Indeed, Bundism—the Yiddish-language Marxism aimed at the "Jewish Street"—built on the latter proposition to create an influential blend of Marxism and nationalism, whereby the Russian-educated Jewish intelligentsia would embrace the Jewish people and lead them to liberation either by teaching them Russian or by transforming Yiddish into a sacred language, with Sholem Aleichem as Pushkin. The Bund prospered briefly in the least urbanized and Russified parts of the Pale, where it tended to appeal to the secularized Jews who had not yet entered the all-Russian youth culture, but ultimately it could not compete with universalist (Russian or Polish) Marxism or Hebrew-based nationalism. Neither Marxism nor nationalism made much sense without a state.[68]

The Jewish nationalism that did offer a solution to the state problem was, of course, Zionism, which had the added advantage of proposing a vision of a consistently Apollonian Jewishness complete with warrior honor and rural rootedness. Spurred by the pogroms of 1903–06, Zionism succeeded in creating a radical youth culture comparable to the Russian one in its cohesion, asceticism, messianism, commitment to violence, and self-sacrificial fervor. Still, it attracted far fewer Jews, and the emigration to Palestine remained tiny compared to the exodus for America (characterized by low levels of income and secular education) and the big cities of the Russian Empire (shaped by government regulations and the high-culture hierarchy to favor the wealthier and the more educated). Zionism appealed to the young and the radical, but most of the young and the radical seemed to prefer "no distinction between Jew and gentile, in the spirit of true equality and brotherhood."

As time went on, this preference seemed to grow stronger. The spread of industrialization and secularization resulted in greater Russification, and greater Russification almost invariably led to world revolution, not nationalism. As Chaim Weizmann, himself a graduate of the Pinsk *Realschule*, wrote to Herzl in 1903,

> In western Europe it is generally believed that the large majority of Jewish youth in Russia is in the Zionist camp. Unfortunately, the opposite is true. The larger part of the contemporary younger generation is anti-Zionist, not from a desire to assimilate as in Western Europe, but through revolutionary conviction.
>
> It is impossible to calculate the number of victims, or describe their character, that are annually, indeed daily, sacrificed because of their identification with Jewish Social Democracy in Russia. Hundreds of thousands of very young boys and girls are held in Russian prisons, or are being spiritually and physically destroyed in Siberia. More than 5,000 are now under police surveillance, which means the deprivation of their freedom. Almost all those now being victimized in the entire Social Democratic movement are Jews, and their number grows every day. They are not necessarily young people of proletarian origin; they also come from well-to-do families, and incidentally not infrequently from Zionist families. Almost all students belong to the

revolutionary camp; hardly any of them escape its ultimate fate. We cannot enter here into the many factors, political, social, and economic, that continuously nourish the Jewish revolutionary movement; suffice to say that the movement has already captured masses of young people who can only be described as children.

Thus, during my stay in Minsk, they arrested 200 Jewish Social Democrats, not one of whom was more than 17 years old. It is a fearful spectacle, and one that obviously escapes West European Zionists, to observe the major part of our youth—and no-one would describe them as the worst part—offering themselves for sacrifice as though seized by a fever. We refrain from touching on the terrible effect this mass-sacrifice has upon the families and communities concerned, and upon the state of Jewish political affairs in general. Saddest and most lamentable is the fact that although this movement consumes much Jewish energy and heroism, and is located within the Jewish fold, the attitude it evidences towards Jewish nationalism is one of antipathy, swelling at times to fanatical hatred. Children are in open revolt against their parents.[69]

Not all those victimized "in the entire Social Democratic movement" were Jews, of course, but it is true that Jewish participation in the Russian "mass-sacrifice" was very substantial in absolute terms and much larger than the Jewish share of the country's population. The Jews did not start the revolutionary movement, did not inaugurate student messianism, and had very little to do with the conceptual formulation of "Russian Socialism" (from Herzen to Mikhailovsky), but when they did join the ranks, they did so with tremendous intensity and in ever growing numbers. No history of Russian radicalism is conceivable without the story of the Jewish children's "open revolt against their parents."

In the 1870s, the overall Jewish share in the Populist movement probably did not exceed 8 percent, but their participation in the student "pilgrimage to the people" circles (the "Chaikovtsy") was much greater. According to Erich Haberer,

Jews comprised a staggering 20 per cent of all Chaikovtsy (that is, 22 out of 106 persons) who were definitely members or close associates of the organization in St. Petersburg, Moscow, Odessa, and Kiev. A breakdown by circles shows that they were well represented in each of these cities with 11 per cent in St. Petersburg, 17 per cent in Moscow, 20 per cent in Odessa, and almost 70 per cent in Kiev. Even more striking is the fact that in the persons of Natanson, Kliachko, Chudnovsky, and Akselrod they were the founders and for some time the leading personalities of these circles. This means that 18 per cent of Jewish Chaikovtsy (four out of twenty-two) belonged to the category of leaders.[70]

In the 1880s, Jews made up about 17 percent of all male and 27.3 percent of all female activists of the People's Will party, and about 15.5 percent and 33.3 percent of all male and female defendants at political trials. In the peak years of 1886–89, the Jews accounted for between 25 and 30 percent of all activists, and between 35 and 40 percent of those in southern Russia. The influential Orzhikh-Bogoraz-Shternberg group, centered in Ekaterinoslav and known for its uncompromising commitment to political terror, was more than 50 percent Jewish, and in the remarkable year of 1898, 24 out of 39 (68.6 percent) political defendants were Jews. Over the two decades 1870–90 Jews made up about 15 percent of all political exiles in Irkutsk province and 32 percent of those in Iakutsk province (probably up to half in the late 1880s). According to the commander of the Siberian military district, General Sukhotin, of the 4,526 political deportees in January 1905, 1,898 (41.9 percent) were Russians and 1,676 (37 percent) were Jews.[71]

With the rise of Marxism, the role of Jews in the Russian revolutionary movement became still more prominent. The first Russian Social Democratic organization, the Group for the Emancipation of Labor, was founded in 1883 by five people, two of whom (P. B. Axelrod and L. G. Deich) were Jews. The first Social Democratic party in the Russian Empire was the Jewish Bund (founded in 1897). The First Congress of the Russian Social Democratic Labor Party (RSDLP) was convened in 1898 in Minsk, at the initiative and under the protection of the Bund activists. At the party's Second Congress in 1903 (which included the Bund delegates), Jews made up at least 37 percent of the delegates, and at the last (Fifth) congress of the united RSDLP in 1907, about one-third of the delegates were Jews, including 11.4 percent of the Bolsheviks and 22.7 percent of the Mensheviks (and five out of the eight top Menshevik leaders). According to the Provisional Government's commissar for the liquidation of tsarist political police abroad, S. G. Svatikov, at least 99 (62.3 percent) of the 159 political émigrés who returned to Russia through Germany in 1917 in "sealed trains" were Jews. The first group of 29 that arrived with Lenin included 17 Jews (58.6 percent). At the Sixth (Bolshevik) party Congress of July–August 1917, which had a larger representation of grassroots domestic organizations, the Jewish share was about 16 percent overall, and 23.7 percent in the Central Committee.[72]

Only in German-dominated Latvia, where nationalist resentment, workers' strikes, and a peasant war coalesced into a single movement under the aegis of the Bolsheviks, did the proportion of revolutionaries in the total population sometimes exceed the Jewish mark. (Antistate activism among Poles, Armenians, and Georgians was not as high but still substantially higher than among Russians because of the way national and social movements reinforced each other.) The Jewish reinforcement was of a different kind: similar to the Russian intelligentsia variety but much more widespread and uncompromising, it consisted in the simultaneous rejection of parental authority and autocratic paternalism. Most Jewish rebels did not fight the state in order to become free Jews; they fought the state in order to become free from Jewishness—and thus Free. Their radicalism was not strengthened by their nationality; it was strengthened by their struggle against their nationality. Latvian or Polish socialists might embrace universalism, proletarian internationalism, and the vision of a future cosmopolitan harmony without ceasing to be Latvian or Polish. For many Jewish socialists, being an internationalist meant not being Jewish at all.[73]

The Russian Social Democrats, too, were fighting a lonely fight. Having rejected the Russian state as the prison-house of nations, declared war on Russian industrialization as both too brutal and too slow, given up on the Russian "people" as too backward or not backward enough, and placed their bets on a world revolution manufactured in Germany, they were perfectly "self-hating" in the Chaadaev tradition of the Russian intelligentsia. And yet, in most cases, their rebellion against their fathers did not quite amount to patricide. The children might reject their parents' religion, habits, attachments, and possessions, but no one seriously proposed switching to the German language or tearing down Pushkin House, the true temple of national faith. Even Lenin believed that Tolstoy was "the mirror of the Russian Revolution" and that Russia's inadequacy might yet prove the world's salvation.

Large numbers of Jewish socialists (following the decline of the Bund after 1907, probably the majority) were more resolute and more consistent. Their parents—like Marx's—represented the worst of all possible worlds because they stood for backwardness and capitalism at the same time. Socialism, for them, meant (as Marx put it) the "emancipation from *haggling* and from *money*, i.e. from practical, real Judaism." Most radical Jewish memoirists remembered struggling with the twin evils of tradition and "acquisitiveness": as far as they were concerned, the Jewish tradition was about acquisitiveness, and acquisitiveness stripped of the Jewish tradition was distilled capitalism, i.e., "practical, real Judaism." The Jews, as a group, were the only true Marxists because they were the only ones who truly believed that their nationality was "chimerical"; the only ones who—like Marx's proletarians but unlike the real ones—had no motherland.

There is nothing specific to Russia about any of this, of course— except that the scale was much greater; the transition from the ghetto to the "life of all the people in the world" more abrupt; and the majority of neutral spaces small, barred, or illegal. The Jews were becoming modern faster and better than were Russian society, the Russian state, or indeed anybody else in Russia. This means that even under a liberal dispensation, the scarcity of neutral spaces would have affected them more than any other group. But the Russian regime was not liberal, and the fact that the Jews were legally excluded from some of those spaces meant that an even larger proportion ended up joining the "little islands of freedom." Anti-Jewish legislation did not start the "Revolution on the Jewish Street" (which often preceded any exposure to the outside world and was directed against Jewishness, not against anti-Jewish legislation), but it contributed a great deal to its expansion and radicalization.

What is remarkable about Jewish disabilities is not that they were worse than those of the Kirgiz, the Aleut, or indeed the Russian peasants, but that they were resented so much by so many. Unlike the Kirgiz, the Aleut, and the peasants, the Jews were moving successfully into elite institutions—only to encounter restrictions based on criteria they considered unfair (punishing success) or obsolete, and thus unfair (religion). The Jewish students, entrepreneurs, and professionals saw themselves as their colleagues' equals or betters, yet they were being treated like the Kirgiz, the Aleut, or the peasants. Those who made it anyway protested against discrimination; many of the others preferred world revolution.

But the Jews were not just the most revolutionary (along with the Latvians) national group in the Russian Empire. They were also the best at being revolutionaries. As Leonard Schapiro put it, "It was the Jews, with their long experience of exploiting conditions on Russia's western frontier which adjoined the pale for smuggling and the like, who organized the illegal transport of literature, planned escapes and illegal crossings, and generally kept the wheels of the whole organization running."[74]

As early as the mid-1870s, according to the People's Will operative Vladimir Yokhelson,

> Vilna became the main conduit for Petersburg's and Moscow's contacts with other countries. To transport books shipped through Vilna, Zundelevich would go to Koenigsberg, where he would meet with the medical student Finkelstein, who was the representative of the revolutionary presses from Switzerland and London. Finkelstein used to study at our rabbinical seminary but had emigrated to Germany in 1872, when an illegal library was found in the seminary's boarding school. . . . Our border connections were used to transport not only books, but also people.[75]

The Jewish revolutionary and educational networks—of people, books, money, and information—were similar to the traditional commercial ones. Sometimes they overlapped—as when students who were also revolutionaries crossed borders and stayed at the houses of their businessmen uncles; when the American soap (Naphtha) millionaire, Joseph Fels, underwrote the Fifth Congress of the RSDLP; or when Alexander Helphand (Parvus), himself both a revolutionary and a millionaire, arranged Lenin's return to Russia in 1917. There was no master plan behind any of this, needless to say, but the fact that the overwhelming majority of ethnically Jewish revolutionaries in the Russian Empire were raised in self-consciously Jewish homes meant that they had acquired some traditional Mercurian skills.

Nor were mobility and secrecy the only traditional Mercurian skills that served the cause of the revolution. Most members of radical circles devoted themselves to the study of sacred texts, revered proficient interpreters of the scriptures, adapted everyday behavior to doctrinal precepts, debated fine points of theory, and divided the world between righteous insiders and lost or malevolent outsiders. Some were better at this than others: the children of intelligentsia parents had been raised on similar commitments, and so had the Jews (Christian dissenters, whom some revolutionary ideologists considered promising recruits, showed no interest in conversion). Even the poorest Jewish artisans joining little islands of freedom had an advantage over nonelite Apollonians because they were converting from one highly literate culture to another, from one debating society to another, from one chosen people to another, from traditional Mercurianism to the modern kind. In all the revolutionary parties, Jews were particularly well represented at the top, among theoreticians, journalists, and leaders. In Russia, as elsewhere in Europe, the Jews were at least as successful at questioning the Modern Age as they were at promoting it.

The remarkable rise of the Jews made a strong impression on Russian society. Highbrow fiction may not have noticed, but many newspapers did, as did various public intellectuals, professional associations, state agencies, political parties (after 1905), and, of course, all those who took part in the anti-Jewish urban riots (pogroms). Everyone agreed that Jews had a special affinity for the Modern Age, and most believed that it was a bad thing.

The reasons for the affinity were familiar. As I. O. Levin wrote ruefully in 1923, "One of the paradoxes of the Jewish fate is undoubtedly the fact that the same rationalism that was one of the causes of their outstanding role in the development of capitalism was also the cause of their no less outstanding participation in the movements directed against capitalism and the capitalist order."[76]

It was a bad thing because (a) the Modern Age, including both capitalism and revolution, was a bad thing, and (b) Jewish preeminence was a bad thing. As K. Pobedonostsev, the tutor and adviser of the last two tsars, wrote to Dostoevsky in 1879, "they have undermined everything, but the spirit of the century supports them." And as Dostoevsky, in his "Diary of a Writer," wrote to the whole reading public in 1877, the spirit of the century equaled "materialism, the blind, insatiable desire for *personal* material prosperity, the thirst for personal accumulation of money at all costs." Humans had always been that way, "but never before have these desires been proclaimed to be the highest possible principle with as much frankness and insistence as in our nineteenth century." Jews may or may not have caused this revolution (Dostoevsky's fiction seemed to suggest that they had not), but they were, he insisted, its truest and most dedicated apostles. "In the very work the Jews do (the great majority of them, at any rate), in their very exploitation, there is something wrong and abnormal, something unnatural, something containing its own punishment."[77]

Most Jewish rebels agreed with Dostoevsky regarding both the Modern Age (capitalism) and the Jewish role (acquisitiveness). Their remedy—world revolution—was a part of the disease as Dostoevsky had diagnosed it, but their aspiration—radical fraternity—was of course very similar to Dostoevsky's own vision of true Christian brotherhood. If the Jews were "possessed," so was Dostoevsky—and so were most of the Zionists, who agreed with Dostoevsky that the Modern Age was destroying the original brotherhood, that the diaspora Jewish society was abnormal and unnatural, and that world revolution was a dangerous chimera. Jabotinsky, like Weizmann, was greatly distressed by the overrepresentation of Jews among Russian socialists. The fact that most revolutionary agitators whom he saw during the "Potemkin days" of 1905 in the port of Odessa were "familiar types with their big round eyes, big ears, and imperfect 'r's" was a bad thing because only true national prophets were capable of leading the masses and because a revolution in somebody else's nation was not worth "the blood of our old men, women, and children."[78]

Most non-Jewish rebels agreed with Dostoevsky regarding capitalism but not (at least not publicly) regarding the Jews, whom they tended to represent exclusively as victims. In the world of the Russian revolutionary intelligentsia, nations were incomplete moral agents: they had virtues and vices, rights and duties, accomplishments and transgressions, but they did not have coherent or comprehensive means of atonement, remorse, penance, or retribution. Membership in a social class, which involved an element of free will, was more of a moral act than membership in a nation. One could, therefore, call for violent retribution against the bourgeoisie or endorse the assassination of anonymous state officials, but one could not, in good conscience, advocate collective responsibility for nations (formal war being a possible exception). Social guilt was a common and virtuous sentiment; national guilt a murky and distasteful one. Antibourgeois bigotry was an oxymoron; national bigotry was, in theory, a taboo (because it was a bourgeois vice). Or rather, it was a vice most of the time, and a virtual taboo with regard to the Jews. Anti-Germanism was taken for granted insofar as it expressed wartime patriotism and a general dislike of the *homo rationalisticus artificialis*; anti-Tatarism (from bloodthirsty history books to ironic portrayals of janitors) was noticed only by Tatars; and the routine attribution of permanent negative traits to various ethnic groups (especially the "Eastern" ones) was a perfectly acceptable means of cultural and moral self-identification. Only the Jews were (most of the time) off-limits—partly because so many of the revolutionary intellectuals' comrades (some of their best friends) were Jews or former Jews, partly because Jews were victims of state persecution, but mostly (since there were other ethnic victims of state persecution who were not off-limits) because they were both fellow elite members and victims of state persecution. They were, uniquely, both remote and near. They were (still) internal strangers.

One reason why Jews were victims of state persecution was that so many of them were becoming elite members. Many of the state officials and leaders of professional associations who presided over Russia's modernization and generally associated the Modern Age with prosperity, enlightenment, liberty, and meritocratic fairness, were disturbed by the extraordinary rate of Jewish accomplishment and Jewish radicalism. Speaking in Kherson in 1875, the minister of enlightenment D. A. Tolstoy declared that the only meaningful educational criterion was academic performance. "Our *gymnasia* should produce aristocrats, but what sort? Aristocrats of the mind, aristocrats of knowledge, aristocrats of labor. God grant that we might have more such aristocrats." In 1882, the same official, as minister of internal affairs, wrote to the tsar commenting on both the Jewish love of learning and the Jewish role in revolutionary activities. By 1888, Tolstoy had become a champion of anti-Jewish admissions quotas. Similarly, the chair of the Governing Council of the St. Petersburg bar and Russia's most prominent lawyer, V. D. Spasovich, who believed in liberal meritocracy as a matter of principle, proposed corporate self-policing when it was revealed, in 1889, that out of 264 apprentice lawyers in the St. Petersburg judicial circuit, 109 were Russian Orthodox and 104 were Jews. "We are dealing with a colossal problem,' he said, "one which cannot be solved according to the rules of cliché liberalism."[79]

Spasovich's problem was possible government intervention. The government's problem was, as the finance minister Kokovtsev put it in 1906, that "the Jews are so clever that no law can be counted on to restrict them." And the main reason they needed to be restricted (according to most high government officials) was that they were so clever. To the extent that tsarist Russia was still a traditional empire, in which each faith and estate performed its own function, the Jews did not fit in because their function was now universal. And to the extent that Russia was a modernizing society with important oases of "cliché liberalism," the Jews did not fit in because they were so successful. In order to "open careers to talent," liberalism has to assume the interchangeability of citizens.

In order to ensure or simulate such interchangeability, it has to employ nationalism. In order to succeed as a creed, it has to remain innocent of the paradox involved. Throughout Europe, Jews revealed the unacknowledged connection between liberal universalism and ethnic nationalism by demonstrating talent without becoming interchangeable. In late imperial Russia, which was inching fitfully from ascriptive traditionalism to cliché liberalism, they became the perfect symbol of why the former was untenable and the latter dangerous.[80]

It was as such a symbol of perilous cleverness that Jews were killed, maimed, and robbed during the urban riots in the Pale in the final half-century of the empire's existence. The Odessa pogrom of 1871 was started by local Greeks, who were losing the competition over trade monopolies, but most of the perpetrators—then and later, as violence increased—were day laborers and other recent migrants from rural areas, who seemed to be losing the competition over modern life. To them, the Jews were the alien face of the city, the wielders of the invisible hand, the old Mercurian stranger turned boss. They were still dangerous traders, one way or another, but their ways were even more mysterious, and many of their children were revolutionaries—the very people, that is, who openly assaulted the sacred but outdated symbols of Apollonian dignity and ascendance: God and Tsar.[81]

When, in 1915, Maxim Gorky published a questionnaire on the "Jewish problem," the most common response was summarized by a reader from Kaluga: "The congenital, cruel, and consistent egoism of the Jews is everywhere victorious over the good-natured, uncultured, trusting Russian peasant or merchant." According to the vox populi from Kherson, the Russian peasant needed to be defended from the Jews because he was still "at an embryonic, infantile stage of development," and according to "U., a peasant," "Jews should undoubtedly receive equal rights but gradually and with great caution, not right away, or before long half of the Russian land, if not all of it, along with the ignorant Russian people, will pass into Jewish slavery." The reserve soldiers D. and S. proposed one solution: "Jews should be given a separate colony, or they'll reduce Russia to nothing." A "Mr. N." proposed another: "My Russian opinion is that all Jews should be wiped off the face of the Russian Empire and that's the end of it."[82]

As everywhere in modern Europe, Jews were vulnerable as triumphant Mercurians without a special ghetto license. In Russia, more than anywhere else, the uprooted Apollonians lacked the rhetorical and legal protection of liberal nationalism—the reassurance that the new state belonged to them even as it seemed so alien; that modernization and homelessness were their gain, not loss; that universal Mercurianism was in fact revitalized Apollonianism. The protection the peasant migrants to the cities did receive (in the form of anti-Jewish restrictions) tended to be mostly counterproductive. The cities of the Pale were dominated by Jews, and more and more of their children, kept there by force and excluded ineffectively from neutral spaces, were joining the rebellion against God and Tsar.

The ones who paid the price were people like Babel's narrator's father, a small shopkeeper who was robbed and humiliated the day his little boy felt such bitter, ardent, and hopeless love for Galina Apollonovna.

> Through the window I could see the deserted street with the vast sky above it and my father with his red hair walking down the road. He did not have a hat, and his thin, flyaway red hair was sticking up; his paper shirtfront was all askew and fastened by the wrong button. Vlasov, an eternally drunken workman in wadded soldier's rags, followed closely on my father's heels.
>
> "Don't you see," he was saying in a hoarse, earnest voice, while touching my father gently with his hands, "We don't need freedom if it gives the Jews freedom to haggle . . . Just give the working man a little bit of life's brightness for his toil, for all this terrible hugeness . . . Just give him some, friend, just give him some, okay . ."
>
> The workman kept touching my father and imploring him about something, while on his face, flashes of pure drunken inspiration alternated with dejection and sleepiness.
>
> "We should all live like the Molokans," he muttered, as he swayed on his unsteady legs, "we've got to live like the Molokans, but without that Old-Believer God of theirs. It's only the Jews who profit from him, the Jews and nobody else . . ."

And Vlasov started shouting in wild desperation about the Old-Believer God who had taken pity only on the Jews. Wailing and stumbling, Vlasov was still chasing after that mysterious God of his, when a Cossack mounted patrol appeared in front of him.

The Cossacks ignored both of them—the drunken pursuer who felt like a victim and begged his prey for mercy, and the tormented victim whose son was triumphing over the Russian boys with fat cheeks even as they were beating Jewish old men. The Cossacks "sat impassively in their high saddles, riding through an imaginary mountain pass and disappearing from view as they turned into Cathedral Street." The little boy was in Galina Apollonovna's kitchen. Earlier that day, he had been hit in the temple by a legless cripple with "a coarse face composed of red meat, fists, and iron." He had been hit with the very dove he had bought to celebrate his admission to the *gymnasium*. Owning doves had been the dream of his life. His dovecote had been built for him by his grandfather, Shoil, who had been murdered earlier that day.

> A goose was frying on the tiled stove; the walls were lined up with pots and pans; and next to the pans, in the cook's corner, was Tsar Nicholas, decorated with paper flowers. Galina washed off the remains of the dove that had dried on my cheeks.
>
> "You'll grow up to be a bridegroom, my pretty little one," she said, kissing me on the mouth with her full lips and turning away.[83]

Babel's narrator would, indeed, grow up to consummate his love for a Russian woman. But Galina Apollonovna was not the only Russian who loved him. There was Efim Nikitich Smolich, in whose athletic breast "there dwelt compassion for Jewish boys," and Piatnitsky, the old *gymnasium* inspector who loved Jewish boys for their love of Pushkin. When, after the exam, Babel's little boy "began to wake up from the convulsion of his dreams," he found himself surrounded by some "Russian boys."

> They seemed to want to push me around or perhaps just to play, but then Piatnitsky suddenly appeared in the corridor. As he passed me he halted for a moment, his frock-coat flowing down his back like a

slow, heavy wave. I glimpsed confusion in that vast, fleshy, lordly back of his, and approached the old man.

"Children," he said to the schoolboys, "I want you to leave this boy alone," and he put his plump, tender hand on my shoulder.[84]

And then there were those—a small minority—who did not pity the Jews for their weakness and their love of old Russia but admired them for their strength and their iconoclasm—those who welcomed the rise of the Modern Age and praised the Jews for bringing it about. They were the Marxists—the only members of the Russian intelligentsia who despised the Russian peasant and the Russian intelligentsia as much as they despised "rotten" liberalism. For them, the Modern Age stood for the transformation—by means of a more or less spontaneous universal patricide—of a city that was symmetrical, bountiful, and wicked into a city that was symmetrical, bountiful, and radiant. There were going to be no tribes under communism, of course, but there was no getting away from the fact that, in the Russian tradition, the symmetrical city, good or bad, was a German creature, and that the Jews, in the words of one of Gorky's correspondents, were "a German auxiliary mechanism."[85] What truly made a Bolshevik was not adherence to a particular dogma but an eager and unequivocal preference for Stolz over Oblomov—except that by the early twentieth century the iconic Stolz might very well be Jewish, not German (or he might be both, one being an auxiliary mechanism of the other). Germans still loomed larger than anybody else, but the Jews had their own special claim on urban virtue. As A. Lunacharsky summed up the story,

> Jews lived everywhere as strangers, but they introduced their urban commercial skills into the different countries of their diaspora and thus became the ferment of capitalist development in countries with lower, circumscribed, peasant culture. This is the reason why the Jews, according to the best students of human development, contributed to an extraordinary degree to progress, but this is also the reason why they drew upon themselves the terrible fury of, first, the lowly peasants, whom the Jews had exploited as traders, usurers, etc., and, second, of the bourgeoisie, which had emerged from the same peasantry.[86]

Lenin was not particularly interested in Jewish history. For him, what capitalism did was "replace the thick-skulled, boorish, inert, and bearishly savage Russian or Ukrainian peasant with a mobile proletarian." Proletarians had no motherland, of course, and there was no such thing as a "national culture," but if one had to think of mobile proletarians in ethnic terms (as the Bund "philistines" were forcing one to), then the Jews—unlike the Russians and Ukrainians—were very good candidates because of the "great, universally progressive traits in Jewish culture: its internationalism and its responsiveness to the advanced movements of the age (the percentage of Jews in democratic and proletarian movements is everywhere higher than the percentage of Jews in the total population)." All advanced Jews supported assimilation, according to Lenin, but it is also true that many of the "great leaders of democracy and socialism" came from "the best representatives of the Jewish world." Lenin himself did, through his maternal grandfather, although he probably did not know it. When his sister, Anna, found out, she wrote to Stalin that she was not surprised, that "this fact" was "another proof of the exceptional ability of the Semitic tribe," and that Lenin had always contrasted "what he called its 'tenacity' in struggle with the more sluggish and lackadaisical Russian character." Maxim Gorky, too, claimed that Lenin had a soft spot for "smart people" and that he had once said, "A smart Russian is almost always a Jew or somebody with an admixture of Jewish blood."[87]

We do not know whether Lenin actually said this, but we know that Gorky did, on numerous occasions. In the 1910s, Gorky was Russia's most celebrated writer, most revered prophetic voice, and most articulate and passionate Judeophile. He was not a member of the Bolshevik party, but he was close to the Bolsheviks where it counted: in his love of the mobile proletarian and his loathing for the Russian and Ukrainian peasant—"savage, somnolent, and glued to his pile of manure" (as Lenin put it elsewhere). Gorky was even more of a Nietzschean than most Bolsheviks: all tradition and religion stood for slavery and mediocrity, and the only proletarian worthy of the name was the etymologically correct proletarian, who embodied absolute freedom because he produced nothing but children (*proles*). The only force capable of releasing the Promethean proletarian from the fetters of "leaden" philistinism was revolution, and the greatest revolutionaries in history had been the Jews.[88]

"The old, thick yeast of humanity, the Jews have always forced the spirit to rise by stirring up restless, noble ideas and inspiring people to seek a better life." Endowed with a "heroic" idealism, "all-probing and all-scrutinizing," the Jews have saved the world from submissiveness and self-satisfaction.

> This idealism, which expresses itself in their tireless striving to remake the world according to the new principles of equality and justice, is the main, and possibly the only, reason for the hostility toward Jews. They disturb the peace of the satiated and self-satisfied and shed a ray of light on the dark sides of life. With their energy and enthusiasm, they have given people the gift of fire and the tireless pursuit of truth. They have been rousing nations, not letting them rest, and finally— and this is the main thing!—this idealism has given birth to the scourge of the powerful; the religion of the masses, socialism.

Nowhere, according to Gorky, were the Jews needed as desperately and, for that very reason, treated as badly as in Russia, where somnolence (Oblomovism) was a treasured national trait, and the transition "from the swamp of oriental stagnation to the broad avenues of Western European culture" a particularly painful challenge. The Jewish prohibition "of all idle pleasure not based on work" is "precisely what we, Russians, lack." For "deep in the soul of every Russian, lord or peasant, there lives a small and nasty devil of passive anarchism, which instills in us a careless and indifferent attitude toward work, society, the people, and ourselves." The more evident is the fact that "the Jews are better Europeans than the Russians," and that, "as a psychological type, they are culturally superior to, and more beautiful than, the Russians," the greater the resentment of the somnolent and the self-satisfied.

> If some Jews manage to find more profitable and beneficial places in life, it is because they know how to work, how to bring excitement to the labor process, how to "get things done" and admire action. The Jew is almost always a better worker than the Russian. It is not something to get mad about; it is something to learn from. In the

matter of both personal gain and service to society, the Jew invests more passion than the long-winded Russian and, in the final analysis, whatever nonsense anti-Semites may talk, they do not like the Jew because he is obviously better, more dexterous, and more capable than they are.[89]

The concept "self-hate" assumes that the unrelenting worship of one's ethnic kin is a natural human condition. To adopt the term for a moment, all national intelligentsias are self-hating insofar as they are—by definition—dissatisfied with their nation's performance relative to other nations or according to any number of doctrinal standards. Gorky's version—the bitter, ardent, and hopeless love of self-described Apollonians for beautiful Mercurians—was becoming increasingly common as more and more "passive anarchists" discovered the powerful but elusive charms of the Modern Age. Inseparable from nationalism (self-love), it was as painful and fragile an infatuation as the one that Mercurians had for Apollonians. The principal attributes of each side (heart/mind, body/soul, stability/mobility, and so on) never changed, but the intensity of mutual fascination increased dramatically—especially in Russia, where the local Apollonians were almost as unprotected by modern state nationalism as the traditional Mercurians were. To put it differently, the Jewish predicament in the age of universal Mercurianism was that they found themselves not only the best among equals but also the only ones without the cover of state nationalism (make-believe Apollonianism). The Russian predicament was that they found themselves not only the worst of all large European aspirants but also the only ones under an unreformed ancien régime (which comforted them not by calling them brothers but by insisting that they were eternal children). The result was love as well as hate: Gorky the self-hating Apollonian loved the Jews as much as Babel the self-hating Jew loved Galina Apollonovna.

The Great War spelled catastrophe for most of Russia's Mercurians. The war among nation-states proved disastrous not only for states without nations (the Russian, Austro-Hungarian, and Ottoman empires), but also for nations without states, especially those that lived as Mercurian strangers among other nations. Fathers and sons (patriarchal empires) did worse than brothers (liberal nation-states), and those who had no family connection to their state did worst of all.

On the Caucasus front, the Ottoman massacres of Armenians and Assyrians led to the influx into Russia of large numbers of refugees, some of whom were later deported internally. But most refugees on Russian territory were entirely of Russia's own making. Over the course of the war, more than a million residents of the Russian Empire defined as alien on the basis of citizenship, nationality, or religion were forcibly expelled from their homes and subjected to deportation, internment, hostage taking, police surveillance, and confiscations of property, among other things. The overwhelming majority of them were Russian Germans and Jews, who were seen as potentially disloyal because of their ethnic connection to enemy subjects, but also—as in the case of the Ottoman Armenians—because they were visible and successful Mercurians. The most widely advertised part of the campaign against them was conducted under the banner of the struggle against "German dominance" in the economy and included the liquidation of firms with "enemy-subject" connections. Anti-Jewish and anti-German pogroms were a regular part of wartime mobilization. The largest of them—in terms of popular participation and financial damage—was the anti-German riot in Moscow on May 26–29, 1915, which resulted in the destruction of about eight hundred company offices and apartments. The common perception that the imperial court (along with its state, style, and capital) was in some sense German played an important part in its final downfall two years later.[90]

Total wars are won by modern nations, and modern nations consist of fraternal native sons. The tsarist state attempted to create a cohesive family by removing "nonnatives" without making meaningful concessions on the fraternity (equality of citizens) front. One result of this policy was the demise of the tsarist state. Another was the end of the special role of Germans as Russia's principal Mercurians. The third was the collapse of the Pale of Settlement and the emergence of the Jews as the Mercurians of a new multinational empire.

The Russian Revolution was a combination of popular uprisings, religious crusades, ethnic wars, colonial conquests, and clashing coalitions. One part of the mix was the Jewish Revolution against Jewishness. Wartime massacres and deportations accompanied by the militarization of apocalyptic millenarianism—anarchist, nationalist, and Marxist—transformed the decades-old rebellion of Jewish children into a massive revolution. During Russia's Time of Troubles of 1914–21, most Jews hid, fled, or moved; tens of thousands were killed. But among those who took up arms, the majority did not stay to defend their parents' lives and property. They had universal brotherhood to fight for.[91]

When Babel's narrator arrived with the Red Cavalry in Galicia, he found "eyeless, gap-toothed" synagogues "squatting on the barren earth"; "narrow-shouldered Jews loitering mournfully at the crossroads"; "hunched-shouldered Jews in waistcoats standing in their doorways like bedraggled birds"; and the all-pervasive smell of sour feces and rotten herring. "The shtetl stinks in the expectation of a new era, and walking through it, instead of human beings, are faded outlines of frontier misfortunes."

It was there, in the "stifling captivity" of Hasidism, among "the possessed, the liars, and the idlers" at the court of "the last rebbe of the Chernobyl dynasty," that he discovered the true prophet of the last exodus.

> Behind Gedali's back, I saw a youth with the face of Spinoza, the powerful brow of Spinoza, and the faded face of a nun. He was smoking and shivering like a runaway prisoner who has just been returned to his cell. Suddenly, ragged Reb Mordche ["a hunchbacked old man no taller than a boy of ten"] crept up to him from behind, tore the cigarette from his mouth and darted back toward me.
>
> "That's Elijah, the Rebbe's son," Mordche wheezed, as he brought close to me the bleeding flesh of his exposed eyelids, "the accursed son, the last son, the disobedient son . . ."
>
> And Mordche shook his small fist at the young man and spat in his face.[92]

This is act 1 of the Jewish Revolution as portrayed by the prophet's "brother," himself a prophet whose "stories were meant to outlive oblivion."[93] Another brother—the official "Young

Communist Poet" Eduard Bagritsky (Dziubin)—remembered his own childhood:

> They tried to dry it out with their matzos,
> They tried to trick it with their candlelight.
> They shoved its face into their dusty tablets,
> Those gates that would remain forever shut.
> The Jewish peacocks on the chairs and sofas,
> The Jewish milk forever going sour,
> My father's crutch, my mother's lacy cap—
> All hissed at me:
>> You wretch! You wretch!
>
> . . . .
>
> Their love?
> But what about their lice-eaten braids,
> Their crooked, jutting-out collar bones,
> Their pimples, their herring-smeared mouths,
> The curve of their horselike necks.
> My parents?
> But growing old in twilight,
> Hunchbacked and gnarled, like savage beasts
> The rusty Jews keep shaking in my face
> Their stubble-covered fists.
>
> . . . .
>
> "You outcast! Pick up your miserable suitcase,
> You're cursed and scorned!
> Get out!"
> I'm leaving my old bed behind:
> "Get out?"
> I will!
> Good riddance!
> I don't care![94]

He did get out—as did Elijah and, of course, Babel and his hero. What they found outside, after 1917, was much bigger than the wonderful and shameful life of all the people in the world; much bigger than Pushkin, Galina Apollonovna, and the little islands of freedom. What they found was the first of the twentieth century's

Wars of Religion, the last war to end all wars, the Armageddon on the eve of eternity.

For those who wished to fight, there was but one army to join. The Red Army was the only force that stood earnestly and consistently against the Jewish pogroms and the only one led by a Jew. Trotsky was not just a general or even a prophet: he was the living embodiment of redemptive violence, the sword of revolutionary justice, and—at the same time—Lev Davydovich Bronstein, whose first school had been Schufer's heder in Gromoklei, Kherson province. The other Bolshevik leaders standing closest to Lenin during the civil war were G. E. Zinoviev (Ovsei-Gersh Aronovich Radomyslsky), L. B. Kamenev (Rosenfeld), and Ya. M. Sverdlov.[95]

These were effects, not causes; icons of a much larger truth. The vast majority of Bolshevik party members (72 percent in 1922) were ethnic Russians; the highest rate of overrepresentation belonged to the Latvians (although after Latvia's independence in 1918, Soviet Latvians became a largely self-selected political émigré community); and none of the prominent Communists of Jewish background wanted to be Jewish. Which is precisely what made them perfect heroes for rebels like Eduard Bagritsky, who did not want to be Jewish, either. Trotsky declared his nationality to be "Social Democratic," and that was the nationality the Bolsheviks represented and Bagritsky fought for: "So that the unyielding earth / Would be drenched in blood, / And a brand-new virgin youth / Sprout up from the bones." Of those fighting on the bones of imperial Russia, the Bolsheviks were the only true priests at the temple of eternal youth, the only crusaders for universal brotherhood, the only party where Eduard Bagritsky and Elijah Bratslavsky could feel at home.[96]

When Babel's narrator next saw him, Elijah the Red Army soldier was dying from his wounds.

> "Four months ago, on a Friday evening, Gedali the junk salesman brought me to your father, Rebbe Motale, but you were not in the Party then, Bratslavsky."
>
> "I was in the Party then," the boy replied, clawing at his chest and writhing in fever, "but I could not abandon my mother . . ."

"And now, Elijah?"

"In a revolution, a mother is but an episode," he whispered softly. "My letter came up, the letter B, and our Party cell sent me to the front. . . ."

"And you landed in Kovel, Elijah?"

"I ended up in Kovel!" he screamed out in desperation. "The damned kulaks broke through our defenses. I took command of a scratch regiment, but it was too late. I didn't have enough artillery. . . ."

Elijah breathed his last. In his little trunk, "all kinds of things were piled up together—the Party propagandist's guidelines and the Jewish poet's notebooks. The portraits of Lenin and Maimonides lay side by side. . . . A lock of woman's hair was inserted in the book of the resolutions of the Sixth Party Congress, and the margins of Communist leaflets were crowded with the crooked lines of Hebrew verses."[97]

That there was a connection between Lenin and Maimonides (and the two Elijahs, of course) is Babel's conjecture; that there were many rebbes' sons in the Red Army is a fact. They fought against ancient backwardness and modern capitalism, against their own "chimerical nationality" and the very foundations of the old world (to paraphrase the "Internationale"). They had no Motherland; they had nothing but their chains to lose; and—unlike many other revolutionaries—they seemed to have an inexhaustible supply of proletarian consciousness, or Social Democratic patriotism.

When M. S. (Eli-Moishe) Altman, the future classicist, was nine years old, he organized a strike against autocracy in his heder. When he was a fourth-grade *gymnasium* student, he wrote a prizewinning essay about Pushkin's "The Bronze Horseman." And when he was in Chernigov as a twenty-two-year-old medical student, he caught up with the revolution.

I foresaw the Bolshevik victory long before the end of the war and printed a special leaflet warning the population of that fact. "We have come to stay!" I wrote in that leaflet. When the Bolsheviks finally did come, they were impressed by the leaflet and, having found out who the author of the warning was, appointed me, a nonmember, as the

> editor of their official newspaper, *The News of the Executive Committee of Chernigov Province.* My life changed completely. I became a fanatical believer in Lenin and the "world revolution" and walked around with such a revolutionary look on my face that the civilian population did not dare come near me. When "we" (the Bolsheviks) took Odessa, I remember staggering down the street like a drunk.[98]

Esther Ulanovskaia grew up in the shtetl of Bershad in Ukraine. As a little girl, she loved Tolstoy, Turgenev, and her grandfather, the rabbi. She dreamed of going to the university and then "straight to Siberia or the gallows."

> Everything about our shtetl annoyed and outraged me. . . . I wanted to fight for the revolution, the people. But "the people" was a rather abstract concept for me. The Jews who surrounded me were not the people—just a bunch of unpleasant individuals, some of whom I happened to love. But the muzhiks, who came to the shtetl on market days, got drunk, swore, and beat their wives, did not look like the people I read about in books, either. It is true that the shtetl Jews were kinder than the Ukrainian peasants, did not beat their wives, and did not swear. But the Jews represented the world I wanted to get away from.[99]

When she was thirteen, she moved to Odessa and joined the "Young Revolutionary International," most of whose members were Jewish teenagers. They already had one Vera (Faith) and one Liubov (Love, or Charity), so Esther became Nadezhda (Hope). "My name Esther ('Esterka' at home), and even its Russian version, Esfir, sounded bad to me. Back in the shtetl everyone had tried to adopt a Russian name; in Odessa, a Jewish name was a sign of frightful backwardness." The civil war provided all those who wanted to escape backwardness—but would never have reached Siberia or the gallows—with the opportunity for self-transformation, self-sacrifice, and ritual slaughter. Vera, Nadezhda, and Liubov, among many others, were moved by the desire to "avenge their comrades and, if necessary, die fighting." At one point, they entered a village, proclaimed Soviet power, and set up a blockade to prevent the peasants from taking their produce to town. There were about a hundred of them, and they were well armed. "I don't know why we needed that blockade," wrote Nadezhda many years later. "I did not question anything and did not notice that the peasants were becoming unhappy." Nadezhda and her friends were fighting for the people in general and no one in particular. Many of them died fighting. Nadezhda survived and went on to become a Soviet secret agent in China, Europe, and the United States.[100]

Babel's narrator (like Babel himself, in December 1917) also escaped pogroms to join the secret police, or the Extraordinary Commission for Combating Counterrevolution and Sabotage. There, at the end of "The Road" (as the story is called), he found "comrades faithful in friendship and death, comrades the likes of whom are not to be found anywhere in the world except in our country." They would remain friends until Babel's death at their hands in January 1940. The first head of the interrogation team investigating Babel's "espionage activity" was a Jewish fugitive from backwardness.[101]

For many young Jews during the civil war, Pushkin Street became "the road" to the world revolution (or to combat against counterrevolution and sabotage, as the case might be). It seemed to be an inexorable, uninterrupted, and universal path of liberation, along which, "Locked in step, / Marched a yellow-faced Chinaman / And a Hebrew with a pale countenance" (as Iosif Utkin, another officially canonized Young Communist poet, put it). The journey was arduous, but the goal was never in doubt—for right there, by their side, was "the poet of the political department" leading the Bolsheviks "to where the shrapnel and the grenades whiz by." As Bagritsky wrote in 1924,

> I took revenge for Pushkin by the Black Sea,
> I carried Pushkin in the Urals through the woods,
> I crawled with Pushkin in the shallow, muddy trenches,
> Lice-eaten, starving, barefoot, and cold!
> My heart would pound wildly with elation,
> The flame of freedom would rise high within my breast,
> When, to the song of bullets and machine guns,
> I'd feel inspired to recite his ringing lines!

The years roll on along their narrow road,
New songs keep boiling up within my heart.

. . . .

The spring's in bloom—and Pushkin, now avenged,
Is with us still, singing of liberty.[102]

The revolutions of 1917 did not have much to do with either Pushkin or the Jews. But the civil war that followed did. Most of the fighting took place in and around the old Pale of Settlement, where ethnic Russians were a minority and Jews made up a large proportion of the urban population. For Polish and Ukrainian nationalists and assorted peasant ("Green") armies, the Jews represented the old Mercurian foe, the new capitalist city, the expansion of Russian high culture, and, of course, Bolshevism (which represented all of the above insofar as it was the religion of the modern city, ethnically Social Democratic but for the time being Russian-speaking). For the Whites, whose movement was hijacked early on by Russian ethnic nationalists and imperial restorationists, the Jews represented all those things that used to be called "German" (a combination of old Mercurianism and new urbanism as a form of "foreign dominance") and, of course, Bolshevism, which appeared to be a particularly contagious combination of old Mercurianism and new urbanism as a form of foreign dominance. For all these groups, the Jews became an enemy that was easy to define and identify. The Ukrainian nationalists, in particular, could succeed only if they conquered the city, but Ukrainian cities were dominated by Russians, Poles, and Jews. The Russians and Poles had their own armies and were rather thin on the ground; the Jews were either Bolsheviks or defenseless shtetl dwellers. To the extent that they ceased to be defenseless, they tended to become Bolsheviks.

The early Bolsheviks did not normally classify their enemies in ethnic terms. The evil they were combating—"the bourgeoisie"—was an abstract concept not easily convertible into specific targets of arrests and executions. This was a serious weakness in a modern war of ascriptive extermination: not only were there no "bourgeois" flags, armies, or uniforms—there were no people in Russia who used the term to describe themselves and very few people who could be thus described according to Marxist sociology. Eventually, this challenge would become grave enough to force the Soviet regime to modify its concept of evil, but during the civil war the Bolsheviks were able to make up in determination whatever they lacked in conceptual clarity.

The Whites, Greens, and Ukrainian nationalists never committed themselves to the wholesale extermination of the Jews. Their detachments murdered and robbed tens of thousands of Jewish civilians, and their secret services singled out certain groups (mostly Jews but also Latvians) for special treatment, but their leaders and their armies as political institutions were equivocal, defensive, or loudly (and sometimes sincerely) indignant on this score. In the end, the Jewish pogroms were seen as violations of discipline that demoralized the troops and undermined the movements' true objectives, which were fundamentally political. Proper enemies were people who held certain beliefs.[103]

The Bolshevik practice was much more straightforward. "The bourgeoisie" might be an elusive category, but no one apologized for the principle of their "liquidation" on the basis of "objective criteria." Property, imperial rank, and education unredeemed by Marxism were punishable by death, and tens of thousands of people were punished accordingly and unabashedly as hostages or simply as "alien elements" within reach. There were many Jews among the "bourgeois," but Jews as such were never defined as an enemy group. The Bolshevik strength lay not in knowing for sure whom to kill, but in being proud and eager to kill individuals as members of "classes." Sacred violence as a sociological undertaking was an essential part of the doctrine and the most important criterion of true membership.

This meant that Jews who wanted to be true members had to adopt physical coercion against certain groups as a legitimate means of dealing with difference. Or rather, they had to become Apollonians. As Babel's Arye-Leib put it, in one of the best-loved passages in Soviet literature:

> Forget for a while that you have glasses on your nose and autumn in your soul. Stop quarreling at your desk and stuttering in public.

Imagine for a second that you quarrel in city squares and stutter on paper. You are a tiger, a lion, a cat. You can spend the night with a Russian woman, and the Russian woman will be satisfied.[104]

A substantial number of Jews heeded Arye-Leib's call. Their overall share of Bolshevik party membership during the civil war was relatively modest (5.2 percent in 1922), but their visibility in city squares was striking. After the February Revolution, all army officers had become suspect as possible "counterrevolutionaries"; the new soldiers' committees required literate delegates; many of the literate soldiers were Jews. Viktor Shklovsky, the literary scholar, estimated that Jews had made up about 40 percent of all top elected officials in the army. He had been one of them (a commissar); he also remembered having met a talented Jewish cellist who was representing the Don Cossacks. In April 1917, 10 out of 24 members (41.7 percent) of the governing bureau of the Petrograd Soviet were Jews.[105]

At the First All-Russian Congress of Soviets in June 1917, at least 31 percent of Bolshevik delegates (and 37 percent of Unified Social Democrats) were Jews. At the Bolshevik Central Committee meeting of October 23, 1917, which voted to launch an armed insurrection, 5 out of the 12 members present were Jews. Three out of seven Politbureau members charged with leading the October uprising were Jews (Trotsky, Zinoviev, and Grigory Sokolnikov [Girsh Brilliant]). The All-Russian Central Executive Committee (VtsIK) elected at the Second Congress of Soviets (which ratified the Bolshevik takeover, passed the decrees on land and peace, and formed the Council of People's Commissars with Lenin as chairman) included 62 Bolsheviks (out of 101 members). Among them were 23 Jews, 20 Russians, 5 Ukrainians, 5 Poles, 4 "Balts," 3 Georgians, and 2 Armenians. According to Nahum Rafalkes-Nir, who represented Poalei-Zion, all 15 speakers who debated the takeover as their parties' official representatives were Jews (in fact, probably 14). The first two VtsIK chairmen (heads of the Soviet state) were Kamenev and Sverdlov. Sverdlov was also the Party's chief administrator (head of the Secretariat). The first Bolshevik bosses of Moscow and Petrograd were Kamenev and Zinoviev. Zinoviev was also the chairman of the Communist International. The first Bolshevik commandants of the Winter Palace and the Moscow Kremlin were Grigorii Isakovich Chudnovsky and Emelian Yaroslavsky (Minei Izraelevich Gubelman). Yaroslavsky was also the chairman of the League of the Militant Godless. The heads of the Soviet delegation at the Brest-Litovsk negotiations were Adolf Ioffe and Trotsky. Trotsky was the face of the Red Army.[106]

When, in March 1919, the Petrograd Soviet, headed by Zinoviev, launched a competition for the best portrait of "a hero of our age," the suggested list of heroes included Lenin, Lunacharsky, Karl Liebknecht, and four Bolsheviks raised in Jewish families: Trotsky, Uritsky (the head of Petrograd's secret police, assassinated in August 1918), V. Volodarsky (Moisei Goldstein, Petrograd's chief censor as the commissar of print, propaganda, and agitation, assassinated in June 1918), and Zinoviev himself.[107]

The Jewish share of the Party's Central Committee in 1919–21 remained steady at about one-fourth. In 1918, about 54 percent of all Petrograd Party officials described as "leading" were Jews, as were 45 percent of city and provincial Party officials and 36 percent of the Northern District commissars. Three out of five members of the presidium of the Petrograd trade union council in 1919, and 13 out of 36 members of the Executive Committee of the Petrograd Soviet in 1920 were Jews. In 1923 in Moscow, Jews made up 29 percent of the Party's "leading cadres" and 45 percent of the provincial social security administration. Their share in the city Party organization (13.5 percent) was three times their share in the general population. Almost half of them were under twenty-five years old (43.8 percent of men and 51.1 percent of women); 25.4 percent of all female Bolsheviks in Moscow were of Jewish background. According to the historian of Leningrad Jewry Mikhail Beizer (and not accounting for pseudonyms),

> It may have seemed to the general population that the Jewish participation in Party and Soviet organs was even more substantial because Jewish names were constantly popping up in newspapers. Jews spoke relatively more often than others at rallies, conferences, and meetings of all kinds. Here, for example, is the agenda of the Tenth City Con-

ference of the Young Communist League (Komsomol), held in Petrograd on January 5th, 1920: Zinoviev made a speech on the current situation, Slosman read the report of the city Komsomol committee, Kagan spoke on political and organizational matters, Itkina greeted the delegates on behalf of female workers, and Zaks represented the Central Committee of the Komsomol.[108]

The secret police did less quarreling in public squares, but it was one of the most public symbols of Bolshevik power. The proportion of Jews in the Cheka as a whole was not very high (compared to what White propaganda often alleged): 3.7 percent of the Moscow apparatus, 4.3 percent of Cheka commissars, and 8.6 percent of senior ("responsible") officials in 1918, and 9.1 percent of all members of provincial Cheka offices (Gubcheka) in 1920. As in the Party, the majority of Cheka members were Russians, and by far the most overrepresented group were the Latvians, consistently and successfully cultivated by Lenin as the Praetorian Guards of the Revolution (35.6 percent of the Moscow Cheka apparatus, 52.7 percent of all Cheka senior officials, and 54.3 percent of all Cheka commissars, as compared to about 0.09 percent in the country as a whole and about 0.5 percent in Moscow). But even in the Cheka, Bolsheviks of Jewish origin combined ideological commitment with literacy in ways that set them apart and propelled them upward. In 1918, 65.5 percent of all Jewish Cheka employees were "responsible officials." Jews made up 19.1 percent of all central apparatus investigators and 50 percent (6 out of 12) of the investigators employed in the department for combating counter-revolution. In 1923, at the time of the creation of the OGPU (the Cheka's successor), Jews made up 15.5 percent of all "leading" officials and 50 percent of the top brass (4 out of 8 members of the Collegium's Secretariat). "Socially alien" Jews were well represented among the Cheka-OGPU prisoners, too, but Leonard Schapiro is probably justified in generalizing (especially about the territory of the former Pale) that "anyone who had the misfortune to fall into the hands of the Cheka stood a very good chance of finding himself confronted with and possibly shot by a Jewish investigator."[109]

Specifically, and very publicly, Jewish names (and some transparent Jewish pseudonyms) were associated with two of the most dramatic and symbolically significant acts of the Red Terror. Early in the civil war, in June 1918, Lenin ordered the killing of Nicholas II and his family. Among the men entrusted with carrying out the order were Sverdlov (head of the the All-Russian Central Executive Committee in Moscow, formerly an assistant pharmacist), Shaia Goloshchekin (the commissar of the Urals Military District, formerly a dentist), and Yakov Yurovsky (the Chekist who directed the execution and later claimed to have personally shot the tsar, formerly a watchmaker and photographer). It was meant to be a secret operation, but after the Whites reoccupied Ekaterinburg, they ordered an official investigation, the results of which, including the Jewish identities of the main perpetrators, were published in Berlin in 1925 (and eventually confirmed). At the end of the civil war, in late 1920–early 1921, Béla Kun (the chairman of the Crimean Revolutionary Committee) and R. S. Zemliachka (Rozaliia Zalkind, the head of the Crimean Party Committee and the daughter of a well-off Kiev merchant) presided over the massacre of thousands of refugees and prisoners of war who had stayed behind after the evacuation of the White Army. For her part in the operation, Zemliachka received the highest Soviet decoration: the Order of the Red Banner. She was the first woman to be thus honored.[110]

But Jewish revolutionaries did not just tower over city squares— they were prominent in the revolutionary remaking of those squares. Natan Altman, who had begun his artistic career by experimenting with Jewish themes, became the leader of "Lenin's Plan for Monumental Propaganda," the founder of artistic "Leniniana" (Lenin iconography), and the designer of the first Soviet flag, state emblem, official seals, and postage stamps. In 1918, he was put in charge of an enormous festival marking the first anniversary of the October Revolution in Petrograd. Fourteen kilometers (8.7 miles) of canvas and enormous red, green, and orange cubist panels were used to decorate—and reconceptualize—the city's main square in front of the Winter Palace. The spatial center of imperial statehood was transformed into a stage set for the celebration of the beginning of the end of time. El Lissitzky (Lazar Markovich [Mordukhovich] Lisitsky) also abandoned the attempt to create a Jewish national form in order to embrace the international artistic revolution and the world revolution as a work of art. His much celebrated "prouns" (the Russian acronym for "projects for the affirmation of the new") included designs for "Lenin's podiums" (huge leaning towers meant to soar above city squares) and the most iconic of all revolutionary posters: "Beat the Whites with the Red Wedge" (the Whites being represented by a white circle).[111]

The revolutionary rebirth was accompanied by revolutionary renamings, which reflected the degree of Jewish prominence. In Petrograd alone, Palace Square, decorated by Natan Altman, became Uritsky Square; the Tauride Palace, where the Provisional Government had been formed and the Constituent Assembly dispersed, became Uritsky Palace; Liteinyi Avenue became Volodarsky Avenue; the palace of Grand Duke Sergei Aleksandrovich became Nakhamkes Palace; the Admiralty Embankment and Admiralty Avenue were named after Semen Roshal; Vladimir Square and Vladimir Avenue were named after Semen Nakhimson; and the new Communist Workers' University (along with various streets and the city of Elisavetgrad) was named after Zinoviev. The royal residences Pavlovsk and Gatchina became Slutsk and Trotsk, respectively. Vera (Berta) Slutskaia had been the secretary of the Vasileostrovsky District Party Committee.[112]

Finally, to return to Arye-Leib's injunction and Babel's first love, there was the matter of spending the night with a Russian woman. Between 1924 and 1936, the rate of mixed marriages for Jewish males increased from 1.9 to 12.6 percent (6.6 times) in Belorussia, from 3.7 to 15.3 percent (4.1 times) in Ukraine, and from 17.4 to 42.3 percent (2.4 times) in the Russian Republic. The proportions grew higher for both men and women as one moved up the Bolshevik hierarchy. Trotsky, Zinoviev, and Sverdlov were married to Russian women (Kamenev was married to Trotsky's sister). The non-Jews Andreev, Bukharin, Dzerzhinsky, Kirov, Kosarev, Lunacharsky, Molotov, Rykov, and Voroshilov, among others, were married to Jewish women. As Lunacharsky (the commissar of enlightenment) put it, echoing Lenin's and Gorky's views but also speaking from personal experience,

> It is with great joy that we view the immense increase in the number of Russo-Jewish marriages. This is the right path. Our Slavic blood still has a lot of peasant malt; it is thick and plentiful, but it flows a little slowly, and our whole biological rhythm is a little too rustic. On the other hand, the blood of our Jewish comrades is very fast flowing. So let us mix our blood and, in this fruitful mixture, find the human type that will include the blood of the Jewish people like delicious, thousand-year-old human wine.[113]

The special relationship between Bolsheviks and Jews—or rather, between the Bolshevik and Jewish revolutions—became an important part of the revolutionary war of words. Many Whites and other enemies of the Bolsheviks equated the two and represented Bolshevism as a fundamentally Jewish phenomenon. This was an effective argument insofar as it made use of some obvious facts to describe the revolution as a form of foreign invasion to be repelled by true patriots. The problem with the argument—for those willing to argue—was the equally obvious size and composition of the Red Army. No one ever claimed that Babel's "Red Cavalry" stories about a Jew trying to join revolutionary Cossacks should have been about a Cossack trying to join revolutionary Jews. And even N. A. Sokolov, the Kolchak government investigator of the tsar's murder who made the point of referring to various rescue efforts as "attempts by the Russian people to save the royal family," made it clear that the Jewish commissars Goloshchekin and Yurovsky had no trouble finding eager regicides (and convinced Bolsheviks) among local factory workers.[114]

Another view assumed that the civil war was, indeed, civil in the sense of being fratricidal, but argued that the Jews bore a special responsibility for the outcome because the Bolshevik doctrine was evil and because the Jews were overrepresented among its authors and principal practitioners. The best-known defense of this view was offered by the prominent monarchist, Russian nationalist, and anti-Semite V. V. Shulgin in a book written in France in 1927. The book was called *What We Do Not Like Them For*. Addressing "them" directly, Shulgin wrote:

> We do not like the fact that you took too prominent a part in the revolution, which turned out to be the greatest *lie and fraud*. We do not like the fact that you became *the backbone and core of the Communist Party*. We do not like the fact that, with your discipline and solidarity, your persistence and will, you have consolidated and strengthened for years to come the maddest and bloodiest enterprise that humanity has known since the day of creation. We do not like the fact that this experiment was carried out *in order to implement the teachings of a Jew, Karl Marx*. We do not like the fact that this whole terrible thing was done *on the Russian back* and that it has cost us Russians, all of us together and each one of us separately, unutterable losses. We do not like the fact that you, Jews, a relatively small group within the Russian population, participated in this vile deed *out of all proportion to your numbers*.[115]

What could be done about this? Probably for the first time in the history of Russian political writing, Shulgin proposed an explicit and comprehensive defense of the principle of ethnic responsibility, ethnic guilt, and ethnic remorse. Anticipating the standard reasoning of the second half of the century, he argued that whereas legally sons should not have to answer for their fathers, morally they should, and do, and always will. Family responsibility is as necessary as it is inescapable, he argued. If Lindbergh's mother is rightfully proud of her son, then Lenin's mother should be ashamed of hers. Nations are families too:

> It cannot be otherwise. All of us, whether we like it or not, reinforce this link every day of our lives. Some miserable Russian exile in a seedy bistro may be "proud" of Russian vodka before some French lowlife. Did he make that vodka himself?! No, he did not, and neither did his father, his grandfather, his distant relative, or even some acquaintance of his; this vodka was invented by Russians about whom this "proud" individual knows absolutely nothing. So what is he

proud of? "What do you mean? Because I am Russian, too, by God!"
This says it all, and the French lowlife does not question the Russian's
right to be proud of "la vodka," because he agrees: every Russian has
the right to be proud of anything done by any other Russian.

What does this mean? This means that all Russians, whether
they like it or not, are connected to each other by a thread that is
invisible but strong, because this *thread has a universal sanction and
recognition*.[116]

The miserable exile is proud of vodka. Others are proud of Tolstoy, Dostoevsky, and Rachmaninoff. "They are proud, and have
every right to be." But if membership in a nation confers pride,
it must, by the same token, impose responsibility. Being proud of
Tolstoy, according to Shulgin, means sharing the blame for Raspu-
tin and Bolshevism.

Shulgin's list of Russian crimes did not go beyond those two,
which seems to mean that Russians had no one but themselves to
apologize to. Not so with the Jews. Since most of the victims of
the Red Terror were Russians, and many of the top perpetrators
(especially in his native Kiev in 1919) were Jews, all Jews owed all
Russians a formal mea culpa. As Shulgin wrote in his newspaper
Kievlianin on October 8, 1919, in the middle of a brutal pogrom
(and thus not without a touch of blackmail),

> Will they understand what they need to do now? Will all those Jews
> who contributed to the catastrophe be publicly cursed in all the Jew-
> ish synagogues? Will the bulk of the Jewish population renounce the
> creators of the "new" world with the same passion with which it as-
> saulted the old? Will the Jews, beating themselves on the chest and
> covering their heads with ashes, repent publicly for the fateful role
> that the sons of Israel played in the Bolshevik frenzy?[117]

And if they do not—if they say that, after all, the Jews as a nation
did not stage the Russian Revolution and should not answer for a
few Jewish Bolsheviks, then the answer should be:

> Fine, *in that case* we did not stage the pogroms, either, and don't
> have anything to do with those few who did: Petliura's men, the
> Ossetians, and assorted riffraff along with them. We don't have any

influence over them. Personally, we did not engage in any pogroms, we tried to prevent pogroms. . . . So if the Jews, all of them, do not plead guilty to the social revolution, then the Russians, all of them, will not plead guilty to the Jewish pogroms. . . .[118]

A few Russian Jewish intellectuals did plead guilty. In a 1923 collection published in Berlin, *Russia and the Jews*, they called on "the Jews of all countries" to resist Bolshevism and to admit the "bitter sin" of Jewish complicity in its crimes. In the words of I. M. Bikerman, "it goes without saying that not all Jews are Bolsheviks and not all Bolsheviks are Jews, but what is equally obvious is the disproportionate and immeasurably fervent Jewish participation in the torment of half-dead Russia by the Bolsheviks." It is true that the Jews suffered immeasurably from the pogroms, but was not the revolution "a universal pogrom"? "Or is condemning a whole social class to extermination . . . a revolution, and killing and robbing Jews a pogrom? Why such honor for Marx and his followers?" And why the continued claim that evil "always comes from others and is always directed at us"? These were very different Jews, after all. According to G. A. Landau, "We were amazed by what we had least expected to encounter among the Jews: cruelty, sadism, and violence had seemed alien to a nation so far removed from physical, warlike activity; those who yesterday did not know how to use a gun are now found among the executioners and cutthroats."[119]

Ia. A. Bromberg, a Eurasianist who did not contribute to *Russia and the Jews* but shared its goals, arguments, and prophetic style, devoted the most impassioned pages of his *The West, Russia, and the Jews* to this remarkable metamorphosis of Mercurians into Apollonians. "The author cannot help remembering his amazement, bordering on shock, at seeing, for the first time, a Jewish soldier as part of a commissar synod, before which he, as a prisoner of the Bolsheviks, was brought for yet another painfully meaningless interrogation." The formerly oppressed lover of liberty had turned into a tyrant of "unheard-of despotic arbitrariness"; the self-effacing negotiator had become the head of "the worst hooligan gangs"; the principled humanist was meting out forced labor for " 'economic espionage' and other fantastic crimes"; the pacifist and draft dodger was haranguing the troops and leading "large military detachments"; and, most strikingly,

> The convinced and unconditional opponent of the death penalty not just for political crimes but for the most heinous offenses, who could not, as it were, watch a chicken being killed, has been transformed outwardly into a leather-clad person with a revolver and, in fact, lost all human likeness. Having joined the mob of other advocates and professionals of "revolutionary justice" representing younger and crueler nations, he is keeping, coldly and efficiently, as if they were regular statistics, the bloody count of the new victims of the revolutionary Moloch, or standing in a Cheka basement doing "bloody but honorable revolutionary work."[120]

The Jewish argument for Jewish "collective responsibility" (Landau's term) was the same as Shulgin's. Given what Bromberg called "the old provincial passion for seeking out and extolling the Jews famous in various fields of cultural life," and especially "the shameless circus around the name of Einstein," one had no choice but to adopt the murderers too. In D. S. Pasmanik's words, "Is the Jewry responsible for Trotsky? Undoubtedly so. Ethnic Jews not only do not renounce an Einstein or an Ehrlich; they do not even reject the baptized Heine and Boerne. And this means that they have no right to disavow Trotsky and Zinoviev. . . . This means reminding the Polish hypocrites, who incite pogroms because of the murder of Budkiewicz, that the head of the Bolshevik inquisition, Dzerzhinsky, is a full-blooded Pole, and reminding the Latvians that, in Soviet Russia, they played the most shameful role of bloodthirsty executioners—along with the Chinese. In other words, we honestly admit our share of the responsibility."[121]

This position proved unpopular (though not entirely sterile).[122] It proved unpopular because it implied that everyone had something to apologize for but provided no universal gauge of culpability; because "an honest admission" seemed to depend on the universal demise of hypocrisy; because neither Shulgin nor "the Latvians" were in a hurry to do their part; because the pogroms had been specifically anti-Jewish while the Bolshevik terror was flexibly antibourgeois; because the Nazis would come to power within ten years; and because national canons consist not of "special, striking, or remarkable" deeds (as Jan T. Gross argues), but of pride-boosting and shame-suppressing tales of triumph, loss, and self-sacrifice. And because, ultimately, nations have no way of expiating their guilt. The language of Bikerman and others was the Christian language of sin, remorse, and penitence, which was meant to apply to mortal individuals with immortal souls. Members of nations might feel ashamed, but nations cannot go to confession, do penance, and eventually appear before their creator. No demand for a national apology can ever be fully complied with—because there is no legitimate source of penance, no agreed-upon quorum of penitents, and no universal authority to judge the sincerity of remorse.[123]

A much more common position among Jewish opponents of the Bolsheviks (and many future historians) was that Bolsheviks of Jewish descent were not Jews. Jewishness, they implied, in a radical departure from the conventional view, was not inherited but freely adopted—and therefore just as freely discarded. Jews were not the Chosen People; Jews were people who chose to be Jews. For some, the choice involved religious observance; for others ("secular Jews"), it amounted to a particular political (moral) affiliation. Simon Dubnow denied the Jewish Bolsheviks the right to call themselves Jews, and the Zionist newspaper *Togblat* proposed, in the Bolshevik spirit, that only persons formally appointed by national parties be considered true representatives of the Jewish masses. This was, of course, the same view as that held by many Russian nationalists: Russian Bolsheviks cannot be Russians because their avowed aim is the destruction of the Russian state, Russian churches, Russian culture, and the Russian peasants (i.e., the "Russian people"). And if they are not Russians, they have got to be Jews.[124]

Another version of this approach was to divide the group in question into the authentic and inauthentic varieties. Lenin argued that each nation possessed two cultures—democratic (good) and bourgeois (bad); I. O. Levin identified Jewish Bolshevism with the "semi-intelligentsia" (as opposed to the real kind), which "had lost the cultural content of old Judaism while remaining alien not only to Russian culture but to any culture at all"; and Lev Kopelev's mother used to explain to her maids and various acquaintances "that there are Jews and then there are Yids; the Jewish people have a great culture and have suffered a lot; Christ, Karl Marx, the poet Nadson, Doctor Lazarev (the best children's doctor in Kiev), the singer Iza Kremer, and our family are all Jews; those who scurry around in the marketplace or at the illegal stock exchange, or work as commissars in the Cheka are Yids."[125]

For the Bolsheviks and their friends, the prominence of Jewish revolutionaries could also be a political liability. In July 1917, Gorky, who never wavered in his admiration for the Jews, called on the Petrograd journalist I. O. Kheisin—who had written an article poking fun at the sickness of the imprisoned tsarina—to show "tact and moral sensitivity" lest anti-Semitic passions obscure the achievements of the revolution. In April 1922, after the civil war, he sent the following message to his friend Sholem Asch, to be passed on to the "Jewish workers of America":

The reason for the current anti-Semitism in Russia is the tactlessness of the Jewish Bolsheviks. The Jewish Bolsheviks, not all of them but some irresponsible boys, are taking part in the defiling of the holy sites of the Russian people. They have turned churches into movie theaters and reading rooms without considering the feelings of the Russian people. The Jewish Bolsheviks should have left such things to the Russian Bolsheviks. The Russian peasant is cunning and secretive. He will put on a sheepish smile for your benefit, but deep inside he will harbor hatred for the Jew who raised his hand against his holy places.

We should fight against this. For the sake of the future of the Jews in Russia, we should warn the Jewish Bolsheviks: "Stay away from the holy places of the Russian people! You are capable of other, more important, deeds. Do not interfere in things that concern the Russian church and the Russian soul!"

Of course, the Jews are not to blame. Among Bolsheviks, there are many agents provocateurs, old Russian officials, bandits, and all kinds of vagabonds. The fact that the Bolsheviks sent the Jews, the helpless and irresponsible Jewish youths, to do these things, does smack of provocation, of course. But the Jews should have refrained. They should have realized that their actions would poison the soul of the Russian people. They should bear this in mind.[126]

The Jewish Bolsheviks were not amused. Esther Frumkina, one of the leaders of the Party's Jewish Section, accused Gorky of taking part in the "attack on the Jewish Communists for their selfless struggle against darkness and fanaticism," and Ilya Trainin, the editor of *The Life of Nationalities* and one of the top Bolshevik experts on the "national question," wrote that the "Stormy Petrel of the Revolution" had finally landed in the "swamp of philistinism." They did take his point, however. Trotsky, according to his own testimony, refused the post of commissar of internal affairs for fear of "providing our enemies with the additional weapon of my Jewishness" (despite Lenin's insistence that there was no task more important than fighting counterrevolution and "no better Bolshevik than Trotsky"). Meanwhile, the minutes of the Politburo meeting of April 18, 1919, included

> Comrade Trotsky's statement that Latvians and Jews constituted a vast percentage of those employed in Cheka frontal zone units, Executive Committees in frontal zones and the rear, and in Soviet establishments at the center; that the percentage of them at the front itself was a comparatively small one; that strong chauvinist agitation on this subject was being carried on among the Red Army men and finding a certain response there; and that, in Comrade Trotsky's opinion, a reallocation of party personnel was essential to achieve a more even distribution of party workers of all nationalities between the front and the rear.[127]

The Bolsheviks kept apologizing for the numbers of Jews in their midst until the subject became taboo in the mid-1930s. According to Lunacharsky:

> The Jews played such an outstanding role in our revolutionary movement that, when the revolution triumphed and established a state, a significant number of Jews entered the institutions of the state. They earned this right with their loyal and selfless service to the revolution. However, this circumstance is seen by anti-Semites as a strike against both the Jews and the revolution.

Moreover, the Jewish proletarian population is predominantly urban and advanced. Naturally, as our country grew and all manner of chains were removed, this population rose in certain proportions to more or less leading positions.

Some conclude from this: "Aha, this means that the revolution and the Jews are in some sense identical!" This enables the counterrevolutionaries to talk about "Jewish dominance," although the explanation is very simple: our revolution was carried out by the urban population, which tends to predominate in leading positions and of which the Jews make up a significant percentage.[128]

Anti-Semites, ethnic nationalists, and advocates of proportional representation were not likely to be satisfied with such simple explanations, but then they would not rise in certain proportions to more or less leading positions until the late 1930s. In the meantime, the Jewish Communist would remain a highly visible part of the official iconography—as a heroic, often tragic figure or simply as a familiar face in the Red Army ranks or at a deputy's desk.

One of the most celebrated books about the civil war was Babel's *Red Cavalry*, an inside story of the painful and never completed transformation of a hiccuping Jewish boy with a swollen blue head into a Cossack hero without fear or mercy. The force that moved him was love—the bitter, ardent, and hopeless first love of a Mercury for an Apollo.

> Savitsky, the commander of the Sixth Division, stood up when he saw me, and I was struck by the beauty of his huge body. He stood up, and with the purple of his riding breeches, the crimson of his rakish little cap, and the decorations hammered onto his chest he sliced the hut in two, the way a standard slices the sky. He smelled of perfume and the cloying freshness of soap. His long legs looked like girls sheathed to the neck in shiny riding boots.
>
> He smiled at me, struck the desk with his whip, and drew toward himself an order that the chief of staff had just finished dictating.[129]

The order was to "destroy the enemy," and the punishment for noncompliance was summary execution administered "on the spot" by Savitsky himself.

> The commander of the Sixth signed the order with a flourish, tossed it to his orderlies, and turned his gray eyes, dancing with merriment, toward me.
>
> I handed him the paper with my appointment to the divisional staff.
>
> "Put it down in the order of the day!" said the commander. "Put him down for every satisfaction except the front one. Can you read and write?"
>
> "Yes, I can," I replied, envying the iron and flower of his youthfulness. "I am a law graduate from St. Petersburg University . . ."
>
> "So you're one of those little geniuses," he shouted, laughing. "And with a pair of glasses on your nose. A little on the mangy side too. They send you fellows down without asking first . . . People have gotten carved up around here for wearing glasses. So, do you plan to stay with us?"
>
> "Yes, I plan to stay with you," I replied before setting off for the village with the quartermaster, to find a place for the night.[130]

Savitsky was to be the Jewish boy's last tutor. The boy had been taught Hebrew, Russian, French, music, and the law, among many other things. His other teachers had included Pushkin, of course, and Zagursky, and Galina Apollonovna, and Efim Nikitich Smolich, who had taught him the names of the birds and the trees, and the Russian prostitute, Vera, who had "taught him her science" in payment for his first story (in "My First Fee"). The job of Savitsky and his beautiful and terrifying Red Cavalrymen was to teach him "the simplest of skills—the ability to kill a man."[131]

One lesson took place in the town of Berestechko, where he saw Bohdan Khmelnytsky's watchtower and heard an old man singing in a childlike voice about bygone Cossack glory.

> Right under my window several Cossacks were preparing to shoot a silver-bearded old Jew for spying. The old man was squealing and

struggling to get away. Then Kudria from the machine-gun detachment took hold of the old man's head and tucked it under his arm.
The Jew grew quiet and stood with his legs apart. With his right hand
Kudria pulled out his dagger and carefully slit the old man's throat,
without splashing any blood on himself. Then he knocked on the
closed window.

"If anyone's interested," he said, "They can come and get him.
He's free for the taking . . ."[132]

The narrator's name—and Babel's civil war pseudonym as a reporter—was Liutov ("the Ferocious One"). His lessons in killing
were numerous, relentless, and multiform. His first prey, soon after
Savitsky's welcome, was a goose.

A stern-looking goose was wandering about the yard, serenely preen-
ing its feathers. I caught up with it and pressed it to the ground; the
goose's head cracked under my boot—cracked and spilled out. The
white neck was spread out in the dung, and the wings flapped convul-
sively over the slaughtered bird.

"Mother of God upon my soul!" I said, poking around in the goose
with my saber. "I'll have this roasted, landlady."[133]

Liutov was rewarded with a place by the fire, the title "brother,"
and a bowl of homemade cabbage soup with pork. He did not become one of the Cossacks, though. His job was to read Lenin aloud
to them, and his heart, "stained crimson with murder, squeaked
and overflowed." He would never master the simplest of skills,
never learn how to truly love a horse, and never lose either the
glasses on his nose or the autumn in his soul. Even as a Cheka employee, Babel would always remain an interpreter. To paraphrase
Osip Mandelstam's epigram, "The horse miaowed, the tomcat
neighed. / The Jew was acting like a Cossack."[134]
That was true of Babel, every one of Babel's doubles, countless
other Jewish boys with glasses who could not swim, as well as all
of Russian literature's "superfluous men" who had never been able
to satisfy a Russian woman. But that was not what made Babel "a
literary Messiah . . . from the sunny steppes washed by the sea," as
Babel himself put it. What made Babel a literary Messiah from the

sunny steppes washed by the sea was his discovery of Jewish Apollonians—Jews who were "jovial, paunchy, and bubbly like cheap wine"; Jews who thought only "of downing a good shot of vodka and punching somebody in the face"; Jews who were kings and "looked like sailors"; Jews who could make a Russian woman named Katiusha "moan, and peal with laughter"; Jews who were taller than the tallest policeman in Odessa; Jews "whose fury contained within it everything that was necessary to rule over others"; Jews who had "murder in their souls"; Jews who could "shuffle their fathers' faces like a fresh deck of cards"; Jews who had well-deserved nicknames like Pogrom and Cossack. Jews who were more like Goliath than David, more like Cyclops and Achilles than Ulysses.[135]

One such Jew—of small stature but "with the soul of an Odessa Jew"—was the blacksmith Jonah Brutman, who had three sons, "three fattened bulls with purple shoulders and feet like spades." The first son followed in his father's trade; the second went off to join the partisans and got killed; and the third, Semen, "went over to Primakov and joined a division of Red Cossacks. He was made commander of a Cossack regiment. He and a few other shtetl boys became the first of an unexpected breed of saber-wielding Jewish horsemen and partisans."[136]

Members of this breed became familiar heroes of Soviet folklore, fiction, and recollection. There are Perets Markish's "Shloime-Ber and Azriel, a shoemaker's sons turned Red Cavalrymen, riding to the front"; there is Izrail Khaikelevich ("Alesha") Ulanovsky, a brawler, sailor, miner, and partisan, who did not like intellectuals and became an NKVD spy; there is the biggest man of the Stalin era, Grigory Novak, the first Soviet champion of the world (in power lifting, in 1946) and the only circus athlete to juggle seventy-pound weights; and there are legendary gangsters, drunkards, and womanizers who, "if there were rings attached to heaven and earth, would grab those rings and pull heaven down to earth." All of them were begotten by Semen Brutman—or possibly Anatoly Rybakov's Uncle Misha, a "recklessly generous and desperately brave" Red army commander, "broad-shouldered and burly, with a chiseled, tanned Mongol face and slanted eyes, a daredevil." Uncle Misha had also left home to become a cavalryman. "He was a kind, devil-may-care, courageous, just, and selfless man. In the revolution he had found a faith to replace the faith of his ancestors; his straight-forward mind could not stand Talmudic hairsplitting; the simple arithmetic of the revolution was more comprehensible to him. The civil war provided an outlet for his burning energy; the simplicity of a soldier's life freed him from the pettiness of human existence."[137]

Such Jews were larger than life, but they were marginal (as most Goliaths are). The Jews who occupied the center stage of early Soviet culture were the unmistakably Mercurian incarnations of Bolshevik Reason, and thus much more familiarly Jewish. All "Party-minded" literature was about the transformation of prole-tarian spontaneity into revolutionary consciousness, or, in mythic (socialist-realist) terms, the taming of a recklessly generous, desper-ately brave, devil-may-care Red Cavalryman into a disciplined, scripture-reading holy warrior. All such proletarians had mentors, and many such mentors were Jews—partly because there were many Jews among Bolshevik mentors, but also because this was a role that called for an authentic, believable Mercurian. The iconic commissar was the consciousness to the spontaneity of the proletar-iat, the head to the body of the revolution, the restless nomad to the inert enormity of the masses. It made sense for the iconic com-missar to be a Jew.[138]

In one of the foundational texts of socialist realism, A. Fadeev's *The Rout* (1926), the Red Partisan commander Iosif Abramovich Levinson is "a tiny man in tall boots, with a long, red wedge of a beard," who looks like a "gnome from a children's book," suffers from a pain in his side, embarrasses himself at Russian skittles, and comes from the family of a used-furniture salesman who "spent his life hoping to get rich but was afraid of mice and played his violin very badly." One of the men under Levinson's command is the shepherd Metelitsa.

> He had always felt vaguely attracted to that man and had noticed on many occasions that it gave him pleasure to ride next to him, talk to him, or simply look at him. He admired Metelitsa not for any outstanding socially useful qualities, of which Metelitsa did not have

very many and which Levinson possessed to a much greater degree, but for the extraordinary physical agility, the animal vitality with which he overflowed and which Levinson himself so sorely lacked. Whenever he saw Metelitsa's nimble figure, ever ready for action, or simply knew that Metelitsa was not far away, he would forget about his own physical weakness and come to believe that he was as tough and tireless as Metelitsa. He was even secretly proud that a man like that was under his command.[139]

The reason a man like that is under his command is that Levinson belongs to the chosen. It was not always clear whether conscious Communists received true knowledge because they were naturally endowed with special qualities (such as an innate sense of justice or an iron will), or whether they developed special qualities as a consequence of receiving true knowledge (through sudden illumination, mortification of the flesh, or formal apprenticeship). Either way, their election as interpreters of the gospel and leaders of the masses was revealed through visible bodily signs, usually the combination of physical corruption and the penetrating gaze so typical of iconic Jews (as well as Christian saints and intelligentsia martyrs). Levinson, for one, had renounced all falsehood when he was a "feeble Jewish boy" with "big naive eyes" staring with "peculiar, unchildlike intentness" from an old family photograph. He never lost that gift: Levinson's "unblinking eyes" could pull a man from the crowd "the way pincers could pull out a nail." "Perfectly clear," "deep as lakes," and "otherwordly," they "took in Morozka [the proletarian daredevil], boots and all, and saw in him many things that Morozka himself was probably unaware of."[140]

Levinson's clairvoyance, however acquired, allows him to "conquer his frailty and his weak flesh" as he leads the often reluctant people to their salvation. Ideologically, he did not have to be Jewish (most of the elect were not), but there is little doubt that for reasons of both aesthetic and sociological verisimilitude, canonical Jewishness seemed an appropriate expression of the Bolshevik vision of disembodied consciousness triumphing over "Oblomov's" inertia.

> "Only here, in our country," thought Levinson, quickening his pace and puffing even more ferociously at his cigarette, "where millions of

people have lived for centuries under the same slow, lazy sun, languishing in filth and poverty, plowing with antediluvian wooden plows, believing in an angry and stupid god—only in a country like this can such lazy and weak-willed, such good-for-nothing people be born. . . ."

Levinson grew very agitated because these were his deepest, most intimate thoughts; because the defeat of all that poverty and misery constituted the only meaning of his life; because there would have been no Levinson at all, but somebody else, had he not been moved by an overwhelming, irresistible desire to see the birth of the new man—beautiful, strong, and kind.[141]

It is for the sake of creating a perfect human being—Apollonian in body and Mercurian in mind—that Levinson steels himself for doing what is "necessary," including the requisitioning of a weeping farmer's last pig and the killing of a wounded comrade too weak to be evacuated. The price he has to pay is as terrible as it is mysterious: "personal responsibility." Clearly analogous to Christian sin, it was both inescapable and ennobling; the greater the personal responsibility for acts ordinarily considered evil, the more visible the signs of election and the inner strength they bespoke. Demonic as well as Promethean, Bolshevik commissars "carried within them" the pain of historical necessity.[142]

In *The Commissars* by Yuri Libedinsky (Fadeev's fellow "proletarian writer" and himself a Jew and a commissar), civil war daredevils are brought together for a special course on military discipline and political education. The man in charge of military training is a former tsarist officer ("military expert"); the chief ideologists are the frail but unbending Jews Efim Rozov and Iosif Mindlov. Both are sickly, stooped, pale-lipped, and bespectacled; both "give up hours of sleep to reading Marx"; both know what is necessary; and both have the inner strength to get it done. Rozov, the head of the district's political department, had been a watchmaker's apprentice when, in March 1917, he saw those "bent, immobile figures" for the last time. "Still, the watchmaker's patient and careful dexterity had become a part of his being and proved useful for his work and struggle." He had become the craftsman of the revolution, the Stolz to its many Oblomovs. "He was different from the unhurried local people. Skinny and short, Rozov moved quickly, abruptly, but without scurrying around, like a knife in the hands of an experienced carver." His mission is "to look over the commissars as if they had been weapons after a battle, make sure they were not dented, cracked, or rusted, and then sharpen and temper them for the next battle."[143]

All revolutionary detachments needed someone like that. In A. Tarasov-Rodionov's *Chocolate* (1922), the martyred Chekist Abram Katzman is stooped, sallow, bespectacled, and hook-nosed; and in Vasily Grossman's "Four Days," the grim Commissar Faktorovich

> despised his feeble body covered with curly black fur. He did not pity or love it—he would not hesitate for a second to ascend a gallows or turn his narrow chest toward a firing squad. Since childhood, his weak flesh had given him nothing but trouble: whooping cough, swollen adenoids, colds, constipation alternating with sudden storms of colitis and bloody dysentery, influenza, and heartburn. He had learned to ignore his flesh—to work with a fever, to read Marx while holding his cheek swollen from an infected tooth, to make speeches while suffering from acute stomach pains. And no, he had never been embraced by tender arms.

It is Faktorovich, however, who, through sheer courage, hatred, and faith, saves his comrades from captivity and uncertainty. For "although his child-sized long underwear kept sliding down ridiculously and his camel-like Hebrew head trembled on its tender neck . . . , there was no doubt that strength was on the side of this true believer."[144]

Nor was there any doubt about the source of true strength in one of the most celebrated poems about the civil war, Eduard Bagritsky's "The Tale of Opanas" (1926). An imitation of Shevchenko's "tales" and Ukrainian folk epics, the poem rethinks and finally resolves the traditional Cossack-Jewish confrontation by translating it into the language of social revolution. The commissar and head of the "requisitioning detachment" Iosif Kogan does what is necessary by confiscating peasant food and executing those who resist. The confused Ukrainian lad Opanas deserts the detachment and ends up joining the army of the peasant anarchist Nestor Makhno.

> O Ukraine! Our native land!
> Autumn's golden harvests!
> In the past, we joined the Cossacks,
> Now we join the bandits!

Opanas kills, robs, loots, and drinks ("Beating Communists and Yids— / What an easy job!") until he is ordered to shoot the captured commissar. Torn by doubt, Opanas suggests to Kogan that he try to escape, but Kogan only smiles, straightens his glasses, and offers Opanas his clothes. The shot rings, and Kogan falls down into the dust, "nose first." Tormented by remorse, Opanas confesses his guilt to a Bolshevik interrogator and is sentenced to be shot. The night before the execution, he is visited in his cell by Kogan's ghost, who smiles sternly and says, "Your life's road, Opanas, / Ends beyond this threshold. . . ."[145]

All these commissars were perfect heroes both because they were Jewish and because they had left their Jewishness behind. Or rather, it was their Jewishness that had allowed them to break with the past. Levinson had "ruthlessly suppressed within himself the passive, languid yearning" for a promise of future happiness—"all those things he had inherited from the humble generations brought up on mendacious fables." Mindlov's wife Leah Sorkina (who died of consumption and revolutionary exhaustion) "had easily abandoned her ancestors' religion—relentless, incomprehensible, and overburdened with tiresome ritual." Some went further. According to M. D. Baitalsky's memoir, the Cheka agent Khaim Polisar "confiscated his father's hardware store for the needs of the revolution." While Grossman's Faktorovich was a Cheka agent, he arrested his uncle, who later died in a concentration camp. "Faktorovich remembered how his aunt had come to the Cheka office to see him and he had told her of her husband's death. She had covered her face with her hands and said: 'Oh my God, oh my God.' "

After Stalin's death, Grossman would return to the character of a Jewish true believer in *Forever Flowing*. Faktorovich would not change (except for the name), but Grossman's language would:

> Was it the age-old chain of abuses, the anguish of the Babylonian captivity, the humiliations of the ghetto, or the misery of the Pale of Settlement that had produced and forged that unquenchable thirst that was scorching the soul of the Bolshevik Lev Mekler?. . .
>
> He served the cause of good and the revolution in blood and without mercy. In his revolutionary incorruptibility, he threw his father into prison and testified against him at a Cheka Collegium meeting. Grimly and cruelly, he turned his back on his sister who begged him to help her husband who had been arrested as a saboteur.
>
> In all his meekness, he was merciless to the heretics. The revolution seemed to him to be helpless, childishly trusting, surrounded by treachery, the cruelty of villains, and the filth of lechers.
>
> And so he was merciless to the enemies of the revolution.[146]

This was a view from the disillusioned future. In the first decade of the revolution, the Bolshevik scorching of the soul was a matter of strength, pride, duty, and "personal responsibility." The soul was being scorched because it had to be—because it was necessary.

In 1922, another proletarian writer, A. Arosev (a childhood friend of V. Molotov and future head of the Soviet Committee for Cultural Ties with Foreign Countries), published a novel entitled *The Notes of Terenty the Forgotten*. One of the characters is the Cheka agent Kleiner, who does not wash very often, always wears the same leather jacket, sleeps on an old trunk, and has the smooth face of a eunuch.

> Kleiner belongs to a special breed. He is a "Chekist" from head to foot.
>
> Perhaps he is the best specimen of that breed. Future generations may not remember his name. His monument may never be built. And yet he is a very loyal man. He is full of a hidden inner enthusiasm. He may seem dry. His conversation is also dry, yet he inspires you when he talks. The sound of his voice seems childish, yet strangely alluring. They say that he has smiled only once in his whole life, and even then

to bad effect: while informing an old lady about the execution of her son, he smiled accidentally out of nervousness. The old lady fainted. Kleiner has never smiled again.[147]

One of Kleiner's ideas is to project executions onto a large screen outside the Cheka building. "It would be a kind of cinema for everyone," he says.

"You mean like in America?"

"Yes, yes, exactly. To teach the people a lesson. So that they'd be scared. The more scared they are, the fewer people we kill . . . I mean . . . execute."

. . . "But such spectacles would only corrupt the people," I said to Kleiner.

"What? What did you say? Corrupt? You are full of prejudices. Peter the Great sent Russian students to the Stockholm anatomical theater and ordered them to tear the corpses' muscles apart with their teeth, so they'd learn how to operate. I bet that didn't corrupt them. What is necessary does not corrupt. Try to understand. What is necessary does not corrupt."[148]

Kleiner himself is incorruptible because he is necessary. "They will probably never build a monument to Kleiner, but they really should: he spent his whole soul on the revolution."[149]

They did build many monuments to Kleiner's commander, Feliks Dzerzhinsky. One used to stand outside the Cheka building in Moscow. Another is Eduard Bagritsky's poem "TBC," in which the pale knight of the revolution appears before a feverish Young Communist poet. "Sharp-angled face, sharp-angled beard," Dzerzhinsky sits down on the edge of the bed and talks to the young man about the heavy burden of the "three-edged frankness of the bayonet," about the need to cut through the "crusty gut of the earth's routine," about the moats closing in over the heads of the executed, and about the "signature on the death sentence spilling out of the hole in the head." And then he intones some of the age's most famous lines:

> Our age is awaiting you out in the yard,
> Alarmed and alert as a well-armed guard.

Go, stand by its side, don't hesitate.
Its solitude is at least as great.
Your enemy's everyone you meet,
You stand alone and the age stands still,
And if it tells you to cheat—then cheat.
And if it tells you to kill—then kill.[150]

The culmination of the story of Jewish commissars in Soviet literature was the famous history of the construction of the White Sea Canal, 1931–34. The book was produced by thirty-six writers (including Gorky, M. Zoshchenko, Vs. Ivanov, Vera Inber, V. Kataev, A. Tolstoy, and V. Shklovsky). The canal was built by labor camp inmates ("reforged" thereby into socially useful citizens). The construction was run by the secret police (the OGPU, the successor to the Cheka). All the top leadership positions were held by Jews: G. G. Yagoda, the OGPU official in charge of the project; L. I. Kogan, the head of construction, M. D. Berman, the head of the Labor Camp Administration (Gulag); S. G. Firin, the head of the White Sea Canal Labor Camp; Ya. D. Rappoport, the deputy head of construction and of the Gulag; and N. A. Frenkel, the head of work organization on the canal.[151]

As portrayed in the *History*, these people were in much better health than their civil war predecessors, but they had lost none of their essential attributes: consciousness, restlessness, ruthlessness, promptness, precision, prodigious powers of penetration, and the optional Jewishness as a confirmation and possibly explanation of all the other attributes. They were the last representatives of the Heroic Age of the Russian Revolution: the age that preferred mobility to stability, boundlessness to borders, proteanism to permanence, consciousness to spontaneity, exile to domesticity, artifice to nature, necessity to beauty, mind to matter, Stolz to Oblomov, those who could not swim to those who could. It was the Mercurian phase of the revolution, in other words; the German Stage without the Germans; the Jewish Age.[152]

No icon better expresses the essence of that age (Kultura 1, in Vladimir Paperny's terminology) than El Lissitzky's *Beat the Whites with the Red Wedge*. The "three-edged frankness of the bayonet" and the "sharp-angled face" of Feliks Dzerzhinsky were aimed at the "crusty gut of the earth's routine" and indeed everything dull, round, or predictably rectangular. According to one of the prophets of the revolutionary avant-garde, Vassily Kandinsky, the triangle was more "sharp-witted" than the square and less philistine than the circle. It was also much more Mercurian than Apollonian, and therefore—stylistically—much more Jewish than Russian. Jewishness was not the only way of representing the triangle, but it was one of the more familiar and aesthetically convincing. Levinson's "red wedge of a beard," Mindlov's angular movements, Rozov's knifelike figure were all references to the traditional and pervasive iconography of Mercurianism. According to one of Ilya Ehrenburg's characters (a Chekist), Lenin might be a sphere; Bukharin was a straight line; but Trotsky, "the chess player and the chief of the steppe hordes, disciplined and lined up under the banner of the twenty-one theses of some resolution—that one is a triangle." And according to Arosev's Terenty the Forgotten, "if I were a futurist artist, I would represent Trotsky as two downward-pointing triangles: a small triangle—the face—on top of a large triangle—the body."[153]

One obvious reading of the wedge-over-circle imagery is violence ("beat the whites"); the other is sex (love). Eduard Bagritsky portrayed both. His poem "February," written in 1933–34 and published posthumously, is about "a little Hebrew boy" who loves books about birds (the same birds, presumably, that adorned Galina Apollonovna's robe and inhabited Efim Nikitich Smolich's realm of "nature"):

> Birds that appeared like weird letters,
> Sabers and trumpets, spheres and diamonds.
>
> The Archer must have been detained
> Above the darkness of our dwelling,
> Above the proverbial Jewish odor
> Of goosefat, above the continuous droning
> Of tedious prayers, above the beards
> In family albums . . .

As a young man, he falls in love with a girl with golden hair, a green dress, and "a nightingale quiver" in her eyes, "all of her as if flung wide open to the coolness of the sea, the sun, and the birds." Every day, as she walks home from school, he follows her "like a murderer, stumbling over benches and bumping into people and trees," thinking of her "as a fabulous bird who had fluttered off the pages of a picture book" and wondering how he, "born of a Hebrew and circumcised on the seventh [*sic*] day," has become a bird catcher. Finally, he gathers up his courage and runs toward her.

> All those books I'd read in the evenings—
> Hungry and sick, my shirt unbuttoned—
> About birds from exotic places,
> About people from distant planets,
> About worlds where rich men play tennis,
> Drink lemonade, and kiss languid women,—
> All those things were moving before me,
> Wearing a dress and swinging a satchel. . . .

He runs beside her "like a beggar, bowing deferentially" and "mumbling some nonsense." She stops and tells him to leave her alone, pointing toward the intersection. And there,

> Fat-bellied and greasy with perspiration,
> Stands the policeman,
>   Squeezed into high boots,
> Pumped up with vodka and stuffed full of bacon. . . .

Then comes the February Revolution, and he becomes a deputy commissar, a catcher of horse thieves and burglars, "an angel of death with a flashlight and a revolver, surrounded by four sailors from a battleship."

> My Hebrew pride sang out as clearly,
> As a tight string stretched out to its limit.
> I would have given much for my forefather
> In his long caftan, his hat with a fox tail
> From under which, like a silvery spiral,
> His earlock crawled out, and a thick cloud of dandruff

Floated over the square of his beard,—
For him to be able to spot his descendant
In this strapping fellow who loomed like a tower
Over the bristling guns and the headlights,
Over the truck that had shattered midnight. . . .

One night, he is sent to arrest some gangsters, and there, in a suffocating brothel reeking of face powder, semen, and sweet liqueur, he finds her—"the one who had tormented me with her nightingale gaze." She is bare-shouldered and bare-legged, half asleep and smoking a cigarette. He asks her if she recognizes him, and offers her money.

Without opening her mouth, she whispered softly,
"Please have some pity! I don't need the money!"

Throwing her the money,
    I barged into—
Without pulling off my high boots, or my holster,
Without taking off my regulation trench coat—
The abysmal softness of the blanket
Under which so many men had sighed,
Flung about, and throbbed, into the darkness
Of the swirling stream of fuzzy visions,
Sudden screams and unencumbered movements,
Blackness, and ferocious, blinding light . . .

I am taking you because so timid
Have I always been, and to take vengeance
For the shame of my exiled forefathers
And the twitter of an unknown fledgling!

I am taking you to wreak my vengeance
On the world I could not get away from!

Welcome me into your barren vastness,
In which grass cannot take root and sprout,
And perhaps my night seed may succeed in
Fertilizing your forbidding desert.

> There'll be rainfalls, southern winds will bluster,
> Swans will make their calls of tender passion.[154]

According to Stanislav Kuniaev, this is the rape of Russia celebrated by "the poet of the openly Romantic ideal Zionism who does not distinguish between messianic ideas and pragmatic cruelty." According to Maxim D. Shrayer, this is "a dream of creating harmony between the Russian and Jewish currents in Jewish history, . . . a dream, if you wish, of a harmonious synthesis, which would lead to the blurring of all boundaries, i.e., to the formation of a Russian-Jewish identity. . . . Sexual intercourse with his former Russian beloved is the modicum of the protagonist's revenge upon and liberation from the prerevolutionary world of legal Jewish inequality and popular anti-Semitic prejudice." And according to the protagonist himself, this is his revenge on the world he "could not get away from"—the world of "goosefat," "tedious prayers," and "cloud[s] of dandruff." The Jewish Revolution within the Russian Revolution was waged against "the shame of exiled forefathers" and for the "Hebrew pride" singing like a string; against the Russia of fat cheeks and for the Russia of Galina Apollonovna. It was a violent attempt to conceive a world of Mercurian Apollonians, a Russia that would encompass the world.[155]

Chapter 4

HODL'S CHOICE: THE JEWS AND THREE PROMISED LANDS

The old man's sons had different worth:
The first was very bright from birth,
The second, not the sharpest tool,
The third one was a perfect fool.

—P. P. Ershov, *The Humpbacked Horse*

Tevye the Milkman had five daughters. (He mentions seven in one place and six in another, but we meet only five, so five it will have to be.) Tsaytl rejected a wealthy suitor to marry a poor tailor, who died of consumption. Hodl followed her revolutionary husband, Perchik, into Siberian exile. Shprintze was abandoned by her empty-headed groom and drowned herself. Beilke married a crooked war contractor and fled with him to America. Chava eloped with a non-Jewish autodidact ("a second Gorky") and was mourned as dead, only to return, repentant, at the end of Sholem Aleichem's book.

Chava's story is not particularly convincing (most of those who abandoned their fathers for Gorky never came back), but it is not altogether implausible because many Jewish nationalists (including such giants of Zionism as Ber Borokhov, Vladimir Jabotinsky, and Eliezer Ben-Yehuda) started out as socialist universalists and worshipers of Russian literature. Most of them never returned to Tevye's house and Tevye's God the way Chava did—in fact, they tended to be more explicit in their rejection of his "diaspora" ways than their Bolshevik cousins and doubles—but they did return to a kind of Jewish chosenness that Tevye would have recognized. (And of course the more readily Tevye would have recognized it, the more explicit they tended to be in their rejection of his diaspora ways.) It seems fair to propose, therefore, that Chava's homecoming stands for her emigration to the Land of Israel, not her improbable return to Tevye's deserted house on the day he was expelled from exile.

A great deal has been written about Chava the Zionist and Beilke the American, representing as they do the two apparently successful solutions to the European Jewish predicament. Even more has been written about the unassuming Tsaytl, who—let us suppose—stayed in rural Ukraine to be forgotten or patronized by the emigrants and their historians; beaten and robbed by Shkuro's and Petliura's soldiers; reformed resolutely but inconsistently by the Soviets (possibly by her own children); martyred anonymously by the Nazis; and commemorated, also anonymously, in the Holocaust literature and ritual. Which is to say, relatively little has been written about Tsaytl's life but a great deal has been written about her death—and about its significance in the lives of Chava's and Beilke's children.

But what about Hodl? Hodl might be celebrated in Russian Soviet history as a "participant in the revolutionary movement" or, if she made the right early choice, as an "Old Bolshevik." She might be remembered in the history of international socialism as a member of the movement's Russian contingent. Or she might be mentioned in the history of Siberia as a prominent educator or ethnographer. She would not, however, be a part of the canonical Jewish history of the twentieth century on the theory that a Bolshevik (assuming this is what she became, along with so many others) could not be Jewish because Bolsheviks were against Jewishness (and because "Judeo-Bolshevism" was a Nazi catchword). Hodl's grandchildren—fully secular, thoroughly Russified, and bound for the United States or Israel—are an important part of the Jewish story; Hodl herself is not.

It is obvious, however, that Hodl's grandchildren would not have entered Jewish history had Hodl not been one of Tevye's daughters—the one he was most proud of. A Marxist cosmopolitan dedicated to the proletarian cause and married to a "member of the human race," she would probably never have gone back to Boiberik or Kasrilevka, would never have had her sons circumcised, would never have spoken Yiddish to any of her children (or indeed her husband, Perchik), and would never have lit candles at a Sabbath dinner. She would, however, have always remained a part of the family—even after she changed her name to something like Elena Vladimirovna (as she was bound to do). "She is God's own Hodl, Hodl is," says Tevye after she leaves, "and she's with me right here all the time . . . deep, deep down. . . ." And of course Perchik, the son of a local cigarette maker but "a child of God's" by adoption and by conviction, was the only son-in-law Tevye admired, considered his equal, and enjoyed "having a Jewish word" with. "He really did seem like one of the family, because at bottom, you know, he was a decent sort, a simple, down-to-earth boy who would have shared all his worldly possessions with us, just as we shared ours with him, if only he had had any. . . ." As far as Tevye was concerned, conversion to Communism was not a conversion at all. Abandoning Judaism for Christianity was an act of apostasy; abandoning Judaism for "the human race" was a family affair. But did not Christianity begin as an abandonment of Judaism for the human race? Did it not start as a family affair? Tevye did not like to think about that . . .[1]

There were not two great Jewish migrations in the twentieth century—there were three. Most of the Jews who stayed in revolutionary Russia did not stay at home: they moved to Kiev, Kharkov, Leningrad, and Moscow, and they moved up the Soviet social ladder once they got there. Jews by birth and perhaps by upbringing, they were Russian by cultural affiliation and—many of them—Soviet by ideological commitment. Communism was not an exclusively or even predominantly Jewish religion, but of the Jewish religions of the first half of the twentieth century, it was by far the most important: more vibrant than Judaism, much more popular than Zionism, and incomparably more viable, as a faith, than liberalism (which forever required alien infusions in order to be more than a mere doctrine). There were other destinations, of course, but they seemed to offer variations on the same theme (minority status within someone else's nation-state), not a permanent Jewish solution to the Jewish problem.[2]

The Modern Age was founded on capitalism and science-centered professionalism. Capitalism and professionalism were fostered, structured, and restrained by nationalism. Capitalism, professionalism, and nationalism were opposed by socialism, which claimed to be both their legitimate offspring and their final vanquisher. The Jews, Europe's traditional Mercurians, were supremely successful at all modern pursuits and thus doubly vulnerable: as global capitalists, professionals, and socialists, they were strangers by definition, and as priests of other tribes' cultural pedigrees, they were dangerous impostors. Mercurians twice over, they were not wanted in a Europe that was all the more fervently Apollonian for being newly and incompletely Mercurianized.

There was a life beyond Europe, however. In the early twentieth century, Jews had three options—and three destinations—that represented alternative ways of being modern: one that was relatively familiar but rapidly expanding and two that were brand-new.

The United States stood for unabashed Mercurianism, nontribal statehood, and the supreme sovereignty of capitalism and professionalism. It was—rhetorically—a collection of *homines rationalistici artificiales*, a nation of strangers held together by a common celebration of separateness (individualism) and rootlessness (immigration). It was the only modern state (not counting other European settler colonies, none of which possessed the iconic power and global reach of the United States), in which a Jew could be an equal citizen and a Jew at the same time. "America" offered full membership without complete assimilation. Indeed, it seemed to require an affiliation with a subnational community as a condition of full membership in the political nation. Liberalism, unlike nationalism and Communism, was not a religion and could not offer a theory of evil or a promise of immortality. It was—especially in the United States, which came closer than any other nation to speaking Liberalese—always accompanied by a more substantial faith (which tended to gain further substance by being "separate from the state"). The role of such spiritual scaffolding might be played by a traditional religion, tribal ethnicity, or both religion and ethnicity (fused, in the case of the Jews, into one harmonious whole). Whatever it was, a Jew became American by subscribing to a particular (at least outwardly religious) definition of Jewishness. As Abraham Cahan, who used to be a "member of the human race" by virtue of being a member of the Russian intelligentsia, wrote in New York in April 1911,

> In many educated, progressive Jewish families people sat down to the Passover *Seder* last night. Twenty years ago, if anyone had heard that a Jewish socialist was interested in a Jewish religious holiday like that, they would have called him a hypocrite. But today, such a thing is perfectly natural.
>
> Twenty years ago a freethinker would not have been allowed to demonstrate any interest in the Jewish people, but today he can![3]

Ia. Bromberg wished to remain a member of both the human race and the Russian intelligentsia and repeatedly ridiculed "the flood of thoughtless, superficial, and banal ethnic boastfulness of the Jewish-American press." As he wrote in 1931,

> In those who used to bring to the altar of the fraternity of nations all the bitterness and pain of centuries-old misery and discrimination, there rose the demon of the most intolerant racial separatism. . . . In recent years, it has been possible to observe the alarming phenomenon of the Protestantization of Judaism, its transformation into one of the countless sects that adorn, in such peculiar fashion, the landscape of American religious life with the loud colors of eccentric provincialism.[4]

The New World looked like the old country. Palestine and Petrograd did not.

The Land of Israel stood for unrelenting Apollonianism and for integral, territorial, and outwardly secular Jewish nationalism. The world's most proficient service nomads were to fit into the Age of Universal Mercurianism by becoming Apollonians. The world's strangest nationalism was to transform strangers into natives. The Jews were to find their true selves by no longer acting Jewish.

Soviet Russia stood for the end of all distinctions and the eventual fusion of all things Mercurian and Apollonian: mind and body, town and country, consciousness and spontaneity, stranger and native, time and space, blood and soil. The challenge of the nation-state was to be solved by the abolition of all nations and all states. The Jewish question was to be solved along with all the questions that had ever been asked.

None of the three options was clearcut, of course; none quite lived up to the billing; and each one contained elements of the other two. In the United States, vestigial establishment tribalism was strong enough to slow down the Jewish ascendance; Communism was the principal religion of the young Jewish intellectuals (to be replaced by Zionism after World War II); and Freudianism, brought by the Jews from Central Europe, would help transform *homines rationalistici artificiales* into potentially well-adjusted champions of things natural. In Palestine, socialism (including collective farms, economic planning, and official trade unionism) became an important part of Zionist ideology, and in the presence of genuine—and undeniably native—Arab Apollonians (the "Polacks of the East," as Brenner once called them), the traditional "diaspora" preference for mind over body and consciousness over spontaneity remained just below the surface (and sometimes rose well above). In early Soviet Russia, carefully selected Mercurians were still leading, teaching, or censuring the overly rotund or rectangular Apollonians; the New Economic Policy created enough opportunities for entrepreneurial creativity to lure some émigré businessmen back to Russia; and various efforts to promote a secular Jewish culture and launch Jewish agricultural settlements seemed to recognize the seriousness of the Zionist challenge.[5]

The three options did not just share some important features— they also shared the same set of people. Tevye's crooked son-in-law was equally willing to ship the old man to America or to Palestine. Tsaytl could have joined any one of her three surviving sisters in their new homes. And then there were the four brothers of Anatoly Rybakov's Uncle Misha (the "kind, devil-may-care, courageous, just, and selfless" Red Cavalryman). One was a "speculator, greedy and cunning." Another, "a simple, calm, and delicate man," worked as a truck driver in America. The third, "a visionary and a daydreamer," left for Palestine but came back after his wife's death. And the fourth became a Soviet prosecutor and spent years renouncing his father the shopkeeper (as well as denouncing and sentencing many more people to whom he was not related). Some of them probably could have exchanged places. Ester Markish's father left Baku for Palestine but then liked what he heard about NEP (the New Economic Policy) and came back to Baku. Tsafrira Merom-skaia's Uncle Sima experimented with pioneer life as a settler in Eretz Israel before settling on pioneer life as a construction worker in western Siberia. Feliks Roziner's father was a Zionist in Odessa and a Communist in Palestine before becoming a Communist in the Soviet Union and eventually a Zionist in Israel. My own grand-mother went first to Argentina, then to "Stalin's Zion" in Birobi-dzhan, and finally to Moscow. One of her brothers stayed in Belo-russia; another stayed behind in Argentina (before moving to Israel), a third became a businessman in Warsaw (before being arrested in the Soviet Union), and the fourth became a Mapai and Histadrut official in Israel.[6]

Whatever the similarities or substitutions, however, there is little doubt that each of these three options took Jews as far as they could go in pursuing one particular facet of modern life—or that all three represented radical alternatives to the status of an overachieving minority in underachieving European nation-states.

The United States was the least radical—the only nonrevolution-ary—option. It was the place "where all the hard-luck cases went" (as Tevye put it); where nostalgia for the shtetl was not an absolute taboo; where Yiddish was spoken in city streets; where Tevye and his "kissing cousin" Menachem Mendl could ply their old trades; where Jews went as whole families (and where succeeding genera-tions of young Jews would keep reenacting the great patricidal re-bellion they had missed out on). America was a Utopia where any-one could become a Rothschild or a Brodsky (or perhaps an Einstein), but it was a familiar Utopia, an Odessa minus the tsar and the Cossacks. According to Bromberg, "This enormous, million-strong ghetto of Brooklyn, the Bronx, and the East Side—what is it if not a concentrated and hypertrophied version of Malaia Arnaut-skaia [in Odessa], Podol [in Kiev], and hundreds of obscure provin-cial towns and shtetls? The streets are paved but unprepossessing and unbelievably dirty, while the strong admixture of Italian, Negro, and Greek-Armenian elements serves only to bring back the memory of the old Moldavian, Gypsy, and the same Greek-Armenian proximity."[7]

Palestine and Soviet Russia were real New Worlds—worlds built for a new breed. If Tevye and Menachem Mendl had been compelled to go there, they would have become silent and invisible both in their children's homes and in the public rhetoric of the two movements (with the possible exception of a brief career for Menachem as a NEP speculator). Palestine and Soviet Russia were the centers of apparently victorious Jewish revolutions against God, patriarchy, strangeness, and everything else Tevye stood for. Both were on the cutting edge of the great European rebellion against universal Mercurianism—a rebellion that included a variety of fascist and socialist movements and was led by Mercurians who desperately wanted to become Apollonians (again). Zionism and Bolshevism shared a messianic promise of imminent collective redemption and a more or less miraculous collective transfiguration. As David Ben-Gurion wrote to his wife Paula in 1918, "I did not want to give you a *small, cheap, secular* kind of happiness. I prepared for you the great sacred human joy achieved through *suffering and pain*. . . . Dolorous and in tears you will arise to the high mountain from which one sees vistas of a New World, a world of gladness and light, shining in the glow of an eternally young ideal of supreme happiness and glorious existence, a world only few will be *privileged* to enter, for only rich souls and deep hearts are *permitted* entry there."[8]

The eternally young ideal was to be realized by eternally young idealists. Both Zionism and Bolshevism labored on behalf of the "next generation" and celebrated full-blooded youthful vigor disciplined by work and war. The youngest of the idealists (who were going to inherit the land or the Earth, depending on the location) were trained for both work and war in various young pioneer organizations that promoted group hiking, marching, singing, and exercising. Boys were to turn into young men (the fate of the girls was, in the early days, not entirely clear); young men were to stay young forever by sacrificing themselves for the cause or stopping time altogether. Both Zionism and Bolshevism exalted well-tanned muscular masculinity and either despised old age or willed it out of existence. The most valued qualities were Apollonian (proletarian or Sabra) solidity, firmness, toughness, decisiveness, earnestness, simplicity, inarticulateness, and courage; the most scorned were Mercurian (bourgeois or diaspora) restlessness, changeability, doubt, self-reflexivity, irony, cleverness, eloquence, and cowardice. "Stalin," "Molotov," and "Kamenev" stood for "steel," "hammer," and "rock." Among the most popular names created by early Zionists were Peled ("steel"), Tzur ("rock"), Even/Avni ("stone"), Allon ("oak"), and Eyal ("ram," "strength"). "We are not yeshiva students debating the finer points of self-improvement," said Ben-Gurion in 1922. "We are conquerors of the land facing an iron wall, and we have to break through it." The original leaders were Mercurians transformed by true faith; their disciples were Apollonians endowed with idealism. Their common descendants would be harmonious new men with new names.[9]

War and hard work were supposed to bring all the true believers together, steeling yesterday's Mercurians and tempering youthful Apollonians. War made peaceful labor possible; peaceful labor drained swamps, conquered nature, made deserts bloom, and tempered human steel still further. The need for war and work perpetuated the culture of asceticism and asexuality, which required more war and work in order to reproduce itself (and thus ensure eternal youth and brotherhood). In both Jewish Palestine (the Yishuv) and Soviet Russia, brotherhood stood for the full identity of all true believers (always the few against the many) and their complete identification with the cause (ardently desired and genuinely felt by most young Jews in both places). Eventually, both revolutions evolved in the direction of greater hierarchy, institutionalized militarism, intense anxiety about aliens, and the cult of generals, boy soldiers, and elite forces, but between 1917 and the mid-1930s they were overflowing with youthful energy and the spirit of fraternal effort, achievement, and self-sacrifice.

They were not equal in scale, however (the Zionist emigration was much smaller than the Soviet one), and they were not equal in prestige. Because the Russian Empire was the main source of all three emigrations, the birthplace of most Zionist and Communist heroes, and the cradle of much of modern Jewish mythology, the migrants to the Soviet interior benefited a great deal from linguistic connection and geographic proximity. In Palestine, Russian shirts, boots, and caps were adopted as the uniform of the early settlers; the flowing Cossack forelock developed into one of the most recognizable trademarks of the young Sabra; Russian songs (both revolutionary and folk) provided the melodies and sometimes the lyrics of many Zionist songs; and the Russian literary canon (both classical and socialist-realist) became the single most important inspiration for new Sabra literature. Ben-Gurion's letter to his wife was written in the language of Russian (and Polish) revolutionary messianism.[10]

In the United States, which had no imminent perfection to offer, the memory of Russia—as the world of Pushkin and Populism—shaped the imagination of many first-generation immigrants. In Abraham Cahan's *The Rise of David Levinsky*, one of the characters (Mr. Tevkin, a Hebrew poet and a Zionist) invokes a common cliché when he says:

> Russia is a better country than America, anyhow, even if she is oppressed by a Tsar. It's a freer country, too—for the spirit, at least. There is more poetry there, more music, more feeling, even if our people do suffer appalling persecution. The Russian people are really a warm-hearted people. Besides, one enjoys life in Russia better than here. Oh, a thousand times better. There is too much materialism here, too much hurry and too much prose, and—yes, too much machinery. It's all very well to make shoes or bread by machinery, but alas! the things of the spirit, too, seem to be machine-made in America.[11]

Tevkin lived in a past that had promised a very different future. In the words of Ia. Bromberg,

> Those who visit the Russian room of the New York Public Library can often see these aging men and women with Jewish features leafing through the canonical and apocryphal writings of the prophets of the old revolutionary underground, the pamphlets printed in Geneva and Stuttgart on thin, "smuggled" paper, the *Russian History* by Shishko, and the appeals by the Committee of the People's Will. The incessant

din and clamor of the "intersection of the world" at Fifth Avenue and Forty-second Street seeps in from outside; the multilevel shrines of the modern Babylon peer in with their thousands of lit-up advertisements. But the thoughts of the readers are far away, following their memories to a mysterious secret meeting in the slums of Moldavanka, Pechersk, and Vyborgskaia, or perhaps to a noisy student rally on Mokhovaia and B. Vladimirskaia, or to the years of lonely contemplation in the smoky and bitter warmth of a Yakut encampment lost in the darkness of the polar night. And looking up at them from the pages of revolutionary memoirs are photographs of young men in Tolstoy shirts, with sunken eyes and obstinate lines by their tightly shut, big, loquacious mouths, and of young girls, penniless martyrs with their touching, thin braids tied above their high, pure foreheads.[12]

There was still hope, however. That past might yet become the future, even for those who had never experienced it. For Alfred Kazin,

Socialism would be one long Friday evening around the samovar and the cut-glass bowl laden with nuts and fruits, all of us singing *Tsuzamen, tsuzamen, ale tsuzamen!* Then the heroes of the Russian novel— *our* kind of people—would walk the world, and I—still wearing a circle-necked Russian blouse "*à la Tolstoy*"—would live forever with those I loved in the beautiful Russian country of the mind. Listening to our cousin and her two friends I, who had never seen it, who associated with it nothing but the names of great writers and my father's saying as we went through the Brooklyn Botanic Garden—"Nice! But you should have seen the Czar's summer palace in Tsarskoye-Selo!"— suddenly saw Russia as the grand antithesis to all bourgeois ideals, the spiritual home of all truly free people. I was perfectly sure that there was no literature in the world like the Russian; that the only warm hearts in the world were Russian, like our cousin and her two friends; that other people were always dully materialist, but that the Russian soul, like Nijinsky's dream of pure flight, would always leap outward, past all barriers, to a lyric world in which my ideal socialism and the fiery moodiness of Tchaikovsky's *Pathétique* would be entirely at home with each other.[13]

But of course they already were entirely at home with each other. For most New York Jewish intellectuals of Kazin's generation, socialism had indeed arrived—exactly where it should have. The land of the free in spirit had become the true Land of the Free; the Russian soul had leapt outward to offer salvation to the world; Russia without a tsar had become that country of pure flight led by young men with obstinate lines by their mouths and young girls with touching braids above their foreheads.

Of the three great Jewish destinations of the first quarter of the twentieth century, one was an actually existing Promised Land. America was a compromise and the promise of a fulfilled Mercurianism; the Jewish state in Palestine was a dream of a handful of idealists; but Soviet Russia was a dream come true, which offered hope and a second home to young American Jews and inspiration (and a possible alternative destination) to Zionist pioneers. In Soviet Russia, young Jews had, in fact, grabbed the "rings attached to heaven and earth" and pulled heaven down to earth (as Babel put it).

Even the enemies of the victorious Jewish Bolsheviks seemed to admit their primacy. In Jabotinsky's *The Five*, a successful Odessa grain merchant's family has the requisite five children. Marusia was born for love and warmth but dies in flames, like a moth; Marko, the dreamer, drowns senselessly in an attempt to save a Russian who does not need or want to be saved; Serezha, the prankster, is blinded by acid; Torik, the careerist, converts to Christianity and disappears without a trace. Only Lika, the Bolshevik and Cheka executioner, is alive and well at the end of the novel. Many young Jewish intellectuals of the 1920s and 1930s disagreed with Jabotinsky's indictment of the revolution: as far as they were concerned, it was Marko, Marusia, and maybe even Serezha (duly "reforged" and reeducated) who had, along with Lika (having first shipped Torik to America), risen to positions of power in Soviet Russia. More important, however, they saw nothing wrong with Lika the Cheka executioner because Lika was both "necessary" and righteous—accepting as she did "personal responsibility" for the pure violence of the socialist revolution. Such was the official view of early Soviet literature and the more or less official view of the non-Soviet Jewish intellectuals.

As Walter Benjamin—with glasses on his nose, autumn in his soul, and vicarious murder in his heart—wrote in 1921, "If the rule of myth is broken occasionally in the present age, the coming age is not so unimaginably remote that an attack on law is altogether futile. But if the existence of violence outside the law, as pure immediate violence, is assured, this furnishes proof that revolutionary violence, the highest manifestation of unalloyed violence by man, is possible, and shows by what means." Over the next fifteen years, Benjamin would become much more direct in his admiration for Lika and her violent religion (he called it a "critique of violence"). He kept planning to go to Jerusalem but traveled to Moscow instead (on a brief excursion: the actual goose killing was Lika's job).[14]

Of the three Jewish utopias, one was in power. Many Jews who did not go to Moscow wished they had. Most young Jews who did go to Moscow pitied or despised those who had not. Roziner's father came back from Palestine and named his son Feliks (after the founder of the Soviet secret police). Agursky's father came back from America and named his son Melib (Marx-Engels-Liebknecht). Mikhail Baitalsky moved from Odessa to Moscow and named his son Vil (Vladimir Ilich Lenin). My great-aunt Bella arrived from Poland and named her son Marlen (Marx-Lenin). The mothers of two of my closest friends (second-generation Muscovites of "Jewish nationality") are named Lenina and Ninel ("Lenin" read backward). Such was the Hebrew of the international proletariat—the true language of paradise.[15]

The journey from the former Pale of Settlement to Moscow and Leningrad was not any less of a migration than the voyage from Odessa to Palestine or from Petrograd to New York. It could take as long and, during the first postrevolutionary years, it might be much more hazardous. Born of revolution, it involved large numbers of people, resulted in a near miraculous transformation, and constituted one of the most important, and least noticed, landmarks in the history of Russia, European Jews, and the Modern Age.

In 1912, the Jewish population of Moscow was about 15,353, or less than 1 percent of the total. By 1926, it had grown to 131,000, or 6.5 percent of the total. About 90 percent of the migrants were under fifty years old, and about one-third were in their twenties. By 1939, Moscow's Jewish population had reached a quarter of a million (about 6 percent of the total and the second largest ethnic group in the city). In Leningrad, the number of Jews grew from 35,000 (1.8 percent) in 1910, to 84,603 (5.2 percent) in 1926, to 201,542 (6.3 percent) in 1939 (also, by a considerable margin, the second largest ethnic group in the city). The numbers for Kharkov are 11,013 (6.3 percent) in 1897; 81,138 (19 percent) in 1926; and 130,250 (15.6 percent) in 1939. Finally, Kiev (in the old Pale of Settlement) had 32,093 (13 percent) in 1897; 140,256 (27.3 percent) in 1926, and 224,236 (26.5 percent) in 1939. On the eve of World War II, 1,300,000 Jews were living in areas that had been closed to them a quarter of a century earlier. More than one million of them, according to Mordechai Altshuler, "were first-generation immigrants in their places of residence outside the former Pale of Settlement."[16]

By 1939, 86.9 percent of all Soviet Jews lived in urban areas, about half of them in the eleven largest cities of the USSR. Almost one-third of all urban Jews resided in the four capitals: Moscow and Leningrad in Russia and Kiev and Kharkov in Ukraine. Nearly 60 percent of the Jewish population of Moscow and Leningrad were between the ages of 20 and 50.[17] In the words (1927) of the Soviet Yiddish poet Izi Kharik,

> So here is a list of all those
> Who have lately departed for Moscow:
> Four shopkeepers, a ritual butcher,
> Eight girls who are going to college,
> A few melameds, and twelve youngsters
> Who went there in search of employment;
> Fat Doba with all of her children,
> Who followed her husband, the tailor,

And Beilke, whose husband, a Gentile,
Is at the Academy there,
And Berele, the wheeler-dealer,
Who seems to have been there forever;
Oh yes—and the good old rabbi,
He, too, has now traveled to Moscow
And brought back all sorts of fine presents,
And has carried on for a year
About the wonders of Moscow,
Where life is so good for the Jews.

.   .   .   .

And everyone's eager to tell you
How wonderful life is in Moscow.[18]

Some of the immigrants engaged in traditional Mercurian trades. The near-total destruction of the prerevolutionary entrepreneurial class and the introduction of NEP in 1921 created extraordinary new opportunities for the four shopkeepers and Fat Doba's husband the tailor, among others. In 1926, Jews constituted 1.8 percent of the Soviet population and 20 percent of all private traders (66 percent in Ukraine and 90 percent, in Belorussia). In Petrograd (in 1923), the share of private entrepreneurs employing hired labor was 5.8 times higher among Jews than in the rest of the population. In 1924 in Moscow, Jewish "Nepmen" owned 75.4 percent of all drugstores, 54.6 percent of all fabric stores, 48.6 percent of all jewelry stores, 39.4 percent of all dry goods stores, 36 percent of all lumber warehouses, 26.3 percent of all shoe stores, 19.4 percent of all furniture stores, 17.7 percent of all tobacco shops, and 14.5 percent of all clothing stores. The new "Soviet bourgeoisie" was Jewish to a very considerable extent. At the bottom of the "Nepman" category, Jews made up 40 percent of all Soviet artisans (35 percent of Leningrad tailors, for example); at the top, they constituted 33 percent of the wealthiest Moscow entrepreneurs (the holders of the two highest categories of trading and industrial licenses). Twenty-five percent of all Jewish entrepreneurs in Moscow belonged to this group (as compared to 8 percent for the city's non-Jewish Nepmen).[19]

The Jewish preeminence in the NEP economy was reflected in their prominence in NEP-era representations of "bourgeois danger." Soviet literature of the 1920s contained a substantial number of loathsome Jewish smugglers, speculators, and seducers of Komsomol girls. One of them was V. Kirshon's and A. Uspensky's Solomon Rubin (in *The Korenkov Affair*), who claimed to be "like a wart: you burn me with acid in one place, and I pop up in another." Another was Sergei Malashkin's Isaika Chuzhachok ("Little Isaiah the Outsider"), who was "small, feeble of body and countenance, and with only three prominent adornments on his spindle-like face: a big red nose; large, yellow fangs; and a pair of beady eyes the color of coffee dregs that, despite Little Isaiah's extraordinary mercuriality, appeared blank and lifeless." Ultimately, however, the Soviet "bourgeois" never became identified with the Jew. The class enemies of NEP-era demonology were primarily Russian peasants ("kulaks"), Russian shopkeepers (*lavochniki*), and Russian Orthodox priests, as well as the largely cosmopolitan pusillanimous "philistines" and foreign capitalists. (In the revised version of *The Korenkov Affair*, known as *Konstantin Terekhin*, the Jewish Nepman Solomon Rubin becomes the anti-Semitic Nepman Petr Lukich Panfilov.) Overall, the proportion of Jews among poster Nepmen seems to have been much lower than the proportion of Jews among real-life Soviet entrepreneurs, and many of the pointedly Jewish fictional capitalists had Bolshevik opposite numbers who were pointedly Jewish themselves. Matvei Roizman's grotesquely devious Aron Solomonovich Fishbein is confronted by the poor blacksmith and workers' faculty student Rabinovich, who moves into his house. More canonically, Boris Levin's war profiteer Morits Gamburg, who "speculated in flour, cloth, shoes, sugar, gramophone needles—anything at all," was renounced by his own son, the sensitive Sergei.

> Sergei Gamburg did not like his parents. . . . He was disgusted by the way his parents were trying to weasel their way into the aristocracy. . . . They had the same lampshade in their house as the Sineokovs. His father had his books, which he never read, rebound to match the new silk upholstery in his office. A grand piano appeared

in the living room, even though no one ever played it. His sister Ida had no musical talent at all, but her music teacher came regularly. . . . They bought a Great Dane the size of a calf. His mother and father, and everyone else in the house, were afraid of that huge dog with its human eyes. . . . They had "Tuesdays" and invited a select company. Sergei knew perfectly well that people came to their place for the food. . . . When his mother said "cucklets," Sergei would wince and correct her, without looking up: "cutlets."

Finally, Sergei resolves to leave home. " 'Speculators,' he thinks of them with revulsion, 'bribe takers, scoundrels.' " His parents' pathetic attempts to stop him cause him to explode.

"You're disgusting," said Sergei through clenched teeth and in a terrible rage. "Do you understand—disgusting. I hate you!" he said as he pushed his father away and jerked at the doorknob.

"Serezha! Sergei! Think about what you are saying!" implored his mother, grabbing him by the sleeve of his trench coat.

"Let him go to hell! To hell! To hell!" screamed his father.

His sister Ida came rushing in, wearing a Ukrainian dress with lots of ribbons. Mimicking and gesticulating, as if she were out of breath, she kept pointing toward her room. This meant: "Quiet, for God's sake, I have people over, and they can hear everything."

Sergei slammed the door behind him, rattling the pink cups in the buffet.[20]

The Jewish Revolution—or violent family romance—was as much a part of NEP and Stalin's Great Transformation as it had been of the Russian revolutionary movement, the Bolshevik takeover, or the civil war. No tsarist decree had condemned Tevye's religion and livelihood as uncompromisingly as might his daughter Hodl—in her new capacity as writer, scholar, or Party official. Kirshon, Roizman, and Levin were all Jews (as well as proletarian writers), and even Malashkin's anti-Semitic book was reportedly much admired by one of the most influential Jews in the Soviet Union, Molotov's wife Polina Zhemchuzhina (Perl Karpovskaia). When NEP came to an end and all remaining private entrepreneurs—with Jewish "fathers" prominent among them—were being hounded, robbed, arrested, and kicked out of their homes, most of the OGPU officials in charge of the operation (including the head of the "hard currency" department of the OGPU Economic Affairs Directorate, Mark Isaevich Gai [Shtokliand]) were Jews themselves. By 1934, when the OGPU was transformed into the NKVD, Jews "by nationality" constituted the largest single group among the "leading cadres" of the Soviet secret police (37 Jews, 30 Russians, 7 Latvians, 5 Ukrainians, 4 Poles, 3 Georgians, 3 Belorussians, 2 Germans, and 5 assorted others). Twelve key NKVD departments and directorates, including those in charge of the police (worker-peasant militia), labor camps (Gulag), counterintelligence, surveillance, and economic wrecking were headed by Jews, all but two of them immigrants from the former Pale of Settlement. The people's commissar of internal affairs was Genrikh Grigorevich (Enokh Gershenovich) Yagoda.[21]

Of the many Russian revolutions, the Jewish version was (by 1934) one of the most implacable and most successful. Yagoda's father had been a goldsmith (or, according to some sources, a pharmacist, engraver, or watchmaker). Ester Markish's father, who had been a wealthy merchant, was tortured in prison by a man named Varnovitsky, currently the head of the "gold expropriation" campaign in Ekaterinoslav and formerly Perets Markish's classmate and fellow Yiddish poet in Berdichev. The Cheka agent Khaim Polisar did not "surprise or offend" any of his Komsomol friends (according to Mikhail Baitalsky, who was one of them) when he confiscated his own father's hardware store. And, of course, Eduard Bagritsky, who publicly renounced his "hunchbacked and gnarled" Jewish parents, was the most popular of all the "Komsomol poets." Mikhail (Melib) Agursky, Anatoly Rybakov, and Tsafrira Meromskaia all had grandparents who were classified as *lishentsy* (persons subject to official discrimination in politics, education, employment, and housing on account of their "class alien" origins or occupations), yet all of them (like Ester Markish, the daughter of a *lishenets*) were proud and privileged members of the Soviet elite. As V. G. Tan-Bogoraz (a former Jewish rebel and a prominent Soviet anthropologist) put it,

In Rogachev, the grandfathers are Talmudists, the sons are Communists, and the grandsons are *tref*—not purified by Jewish circumcision. And so a grandfather smuggles such uncircumcised contraband into the synagogue with him and seats him on a table, next to a huge volume in a leather binding that smells of mice and decay.

"What are you going to be when you grow up, Berka?" To which Berka responds with much deliberation and self-importance: "First of all, my name is not Berka but Lentrozin [Lenin-Trotsky-Zinoviev], and as for what I am going to be—I am going to be a Chekist."[22]

There was little to prevent young Berka from realizing his dream (once he had dropped "Lentrozin" to become Boris), and nothing at all to keep him from leaving Rogachev for Moscow or Leningrad. There, chances are, he would have gone to school—and done very well. The Jews were, consistently and by a substantial margin, the most literate group in the Soviet Union (85 percent, as compared to 58 percent for Russians, in 1926; and 94.3 percent, as compared to 83.4 percent for Russians, in 1939). Relatively free access to public education, coupled with the destruction of the prerevolutionary Russian elite and the relentless official discrimination against their children, created unprecedented opportunities (by any standard anywhere) for Jewish immigrants to Soviet cities. Of the two traditional Jewish pursuits—wealth and learning—one led into the NEP trap. The other, also facilitated by the absence of well-prepared competitors, was the ticket to success in Soviet society. Most Jewish migrants, and almost all the young ones, chose the latter.[23]

By 1939, 26.5 percent of all Jews had had a high school education (as compared to 7.8 percent of the population for the Soviet Union as a whole and 8.1 percent of Russians in the Russian Federation). In Leningrad, the proportion of high school graduates among Jews was 40.2 percent (as compared to 28.6 percent for the city as a whole). The number of Jewish students in the two upper grades of Soviet high schools was more than 3.5 times their share in the general population. Education was one of the top priorities of a Marxist regime that came to power in a country it considered "backward" and in a manner it described as inverted. The mission of the Soviet state ("superstructure") was to create the economic preconditions ("base") that were supposed to have brought it into existence. Forced industrialization was deemed the only way to correct history's mistake; mass education of the "conscious elements" was viewed as the key to successful industrialization; the Jews were seen as the most educated among the conscious and the most conscious among the educated. For the first twenty years of the regime's existence, the connection seemed to hold.[24]

Between 1928 and 1939, the number of university students in the Soviet Union increased more than fivefold (from 167,000 to 888,000). The Jews could not quite keep up—not only because there was a limit on how many students a small ethnic group (1.8 percent of the population) could provide, but also because many of them were not eligible for the preparatory "workers' departments" that the regime was using as an important tool of upward mobility, and because various "affirmative action" programs in the non-Russian republics included preferential admissions for "indigenous" nationalities, as a result of which, for example, the Jewish share of all university students in Ukraine fell from 47.4 percent in 1923/24 to 23.3 percent in 1929/30. Still, Jewish performance was second to none. In the ten years between 1929 and 1939, the number of Jewish university students quadrupled from 22,518 to 98,216 (11.1 percent of the total). In 1939, Jews made up 17.1 percent of all university students in Moscow, 19 percent in Leningrad, 24.6 percent in Kharkov, and 35.6 percent in Kiev. The share of college graduates among Jews (6 percent) was ten times the rate for the general population (0.6 percent) and three times the rate for the urban population (2 percent). Jews constituted 15.5 percent of all Soviet citizens with higher education; in absolute terms, they were second to the Russians and ahead of the Ukrainians. One-third of all Soviet Jews of college age (19 to 24 years old) were college students. The corresponding figure for the Soviet Union as a whole was between 4 and 5 percent.[25]

The most striking consequence of the migration of Jews to Soviet cities was their transformation into white-collar state employees. As early as 1923, 44.3 percent of Moscow Jews and 30.5 percent of Leningrad Jews belonged to that category. In 1926, the white-collar share of all employed Jews was 50.1 percent in Moscow and 40.2

percent in Leningrad (compared to 38.15 and 27.7 percent for non-Jews). By 1939, these percentages had reached 82.5 percent in Moscow and 63.2 percent in Leningrad. From the inception of the Soviet regime, the unique combination of exceptionally high literacy rates and a remarkable degree of political loyalty ("consciousness") had made Jews the backbone of the new Soviet bureaucracy. The Party considered old tsarist officials—and indeed all non-Bolsheviks educated before the revolution—to be irredeemably untrustworthy. They had to be used (as "bourgeois experts") for as long as they remained irreplaceable; they were to be purged (as "socially alien elements") as soon as they became expendable. The best candidates for replacing them (while the proletarians were "mastering knowledge") were Jews—the only members of the literate classes not compromised by service to the tsarist state (since it had been forbidden them).[26] As Lenin put it, "The fact that there were many Jewish intelligentsia members in the Russian cities was of great importance to the revolution. They put an end to the general sabotage that we were confronted with after the October Revolution. . . . The Jewish elements were mobilized . . . and thus saved the revolution at a difficult time. It was only thanks to this pool of a rational and literate labor force that we succeeded in taking over the state apparatus."[27]

The Soviet state urgently needed new professionals, as well as officials. Jews—especially young Jews from the former Pale—answered the call. In 1939 in Leningrad, Jews made up 69.4 percent of all dentists; 58.6 percent of all pharmacists; 45 percent of all defense lawyers; 38.6 percent of all doctors; 34.7 percent of all legal consultants; 31.3 percent of all writers, journalists, and editors; 24.6 percent of all musicians; 18.5 percent of all librarians; 18.4 percent of all scientists and university professors; 11.7 percent of all artists; and 11.6 percent of all actors and directors. In Moscow, the numbers were very similar.[28]

The higher one looks in the status hierarchy, the greater the Jewish share. In 1936/37, Jewish students made up 4.8 percent of all Moscow schoolchildren in grades one through four, 6.7 percent in grades five through seven, and 13.4 percent in grades eight through ten. Among university students, their proportion (in 1939) was

17.1 percent, and among university graduates 23.9 percent. Three percent of all Soviet nurses and 19.6 percent of all physicians in 1939 were Jews. In Leningrad, Jews constituted 14.4 percent of all store clerks and 30.9 percent of all store managers. In the Soviet Army in 1926, the proportion of Jews in military academies (8.8 percent) was almost twice their share of Soviet commanders (4.6 percent) and four times their share of all servicemen (2.1 percent). In the Russian Republic in 1939, Jews made up 1.8 percent of all schoolteachers and 14.1 percent of all researchers and university professors (the corresponding figures for Belorussia and Ukraine were 12.3 and 32.7 percent; and 8 and 28.6 percent).[29]

It was at the very top of the Moscow and Leningrad cultural elite that the Jewish presence was particularly strong and—by definition—visible. Jews stood out among avant-garde artists (Natan Altman, Marc Chagall, Naum Gabo, Moisei Ginzburg, El Lissitzky, Anton Pevsner, David Shterenberg); formalist theorists (Osip Brik, Boris Eikhenbaum, Roman Jakobson, Boris Kushner, Viktor Shklovsky, Yuri Tynianov); "proletarian" polemicists (Leopold Averbakh, Yakov Elsberg, Aleksandr Isbakh, Vladimir Kirshon, Grigory Lelevich, Yuri Libedinsky); innovative moviemakers (Fridrikh Ermler, Iosif Kheifits, Grigorii Kozintsev, Grigorii Roshal, Leonid Trauberg, Dziga Vertov, Aleksandr Zarkhi); and Komsomol poets (Eduard Bagritsky, Aleksandr Bezymensky, Mikhail Golodnyi, Mikhail Svetlov, Iosif Utkin).

Jews were prominent among the most exuberant crusaders against "bourgeois" habits during the Great Transformation; the most disciplined advocates of socialist realism during the "Great Retreat" (from revolutionary internationalism); and the most passionate prophets of faith, hope, and combat during the Great Patriotic War against the Nazis (some of them were the same people). When the Society of Militant Materialist Dialecticians was founded in 1929, 53.8 percent of the founding members (7 out of 13) were Jews; and when the Communist Academy held its plenary session in June 1930, Jews constituted one-half (23) of all the elected full and corresponding members. At the First Congress of Soviet Writers in 1934, Jews made up 19.4 percent of all delegates (behind the Russians with 34.5 percent and ahead of the Georgians with 4.8

percent and the Ukrainians with 4.3 percent), and 32.6 percent of the Moscow delegation. Between 1935 and 1940, 34.8 percent of all new members of the Moscow branch of the Writers' Union were Jews (85 out of 244). Most of the popular Soviet mass songs were written and performed by immigrants from the former Pale of Settlement, and when the time came to identify the victorious revolution with the classical musical canon, the overwhelming majority of the performers were Jewish musicians trained by Jewish teachers (45 percent of all teachers at Moscow and Leningrad conservatories appointed in the 1920s were Jews). The Soviet Union competed against the capitalist world in every aspect of life, but before its athletes began to participate in international competitions in the 1940s, there were only two spheres in which the land of socialism confronted the "bourgeois world" directly, openly, and according to conventional rules: chess and classical music. Both were almost entirely Jewish specialties, and both produced some of the most celebrated and highly rewarded public icons of the 1930s, among them the future chess world champion Mikhail Botvinnik and a whole pantheon of Soviet music laureates including David Oistrakh, Emil Gilels, Boris Goldstein, and Mikhail Fikhtengolts.[30]

And then there was war. The Spanish civil war was narrated for Soviet citizens by the country's most famous journalist, Mikhail Koltsov (Fridliand), and conducted on their behalf by some of the country's best secret agents and diplomats, most of them Jews. During the war against the Nazis, the Soviet regime spoke with two voices: the mouthpiece of Russia's rage and revenge was Ilya Ehrenburg (Stalin's main cultural ambassador), while the sublime baritone of the socialist state belonged to Yuri Levitan (Soviet radio's official announcer). At least 40 percent of Moscow writers killed during the war were Jews. One of them was my maternal grandfather, Moisei Khatskelevich Goldstein, an immigrant from Poland by way of Argentina, who wrote to my ten-year-old mother in February 1943: "On the 25th anniversary of the glorious Red Army, in whose ranks I now serve, my wish is that you do well in school, as the great Party of Lenin-Stalin demands." A month later, shortly before his death, he wrote, in imperfect Russian, to my grandmother:

It is hard to imagine the suffering of the people who were under the German occupation. For millennia to come, people will tell stories and sing songs about the suffering of the Russian woman. Her husband has been killed, her children taken away, her house burnt down, and yet there she stands, amid the ruins of her house, like a monument, a living image of the will to live. She lives, and will live on.[31]

———————

Some of the Jewish members of the Soviet cultural elite were old rebels like Tevye's Hodl, F. A. Moreinis-Muratova, and V. G. Tan-Bogoraz, who left their blind fathers to fight the tsar and came of revolutionary age in the underground world of terrorist conspiracies, reading circles, Party conferences, and Siberian exile. A few of them would remain active "builders of socialism" into the 1930s, but all would be forever "old" by virtue of being the living progenitors and dutiful memoirists of the socialist revolution.

Some—like Natan Altman, El Lissitzky, and David Shterenberg—joined the revolution through the back door of the avantgarde and went on to paint its facade during the early years of poster messianism, and then again during Stalin's Great Transformation.

Some, like "Hope" Ulanovskaia, Eduard Bagritsky, or Babel's Elijah Bratslavsky, renounced their parents to become children of the civil war. Their revolution stood for the cavalry attacks, bandits' bullets, and campfire brotherhood of the last and decisive battle against the old "world of violence" (to quote the "Internationale"). The most faithful chronicler of that generation and the author of two of its greatest anthems—"Granada" (about a Ukrainian boy who died for the happiness of poor peasants in faraway Spain) and "Kakhovka" (about "our girl in a trench coat" who walked through a burning town to "the machine gun's even roll")—was Mikhail Svetlov (Sheinkman). As a little Jewish boy in Ekaterinoslav, he used to be frightened of his rabbi's morbid tales—but not anymore.

> Now I wear a leather jacket,
> Now I'm tall—and the rabbi is small.

He is ready—"if necessary"—to burn down the old temple, and he looks forward to a fiery apocalypse "when the old rabbi dies under the collapsed wall of his synagogue." The death of the rabbi signals the birth of the Bolshevik.

> The red flag overhead,
> The flashing bayonet,
> The armored car.
> This was the dawn of the holy day
> The Bolshevik was born.
>
> .   .   .   .
>
> I stand before my Republic,
> I have come from the distant South.
> I have placed all my weakness—truly—
> Under arrest.

The participants in the battle would carry the memory of that day—and the hope of its reenactment, over and over again—for as long as they lived. Few of them lived as long as Svetlov (who died, his youth "aged" but not used up, in 1964), but none of them—Chekist or poet (they made no such distinctions themselves)—would ever grow old. The son of a Jewish artisan from Zhitomir, author of the official Komsomol song ("The Young Guard," 1922), and one of the Party's most uncompromising crusaders against old age and degenerate art, Aleksandr Bezymensky wore his Komsomol badge until his death at seventy-five. He did not need to wear it: "My very old mother, who is but a speck / In our struggle, / Cannot understand that my Party card / Is a part of me." Nor did he need to die:

> People! Sharpen your swords and knives!
> People! Wouldn't you rather
> Live forever?
> These are the thieves of your lives:
> Sleep and death.
> Death to both![32]

And then there were those—"the younger brothers"—who were raised by the Komsomol of the 1920s to "besiege the fortresses" of the First Five-Year Plan. Too young to have fought in the civil war and too "young at heart" to live in peace under NEP, they battled vulgarity, cupidity, mediocrity, inequality, patriarchy, and, above all, "philistinism." As one of them, Lev Kopelev, described the evil they were up against,

NEP stood for private stores and small shops stocked much more abundantly and decorated much more colorfully than the drab workers' cooperatives; dolled-up men and women in restaurants, where bands blared through the night, and in the casinos, where roulette wheels spun and dealers screamed "The Bets are down!"; girls with bright lipstick in short dresses who walked the streets at night accosting single men or laughing shrilly in cabs.

NEP stood for farmers' markets swarming with dirty, brightly colored crowds: kulak carts drawn by overfed horses, loud women hawking their goods, unctuous speculators, and ragged street children black with dirt.

NEP stood for newspaper reports about village correspondents killed by kulaks; trials of embezzlers, bribe-takers, and quacks; satirical stories about moral corruption, settling-down, and formerly honest Communist lads from the working class becoming bureaucrats and time-servers sucked in by the swamp of philistinism.[33]

To keep their faith amid corruption and imperfection, Party and Komsomol members had to continuously cleanse themselves of impure thoughts—while the Party and Komsomol continuously cleansed their ranks of impure members. Baitalsky's Komsomol comrade Eve (who bore him a son they named Vil, and whom he never formally married because it would have been a philistine thing to do) was the daughter of a poor shtetl tailor.

Everything she did, every step she took, Eve dedicated to the revolution. Every single moment was lived with enthusiasm, whether it was volunteer work unloading coal at the port or the study of Russian grammar in a workers' club. Having been unable to attend school as a child, she took up the study of grammar late in life, but in the firm conviction that she was doing it not for herself, but for the proletarian revolution. Looking back at my own life and that of my companion, I can see: most of Eve's actions were like solemn religious performances.[34]

Hope for universal redemption depended on personal righteousness and on the imminent triumph of the revolution. When, after the murder of Kirov, all deviationists had to be purged, Eve banished Baitalsky (a onetime Left Oppositionist) from her house. When, in 1927, war seemed imminent, Mikhail Svetlov looked forward to "marching westward" again ("The Soviet bullets / Will fly like before . . . / Comrade commander, / Open the door!"). And when, in 1929, the final offensive against the countryside was getting underway, he—ever the voice of Komsomol activism—asked for his civil war wound to be opened so that the old bullet lodged in his flesh might be reused. "The steppes are ablaze, my friend, / My lead is needed again!"[35]

They got their wish. The veterans of the civil war and the "Komsomols of the 1920s" were in the forefront of the great battles of the First Five-Year Plan. They vanquished the unctuous shopkeepers, "reforged" the shrill streetwalkers, purged the morally corrupt, and "liquidated the kulaks as a class." It was a time to be firm: according to Kopelev—who took part in the confiscation of peasant property in Ukraine, witnessed the famine that followed, and attempted to reconstruct, many years later, the way he had felt then—"You mustn't give in to debilitating pity. We are the agents of historical necessity. We are fulfilling our revolutionary duty. We are procuring grain for our socialist Fatherland. For the Five-Year Plan." For Kopelev, and for most Jewish and non-Jewish members of the new Soviet intelligentsia, it was a time of revolutionary enthusiasm, self-sacrificial work, genuine comraderie, and messianic expectation. It was the eagerly anticipated reenactment of the civil war that provided those who had missed the revolution with their own "rebellious youth"—a youth that was meant to last forever (and, in many cases, did).[36]

Finally, there were the members of the Moscow and Leningrad elite born in the 1920s, when the erstwhile revolutionaries got around to starting their own families. Children of the new regime—Hodl's children—they were the first postrevolutionary generation, the first fully Soviet generation, the first generation that did not rebel against their parents (because their parents had done it once and for all). Most of them grew up in downtown Moscow and Leningrad and went to the best Soviet schools (usually housed in former *gymnasia* or aristocratic mansions). The proportion of Jews among them was particularly high, probably higher than among previous cohorts. As Tsafrira Meromskaia wrote, using the sarcasm and categories of another age,

> Our school was in the center of the city [Moscow], where the privileged classes of the classless society lived, so the children were of a certain kind too. As for the national composition of the student body, the "Jewish lobby" was absolutely dominant. All those Nina Millers, Liusia Pevzners, Busia Frumsons, Rita Pinsons, as well as Boria Fuks and company, overshadowed in every way the occasional Ivan Mukhin or Natasha Dugina. This elite studied with brilliance and ease, setting the tone for all activities without exception.[37]

They went to theaters, read the nineteenth-century classics, and spent summers at dachas or on the Black Sea in ways that recalled those nineteenth-century classics. Many of them had peasant nannies who, in later memoirs, would become faithful reflections of the old revolutionaries' peasant nannies (and ultimately of Pushkin's Arina, the immortal prototype of all peasant nannies). Inna Gaister, whose father was an immigrant from the Pale and a prominent theorist of collectivization, was raised by Natasha Sidorina from the village of Karaulovo outside of Riazan. Raisa Orlova (who lived on Gorky Street not far from Meromskaia and the Bagritskys, and across the river from Gaister's "House of Government") had a nanny who liked an occasional shot of vodka and worshiped her good-natured and simple-hearted peasant God.

> Actually, there were two gods rather than one in my childhood. My very old grandmother—my mother's mother—also lived in our apartment. She slept in a small room off the entryway, and I always picture her lying in bed. . . . Her room was stuffy, foul-smelling, and for some reason frightening. Grandmother would tell me about her God and about the Bible. Grandmother's God—unlike Nanny's—was mean,

and was always throwing rocks and fighting wars. For the longest time, those rocks would remain my only memory of the Bible. Perhaps that was because Nanny and Grandmother kept feuding with each other, and I was always on Nanny's side.[38]

Orlova's grandmother was indistinguishable from Babel's and Mandelstam's. Her mother asked to hear Pushkin on her deathbed. Her nanny's name was Arina.

Pushkin Street stretched from the dark rooms of the old Pale to the center of both Russia and the Soviet Union (in the late 1930s, three-quarters of all Leningrad Jews lived in the seven central districts of the old imperial capital). Hodl's children grew up speaking the language of Pushkin and the language of revolution. They spoke both natively, and they spoke them more fluently and with greater conviction than anyone else. They were the core of the first generation of postrevolutionary intelligentsia—the most important and most influential generation in the history of the Soviet cultural elite. They considered themselves the true heirs of Great Russian Literature and the Great Socialist Revolution at the same time. As Baitalsky put it, "we inherited the moral ideals of all the generations of the Russian revolutionary intelligentsia: its nonconformity, its love of truth, its moral sense." And as the same Baitalsky put it a few pages later, "we all prepared ourselves to be agitation and propaganda officials." Only those of them who died during World War II succeeded in creating a sublime blend of the two. The survivors would have to choose.[39]

But back in the 1930s, when they were young and, by most accounts, happy, their greatest challenge was to discover a language worthy of paradise. As one of Raisa Orlova's classmates (Anna Mlynek) said in a famous—and apparently deeply felt and passionately received—speech at a nationwide high school graduation ceremony in 1935,

> Comrades, it is difficult to speak today, but there is so much I would like to say, so much that needs to be said. One searches for the right words to respond to our dear older comrades, the right words that would express the feelings that fill our hearts—but what words would do our lives justice? . . .

The highest mountain on earth—Mount Stalin—has been conquered by our country. The best subway in the world is our subway. The highest sky in the world is our sky: it has been raised by our aviators. The deepest sea is our sea: it has been deepened by our divers. In our country, people fly, run, study, draw, and play faster, farther, and better than anyone else in the world! . . .

That is what is expected of us—the first generation produced by the revolution.[40]

In the second half of the 1930s, the most prestigious Soviet university was the Institute of History, Philosophy, and Literature (IFLI), headed by R. S. Zemliachka's sister A. S. Karpova (Zalkind) and known as the "Communist Lycée" (by analogy with the aristocratic Tsarskoe Selo Lycée, attended by Pushkin and forever associated with joyous creativity, lifelong friendships, auspicious beginnings, and, above all, poetry). IFLI had all of those things in great abundance. According to Orlova's recollections, "The cult of friendship reigned supreme. We had our special language, our Masonic signs, and a very strong sense of belonging. Friendships were formed overnight and lasted a long time. And even now [1961–79], whatever the moats and precipices that divide some of us, I find myself saying: 'God help you, dear friends.' "[41]

The quotation is, of course, from Pushkin. The most popular IFLI teachers (Abram Belkin, Mikhail Lifshits, and Leonid Pinsky) were professors of literature, and the most charismatic students (also predominantly Jewish) were poets, critics, and journalists. As Kopelev wrote about Belkin, "he did not just love Dostoevsky—he professed Dostoevsky's work as a religious doctrine." And as David Samoilov wrote about Pinsky, "in the old days he would have become a famous rabbi somewhere in Hasidic Ukraine, a saint and an object of worship. In fact, we worshiped him too. He was a great authority, a famous interpreter of texts." But it was not their professors that the IFLI poets worshiped—it was their "age," their youth, their generation, their fraternity, and their art.

We would talk until we were hoarse and recite poetry until we were blue in the face. We would sit around long past midnight. I remember how I ran out of cigarettes once, around two in the morning. We walked about five kilometers through the city, to an all-night store near Mayakovsky Square. Then we walked back and continued our argument in the haze of tobacco smoke.[42]

Many of these boys and girls were the unself-conscious children of Jewish immigrants living the life of the Russian intelligentsia—*being* the Russian intelligentsia. They were not concerned about where their parents had come from because they knew themselves to be the descendants of the Russian intelligentsia, the true heirs of the sacred fraternity that their parents had joined, helped destroy, and then—unwittingly—labored to reconstitute. At IFLI, the uncontested prophet of "the generation" was Pavel Kogan, the author of one of the most popular and durable Soviet songs ever written: "The Brigantine."

> I am sick of arguing and sitting,
> And of loving faces wan and pale . . .
> Somewhere in a distant pirate city
> A brigantine's about to set sail . . .
>
> The old captain, windswept like a sea rock
> Lifted anchor, leaving us behind.
> Let us say farewell, and wish him true luck
> Raising glasses filled with golden wine.
>
> Let us drink to the pirates and strangers
> Who despise the cheap comforts of home,
> Let us drink to the proud Jolly Roger,
> Flapping fearlessly over the foam.

The revolution was over; the captain had sailed away; and the poet's peers had matured along with their country. But of course the revolution was not over, and the poet's peers had not matured any more than had their country—where, according to Kogan, "even in the winter, it was forever spring." Stalin's Russia was a land of perpetual bloom, youth, and warmth (such was the reality of "socialist realism"), the land of "roads through eternity" and "bridges over time." For the eternally young, there were always wars to wage—

> In the name of our fierce adolescence,
> In the name of the planet we've wrested
> From the plague,
> From the blood,
> From the winter
> And from obtuseness.
> In the name of the War of 1945,
> In the name of the Chekist stock.
> In
> The name!

This was written in 1939, when Kogan was twenty-one years old and the war was two (not six) years away. Kogan's comrades were going to be worthy of their Chekist predecessors because they came from the same stock and wielded the same wedge against the same "obtuseness" and "cheap comforts." Kogan's most famous lines were these: "I've never loved the oval, / I'm keen on sketching angles." His "age" was ultimately the same as Bagritsky's: "awaiting you out in the yard" and demanding blood sacrifices.

> I understand it all, it's no great mystery.
> Our age is speeding down its iron trail.
> I understand, and I say: "Long live history!"—
> And throw myself head-first upon the rail.

One of Kogan's last poems, "The Letter," was written in December 1940. "We've lived to see the day," he wrote.

> We, the high-browed boys of a remarkable revolution—
> Dreamers at ten,
> Poets and punks at fourteen.
> Put down on casualty lists at twenty-five.[43]

Kogan was killed in 1942, when he was twenty-four years old. His novel in verse, which was conceived—almost sacrilegiously— as his generation's *Eugene Onegin*, remained unfinished. His best "Monument" is a poem by his fellow bard Boris Slutsky (who would do so much to reclassify—and immortalize—the graduates of the Communist Lycée as the "war generation").

> Let's do a little boasting
> Now that the fighting's done.
> We did our share of toasting,
> We had our drinking fun.
> Yet somehow we all shared
> A faith in future rockets:
> My friends were well prepared
> To do their job as prophets.[44]

Some of those who survived to become "the war generation" would go on to become "the generation of the sixties" and eventually the oldest of the "foremen" of Gorbachev's perestroika. But in the 1930s (before "the fight was done"), they were still the eternally young boys and girls of the remarkable revolution. What all the members of the prewar Soviet elite had in common was their total identification with their "age"; their belief that they—and their country—were the embodiment of the revolution; their conviction that, as Kopelev put it, "the Soviet power was the best and most just power on earth." All of them—from Hodl to Hodl's children—were ready and willing to do their job as prophets.[45]

Most members of the new Soviet elite were not Jews, and most Jews were not members of the new Soviet elite. But there is no doubt that the Jews had a much higher proportion of elite members than any other ethnic group in the USSR. In absolute terms, they were second to the Russians, but if one divides the elite into groups whose members came from the same region, shared a similar social and cultural background, and recognized each other as having a common past and related parents, it seems certain that Jews would have constituted the largest single component of the new Soviet elite, especially (or rather, most visibly) its cultural contingent. They tended to be the poets, the prophets, and the propagandists. According to David Samoilov, a member of the Kogan generation who was born in Moscow to a Jewish doctor from Belorussia and went on to become one of the most eloquent chroniclers of the

Soviet cultural elite, Jews had filled "the vacuum created by the terrorist regime" and then graduated from a "social stratum" to become a "part of the nation." The Jews, he believed, represented "a certain kind of mentality, a branch of the Russian intelligentsia in one of its most selfless variants."[46]

In effect, the role of the Jews in the prewar Soviet Union was similar to the role of the Germans in imperial Russia (or the role of Phanariot Greeks in the Ottoman Empire, among other instances). Mercurian nations in cosmopolitan empires, they represented modernity and internationalism among Apollonians doomed to becoming Mercurians. Closely associated with Mercurianizing regimes at their inception, they were used by those regimes as models, missionaries, surrogates, eager converts, and incorruptible officials. Both the tsar's Germans and the Soviet Jews identified themselves with their states because they shared those states' goals, were good at implementing them, and benefited tremendously from both their loyalty and their ability (for as long the regimes remained cosmopolitan). Both served as bureaucrats, elite professionals (including scholars), and leading officials in those most Mercurian of all state functions: diplomacy and the secret service. The Russian Germans were traditional Mercurians who tended to maintain their external strangeness and internal cohesion as a prerequisite for the continued performance of their mediating roles. The Soviet Jews were moderns who had abandoned traditional Mercurianism in order to overcome their strangeness and create a society that would dispense with all forms of mediation—only to find themselves performing traditional Mercurian functions almost identical to those of their imperial German predecessors (and in many ways similar to those of their own grandparents in the German and Polish lands).

One crucial difference (which was probably due to the unplanned and unpremeditated nature of the Jewish transformation into specialized Soviet Mercurians) was the much greater proportion of Soviet Jews (compared to the Russian Germans) among those who thought of themselves as members of the Russian intelligentsia. In imperial Russia, there was a distinction, largely inconsistent but always insisted upon, between the prophetic spokesmen for the country's Apollonian "people" and the unapologetically Mercurian modern professionals, some of them allied with the state and many of them Germans (real or metaphoric). In the Soviet Union of the 1930s, most people who thought of themselves as members of the intelligentsia were both prophetic spokesmen for the country's Apollonian "people" and unapologetically Mercurian modern professionals, all of them allied with the state and many of them Jews. David Samoilov tried to draw the line between the two, or rather, to extend the line that seemed so clear in the 1970s and 1980s back into the 1920s and 1930s. Among the Jewish immigrants to Soviet cities, he wrote in his memoirs, "there were both the Jewish members of the intelligentsia, or at least the material out of which the intelligentsia would be made, and the many-thousand-strong detachments of red commissars and Party functionaries, dehumanized, raised by the wave, intoxicated by power." Tsafrira Meromskaia, born two years later (in 1922), assumed that she belonged to the intelligentsia by virtue of her Jewish origins in combination with her elite upbringing and social success. Describing the communal apartment in which her family, newly arrived in Moscow, lived in the late 1920s before moving to an elite building on Tverskaia, she mentions the apartment's former owner and his "overripe daughter with straight greasy hair the color of rotten straw and deep-set eyes with colorless eyelashes"; "the proletarian Gurov, who had done well for himself by trading his heavy hammer for a job as a seeing eye of the Soviet security agencies"; the "prosperous chief accountant, Comrade Rubinchik, with his smooth, childless wife"; the "semiresponsible" Party official with his "irresponsible" mother-in-law; the engineer Fridman with his wife and two small children; and finally "the representatives of the Soviet intelligentsia": Meromskaia's own family. Meromskaia's grandparents had been traditional Jews from the Pale of Settlement; her parents had both gone to prerevolutionary *gymnasia* and then to the Kiev University law school. Under the Soviets, her father (born Abram Mekler) had become a prominent journalist at the *Peasant Newspaper* and *Izvestiya*. Her aunt had become a film director and producer; her mother never worked.[47]

Being a Soviet *intelligent* of the 1930s meant being both fully Soviet (committed to the building of socialism) and a true *intelli-*

gent (committed to the preservation of the cultural canon). One reason Meromskaia ended up living in an elite house was that she lived with Pushkin.

> That's right. He was always with me. I always checked my feelings, opinions, and tastes by asking myself: What would he have said, decided, thought, believed?
>
> I remember asking my dad when I was about five, "Did they have ice cream in Pushkin's day?" It was important for me to know whether he had had the opportunity to enjoy it as much as I did.
>
> Later I read everything ever written about him. I knew all the houses in Moscow where he had lived or stayed, the places where his friends had lived, and of course the famous church where he was married.
>
> When in Leningrad, I never failed to visit his last apartment on the Moika; the site of his duel on the Chernaia Rechka, and the church where his funeral service was held. I saw the city through his eyes. I went to Tsarskoe Selo, where he had attended the lycée. Traveling around Bessarabia, I kept thinking of his "Gypsies." And then there was Mikhailovskoe and Trigorskoe, where I could wander in the park to my heart's content. In the Crimea, I saw the sea through his eyes.[48]

Much later, she made a pilgrimage to Tolstoy's grave at Yasnaia Poliana—to "listen to the silence" and to experience the "feeling of being a part of something important, powerful, and pure." Raisa Orlova had already been there: she and her first husband Leonid Shersher (an ethnic Jew and an IFLI poet) had spent their "honey week" there.[49]

In the 1930s, all college-educated Soviets—and especially Hodl's children—lived with Pushkin, Herzen, Tolstoy, Chekhov, and an assortment of Western classics as much as they lived with industrialization, collectivization, and cultural revolution. Samuil Agursky, a top official in the Party's Jewish Section and the greatest Soviet enemy of the Hebrew language and Zionism, raised his son Melib (who did not speak Yiddish) on "Heine, Diderot, Shakespeare, Schiller, Plautus, Goethe, Cervantes, Thackeray, Swift, Beranger, and much else. Father also bought a lot of prerevolutionary literature, especially the Niva supplements, which contained Gogol, An-

dreev, Hamsun, Ibsen, and Goncharov. We also had Sir Walter
Scott, Byron, Rabelais, Maupassant, Hugo, Pushkin, Gorky, Tolstoy, Turgenev, Lermontov, Chekhov, Belinsky, Derzhavin, Veresaev,
and Nadson. As for Soviet literature, we had curiously little of it,
except for Mayakovsky, Sholokhov, and Furmanov."[50]

The combination of all of the "great books" (paintings, sym-
phonies, ballets) ever created with faith in Party orthodoxy was
known as socialist realism. In the 1930s, "world culture" and its
ever growing Russian component informed and molded Soviet socialism the way classical, baroque, and Gothic architecture shaped
Soviet cities and dwellings. When Evgenia Ginzburg, a privileged
Communist intellectual and the wife of a high Party official, found
herself in cattle car no. 7 on the way to a labor camp, she kept up her
own spirit and that of her fellow inmates by reciting from memory
Griboedov's *Woe from Wit* and Nekrasov's *The Russian Women*.
When the eavesdropping guards accused her of having smuggled in
a book, she proved her innocence—and revealed theirs—by reciting
the whole text of *Eugene Onegin*. The head guard sat in judgment.
"At first [he] wore a threatening expression: she'd get stuck in a
minute, and then he'd show her! This gave way by degrees to as-
tonishment, almost friendly curiosity, and finally ill-concealed delight." He asked for more. "So I went on. The train had started
again, and the wheels kept time to Pushkin's meter."[51]

Vasily Grossman's *Life and Fate* was to do for the Great Patriotic
War what Leo Tolstoy's *War and Peace* had done for the "Patriotic
War of 1812." The central character is an ethnic Jew who, before
the war, "never thought of himself or his mother as Jewish." His
mother, a doctor, had thought of herself as Jewish once, but that
was many years ago, before Pushkin and the Soviet state "had made
her forget." When the Nazis forced her to remember, she had to
pack up her things and move to the ghetto.

> I got a pillow, some bedclothes, the cup you once gave me, a spoon,
> a knife and two plates. Do we really need so very much? I took a few
> medical instruments. I took your letters; the photographs of my late
> mother and Uncle David, and the one of you with your father; a
> volume of Pushkin; *Lettres de mon moulin*; the volume by Maupassant

with *Une vie*, a small dictionary. . . . I took some Chekhov—the volume with "A Boring Story" and "The Bishop'—and that was that, I'd filled my basket.[52]

Evgeny Gnedin, whose birth in 1898 had been announced by his father, Parvus, as the birth of an enemy of the state with no Motherland, went on to become the head of the Press Department of the People's Commissariat for External Affairs. His whole generation, he wrote in his memoirs, was formed by "two currents of intellectual life: the socialist revolutionary ideology and the humane Russian literature." During the collectivization of the peasants, he worked as an "agitator," and when he was later locked up naked in a cold punishment cell for a crime he had not committed, he recited Pushkin, Blok, Gumilev, and Viacheslav Ivanov, along with his own poetry.[53]

Lev Kopelev was a collectivizer, poet, and Gulag inmate too. He was also an IFLI student, a bilingual Russian-Ukrainian speaker, and a card-carrying citizen of the world ("Satano," in Esperanto). One thing Kopelev was not—as far as he was concerned—was a Jew. He did identify himself as "Jewish" on standard Soviet forms and his internal passport, but that was because he did not want to be seen as "a cowardly apostate," and—after World War II—because he did not want to renounce those who had been murdered for being Jewish. "I have never heard the call of blood," he wrote, "but I understand the language of memory. . . . That is why in all the formal questionnaires, to all the official questioners, and to anybody who is just curious, I have always said and will always say: 'Jew.' But to myself and my close friends, I speak differently."

To himself and his close friends, Kopelev spoke the language of international Communism, Soviet patriotism, and world culture, which—to him, his close friends, and all Jewish immigrants to the Soviet capitals—was Russian. As Mayakovsky put it, and Kopelev repeated "as his personal conviction,"

> I would have learned Russian—
> If only because
> That language was spoken by Lenin.

But since he had learned it as a native language, as Lenin had, he had no choice but to create the rest of the world in its image. "My feelings and my perception of the world were formed and developed, above all, by the Russian word, Russian mentors, and Russian translations of Shakespeare, Hugo, Dickens, Mark Twain, and Jack London." For Hodl and her children, Pushkin Street and the road to socialism were one and the same thing. "To be Russian," wrote Kopelev, quoting Dostoevsky's "Pushkin Speech," "means being a Universal Human Being."[54]

The mass migration of Jews to the big cities, their close identification with Bolshevism, and their emergence as the core of the new Soviet Russian intelligentsia provoked hostility among those who objected to the arrival of these new immigrants, did not approve of Bolshevism, or could not, for various reasons, join the new Soviet Russian intelligentsia. "If you only knew what the city's population looks like," wrote one Leningrad resident to a friend in the United States in 1925, "what kind of revolting Jewish types you run into—with earlocks, speaking their croaking, hiccuping jargon." And as another one wrote to a correspondent in Yugoslavia three months later, "the sidewalks are filled with people in leather jackets and gray trench coats, spitting sunflower seeds in your face, and there are so many Jews with long earlocks feeling totally at home that you might as well be in Gomel, Dvinsk, or Berdichev." One Muscovite, in a letter sent to Leningrad in April 1925, felt the same way: "I don't go to public places anymore and try not to walk around too much because of the aggravation of having to look at Jewish faces and Jewish store signs. Pretty soon, a Russian sign will become a rarity in Moscow, or I should say, in New Berdichev. This Soviet nation is everywhere; I make the point of not reading newspapers or servile literature."[55]

The association of Jews with the Soviet state was a common theme in the anti-Jewish letters intercepted by the Leningrad secret police in the mid-1920s. "The Jewish dominance is absolute" (October 1924); "the whole press is in the hands of the Jews" (June

1925); "the Jews, for the most part, live extremely well; everything, from trade to state employment, is in their hands" (September 1925); "every child knows that the Soviet government is a Jewish government" (September 1925). Some members of the prerevolutionary elite, in particular, resented the "antibourgeois" quotas in educational institutions and the subsequent rise of the Jewish immigrants as both prominent new *Kulturträger* and leading "proletarian" iconoclasts. The art historian A. Anisimov wrote to a colleague in Prague (in November 1923), "Out of 100 applicants to Moscow University, 78 are Jews; thus, if the Russian university is now in Prague, the Jewish one is in Moscow." The father of a student about to be "purged" for alien origins wrote to a friend or relative in Serbia: "Pavel and his friends are awaiting their fate. But it's clear that only the Jerusalem academics and the Communists, Party members generally, are going to stay." And according to the wife of a Leningrad University professor, "in all the institutions, only workers and Israelites are admitted; the life of the intelligentsia is very hard."[56]

Mikhail Bulgakov, who thought of the Soviet regime as above all the reign of vile plebeians with "dogs' hearts," considered Jews important (if clearly secondary) instigators and beneficiaries of what had happened to "the great city of Moscow." As he wrote in his diary on December 28, 1924, after a public reading of his "Fatal Eggs" at a meeting of the fashionable "Nikitin Saturdays," "there were about thirty people there, not one of them a writer and none with any understanding of Russian literature. . . . These 'Nikitin Saturdays' consist of stale, slavish, Soviet riffraff, with a thick Jewish admixture." A week later, accompanied by his friend M. (Dmitry Stonov, a writer and a Jewish immigrant from the Pale of Settlement), he visited the editorial offices of the *Godless* magazine.

> The circulation is 70,000, as it turns out, and it is going fast. The offices are filled with unbelievable scum coming and going. There is a little stage, some kind of curtains, decorations. . . . On the stage there is a table; on the table there is some kind of holy book, perhaps the Bible, with two heads hovering above it.
>
> "Reminds me of a synagogue," said M. as we walked out. . . .

That very night, I skimmed the issues of the *Godless* and was stunned. The point is not just that this is a sacrilege, although the sacrilege is, of course, boundless, formally speaking. The point is that they represent Christ, Christ himself, as a scoundrel and a cheat. It is not hard to see whose work it is. This crime is immeasurable.[57]

The Party took such views seriously. According to the August 1926 Agitprop report to the Central Committee secretariat, "The sense that the Soviet regime patronizes the Jews, that it is 'the Jewish government,' that the Jews cause unemployment, housing shortages, college admissions problems, price rises, and commercial speculation—this sense is instilled in the workers by all the hostile elements. . . . If it does not encounter resistance, the wave of anti-Semitism threatens to become, in the very near future, a serious political question."[58]

The Party did offer some resistance, and the wave of anti-Semitism never became a serious political question (as far as the Party was concerned). One method of dealing with the threat was surveillance and repression. Most of the letters read by the secret police (in 1925, approximately fifteen hundred a month by the Leningrad Political Control Office alone) were accompanied by "memoranda" that included the names of the sender and addressee as well as excerpts relevant to the work of specific OGPU departments. All the letters quoted above (except the Anisimov one, which comes from a different source) were passed on to the Counterrevolution Department (KRO) or the Secret-Operational Department (SOCh) of the OGPU for further action. In March 1925, seven Russian nationalists were shot for advocating the toppling of the "Communist-Jewish" regime and the deportation of all Soviet Jews to Palestine (among other things).[59]

In another—inconsistent, uncoordinated, and more or less individual—strategy, prominent officials of Jewish descent took care to avoid undue prominence or to play down their Jewish descent. Trotsky claimed to have refused the post of commissar of internal affairs for fear of providing the enemies of the regime with additional anti-Semitic ammunition, and Molotov recalled that after Lenin's death, the ethnic Russian Rykov was chosen over the more competent Kamenev as the new head of the Soviet government (Sovnarkom) because "in those days Jews occupied many leading positions even though they made up a small percentage of the country's population." Neither Trotsky nor Kamenev considered themselves Jews in any sense other than the narrowly genealogical ("ethnic") one, but of course it was the narrowly genealogical sense that was dominant (and, after the introduction of the passport system in 1933, more or less compulsory) in Soviet "nationality policy." When in 1931 Molotov requested information on the ethnic breakdown of the members of the Central Executive Committee of the third convocation, both Trotsky and Kamenev were included on the list of those who did not fill out the delegates' questionnaire but whose nationality was "common knowledge." The nationality of Emelian Yaroslavsky (Gubelman) and Yuri Larin (Lurie) was less well known; both were leading Soviet spokesmen on the question of anti-Semitism, and both consistently referred to Jews in the third person.[60]

But of course the most sensitive "nationality" of all was Lenin's. In 1924 Lenin's sister Anna discovered that their maternal grandfather, Aleksandr Dmitrievich Blank, had been born Srul (Israel), the son of Moshko Itskovich Blank, in the shtetl of Starokonstantinov in Volynia. When Kamenev found out, he said, "I've always thought so," to which Bukharin allegedly replied: "Who cares what you think? The question is, what are we going to do?" What "they," or rather, the Party through the Lenin Institute, did was proclaim this fact "inappropriate for publication" and decree that it be "kept secret." In 1932 and again in 1934, Anna Ilinichna begged Stalin to reconsider, claiming that her discovery was, on the one hand, an important scientific confirmation of the "exceptional ability of the Semitic tribe" and "the extraordinarily beneficial influence of its blood on the offspring of mixed marriages"; and, on the other, a potent weapon against anti-Semitism "owing to the prestige and love that Ilich enjoys among the masses." Lenin's own Jewishness, she argued, was the best proof of the accuracy of his view that the Jewish nation possessed a peculiar " 'tenacity' in struggle" and a highly revolutionary disposition. "Generally speaking," she concluded, "I do not understand what reasons we, as Communists, may have for concealing this fact. Logically, this does not follow from the recognition of the full equality of all nationalities." Stalin's response was an order to "keep absolutely quiet." Anna Ilinichna did. The enemies of the regime were deprived of additional anti-Semitic ammunition.[61]

Another way of dealing with the overrepresentation of Jews at the top of Soviet society was to move some of them to the bottom— or rather, to turn the Jews into a "normal" nationality by providing the Mercurian head with an Apollonian body. In the 1920s and early 1930s, Soviet nationality policy consisted in the vigorous promotion of ethnic diversity, ethnic autonomy, and ethnoterritorial institutional consolidation. According to the Party orthodoxy (as formulated by Lenin and Stalin before the revolution), the injustices of the tsarist "prisonhouse of nations" could be overcome only through sensitivity, tact, and various forms of "affirmative action" (to use an apt anachronism). The formerly oppressed peoples felt strongly about their cultural peculiarities because of their history of oppression. The end of that oppression and a pointed promotion of national peculiarities would inevitably lead to the disappearance of national mistrust and—as a consequence—of undue preoccupation with national peculiarities. As Stalin put it back in 1913, "a minority is discontented . . . because it does not have the right to use its native language. Allow it to use its native language and the discontent will pass by itself." The passing of ethnic discontent would result in the demystification of ethnic groups and their ultimate fusion under communism. Nationality, as every Marxist knew, was a facade that concealed the reality of class struggle. Bolshevik multiculturalism was like politeness: nothing was valued as highly and cost as little (or so the Bolsheviks thought). By promoting the "national form," the Party was reinforcing the "socialist content." Diversity was the surest path to unity. The greatest monument to this dialectic was the first ethnoterritorial federation in the history of the world: the Union of Soviet Socialist Republics.[62]

The Jews were considered a formerly oppressed Soviet nationality and were treated like all the other formerly oppressed Soviet nationalities (all except the Russians, that is). Religion was a bad thing, of course, as was the use of scriptural languages for secular purposes (the Muslims had to abandon Arabic script), but a modern, secular national culture was a very good thing indeed. In the case of the Jews, this meant the creation of several special ethnoterritorial units in Ukraine and the Russian Republic and a massive promotion of the Yiddish language, theater, press, schools, and literature (complete with a large-scale celebration of Sholem Aleichem as the Jewish Pushkin). The enthusiasm of the Bolshevik Yiddishists was great, but the overall results—by 1934, when the Soviet state paused to take a breath—were meager. The problem was not Zionism, Hebraism, or Judaic traditionalism, which were negligible irritants compared to the challenges that the Soviet culture-building effort encountered in Central Asia, for example. The problem was that, according to the official Marxist blueprint, the Jews were too far ahead of the Soviet culture-building effort. There were many Soviet nationalities without compact homelands and many more Soviet nationalities that seemed unable to separate religion from ethnicity, but no other Soviet nationality was as top-heavy, in class terms (resembling, like the iconic Trotsky, a downward-pointing triangle); as heavily represented at the Soviet top; or as little interested in either the state's attack on its religion or the state's promotion of its "national culture." No other ethnic group was as good at being Soviet, and no other ethnic group was as keen on abandoning its language, rituals, and traditional areas of settlement. No other nationality, in other words, was as Mercurian (all head and no body) or as revolutionary (all youth and no tradition).[63]

Accordingly, in one crucially important sense, the "normalization" of the Jews was the reverse of the "modernization" of all the other Soviet nationalities. The purpose of fostering ethnic units, cultures, cadres, and institutions was to eliminate nationalist obstacles on the way to socialist urbanization, education, and cosmopolitanism. The Jews, however, were so heavily urbanized, so well educated, and so eager to become cosmopolitan (by way of secularization, intermarriage, and language shift) that Soviet nation building seemed either irrelevant or counterproductive (to both the Party and most Jewish consumers). Commendably but also dangerously, the Jews seemed much more Soviet than the rest of the Soviet Union. Moreover, those Jews who had stayed behind in the old shtetls as traditional traders and artisans did not fit into either the new Soviet economy or the peasant-into-worker-into-New-Man Marxist progression, whatever language they spoke. And so, in the name of equality and in order to deal with the threat of anti-Semitism on the one hand and capitalism on the other, the Party supported Yuri Larin in his attempt to turn at least 400,000 urban Jews into farmers—an attempt that, according to Larin's opponent Kaganovich, contained "elements of Zionism," and that, however one looks at it, was the mirror image of both Marxist theory and Soviet practice.[64]

Larin and most of his supporters (including the ones in the United States, who provided most of the financing) wanted to locate the center of new Jewish agriculture—and eventually "the national Jewish republic"—in northern Crimea and in the adjacent areas of the Kuban and southern Ukraine. This plan, and the early phases of its implementation in 1926–27, proved a serious political challenge because of strong resistance on the part of local officials, especially the head of the Crimean Autonomous Republic Veli Ibraimov, who claimed to speak on behalf of the Crimean Tatar population and was lobbying for the return to the Crimea of hundreds of thousands Tatar exiles living in Turkey. In October 1926, Larin wrote a letter to the Central Committee of the Party accusing Ibraimov of inciting pogroms, defending kulak interests, and "serving the nationalist-chauvinist aspirations of the part of the Tatar bourgeoisie that advocates a Turkish orientation." Larin's complaint may or may not have been a factor in Ibraimov's 1928 execution on charges of espionage for Turkey; either way, the demise of the Crimean project's most determined foe came too late to prevent the demise of the Crimean version of Jewish Apollonization. On March 28, 1928, the Soviet government approved the creation of a Jewish agricultural settlement in a remote part of the Soviet Far East not assigned to any other ethnic group (the local hunting and gathering population had no clout in the capital and no apparent intention to engage in agriculture). In 1930, Birobidzhan was proclaimed a Jewish National Region; in 1931, my grandparents arrived there from Buenos Aires by way of Hamburg and Leningrad; in 1932, their first daughter froze to death;

later that same year, they moved to Moscow (leaving my grandmother's sister and her family behind). The idea of settling on the land—especially such inhospitable land—made little sense to most Soviet Jews, less sense to conceptually consistent Soviet Marxists, and almost no sense whatsoever at the time of the most intense industrializing drive ever attempted by any state and the most resolute assault on the Apollonian countryside ever undertaken by any urban civilization.[65]

Thus the brunt of the struggle against the "wave of anti-Semitism" had to be borne by those responsible for agitation and propaganda. In August 1926, the Central Committee's Agitprop conducted a special meeting on the subject, and in December 1927 Stalin launched a massive public campaign against anti-Semitism by declaring to the delegates of the Fifteenth Party Congress, "This evil has to be combated with utmost ruthlessness, comrades." For the next four years, the Party sponsored countless formal appeals, celebrity speeches, mass rallies, newspaper exposés, and show trials aimed at eradicating the evil. In 1927–32, Soviet publishing houses produced fifty-six books against anti-Semitism, and at the height of the campaign in 1928–early 1930s, articles on the subject appeared in the Moscow and Leningrad newspapers almost daily. The campaign fizzled out in 1932, but as late as 1935 the newly dismissed commandant of the Moscow Kremlin R. A. Peterson had to apologize to the Party Control Commission for saying that one way to combat anti-Semitism was not to hire Jews. On May 22, 1935, the secretary of the Writer's Union A. S. Shcherbakov wrote to the Central Committee secretaries Stalin, Andreev, and Ezhov, recommending that the poet Pavel Vasiliev be punished for an anti-Semitic brawl. On May 24 *Pravda* published an article condemning Vasiliev for anti-Semitic "hooliganism," and within days he was arrested and sentenced to three years in a labor camp. And on May 17–23, 1936, the federal public prosecutor A. Ia. Vyshinsky was assigned to a widely publicized murder case (the first one of his career and presumably a dress rehearsal for the first "Moscow Trial," which was to take place within a few months). Konstantin Semenchuk, the head of the polar station on Wrangel Island, and Stepan Startsev, his dog-sled driver, were accused of murdering the expedition's doctor, Nikolai Lvovich Vulfson, and planning to kill his wife, Gita Borisovna Feldman. Anti-Semitism was one alleged motive; Vulfson's and Feldman's selfless defense of state property and Soviet nationality policy was another. No evidence was presented; none was needed (according to Vyshinsky, who proclaimed *cui prodest*, "who benefits," to be his main legal principle); and none existed (according to Arkady Vaksberg, who claims to have seen the file). Both defendants were shot.[66]

The campaign against anti-Semitism was part of the Great Transformation policy of vigorous "indigenization" and "internationalism." Between 1928 and about 1932–34, the Party demanded the widest possible use of the largest possible number of languages, the aggressive promotion of "national cadres," and the tireless celebration of ethnic differences, peculiarities, and entitlements. Once again, however, the Jews were in a special position because, according to both anti-Semites and philo-Semites (as well as some Jews), their main peculiarity was their denial of possessing any peculiarities, and their chief entitlement was to being considered exceptionally good Russians and Soviets—and thus exceptional among nationalities. Before the mid-1930s, "Russian" and "Soviet" were the only two nationalities that were not seen as properly ethnic—or rather, as having a politically meaningful national form. Both were immune from nationality policy because both were defined exclusively in class terms. And so, mutatis mutandis, were most Moscow and Leningrad Jews. Or rather, they were supposed to be a part of the nationality policy but did not seem interested, and they were often defined in (upper-)class terms but were not supposed to be. They seemed to be a nationality without form—a caste of exemplary Soviets.

But what did this mean, and why was this so? The Soviet campaign against anti-Semitism consisted of two elements: an attempt to combat anti-Jewish prejudice, jealousy, and hostility (old and new), and an attempt to explain why the Jews occupied such a peculiar place in Soviet society. The two fundamental approaches were (a) the Jews did not occupy a peculiar place in Soviet society; and (b) the Jews occupied a peculiar place in Soviet society for perfectly wholesome and understandable reasons. Approach (a) implied that anti-Semitism was a form of false consciousness inherited from the old regime; approach (b) suggested that anti-Semitism was a form of jealousy that could be cured through a combination of Jewish normalization and Apollonian modernization. Most Soviet authors used both approaches. According to Emelian Yaroslavsky, propaganda about Jewish overrepresentation among Soviet leaders was being spread by the enemies of the revolution. "What do they care that in the Communist Party, which has 1,300,000 members and candidate members, there are more than 1,000,000 Russians, Ukrainians, Belorussians, and other non-Jews!" And as for future leaders, "even the tsarist government allowed the Jews to make up 10 percent of all university students, but under the Soviet government that number has barely reached the average of 13 percent for all institutions of higher education." On the other hand, argued Yaroslavsky, anti-Semitism could not be defeated unless the proportion of Jewish workers ("which is still totally insufficient") and that of Jewish peasants ("the center of gravity in the struggle against anti-Semitism") were increased dramatically.[67]

Larin went much further. He did say that the Jews were far from being "preeminent, overabundant, dominant, and so on" among Soviet leaders, even though they had "spilled more blood ["than the workers of other nationalities"] in the struggle for freedom, for the liberation of our country from landowners and capitalists, from tsarism." Larin's main point, however, was to explain why the Jews were, indeed, overrepresented (about 19 percent of the total in 1929) "in the apparatus of public organizations," including "both elected and appointed members of trade union boards, provincial administrations, Party committees, and similar organs." The reason, he suggested, was that "the Jewish worker, because of the peculiarity of his past life and because of the additional oppression and persecution he had to endure for many years under tsarism, has developed a large number of special traits that equip him for active roles in revolutionary and public work. The exceptional development of the special psychological makeup necessary for leadership roles has made Jewish revolutionary workers more capable of gaining prominence in public life than the average Russian worker, who lived under very different conditions."

There were three main reasons for this, according to Larin. First, the economic "struggle for survival' in overcrowded shtetls had created unusually active, resilient, and determined individuals. "In other words, the conditions of everyday life produced in urban Jews a peculiar, exceptional energy. When such individuals became factory workers, underground revolutionaries, or, upon arrival in Moscow after the revolution, employees in our institutions, they moved up very quickly because of this energy—especially because the bulk of our Russian workers were of peasant origin and thus hardly capable of systematic activity."

The second reason for the Jewish preeminence was a strong sense of solidarity among them. Because of discrimination against Jewish workers under the old regime, "there developed, among this segment of the Jewish people, an unusually strong sense of solidarity and a predisposition toward mutual help and support. This exceptionally strong solidarity was very useful in both revolutionary struggle and Party work, and is generally one of the fundamental class virtues of the proletariat. . . . Consequently, within the revolutionary movement, Jewish workers were bound to move up into the revolutionary apparatus at a much higher rate than was their share of the proletariat as a whole."

The third advantage that the Jews had over the Russians, according to Larin, was their generally higher level of culture (*kul'-turnost'*). Because education had always been the main path to Jewish emancipation and because of the long Jewish tradition of literacy and urban life, "tens of thousands of Jewish laboring youth used to spend long years, night in night out, bent over their books, in an attempt to break out of the narrow circle of restrictions. It rarely worked . . . , but the higher cultural level acquired in this manner went on to benefit the revolutionary struggle."[68]

There was nothing inherently wrong with Jewish excellence, according to Party ideologues (Jewish or not), but it did offend against the principle of full national equality and led to the growth of anti-Semitism. Larin's remedies were the same as Yaroslavsky's and everyone else's: Jewish normalization (especially through agricultural settlement), non-Jewish modernization (espe-

cially through education), and a concerted campaign of conscious-
ness-raising among non-Jews on the subject of Jewish excellence
(to the effect that it did not exist or existed for good but temporary
reasons).

The most remarkable thing about these remedies was that two
of them worked as intended. The Jewish normalization project was
a failure, but the combination of the public assault on anti-Semitism and the dramatic expansion of educational and employment
opportunities for hundreds of thousands of Apollonians during the
First Five-Year Plan seem to have borne fruit. It is possible, of
course, that the problem was not widespread in the first place: in
Izmozik's study of intercepted mail, only 0.9 percent of all letters
opened by the Leningrad secret police between March 1925 and
January 1926 (67 out of 7,335) contained negative comments
about Jews. It is also quite probable that, especially in the former
Pale, both traditional anti-Semitism and the new resentment over
Jewish prominence in the Soviet state simmered just below the surface, occasionally glimpsed despite official prohibitions and camouflage. What does seem striking, in any case, is that virtually all memoirists writing about Moscow and Leningrad intelligentsia life in
the 1930s seem to agree that there was no anti-Jewish hostility and
generally very few manifestations of ethnic ranking or labeling.
Allowing for a degree of nostalgic wishful thinking and for the fact
that most of these memoirists are elite members writing about elite
institutions, it seems fair to conclude that the new-minted, self-
confident, optimistic, and passionately patriotic Soviet intelligentsia of the 1930s included a very substantial proportion of ethnic
Jews and a remarkably small number of their detractors. The prominent philosopher Vitaly Rubin went to a top Moscow school. More
than half of his classmates were Jewish.

> Understandably, the Jewish question did not arise there. Not only
> did it not arise in the form of anti-Semitism; it did not arise at all. All
> the Jews knew themselves to be Jews but considered everything to
> do with Jewishness a thing of the past. I remember thinking of my
> father's stories about his childhood, heder, and traditional Jewish up-

bringing as something consigned to oblivion. None of that had anything to do with me. There was no active desire to renounce one's
Jewishness. This problem simply did not exist.[69]

The Soviet Union was building a unique blend of Apollonianism
and Mercurianism, and the rapidly expanding Soviet intelligentsia
consisted of grateful young beneficiaries. The children of Jews were
acquiring Apollonian bodies and belligerence; the children of
"workers and peasants" were gaining Mercurian cleverness and mobility. Both despised their parents (for the half-humans they were),
and both were being trained as brothers, as well as prophets. Vasily
Stalin once told his little sister Svetlana, "Our father used to be a
Georgian." Or, as Sholem Aleichem's little Motl put it, "I am lucky,
I'm an orphan."[70]

The story of the Jewish social rise, Jewish patricide, and Jewish
conversion to non-Jewishness (of whatever kind) is of course not
peculiar to the Soviet Union. What is peculiar is that there was
no preexisting elite to compete with or alienate, no special membership fee analogous to baptism, and—up until the late 1930s—no
official discrimination of any kind (given total ideological purity,
of course). Hodl's husband Perchik, who had always considered
himself a "member of the human race," would have become one
de jure and possibly by profession when he arrived in Moscow after
the Bolshevik Revolution. Assuming he did not die in the civil war
and did not join an opposition, there is a good chance he might
have ended up running a publishing house, a People's Comissariat,
and perhaps even a special agency directly responsible for ideological purity.

Indeed, the Soviet secret police—the regime's sacred center,
known after 1934 as the NKVD—was one of the most Jewish of
all Soviet institutions. In January 1937, on the eve of the Great
Terror, the 111 top NKVD officials included 42 Jews, 35 Russians,
8 Latvians, and 26 others. Out of twenty NKVD directorates,
twelve (60 percent, including State Security, Police, Labor Camps,

and Resettlement [deportations]) were headed by officers who identified themselves as ethnic Jews. The most exclusive and sensitive of all NKVD agencies, the Main Directorate for State Security, consisted of ten departments: seven of them (Protection of Government Officials, Counterintelligence, Secret-Political, Special [surveillance in the army], Foreign Intelligence, Records, and Prisons) were run by immigrants from the former Pale of Settlement. Foreign service was an almost exclusively Jewish specialty (as was spying for the Soviet Union in Western Europe and especially in the United States). The Gulag, or Main Labor Camp Administration, was headed by ethnic Jews from 1930, when it was formed, until late November 1938, when the Great Terror was mostly over. As Babel (himself a onetime secret police employee, a friend of some prominent executioners, and ultimately a confessed "terrorist" and "spy") described one of his characters, one nicknamed A-Jew-and-a-Half, "Tartakovsky has the soul of a murderer, but he is one of us, he is our flesh and blood."[71]

There was, of course, no separate Jewish interest that these people had in common—any more than the German officials and professionals in imperial Russia had had a special German interest. On the contrary, all these groups made perfect policemen and plenipotentiaries precisely because of their Mercurian training and their uniquely Mercurian rootlessness. The rise of the nation-state had made internal strangeness impossible (the very traits that had signified loyalty now suggested treason), but the Soviet Union was neither an Apollonian empire nor a nation-state, and Soviet Jews were no ordinary Mercurians. Before the mid-1930s, the USSR was a relentlessly universalist Centaur state that aspired to a perfect combination of Mercurianism and Apollonianism (with a temporary emphasis on the former, given Russia's excess of the latter). The Jews played a central role in this endeavor both because they were traditional Mercurians and because they were so eager to become Apollonians. Their parents provided them with the skills necessary for success in Soviet society; their rebellion against their parents made them unusually consistent at Soviet internationalism. Jews were relatively numerous in the chambers of power because of their Jewish energy and education, and because of their singular commitment to socialism (Jewish non-Jewishness). Apollonized Mercurians did better than Mercurianized Apollonians.

In any case, in early 1937 Hodl the Muscovite would not have been allowed to correspond with her sisters, but she probably would have been living in elite housing in downtown Moscow (not far from Meromskaia, Gaister, Orlova, Markish, and so many others), with access to special stores, a house in the country (dacha), and a live-in peasant nanny or maid (the Markishes had both). At least once a year, she would have traveled to a Black Sea sanatorium or a mineral spa in the Caucasus.

If Hodl had written her memoirs in the 1930s, they would have been about her revolutionary youth. Hodl's life as she would have remembered it had no childhood (except perhaps a brief mention of her family's poverty), no Kasrilevka, and no Tevye. It had no adulthood and no old age. The revolution turned preexisting revolutionaries into "Old Bolsheviks," and Old Bolsheviks had nothing but their revolutionary youth to remember (or look forward to). The 1930s Soviet present belonged to Hodl's daughters' happy childhood.

Hodl's daughters' memoirs all have childhoods—happy 1930s childhoods and happy 1930s adolescence. They adored their nannies and their parents (but not necessarily their grandparents—supposing Tevye was still around, living quietly in Hodl's new apartment). They loved their schools, their teachers, and their friends. They took piano lessons, worshiped famous tenors, and knew all the Maly Theater actors. They read a lot of nineteenth-century novels and lived nineteenth-century intelligentsia lives. Their memories of New Year celebrations are versions of canonical Christmas reminiscences, and their descriptions of their dacha summers are Nabokovian evocations of the Russian gentry's paradise lost. Even Meromskaia's sarcasm—in a book entitled *Nostalgia? Never!*—dissolves in the presence of the Soviet version of manorial Arcadia.

Oh, those vistas and evenings outside of Moscow, in the dacha settlements with their wooden houses with open verandas overlooking small gardens enclosed by picket fences or wildly overgrown yards, which were, in effect, fenced-in sections of the woods complete with mushrooms and berries. The cultivated ones overflowed with lilacs, jasmine, and wild cherry. The flower beds smelled of mignonette and looked bright and pretty thanks to the pansies and all sorts of other members of the friendly flower family. Under the windows, the Romantic *dachniki* planted aromatic nicotiana, nondescript during the day but sweetly pungent at night, while the more pragmatic ones planted gorgeous dahlias, which looked nice but would not get stolen. Beyond the gate, there was a narrow beaten path running alongside the fence. And somewhere close by there was always a river or lake, and, of course, the woods: the mixed forests south of Moscow and the dry, warm pine forests to the north and west—the tall, slender trunks smelling of resin, and the ground strewn with black pinecones half covered by yellow needles.

In the evenings, after a "long day's work," we would wash ourselves with warm water heated by the sun and put sandals on feet hardened by many hours of barefooted recklessness. And then we would join the grownups over evening tea or, more often, talk endlessly, into the night, with our girlfriends—and with the boys too. From each terrace came the sounds of the gramophone: sultry tangos, Utesov, Shulzhenko, the semibanned Leshchenko, sometimes Ellington's "Caravan," but mostly "Me and My Masha by the Samovar."

Gradually, all these familiar dacha sounds would die down, the *dachniki* would go to bed, and night silence would fall, interrupted by an occasional train whistle or the beckoning call of mothers and grandmothers. The moon would emerge slowly from behind the trees. A slight smell of smoke would hang in the air.[72]

Most of the *dachniki*—and generally most members of the Soviet "new class"—were not Jews. But few Soviet groups, however defined, had as good a chance of finding themselves among Meromskaia's *dachniki* as did the immigrants from the former Pale of Settlement. More of Hodl's children than just about anybody else's had the proverbial Soviet "happy childhoods."

In 1937, Inna Gaister's grandmother Gita came from Poland to Moscow to see her children. She had seven sons and daughters. The youngest still lived with her; all the others had moved to Moscow. Rakhil (Inna's mother), a Party member since 1918, worked as an economist at the People's Comissariat of Heavy Industry; her husband, Aron Gaister, was deputy commissar of agriculture; their youngest daughter, Valeria, was named after Valerian Kuibyshev, one of Stalin's top lieutenants. Khaim, a civil war veteran married to an ethnic Russian, was deputy head of the Military Chemical Academy in Moscow. Veniamin was a history Ph.D. ("doctor of sciences") and a researcher at the Institute of World Economy and International Politics. Lipa was an engineer at a factory; her first husband was a Soviet secret agent in Hungary, her second an engineer at the Moscow Automobile Plant. Pinia was a navy pilot, a student at the Air Force Academy, and, like Khaim, a colonel. Also like Khaim, he was married to a Russian woman. They named their son Valery, after the famous Soviet pilot Valery Chkalov. Adassa had immigrated to the Soviet Union illegally in 1923; she had since graduated from college and was working as a chemical engineer. Finally, Leva had arrived in 1932, gone to work at the Moscow Automobile Plant, and enrolled as a student by correspondence in the Bauman Superior Institute of Technology.

Grandma Gita did not speak Russian, so Adassa met her at the border town of Negoreloe. From the Belorussky Railway Station she was taken to Lipa's in my father's car. That night all seven children and their spouses came to see her. Many years had gone by since they, as young people, had left the family home. We can only guess what her hopes for them may have been back then. What kind of fate had she asked God to grant her uneducated children from a miserable Jewish shtetl? And now here she was, surrounded by prosperous people with all kinds of degrees: engineers, colonels, Ph.D.'s. As far as she was concerned, my mother, for example, was "Madame Minister's Wife"! She had a lot of grandchildren too. All her life she had been tied to her garden and her cow. My great-great-grandfather, Grandma Gita's grandfather, had been a rabbi who had written famous Talmudic commentaries called "Elijah's View." Her own literacy was limited to reading Hebrew prayers and painstakingly composing letters in her own shtetl dialect.

I was there that night. According to the Jewish custom, Grandma was wearing a wig. It was red. I was also surprised that she was eating off special plates that she had brought with her from Poland. She sat proudly at the head of the table in the place of honor. I also remember her full dark skirts that reached the ground. That night must have been the first time in her life that she was truly happy.[73]

We do not know how happy Grandma Gita (who could not speak with her grandchildren) truly was or whether she had been truly happy before, but we can be certain that her children, grandchildren, and in-laws sitting around the table were genuinely proud of their accomplishments and fully convinced that Grandma Gita had never been truly happy before. They also knew—beyond all doubt and reflection—that their lives were a part of History and thus incommensurate with the lives of their kinsmen languishing in America and Palestine. Tevye loved all his daughters, of course; Hodl (who was approximately the same age as Rakhil Kaplan, Gita's oldest daughter and Inna Gaister's mother) worried about her sisters Beilke and Chava; Hodl's children felt nothing but pity for their overseas cousins (on those rare occasions when they thought about them at all).

When Hope Ulanovskaia and her husband were told in 1931 that their next posting as Soviet secret agents would be to America, and not Romania, as they had supposed, Hope was "terribly upset."

> The First Five-Year Plan was underway; people were building socialism, making sacrifices. At least in Romania we would not have had an easy life. We might have had enough to eat, but at any moment we could have been arrested by the secret police. But in America, as everyone knew, Soviet espionage was not of great interest to anybody. I knew about America from Upton Sinclair and Theodore Dreiser, and the very thought of going there was revolting to me.[74]

America did prove a rather unpleasant place, if not quite as unpleasant as Hope had been led to believe. "I knew that America was the classic capitalist country, the most disgusting place in the world, and was anxious to see all the 'ulcers' of capitalism as soon as possible." She saw the lines at Salvation Army soup kitchens, the "frightful enormity of stone" ("like a well"), and the "real despair" of unemployment, but she also found informality, prosperity, and many good friends (especially Whittaker Chambers, whom she and her husband knew as "Bob"). Most important, she found her favorite aunt and uncle, who had left their native Bershad because of family trouble and still knew her as "Esterka." Uncle had his own window-cleaning business but had had to let his assistant go because of the Depression. "He had a five-room apartment; they took baths every day and drank orange juice in the morning. In other words, they had become real Americans." Neither Hope nor Uncle himself was much impressed, however.

> Uncle was unhappy with capitalism and very interested in how people lived in the Soviet Union. He had heard about this person's son becoming a doctor and that person's daughter an engineer, and was very unhappy that his own children had not gone to college. He had wanted his younger son, Srulikl, who was now Sidney, to be a dentist, but he had become an ardent Communist, dropped out of school, and was working for a Communist newspaper in Baltimore. The older one, David, was a worker, a member of a leftist trade union. Aunt was complaining that her children were reproaching her: Why had she taken them out of the Soviet Union? Uncle asked me: "Do you think I'd be better off there?" I wanted to be honest: "I would not leave the Soviet Union if I were offered all the riches of Morgan. But I'll be frank with you, Uncle: you may be a window washer, but you live better than our engineers. We don't drink orange juice in the mornings and don't eat chicken. Nobody has apartments like yours. We, for example, live in one room."
>
> . . . Then my cousins arrived. They listened to me with rapt attention. . . . I was telling them: "You see, workers in our country feel that they are the true masters of the land. Through blood and sweat, we are building a beautiful building. When we finish, we'll have everything." How they listened to me! They loved me. They believed me. We had grown up together.[75]

She believed it too. She meant every word. But she was also right about the difference in material conditions—a difference caused by America's greater wealth and Jewish American economic success. The Jews had done well in America—much better, in fact, than any other immigrant community and better, as far as social mobility was concerned, than most native-born Americans. The Russian Jews were the latest, largest, and most specialized of the Mercurian immigrants, and they acted and succeeded accordingly. They arrived as families (about 40 percent of the Jewish immigrants were female, and 25 percent children); intended to stay (the average rate of repatriation from the United States was 7 percent for the Jews, 42 percent for everyone else); became fully urbanized; took almost no part in the competition for unskilled jobs; included an extraordinarily high proportion of entrepreneurs (in New York in 1914, every third male immigrant); and did business the old-fashioned Mercurian way—by relying on cheap family labor, long hours, low profit margins, ethnic solidarity, vertical integration, and extremely high rates of standardization, specialization, and product differentiation. In New York, in particular, the Russian Jewish immigrants took advantage of their traditional skills and old-country experience to monopolize and revolutionize the clothing industry (in 1905 the city's largest, worth $306 million and employing one-fourth of New York's industrial labor force). By 1925, 50 percent of New York's Russian Jewish heads of households were in white-collar occupations, almost exclusively through entrepreneurship. As Andrew Godley put it, "most Jewish immigrants . . . rose from the direst of poverty to positions of economic security and social respectability within fifty years when most of those around them did not."[76]

The story was a familiar one: business success followed by success in the educational system and the professions. At the end of World War I, Harvard's Jewish enrollment was about 20 percent, and Columbia's about 40 percent. In 1920, City College of New York and Hunter College were 80 to 90 percent Jewish. In 1925, more than 50 percent of the children of Jewish immigrant businessmen had white-collar jobs that required formal education. According to an Industrial Commission report, "In the lower schools the Jewish children are the delight of their teachers for cleverness at their books, obedience, and general good conduct." And according to one bemused Boston prep school student, "Jews worked far into each night, their lessons next morning were letter perfect, they took obvious pride in their academic success and talked about it. At the end of each year there were room prizes given for excellency in each subject, and they were openly after them. There was none of the Roxbury solidarity of pupils versus the master. If anyone reciting made a mistake that the master overlooked, twenty hands shot into the air to bring it to his attention."[77]

In the Soviet Union and the United States, the children of Jewish immigrants were going to school at about the same time and with the same degree of eagerness and excellence. In both places, the dramatic expansion of the educational systems coincided with the Jewish influx and helped accommodate it. And in both places, there arose—eventually—"the Jewish problem" of excessive success. In the Soviet Union, the state responded by expanding enrollments and intensifying affirmative action programs for "workers and peasants" and titular ethnics. As Larin put it, not without some defensiveness, "we cannot do what the tsarist government used to do: pass a law mandating that Jewish workers be accepted by workers' preparatory departments at a lower percentage rate than the Russian workers, or that Jewish intellectuals and artisans be enrolled in colleges in smaller proportions, relative to their total population, than their Russian counterparts." In the United States, most top colleges could not do what the tsarist government used to do, either, but they could—and did—use indirect methods, such as regional quotas or "character" tests, to combat the "Jewish invasion."[78]

The most notable thing about Jewish students in the Soviet Union and Jewish students in the United States was the fact that whereas Soviet colleges produced Communists, the American colleges also produced Communists. As Thomas Kessner put it, "The immigrant generation sought security for their children and as they understood it this required American education. In the process they propelled their children away from themselves, producing a generation gap of enormous proportions, resulting in conflicts of fierce intensity often beyond reconciliation. While other groups held their offspring firmly to the old ways, the Eastern Europeans did not pass on the moral norms of their past. Instead they passed their children on to America."[79]

In other words, America was reproducing the familiar European pattern. The Jewish emergence from the ghetto and success in the expanded marketplace were followed by the Jewish Revolution against Jewishness as the "chimerical nationality" of capitalism. Jews were, proportionately, much more Marxist than the international proletariat because they were much more like Marx. In America, they were even more so because America was the promised land of *homines rationalistici artificiales*, a country of chimerical nationality with no Goethe-Schiller cult or messianic intelligentsia to replace the lost Jewishness. One strategy was to retain the Jewishness, recover it if it seemed lost, and possibly reform it by means of a peculiarly American procedure that Bromberg called the "Protestantization of Judaism." Another was to form one's own messianic intelligentsia, "the Movement." Most of the "New York intellectuals" of the 1930s were the children of Russian Jewish immigrants. They were not modern intellectuals involved in "cultural production"—they were the overseas chapter of the Russian intelligentsia, the true believers in the temple of eternal youth, the priests of proletarian politics, the denizens of "the little islands of freedom" in an evil empire that, according to one City College graduate, "resisted the analysis of Marx the way other lands in other times had resisted the thunderous anguish of Isaiah."[80]

Like old Russia's little islands of freedom, the American ones were not uninhabited. According to David A. Hollinger, the new cosmopolitan intelligentsia in the United States "was formed by the amalgamation of two antiprovincial revolts, one manifest especially among well-to-do WASPs of native stock, directed against the constraints of 'Puritanism,' and the other manifest especially among the sons of immigrants, directed against the constraints of Jewish parochialism, particularly as identified with Eastern Europe." As Joseph Freeman, a refugee from the Pale of Settlement to Communism by way of Columbia University, saw it (through Matthew Arnold's prism), both groups were moving, at the same time, "from Moses and Jesus to Venus and Apollo, from a common 'Judeo-Christian asceticism' to a Hellenistic 'refuge of souls in rebellion against puritan bondage.' " Like Abraham Cahan's Vilna circle

("No distinction between Jew and gentile! In the spirit of true equality and brotherhood!"), Freeman's refuge was a new family without fathers, in which "Nordic Americans" communed with Jews and Negroes, and which "represented that ideal society which we all wanted, that society in which no racial barriers could possibly exist."[81] They—the Jews among them, at any rate—had inherited the entirety of human history in order to transcend it. "By the time we were leaving the university we were no longer, culturally, Jews. We were Westerners initiated into and part of a culture which merged the values of Jerusalem, Egypt, Greece and ancient Rome with the Catholic culture of the Middle Ages, the humanistic culture of the Renaissance, the equalitarian ideals of the French Revolution, and the scientific concepts of the nineteenth century. To this amalgam we added socialism, which seemed to us the apex, so far, of all that was greatest in Western culture."[82]

They were, like Mandelstam's mother's Vilna friends, a self-conscious "generation" following "luminous personalities" toward "self-immolation" (vicariously, as it turned out, except for the few who became Hope Ulanovskaia's secret agents). They were an army of fraternal prophets. They were "the Movement."

According to Isaac Rosenfeld's recollection of life at the University of Chicago in the 1930s,

> The political interest colored practically every student activity on campus, with the major division drawn between Stalinists (who dominated the American Student Union) and the Trotskyites (who worked through the local chapter of the Young People's Socialist League). The two Marxist groups, with their symps and associates, spoke bitterly about, but never to, each other and avoided all contact, except to heckle, and occasionally strong-arm, each other's meetings. Politics was everywhere, in a measure, one ate and drank it; and sleep gave no escape, for it furnished terror to our dreams. . . . Liaisons, marriages, and divorces, let alone friendships, were sometimes contracted on no other basis than these issues. . . . Politics was form and substance, accident and modification, the metaphor of all things.[83]

It was Soviet politics, or perhaps socialist anti-Soviet politics, or rather, prophetic politics in the shadow of the Soviet Union, that was the metaphor of all things. Beilke's children agreed with Hodl's children that History (as future, not past) was unfolding in Moscow. The USSR might be on the straight road to perfection, or it might have taken a wrong turn somewhere; either way, the USSR is where the "accursed questions" were being answered and the "last and decisive battles" were being waged. Most of the secret agents recruited by the Ulanovskys in America were Russian Jews or their children, and there is little doubt that Trotsky's greatest appeal was that he was both Jewish and Russian: a perfect Mercurian Apollonian, a fearsome warrior with glasses on his nose (he was, in effect, the Israel of the 1930s; or rather, Israel would become the Trotsky of the next Jewish American generation). According to Irving Howe, no major figure of the twentieth century "combined so fully or remarkably as did Trotsky the roles of historical actor and historian, political leader and theorist, charismatic orator and isolated critic. Trotsky made history, and kept an eye on history. He was a man of heroic mold, entirely committed to the life of action, but he was also an intellectual who believed in the power and purity of the word."[84]

Some Jewish American rebels in the 1930s were also the children of Jewish Russian rebels—the ones who spent hours in the New York Public Library "leafing through the canonical and apocryphal writings of the prophets of the old revolutionary underground." For them, socialism began at home—as "one long Friday evening around the samovar and the cut-glass bowl laden with nuts and fruits, all of us singing *Tsuzamen, tsuzamen, ale tsuzamen!*"; or as heated arguments among uncles and aunts about the dictatorship of the proletariat and the treachery of the revisionists. When Daniel Bell converted from Judaism to the Young People's Socialist League, his family's main worry was whether he had joined the right sect.[85]

But most Jewish American parents in the 1920s and 1930s were not rebels, so most Jewish American rebels renounced their parents as well as the cold world they had launched them into. As in Europe outside the Soviet Union, Jewish parents and capitalism seemed to take turns representing each other ("the *social* emancipation of the Jew is the *emancipation of society from Judaism*"). Much of early

Jewish American literature was about Jewish boys questioning their legitimacy and about Jewish entrepreneurs selling their soul to the devil. Isaac Rosenfeld's underground young man in *Passage from Home* hates his father and would rather have another one; Henry Roth's "cellar" boy in *Call It Sleep* is hated by his father, who would rather have another son (of whose parentage he would be certain). Both Abraham Cahan's David Levinsky and Budd Schulberg's Sammy Glick lose their fathers, lose themselves, and produce no children as they climb up in search of wealth and status.

Tevye's American daughter (Beilke), his Soviet daughter (Hodl), and their children all agreed about what each destination stood for. For David and his mother in *Call It Sleep*, New York was a "wilderness." For Boris Erlich in Babel's "Jewess," the Soviet Union was both his home and his masterpiece.

> Boris showed her Russia with so much pride and confidence, as if he, Boris Erlich, had himself created Russia, as if he owned it. And to some extent, he did. There was in everything a drop of his soul or of his blood, the blood of the corps commissar (of the Red Cossacks)— from the international train cars to the newly built sugar factories and refurbished train stations.[86]

For Beilke and her children, language and "tonguelessness" were sources of agony and fascination; for Hodl and her children, "the clear and pure Russian sounds" came naturally (or so they seem to have felt). Beilke's children despised their father Podhotzur, the brash businessman and social climber; Hodl's children adored their father, Perchik, the ascetic revolutionary and hardworking official. Beilke's children were uncertain Jews and incomplete Americans; Hodl's children were native-born Russians and perfect Soviets.

But what about Chava's children in Palestine? Their Moscow cousins were too close to the center of the world and the end of history to pay much attention (other than to extend a generic promise of salvation), while the ones in New York were too busy looking toward Moscow (or doing business). One of Beilke's daughters may have preferred Eretz Israel to the Soviet Union, but her voice was drowned out by the chorus of world revolution.

Meanwhile, Chava's children were living a revolution of their own—building, consistently and unapologetically, socialism in one country. Like their Soviet cousins, they were the first generation: "first" because they were Sabras (the Yishuv's firstborn) and a self-conscious "generation" because they knew that they all belonged to the fraternity of fulfilled prophecy and eternal youth. In the words of Benjamin Harshav, "The cell of life was not the family but the age group sharing a common ideology and reading the new Hebrew journalism. Theirs was a consciousness of the end of all previous history: the end of two thousand years of exile and the end of thousands of years of class warfare—in the name of a new beginning for man and Jew." And, like their Soviet cousins, they had little use for Tevye. Or rather, Hodl's children pitied Tevye when they thought of him at all: most of them knew that Sholem Aleichem was the Yiddish Pushkin even if they had never read *Tevye the Milkman*, and many of them had heard of Mikhoels's Yiddish theater even if they never went there. In Eretz Israel, the repudiation of Tevye was the cornerstone of the new community, the true beginning of the new beginning for man and Jew. According to Harshav, "it was a society without parents, and for the children growing up, without grandparents; the former admiration for grandfather as the source of wisdom was turned upside down, and the orientation of life was toward the utopian future, to be implemented by the next generation."[87]

The American cousins questioned—and sometimes disowned—their fathers. The ones in the Soviet Union and Eretz Israel joined their mothers and fathers in disowning their grandfathers. The task of the "next generation" was to show themselves worthy of their parents by completing the patricidal revolution they had begun. As a fourteen-year-old boy wrote to his parents from Kibbutz Yagur in 1938, "I feel happy that the yoke of the general good has been laid on me, or more precisely, that I have placed the yoke of the general good on my own back and bear it. . . . I desire, as they say, to put myself at the service of my people and land and the world and the workers and everything, so that I can fix and renew things."[88]

Like the first Soviet generation and the true believers among their American cousins, the first Sabra generation lived in a world where politics was "the metaphor of all things." The kibbutz, the moshav, the school, the youth movement, and the military were closely interrelated, mutually dependent, and ultimately subordinate to the political leadership and the cause of Zionist redemption. The Sabra loved their teachers, who were prophets, and worshiped their military commanders, who were teachers. Kindergartens had "Jewish National Fund corners" analogous to Soviet "red corners" (Communist shrines), and the Palmach (the elite strike force of the Jewish military organization, the Haganah) had political officers analogous to Soviet commissars. Both generations lived amid relentless and mostly spontaneous political unanimity; both grew up among living saints and proliferating memorials; both drained swamps and made deserts bloom; and both struggled to merge the personal and the communal into one heroic story of timelessness regained. As David Ben-Gurion proclaimed in 1919, "a distinction between the needs of the individual and the needs of the nation has no basis in the lives of the workers in Eretz Israel." And as one young Sabra wrote in his diary in 1941, the "memories of private events" had begun to overshadow the "national historical background" in the chronicle of his life. "I will now correct this imbalance and write about enlistment and those who evade it, about the death of Ussishkin and the death of Brandeis, about the wars of Russia. . . . Why should I not write about these things in my diary? These facts are history and will always be remembered, while the details of individuals go astray and get lost in oblivion. Get lost and vanish."[89]

The Yishuv was no Soviet Union. It was small, particularist, and proudly parochial. Its unity was entirely voluntary (defectors were despised but free to go), and its warrior energy was directed outward, at the easily identifiable non-Jews. It was messianic but also one among many, unique but also "normal," in the familiar nationalist mold (which was mostly biblical in the first place). As one Herzliya Gymnasium student wrote in 1937, "this is the nation that has produced great heroes, zealous for freedom, and from whom rose prophets who prophesied the rule of justice and honesty in the world—because this nation is a heroic and noble nation and only the bitter and harsh life of Exile debased it, and this nation is still destined to be a light unto the nations."[90]

Zionism and Soviet Communism were both millenarian rebellions against capitalism, "philistinism," and "chimerical nationality." But Zionism belonged to the integral-nationalist wing of the twentieth-century revolution against modernity and shared much of its rhetoric and aesthetic. In the 1930s, Chava's children did more hiking, exercising, and singing around the campfire than did their Soviet cousins; talked more about the healthy (masculine) body; communed more passionately with nature (in a year-round dacha pastoral); and spent a lot more time learning how to shoot. The Soviets were trying to create a perfect mix of Mercurianism and Apollonianism; the Zionists were trying to transform Mercurians into Apollonians. The Soviets were erasing the differences between town and country by building cities; the Zionists were overcoming the diaspora urbanism by building villages. Hodl's children wanted to be poets, scholars, and engineers; Chava's children wanted to be armed farmers and "Hebrew commanders." Beilke's children wanted to be somebody else's children—preferably Hodl's.

If Hodl's husband, Perchik, did indeed become a people's commissar, publishing house director, secret police official, or a prominent Old Bolshevik, his family's prosperity and his children's happy childhoods were likely to end during the so-called Great Terror of 1937–38. Soviet socialism strove for complete human transparency in pursuit of equality; the full coincidence of every person's life with the story of world revolution (and ultimately with the story of Stalin's life as recorded in the "Short Course of the History of the All-Union Communist Party"). Having vanquished its military enemies and political opponents, destroyed all "exploiting classes," replaced (or "reforged") the "bourgeois specialists," suppressed internal dissenters, nationalized both peasants and pastoralists, and built, by 1934, "the foundations of socialism," the regime had no open and socially classifiable enemies left. Impurities persisted, however—and so, having proclaimed victory over the past, the regime turned on itself. Watched over by Stalin, committed to boundless violence, haunted by the demons of treason and contagion, and transported by the frenzy of self-flagellation and mutual suspicion, the high priests of the revolution sacrificed themselves to socialism and its earthly prophet. As Nikolai Bukharin wrote to Stalin from prison,

> There is something *great and bold about the political idea* of a general purge. . . . This business could not have been managed without me. Some are neutralized one way, others in another way, and a third group in yet another way. What serves as a guarantee for all this is the fact that people inescapably talk about each other and in doing so arouse an *everlasting* distrust in each other. . . .
>
> Oh Lord, if only there were some device which would have made it possible for you to see my soul flayed and ripped open! If only you could see how I am attached to you, body and soul. . . . No angel will appear now to snatch Abraham's sword from his hand. My fatal destiny shall be fulfilled. . . .
>
> I am preparing myself mentally to depart from this vale of tears, and there is nothing in me toward all of you, toward the party and the cause, but a great and boundless love. . . .
>
> I ask you one last time for your forgiveness (only in your heart, not otherwise).[91]

And as Nikolai Ezhov, who presided over Bukharin's execution, later stated on the eve of his own,

> During the 25 years of my party work I have fought honorably against enemies and have exterminated them. . . . I purged 14,000 Chekists. But my great guilt lies in the fact that I purged so few of them. . . . All around me were enemies of the people, my enemies. . . . Tell Stalin that I shall die with his name on my lips.[92]

The revolution had finally gotten around to eating its own children—or rather, its own parents, because Hodl and especially Perchik were much more likely to be arrested and shot than the youthful members of the "first Soviet generation." The revolution was as patricidal as the original revolutionaries had been, and no one was as puzzled by this as the original revolutionaries themselves. According to Hope Ulanovskaia, who had recently returned from the United States,

> Once, when after yet another arrest, I asked: "What is going on? Why? What for?" your father [i.e., her husband, an agent of the Main Intelligence Directorate] replied calmly: "Why are you so upset? When I told you how the White officers were being shot in the Crimea, you weren't upset, were you? When the bourgeoisie and the kulaks were being exterminated, you used to justify it, didn't you? But now that it's our turn, you ask: How, why? This is the way it's been from the very beginning." I reasoned with him: "I understand that it's terrible when people are killed, but before we always knew that it was for the sake of the revolution. Now nobody is explaining anything!" And so we started looking into our past, trying to determine when it had all started.[93]

The Ulanovskys were looking into their past in their own apartment; most of their friends and colleagues were doing it in their interrogation cells. Every prison confession was a (coauthored) attempt to determine the sources of treason, and every public pronouncement was a comment on the origins of perfection. As Babel had said in his speech at the First Congress of Soviet Writers in 1934,

> In our day, bad taste is no longer a personal defect; it is a crime. Even worse, bad taste is counterrevolution. . . . As writers, we must contribute to the victory of a new, Bolshevik taste in our country. It will not be an insignificant political victory because, fortunately for us, we do not have victories that are not political. . . . The style of the Bolshevik epoch is calm strength and self-control; it is full of fire, passion, power, and joy. Who should we model ourselves on? . . . Just look at the way Stalin forges his speech, how chiseled his spare words are, how full of muscular strength.[94]

Babel was executed for bad taste—for not mastering the style of the epoch, not having enough calm strength and self-control, not being able to forge himself like Stalin. Because, unfortunately for him, there was nothing in Stalin's Soviet Union that was not political and muscular. Babel was executed by his own creatures and his only true love: those who could "shuffle their fathers' faces like a fresh deck of cards"; those "whose fury contained within it everything that was necessary to rule over others"; those who had "murder in their souls"; those who had mastered "the simplest of skills—the ability to kill a man." The name of Babel's first interrogator was Lev Shvartsman.

Mikhail Baitalsky was arrested and sent to a camp. My grandmother's brother Pinkus, a visiting businessman from Poland, was arrested and sent to a camp. My grandfather, Moisei Khatskelevich Goldstein, was arrested, tortured, and released a year and a half later, after Ezhov's ouster. Tsafrira Meromskaia's childhood ended when her parents were arrested. And so did Inna Gaister's. Of Grandma Gita's children and in-laws gathered around the table at her welcome dinner, at least ten were arrested.

> After the arrests of Lipa and my mother, Grandma Gita had been living with Adassa. After Adassa was taken to prison, Grandma had moved in with Veniamin. In early December Elochka, Lipa's daughter, came home from school one day and found Grandma Gita sitting on the stairs in front of their apartment. Veniamin, without warning Niuma [Lipa's husband] or Leva, had brought her there and left her by the locked door. Grandma moved in with Niuma. I would often see her there. She was no longer the same proud and happy Grandma I had seen arrive from Poland. I can still picture her with her red wig all twisted round and her bun hanging over her ear. She could not understand why her children had been imprisoned. She kept pacing up and down the apartment, intoning: "It's all my fault. I have brought grief to my children. I must return home immediately. As soon as I leave, things will get better again." She was saying all this in Yiddish. Of course, Elochka and I could not understand a word of what she was saying, so Leva had to translate for us.[95]

Members of the political elite suffered disproportionately during the Great Terror. Because Jews were disproportionately represented within the political elite, they were prominent among the victims. Many of Evgenia Ginzburg's fellow passengers on the train bound for the Kolyma camps were Jewish Communists, and the same was true of Roziner's mother's cellmates at the Butyrki prison in Moscow. There were other women there, "but intelligentsia Communists, including my mother, kept apart from them. Practically all of them were Jews, all believed unconditionally in the purity of the Party, and every one of them thought that she had been arrested by mistake." Roziner's mother, Iudit, had graduated from a heder and spent two years in a Jewish *gymnasium* in Bobruisk before moving (in 1920) to Moscow, where she had become a student at the city's best school (the Moscow Exemplary School-Commune). After a short stint in Palestine, where she had joined the Communist Party, Iudit had returned to the Soviet Union.[96]

Members of the political elite suffered disproportionately, but they were not the majority of those affected. The Jews, who were not numerous among nonelite victims, were underrepresented in the Great Terror as a whole. In 1937–38, about 1 percent of all Soviet Jews were arrested for political crimes, as compared to 16 percent of all Poles and 30 percent of all Latvians. By early 1939, the proportion of Jews in the Gulag was about 15.7 percent lower than their share of the total Soviet population. The reason for this was the fact that the Jews were not targeted as an ethnic group. None of those arrested during the Great Terror of 1937–38—including Meromskaia's parents, Gaister's relatives, and my grandfather—was arrested *as a Jew*. The secret police did put together several Jewish-specific cases, but they were all politically (not ethnically) defined. Iudit Roziner-Rabinovich, for example, was arrested during the sweep of "Palestinians," but her interrogator (himself Jewish) was interested in Zionist organizations, not nationality. Samuil Agursky, the great crusader against Zionism, Moyshe Litvakov, his political enemy and fellow leader of the Party's Jewish Section, and Izi Kharik, the Yiddish "proletarian" writer and the author of the poem about the exodus to Moscow, were all arrested as part of the attack against former Bundists (real or imaginary). At the same time, similar campaigns were being waged against the former members of all the other non-Bolshevik parties, including the Socialist Revolutionaries, the Mensheviks, the Ukrainian Borotbists, the Azerbaidjani Mussavatists, and the Armenian Dashnaks, among others. And while Jewish national districts and schools were closed down, all other national districts and schools were closed down too, many of them more brutally and abruptly than the Jewish ones ("national" meant an ethnically defined unit within a different ethnically defined unit, such as Jewish or Polish districts and schools in Ukraine).[97]

Indeed, Jews were the only large Soviet nationality without its own "native" territory that was not targeted for a purge during the Great Terror. Ever since the revolution, the regime had been promoting ethnic particularism in general and diaspora communities (those with "national homes" across the border) in particular. One of the reasons for the latter policy was to offer the neighboring peoples clear and tangible proof of Soviet superiority. A special Politburo decree of 1925 had mandated that the national minorities of the Soviet border regions receive a particularly generous portion of national schools, national territories, native-language publications, and ethnic hiring quotas. The idea behind the "Piedmont Principle" (as Terry Martin calls it) was to instruct, inspire, and influence the peoples of neighboring countries—and perhaps offer them an alternative home. Starting in the mid-1930s, however, as the fear of contagion grew and the nature of the enemy seemed harder to determine, it became painfully obvious to the professionally paranoid that the opposite of inspirational influence was hostile penetration, and that cross-border kinship meant that bad Soviets, and not just good foreigners, might seek an alternative home. Between 1935 and 1938, the Chinese, Estonians, Finns, Germans, Iranians, Koreans, Kurds, Latvians, and Poles were all forcibly deported from border regions on the theory that their ethnic ties to neighboring non-Soviets made them uniquely susceptible to alien penetration. And in 1937–38, all diaspora nationalities of the Soviet Union became the subject of special "mass operations" involving quotas of arrests and executions. Twenty-one percent of all those arrested on political charges and 36.3 percent of all those executed were the targets of "national operations." Eighty-one percent of all those arrested in connection with the "Greek operation" were executed. In the Finnish and Polish operations, the execution rates were 80 and 79.4 percent.[98]

The Jews did not seem to have an alternative home. Unlike the Afghans, Bulgarians, Chinese, Estonians, Finns, Germans, Greeks, Iranians, Koreans, Macedonians, Poles, and Romanians, they were not seen as naturally attractive to foreign spies or congenitally weak as loyal Soviets. In 1939, Soviet publishing houses produced fourteen different titles by Sholem Aleichem on the occasion of his eightieth birthday; the State Museum of Ethnography in Leningrad organized the exhibition *Jews in Tsarist Russia and the USSR*; and the director of the State Jewish Theater, Solomon Mikhoels, received the Lenin Order, the title "People's Artist of the USSR," and a place on the Moscow City Soviet. Most Soviet Jews were not directly affected by the Great Terror, and of those who were, most suffered as members of the political elite. Because the people promoted to replace them tended to be former peasants and blue-collar workers, the Jewish share in the Party and state apparatus dropped precipitously after 1938. Because the cultural and professional elite was not hit as hard and experienced no significant turnover, the Jewish preeminence among top professionals remained intact.[99]

And then two things happened. In the second half of the 1930s, following the establishment of High Stalinism and especially during the Great Patriotic War, the Soviet state—now manned by newly promoted ethnic Russians of peasant and proletarian origins—began to think of itself as the legitimate heir to the Russian imperial state and Russian cultural tradition. At the same time, following the rise of Nazism and especially during the Great Patriotic War, more and more Soviet intelligentsia members—now branded inescapably with biological ethnicity—began to think of themselves as Jews.

The Soviet Union was neither a nation-state nor a colonial empire nor a United States of interchangeable citizens. It was a large section of the world that consisted of numerous territorially rooted nationalities endowed with autonomous institutions and held together by the internationalist ideology of world revolution and a cosmopolitan bureaucracy of Party and police officials. It was designed that way and claimed to remain so until its collapse in 1991, but in fact both the ideology and the bureaucracy began to change after about 1932 as a result of the radical collectivization of industry, agriculture, politics, and speech during the "Stalin Revolution." The newly completed command economy and the newly unified socialist-realist society seemed to require greater transparency, centralization, standardization, and thus—among other things—a unionwide lingua franca and a streamlined system of communications. By the end of the 1930s, most ethnically defined soviets, villages, districts, and "minority" schools had been sacrificed on the altar of a symmetrical federation of relatively homogeneous proto-nation-states and a few ethnic subunits too well entrenched to uproot (most of them in the Russian Republic).

Modern states require nations at least as much as modern nations require states. By representing and embodying political communities that share a common space, economy, and conceptual currency, they tend to become "ethnicized" in the sense of acquiring a common language, purpose, future, and past. Even the epitome of non-ethnic liberal statehood, the United States of America, has created a nation bound by a common language-based culture and thus by a sense of kinship more tangible and durable than the cult of a few political institutions. The Soviet Union's version of "the American people" was Sovietness, of course, but the Soviet Union was an ethnoterritorial federation in which each unit had its own native language and native speakers (except for the Russian Federation, which was still doing penance for its imperial past while also serving as an example of an ethnicity-free society). For the first fifteen years or so, Sovietness seemed to refer to the sum total of all native languages without exception plus a Marxist cosmopolitanism centered in Moscow. After Stalin's Great Transformation, however, the language of Marxist cosmopolitanism became the lingua franca of the entire Soviet command society. That language was Russian (not Esperanto, as some people proposed)—and Russian, in addition to being the language of Marxist cosmopolitanism, was the proud possession of a very large group of people and the revered object of a powerful Romantic cult. Moreover, it was the everyday language of top Bolshevik officials, most of whom (including the important

Jewish contingent) were members of the Russian intelligentsia as well as revolutionaries of "the Social Democratic nationality." Equally devoted to Pushkin and world revolution, they did not sense any tension between the two because most of them believed that Pushkin and the world revolution were fraternal twins. In a familiar paradox of nationalism, the Soviet advance toward modernization and unification led to the "Great Retreat" toward the *Volk*. The leap into socialism resulted in Russification.

The Soviet Union never became the Russian nation-state, but the country's Russian core did acquire some national content (although not as much as the other union republics), and the overarching concept of Sovietness did come to rely on elements of Russian nationalism (although never conclusively or consistently). "Russian" and "Soviet" had always been related: first as the only nonethnic peoples of the USSR and eventually as partially ethnicized reflections of each other: the Russianness of the Russian Republic was relatively underdeveloped because the Sovietness of the Soviet state was predominantly Russian.

When, during the civil war, Lenin appealed to the revolutionary workers and peasants to defend their "Socialist Fatherland," the Russian word "Fatherland" could not be stripped of its presocialist connotations whether Lenin wanted it to be or not (he probably did not). When, during the mid-1920s, Stalin called on the Party to build "socialism in one country," at least some Party members must have associated that country with the one in which they were born. And when, in 1931, Stalin urged the Soviet people to industrialize or perish, his reasoning had more to do with Russian national pride (as he understood it) than with Marxist determinism:

> To slacken the tempo would mean falling behind. And those who fall behind get beaten. But we do not want to be beaten. No, we refuse to be beaten! One feature of the history of old Russia was the continual beatings she suffered because of her backwardness. She was beaten by the Mongol khans. She was beaten by the Turkish beys. She was beaten by the Swedish feudal lords. She was beaten by the Polish and Lithuanian gentry. She was beaten by the British and French capitalists. She was beaten by the Japanese barons. All beat her—be-

cause of her backwardness, because of her military backwardness, cultural backwardness, political backwardness, industrial backwardness, agricultural backwardness. They beat her because to do so was profitable and could be done with impunity. . . . In the past we had no fatherland, nor could we have had one. But now that we have overthrown capitalism and power is in our hands, in the hands of the people, we have a fatherland, and we will uphold its independence.[100]

The "mature" Stalinist state ensured the "friendship of the peoples of the USSR" by promoting the nationalism of the non-Russian republics (complete with the officially sponsored and highly institutionalized cults of national bards and ethnic roots). It cemented that friendship by promoting the cult of the Russian people, language, history, and literature (as a common Soviet asset, not as the exclusive property of the Russian Republic, which remained a ghost entity until the end of the Soviet Union). In 1930, Stalin ordered the proletarian poet Demian Bedny to stop carrying on about the proverbial Russian sloth. "The leaders of the revolutionary workers of all countries are avidly studying the edifying history of the Russian working class, its history and the history of Russia. . . . All this fills (cannot but fill!) the hearts of the Russian workers with the feeling of revolutionary national pride capable of moving mountains, of working miracles." Bedny was too proletarian a poet to get the point. On November 14, 1936, a special Politburo decree banned his comic opera *Warriors* for "slandering the warriors of the Russian historical epics, the most important of whom live on in popular consciousness as the representatives of the heroic traits of the Russian people." Several months earlier, Bukharin had been attacked for calling the Russians "a nation of Oblomovs," and a few days before that (on February 1, 1936), a special *Pravda* editorial had formally announced that the Russian people were "first among equals" in the family of Soviet nations. By the end of the decade, patriotism had superseded world revolution, "traitors to the motherland" had replaced class enemies, most of the newly Latinized languages had been switched to Cyrillic, and all non-Russian schools in the Russian regions of the Russian Federation had been closed down. The study of Esperanto had become illegal, and the study of Russian had become obligatory. In May 1938, Boris Volin (an education official and the former chief censor) summarized the new orthodoxy in an article entitled "The Great Russian People," published in the Party's main theoretical journal:

> The Russian people have every right to be proud of their writers and poets. They have produced Pushkin, the creator of the Russian literary language, the founder of modern Russian literature, who enriched humanity with his immortal artistic creations. . . . The Russian people have every right to be proud of their scientists, who have provided more evidence of the inexhaustible creative genius of the Russian people. . . . The musical gifts of the Russian people are rich and diverse. . . . No less powerful are the manifestations of the Russian popular genius in the realm of fine arts and architecture. . . . The Russian people have created a theater that, one can say without exaggeration, has no equal in the world. . . .
>
> The Judas Bukharin, moved by his hatred of socialism, slandered the Russian people by describing them as "a nation of Oblomovs.". . . This is base slander against the Russian nation, against the courageous, freedom-loving Russian people, who have struggled and toiled tirelessly to forge their happy present and are in the process of creating an even happier and more beautiful future. . . . The great Russian people find themselves in the forefront of the fight against the enemies of socialism. The great Russian people are at the head of the struggle of all the peoples of the Soviet land for the happiness of mankind, for communism.[101]

At first, nothing seemed to suggest that the new role of the "Great Russian People" was incompatible with the continued openness of the Soviet cultural elite to the Jewish immigrants from the former Pale. Indeed, some of the leading ideologues of Russian patriotism (including Boris Volin, the jurist I. Trainin, the critic V. Kirpotin, and the historian E. Tarle) were ethnic Jews themselves. The young Lev Kopelev had not been alone in being impressed by Stalin's "We do not want to be beaten" speech. "It was then that I, a convinced internationalist, a Soviet patriot, and a representative of the newly formed multinational Soviet people, began to feel an acute sense of hurt and injustice on behalf of Russia, Russian history, and the Russian word."

> I was very pleased with this new turn in political propaganda and historical research, this decisive rejection of national nihilism. The Party confirmed and affirmed what I had felt since childhood and become conscious of in my youth.
>
> Such concepts as the "Motherland," "patriotism," the "people," and "national" were being restored. And I mean *restored*—because previously they had been toppled, overthrown. . . .
>
> I enjoyed the films about Peter the Great, Alexander Nevsky, and Suvorov; I liked the patriotic poems by Simonov, the books by E. Tarle and the "Soviet Count," Ignatiev; I reconciled myself to the return of officers' ranks and epaulets.
>
> My childhood attachment to the historical tales of our land came back to life in an adult form. And the never forgotten sounds of "Poltava" and "Borodino" rang out with renewed force.[102]

No one knew "Poltava" as thoroughly as Babel's and Marshak's Jewish boys—or their Soviet children. When the Great Patriotic War began, those children (Pavel Kogan's "generation") found themselves "amid the dust of battle" restaging both Poltava and the revolution. Boris Slutsky was a young political officer who spoke to the troops "on behalf of Russia":

> And I remind them of our native land.
> They're silent, then they sing, then they rejoin the battle.[103]

Slutsky's friend David Samoilov was his company's Komsomol leader. While waiting to go to the front, he wrote a paper on Tolstoy's *War and Peace*.

> What I (and perhaps someone before me) was trying to do was discern—through Tolstoy's eyes—the shape of socialism, of social equality, in the structure of the patriotic war. . . . A literary young man was seeking a confirmation of his state not in life, which he did not know, but in literature, which provided a firm support for the spirit. The point (as I sensed very deeply) was to leave behind the idea of intelli-

gentsia exclusivity, or rather, the idea of the primacy of obligations over rights. I needed to shed this idea, which had been instilled in me—unwittingly—by my environment, upbringing, education, the IFLI elitism, and my dream of poetic talent and special election.[104]

He found exactly what he was looking for: the Great Patriotic War as a reenactment of the Patriotic War of 1812 and his own spiritual journey as a reflection of Pierre Bezukhov's—and possibly of Babel's, too, for the story of the Jewish runt's "awakening" is but an ethnic version of the canonical Mercurian-Apollonian (intelligentsia-people) encounter. "The exhilaration I felt," wrote Samoilov, "came from the feeling of having common duties shared by all, and at the same time from the perception of a special value of my own individuality as equal to any other." Before long, Samoilov found his very own Platon Karataev and his very own Efim Nikitich Smolich. "The only person in our unit who truly revered spirituality and knowledge was Semyon Andreevich Kosov, a plowman from the Altai. A man of large stature and enormous strength, he felt a special tenderness for all those weaker than he was, be they animals or human beings. He suffered from hunger more than anyone else, and sometimes I would give Semyon my soup, while he would hide a tiny lump of sugar for me. But it was not this exchange that sustained our friendship—it was the mutual attraction of the strong and the weak."[105]

Samoilov combined weakness with knowledge because he was a Russian *intelligent* and because he was a Jew. For him, the "Russian people" he loved and wanted to share duties with were both an alien tribe (the Russians) and an alien class (the people). This was an old Romantic equation, of course, but it seems to have been more passionately felt by first-generation intelligentsia members freshly liberated from "tonguelessness." In Samoilov's version of Mandelstam's immersion in the "rootedness and the sound of Great Russian speech, slightly impoverished by intelligentsia conventions," Semyon stood for language as both life and truth. "Semyon's wisdom came not from reading but from all the experiences that had accumulated in popular speech. Sometimes I felt that he had no thoughts of his own, just clichés for all occasions. But now I understand that we also speak in clichés, except that we quote inaccurately and haphazardly. Our signs may be individualized but they are pale as speech acts. The people swim in the element of speech, washing their thoughts in it. We use speech to rinse our mouths."[106]

Sharing duties with Semyon was an immaculate culmination of Babel's and Bagritsky's first loves. During the Great Patriotic War, the Jewish Revolution against Jewishness seemed to achieve—finally—a perfect fusion of true internationalism and rooted Russianness, knowledge and language, mind and body. Samoilov and Semyon were fighting shoulder to shoulder "on behalf of Russia," the world's savior. Samoilov the poet was Semyon's true heir. "Semyon . . . belonged to the Russian folk culture, which has now faded away almost completely along with the disappearance of its carriers, the peasants. This culture lived for many centuries and became an inherent part of the national culture, having dissolved into the geniuses of the nineteenth century, above all Pushkin."[107]

Samoilov's fulfillment was platonic, fraternal, and mostly verbal. Margarita Aliger's passion was a direct—and self-consciously female—response to Babel's "First Love," "First Goose," and "First Fee." Her long poem "Your Victory" (1945–46) is the story of an all-conquering love between a beautiful Jewish girl from "Russia's southern coast," who "escaped the prison of warm rooms and favorite books," and a "savage, fearless, and obstinate" boy from a Cossack village, who "stole watermelons and teased girls." They both belonged to the generation conceived by the revolution, raised to the sounds of the "Internationale," and tempered by the First Five Year Plan—a generation that "will never grow old" and "will never learn how to save money or keep goods under lock and key." They shared hopes, friends, and their faith; they got married in Turkmenistan, where she was a Komsomol official; and they moved to Moscow, where they received a new apartment with "two rooms, a balcony, a hallway." They were in love, but they had different "characters" and different "souls," and their last and decisive revolutionary battle was the one for mutual discovery, recognition, and acceptance. Or rather, it was her personal battle to learn how to "live in dignity" with someone as "huge, frightening, good, perfidious, faithful, and confused" as he was.

> Whose muse will do you justice,
> The frightening, virtuous, bold,
> The heart of both light and darkness,
> The soul of the child and the artist,
> The wonderful Russian soul?
>
> . . . .
>
> When, gradually, you unearth
> Your husband's most hidden riches,
> You see that he's so much worse
> And better than what you had pictured.
> That everything you had imagined,
> All things you'd longed to admire
> Are trivial, slight, and wretched
> Compared to this blackness and fire.

He was doubly different, desirable, and enigmatic because he was both a man and a Russian—the way Samoilov's Semyon was both a "man of the people" and a Russian. Eventually, Aliger's protagonist (perhaps Margarita too) understands that "there is no other path and no other fate" for her, but it is only during the Great Patriotic War, when he leaves for the front and she stays behind to share (as poet and political "agitator") "the miraculous faith of the Russian people," that she makes her final commitment and promises to bear him a daughter in his image. "You can give her any name you like."

But it is too late: because he will never come back from the front and they will never have children. The moment of greatest intimacy and true fulfillment (as compared to Babel's and Bagritsky's flailing adolescent attempts) is the beginning of the end of the Russian-Jewish First Love. The reason is "blood."

Chased out of Odessa by the Nazis and wandering somewhere in the Tatar wilderness, Margarita's mother loses her usual "serenity and nobility" and acquires "a frightening, charred resemblance / To those who have no homeland." Why is that? Are they not at home in the Soviet Union?

> Staying warm by the stove somehow,
> Improvising a table to set,
> "We are Jews," said my mother, "How
> Could you ever, how dared you forget?"

Margarita is not sure what she means. She does have her Motherland, after all, one she loves all the more because "you don't get to choose it."

> Yes, I dared! Can't you see, I dared!
> There was so much else I could love.
> Why would I—why should I have cared,
> When so blue was the sky above?

Is Motherland—is nationality—not about "Pushkin's golden tales," "Gogol's enchanting voice," "Lenin's expansive gesture," and "the unsparing love of a wild Russian man"? Not entirely, as it turns out.

> Our freedom's firstborn generation,
> Raised in blissful ignorance of Hell,
> We forgot about our ancient nation,
> But the Nazis—they remembered well.
> We all knew that war demanded valor,
> Not that it required one final choice;
> We all knew that human blood had color,
> Not that it might also have a voice.
> When the scythes of Death began to mow,
> We found out that Hell had several rungs;
> When the time came for the blood to flow,
> It cried out in many different tongues.
> As I listen to the mortal moaning,
> I discern one voice I can recall.
> And each day gets louder, more imploring,
> Blood's insistent, subterranean call.[108]

The Nazis classified people, particularly the Jews, according to the voice of their blood. Most people, and particularly the Jews, responded by hearing their blood's call. Nowhere did it make more sense than in the Soviet Union, where all citizens, including the Jews, were classified by blood and expected to listen earnestly to its call.

From its inception, the Soviet state had been promoting ethnicity as a remedy against the memory of oppression. In the absence of new oppression, ethnicity was—eventually—going to die from an overdose of oxygen (the way the state itself was going to wither away as a consequence of being strengthened). In the meantime, the state needed to know the nationality of its citizens because it needed to delimit ethnic territories, teach native languages, publish national newspapers, and promote set percentages of indigenous cadres to a variety of positions and institutions. The state kept asking its citizens about their nationality, and they kept answering, over and over again—first according to their self-perception or self-interest and then according to their blood (whether they liked it or not).

With the introduction of the internal passport system in 1932, nationality became a permanent label and one of the most important official predictors of admissions and promotions in the Soviet Union. When, at the age of twenty, Lev Kopelev received his first passport, he did what many of Hodl's children would do: he chose to be a Jew. Russian and Ukrainian by culture and conviction, he "had never heard the call of blood" but he did understand "the language of memory," as he put it, and he believed that to renounce his parents, who had always thought of themselves as Jews, would be "a desecration of their graves." What made his choice easier was the fact that it did not make any difference. One could benefit from being an Uzbek in Uzbekistan or a Belorussian in Belorussia; "Jewish" and "Russian" were—back in 1932—virtually interchangeable (both inside and outside of the Russian Republic).[109]

But the Kopelev option proved short-lived. As the Soviet Union became more thoroughly ethnicized, ethnic units became more rooted (in history, literature, and native soil), and personal ethnicity became exclusively a matter of blood. When it came to killing enemies, in particular, biological nationality proved far superior to fluid political and class affiliations. On April 2, 1938, as most diaspora ethnic groups were being purged, a special secret police instruction introduced a new, strictly genetic, procedure for determining nationality.

> If one's parents are Germans, Poles, etc., irrespective of where they were born, how long they have lived in the USSR, or whether they have changed their citizenship, etc., the person being registered cannot be classified as Russian, Belorussian, etc. If the nationality claimed by the person being registered does not correspond to his native language or last name (for instance, the person's name is Müller or Papandopoulo but he calls himself a Russian, Belorussian, etc.), and if the real nationality of the person in question cannot be determined at the time of registration, the "nationality" line is not to be filled in until the applicant produces written proof.[110]

Germans, Poles, and Greeks were subject to "mass operations"; Jews and Russians were not, but the procedure was the same for everyone. When the Nazis came, most Soviets had no trouble understanding their language.

When the Nazis came, most of Hodl's children knew that they were, in some sense, Jews. They may never have been to a synagogue, seen a menorah, heard Yiddish or Hebrew, tasted gefilte fish, or indeed met their grandparents. But they knew they were Jews in the Soviet sense, which was also—in essence—the Nazi sense. They were Jews by blood.

When the Nazis came, they began killing Jews according to their blood. Inna Gaister's Grandma Gita was killed soon after she returned home, and so was Mikhail Agursky's grandmother and also his great-aunt, and so was my grandmother's only brother who did not emigrate from the Pale, and so was Tsaytl, Tevye's daughter, who stayed in their native Kasrilevka, and so were most of her children, grandchildren, friends, and neighbors.

> Killed were the old artisans and experienced craftsmen [wrote Vassily Grossman on reentering Ukraine in the fall of 1943]: tailors, hatters, cobblers, tinsmiths, jewelers, painters, furriers, and bookbinders;

killed were the workers: porters, mechanics, electricians, carpenters, stonemasons, and plumbers; killed were the wagoners, tractor operators, truck drivers, and cabinetmakers; killed were the water carriers, millers, bakers, and cooks; killed were the doctors: physicians, dentists, surgeons, and gynecologists; killed were the scientists: bacteriologists, biochemists, and directors of university clinics, killed were the history, algebra, and trigonometry teachers; killed were the lecturers, assistant professors, masters and Ph.D.'s; killed were the civil engineers, architects, and engine designers; killed were the accountants, bookkeepers, salesmen, supply agents, secretaries, and night guards; killed were the grade school teachers and seamstresses; killed were the grandmothers who knew how to knit socks, bake tasty cookies, cook chicken soup, and make apple strudels with nuts, as well as the grandmothers who could not do any of those things but could only love their children and their children's children; killed were the women who were faithful to their husbands and the loose women too; killed were the beautiful girls, serious students, and giggly schoolgirls; killed were the plain and the foolish; killed were the hunchbacks, killed were the singers, killed were the blind, killed were the deaf, killed were the violinists and pianists, killed were the two- and three-year-olds; killed were the eighty-year-old men with their eyes clouded by cataracts, their cold transparent fingers, and soft voices like rustling paper; and killed were the crying babies suckling at their mothers' breasts to the very last moment.[111]

And for every one of their surviving relatives, for all Jews by blood, as for Margarita Aliger, the spilled blood spoke in their mother tongue. As the Polish Jewish poet Julian Tuwim put it,

I hear voices: "Very well. But if you are a Pole, why do you write 'We—Jews?' " I reply: "because of my blood." "Then it is racialism?" Nothing of the kind. On the contrary. There are two kinds of blood: the blood that flows in your veins and the blood that flows out of them. . . . The blood of Jews (not "Jewish blood") flows in deep, broad streams; the dark streams flow together in a turbulent, foaming river, and in this new Jordan I accept holy baptism—the bloody, burning brotherhood of the Jews.[112]

Tuwim's syllogism was as faulty as it was powerful. He did not call on all decent people to call themselves Jews—he was calling on all Jews by blood to become Jews by national faith (and by open declaration) because of the blood of Jews (Jewish blood) that the Nazis were spilling. Ilya Ehrenburg was—uncharacteristically—more straightforward. One month after the Nazi invasion of the Soviet Union, he said:

> I grew up in a Russian city. My native language is Russian. I am a Russian writer. Now, like all Russians, I am defending my homeland. But the Nazis have reminded me of something else: my mother's name was Hannah. I am a Jew. I say this with pride. Hitler hates us more than anyone else. And that does us credit.[113]

Jewishness, like Russianness (only more so, because of its Mercurian past) was ultimately about parents and their children. In Grossman's *Life and Fate*, the protagonist's mother writes to her son from the ghetto, shortly before her death:

> I never used to feel Jewish: all my friends growing up were Russian; my favorite poets were Pushkin and Nekrasov; and the play that reduced me to tears, together with the whole audience—a congress of Russian village doctors—was Stanislavsky's production of *Uncle Vanya*. And, Vitia dear, when I was fourteen and our family decided to emigrate to South America, I told my father: "I'll never leave Russia—I'd rather drown myself." And so I didn't go.
>
> But now, during these terrible days, my heart is filled with a maternal tenderness toward the Jewish people. I never knew this love before. It reminds me of my love for you, my dearest son.[114]

Her son, Viktor Pavlovich (in fact, "Pinkhusovich," but his mother had Russified his patronymic) Shtrum becomes Jewish because of his love for his mother—because of what the Nazis are doing to her.

> Never, before the war, had Viktor thought about the fact that he was a Jew, or that his mother was a Jew. Never had his mother spoken to him about it—either during his childhood or during his years as a

student. Never while he was at Moscow University had one student, professor, or seminar leader ever mentioned it.

Never before the war, either at the institute or at the Academy of Sciences, had he ever heard conversations about it.

Never—not once—had he felt a desire to speak about it to [his daughter] Nadya, to explain to her that her mother was Russian and her father Jewish.[115]

His mother's last letter would force him to hear the "call of blood." The sight of the liberated areas—"Ukraine without the Jews," as Grossman called it—might cause it to grow even louder. And the gradual rise of unabashed popular anti-Semitism—first in the Nazi-occupied territories, then in remote evacuation centers, and eventually in the Russian heartland—might make it impossible to resist. Ukraine, in particular, had been the main stage for the old Pale's "two solitudes," the revolution's bloodiest pogroms, and the Soviet state's war against the peasants (at least some of whom identified the Soviet state with the Jews—from anti-Semitic habit and because of Jewish visibility in the Party). Now, after "three years of constant exposure to relentless, exterminatory, anti-Semitic rhetoric and practices" (as Amir Weiner puts it), some Soviet citizens seemed to be saying, for the first time in around two decades, that they preferred their Ukraine "without the Jews."[116]

Perhaps most important, and most fateful for "state Jews" like Shtrum and Hodl's children, the Party kept strangely silent (for the time being)—silent about the new anti-Semitic talk, about the Kiev pogrom of September 1945, and about what had happened to Soviet Jews under the Nazis. The experience of a total ethnic war had made the newly ethnicized Soviet regime even more self-conscious about blood and soil, or rather, about the blood of those who had a formal claim to the Soviet soil. The Jews were not a regular Soviet nationality, and this seemed to mean that they were not entitled to their own martyrs, their own heroes, and perhaps even their own national existence. And this, after what had happened to his mother and all of her friends and neighbors, might force Viktor Shtrum to rethink both his Soviet patriotism and his Jewish nationality.[117]

This would not happen until late in the war, however. In the early stages, when more and more Soviet soil was being overrun by the Nazis, and more and more Soviet patriots of Jewish nationality were heeding the call of blood without ceasing to be Soviet patriots, the Party had not been shy about proclaiming its commitment to Jewish martyrs, heroes, and national existence. Two months after the invasion, it had sponsored "An Appeal to World Jewry" signed by four well-known Yiddishists and several Soviet cultural celebrities of Jewish background, including the Bolshoi conductor S. Samosud, the physicist Petr Kapitsa, and the chief socialist-realist architect Boris Iofan (who was still at work on the ultimate public building of all time, the Palace of the Soviets). On the day the appeal was published (August 24, 1941), a special "rally of the representatives of the Jewish people" was broadcast by Radio Moscow to the Allied countries. Both the written appeal and the radio addresses referred to their audience as "brother-Jews the world over," emphasized the role of the Jews as the primary victims of Nazism, expressed pride in the heroism of their fighting "kinsmen," and called on those who were far from the battlefields for help and support. In the words of the published document, "Throughout the tragic history of our long-suffering people—from the time of Roman domination through the Middle Ages—there has never been a period that can compare to the horror and calamity that fascism has brought to all humanity and, with particular ferocity, to the Jewish people."

In this hour of horror and calamity, it turned out that the Jewish people—"ethnic" or religious, Communist, Zionist, or traditionalist—were one family. As the director of the State Jewish Theater, Solomon Mikhoels, put it,

> Along with all the citizens of our great country, our sons are engaged in battle, dedicating their lives and blood to the great patriotic war of liberation, being waged by the Soviet people.
>
> Our mothers themselves are sending their sons into this battle for justice, for the great cause of our free Soviet homeland.
>
> Our fathers are fighting alongside their sons and brothers against the enemy who is ravaging and annihilating the people.

And you, our brothers, remember that here in our country, on the battlefields, your fate as well as the fate of the countries you live in is being decided. Don't be lulled by the thought that Hitler's brutal savagery will spare you.

Of all the brothers and sisters living outside of the Soviet Union and occupied Europe, the largest number lived in America. It was to them that most of the appeals were directed, and it was from them that the strongest fraternal sentiment was expected. In the words of Ilya Ehrenburg, "There is no ocean behind which you can hide. . . . Your peaceful sleep will be disturbed by the cries of Leah from Ukraine, Rachel from Minsk, Sarah from Białystok—they are weeping over their slaughtered children."[118]

Mikhoels, Ehrenburg, and others were moved by the "call of blood" and moral outrage. The Soviet officials who sponsored the rally and edited the speeches were mostly interested in financial assistance and the opening of a second front. (Although some of them may have heard the call of blood too: the head of the Soviet external propaganda apparatus, Solomon Lozovsky, was himself an ethnic Jew, as were the Soviet ambassadors to Great Britain and the United States, I. M. Maisky and K. A. Umansky, who met with Chaim Weizmann and David Ben-Gurion in 1941 as part of the Soviet effort to court world Jewish organizations.) In late 1941–early 1942, the Soviet Bureau of Information created a special Jewish Anti-Fascist Committee. Its purpose (like that of several others formed at the same time: the Women's, Scholars', Slavic, and Youth Committees) was to cultivate a specialized overseas constituency for the benefit of the Soviet war effort. The JAFC's main task was to raise money in the United States. The committee's leaders were Mikhoels, Soviet Jewry's most recognizable face, and Shakhno Epstein, a journalist, the Party's Jewish Section veteran, and a former Soviet secret agent in the United States.[119]

During World War II, the Soviet state received around $45 million from various Jewish organizations, most of them U.S.-based. The greatest fund-raising effort of all was the North American tour undertaken in the summer and fall of 1943 by Mikhoels and a member of JAFC's presidium, Itsik Fefer, a Yiddish writer and secret police informer. Mikhoels and Fefer spoke at mass rallies (the one at the Polo Grounds in New York was attended by about fifty thousand people); negotiated with the leaders of the World Jewish Congress and World Zionist Organization (in ways that had been approved by Soviet officials); and met with—among many others—Albert Einstein, Charlie Chaplin, Eddie Cantor, Theodore Dreiser, Thomas Mann, and Yehudi Menuhin. The visit was enormously successful: American audiences responded eagerly to the Soviet Jewish appeals, and both Mikhoels and Fefer were greatly impressed by the wealth, influence, and generosity of American Jewish organizations. The tour's chief organizer was Ben-Zion Goldberg, a pro-Soviet Yiddish journalist, immigrant from the Russian Empire, and Sholem Aleichem's son-in-law. Some of Tevye's surviving children and grandchildren were finally getting together again.[120]

Within the Soviet Union, Tevye's surviving children and grandchildren—including those, like Viktor Shtrum, who had never considered themselves Jewish—were finally getting together again, in ways that threatened to overwhelm the Jewish Anti-Fascist Committee. As Perets Markish stated at the JAFC Second Plenary Session in February 1943, "A colonel from one of the tank units came up to me a while ago. 'I am a Jew,' he said, 'and I would like to fight as a Jew. I would like to contact the appropriate authorities to suggest forming separate Jewish units.' . . . Then I asked him: 'How effective do you think such units will be?' And he replied: 'Uniquely effective. The Jewish soldiers have only one choice: to kill the enemy or perish.' "[121]

A year later, a first lieutenant teaching at the Penza Artillery Academy wrote to Mikhoels asking for help in getting transferred to the front. "I, too, am a Jew, and I have a personal score to settle with Hitler's gang. The German thugs massacred my relatives who were living in Odessa and destroyed our happy, quiet life. And I want to take revenge for it. Revenge, revenge, and more revenge, in every place and at every moment."[122]

As the Soviet Army rolled westward, the demands for a specifically Jewish answer to the specifically Jewish suffering became one "insistent, subterranean call." Soviet Jews were writing to the Anti-Fascist Committee asking for help in burying and commemorating the dead, chronicling Jewish martyrdom and heroism, regaining access to prewar homes, and combating growing anti-Semitism. But more than anything else, they were writing about the insistent, subterranean call itself. As one war veteran put it in a letter to Mikhoels, "Let us not be ashamed of our blood. And what is more, in our country we Jews are not poor relations. I have grown convinced that Israel lived, lives, and will go on living forever and ever. My eyes are full of tears. They are not tears of grief, but of joy."[123]

Another one, a lieutenant of the guards and a "senior engineer," addressed the entire committee:

> I make this appeal to you as a member of the younger generation of adult Jews.
>
> We see in you the representatives of a Great Nation—a nation of genius and martyrdom. Through you we express our hope for a distinctive statehood and national-cultural autonomy. We cannot allow the disappearance of a wonderful nation that gave the world some of its brightest luminaries and has preserved, through centuries of persecution, death, and suffering, the banner of humanism and internationalism, an unparalleled thirst for creativity, exploration, and invention, the dream of a happily reunited mankind, and a faith in progress.
>
> You are the only headquarters of that wonderful nation in the USSR. Only you can assure the preservation of our Great Nation of prophets, innovators, and martyrs.[124]

Some members of the committee were wary of usurping the Party's role. (As one Old Bolshevik and experienced Party and state official, M. I. Gubelman, put it, "the nationalities question in our country has been sufficiently addressed by Comrade Stalin and needs no further amendments.") But many, especially the Yiddish writers in the committee's presidium, seem to have felt that they did, in a sense, represent the Jewish people, and that the Jewish people required special consideration because of the national tragedy that had befallen them and because the survivors of that tragedy were *their* people, *their* blood relatives.[125]

The boldest political initiative that resulted from this sentiment was the February 1944 letter to Stalin, in which the committee leaders Mikhoels, Epstein, and Fefer proposed the creation of a Jewish Soviet Socialist Republic in the Crimea. First, they argued, the Jewish refugees from the Nazi-occupied territories had no homes or families to go back to; second, the creation of national intelligentsias among "fraternal peoples" had rendered the professionals of "Jewish nationality" superfluous; third, the existing Yiddish cultural institutions were too few and too scattered to meet Jewish cultural requirements; and fourth, the war had led to a resurgence of anti-Semitism and, as a reaction to it, Jewish nationalism. The existing Jewish Autonomous Region in the Far East, they concluded, was too remote from the "main Jewish toiling masses" and thus incapable of solving "the administrative and legal problem of the Jewish people" in the spirit of the "Leninist-Stalinist nationalities policy."[126]

The Politburo members Kaganovich, Molotov, and Voroshilov (the first Jewish, the latter two married to Jewish women) seemed cautiously sympathetic, but Stalin did not like the idea and the project died a slow bureaucratic death (despite a brief flare of enthusiasm following the deportation of the Crimean Tatar population to Central Asia and Kazakhstan). The alternative plan of resettling the Jews in the former Republic of Volga Germans appealed to Fefer and Perets Markish as an act of "historical justice" but was vetoed by Molotov as another quixotic attempt to put "an urban nation . . . on a tractor." The "Jewish problem," it appeared, could not be solved in the spirit of the Leninist-Stalinist nationalities policy.[127]

Disappointing as these reverses may have been, they occurred in the dark recesses of "apparatus" politics and concerned the wartime refugees from the former Pale of Settlement, not their kinsmen in the capitals (Tsaytl's surviving children, not Hodl's). Everything changed, however, after the creation of the State of Israel in Palestine. In an attempt to put pressure on Britain and acquire an ally in the Middle East, the Soviet Union had supported a separate Jewish state, supplied Jewish fighters with arms (via Czechoslovakia), and promptly recognized Israel's independence. It was inside the USSR, however, that the official encouragement of Zionism produced the most striking and—for Soviet officials—disconcerting results. Assuming that they were within the boundaries of the official policy, or possibly no longer caring whether they were or not, thousands of Soviet Jews, most of them Jews "by blood" from Moscow and Leningrad, took the occasion to express their feelings of pride, solidarity, and belonging. As one Moscow student wrote to the JAFC,

> Please help me join the Israeli Army as a volunteer. At a time when the Jewish people are shedding their blood in an unequal struggle for their freedom and independence, my duty as a Jew and a Komsomol member is to be in the ranks of their fighters.
>
> I am twenty-two years old; I am in good physical shape and have sufficient military training. Please help me fulfill my duty.[128]

Before the war, being a Komsomol member of Jewish descent had meant being an internationalist and, for Hodl and her children, an avid follower of Russian high culture. After the war—and apparently still in the spirit of Leninst-Stalinist nationalities policy—it meant being a proud ethnic Jew too. As another Muscovite wrote two days earlier, "there is no doubt that the government of the USSR will not hinder this effort [of sending arms and volunteers to Palestine], just as it did not hinder the campaign of aid to Republican Spain." Jewish national redemption equaled anti-Fascism equaled Soviet patriotism. "A tremendous change has taken place in our lives: our name—'Jew'—has been raised so high that we have become a nation equal to other nations. At present, a small handful of Jews in the State of Israel is conducting an intense struggle against Arab aggression. This is also a struggle against the English empire. It is a struggle not only for an independent State of Israel, but also for our future, for democracy and justice."[129]

Comrade Stalin and the Soviet government, according to another letter to the JAFC, "had always helped independence fighters" (unlike "the English and American scum," who are "inciting, and will *always* incite, the Arabs"). Ultimately, however, the Jewish cause in Palestine was the cause of all Jews because all Jews were related by blood and because of what they had all been through. "Now [wrote another JAFC correspondent], when a war to the death is being waged, when the war is getting more and more intense, when our brothers and sisters are shedding their blood, when the fascist Arab gangs supported by Anglo-American imperialism are trying to strangle the heroic Jewish people and drown them in blood, we, Soviet Jews, cannot sit and wait in silence. We must actively help those self-sacrificial heroes triumph, and active help means fighting alongside our brothers."[130]

As Fefer would later describe the May days of 1948, "we were under siege. Dozens of people would come every day." And as G. M. Kheifets (Fefer's deputy in the JAFC, the committee's principal secret informer, and formerly the head of Soviet espionage on the West Coast of the United States) reported to the Central Committee of the Party, most visitors wanted to go to Palestine as volunteers.

> The majority of the petitioners speak not just for themselves, but on behalf of their colleagues and schoolmates. The largest number of requests are from students of Moscow institutions of higher learning: the Law Institute, the Chemistry Institute, the Foreign Language School, the Institute of Chemical Machine-Building, and others. There are also petitions from Soviet employees—engineers from the Steel Research Center and the Ministry of Armaments—as well as Soviet Army officers. As their motive, the petitioners cite their desire to help the Jewish people in their struggle against English aggression, on behalf of the Jewish state.[131]

Indeed, some went so far as to make "unheard-of, shocking" statements (as one JAFC presidium member described them) to the effect that Palestine was their homeland. But what was even more unheard-of and shocking was that thousands of people were making such statements publicly and collectively. On September 3, 1948, the first Israeli ambassador to the USSR, Golda Meyerson (later Meir), arrived in Moscow. What followed was a series of improvised, spontaneous, and unsupervised political rallies—something the Soviet capital had not seen in more than twenty years. For Golda Meir, who had been born in the Russian Empire, visiting the Soviet Union was a kind of homecoming. On the very first Saturday after her arrival, she went to the Moscow synagogue and, having greeted the rabbi, broke into tears. The purpose of her visit, however, and of course the purpose of the new state she represented, was to remind the Jews of all countries that their true home was not their home. During the next month, every one of her public appearances was accompanied by a demonstration of Soviet Jewish identification with Israel. On October 4, 1948, on Rosh Hashanah, thousands of people came to the Moscow synagogue to see her. Some cried, "Shalom"; most had probably never been to a synagogue before. And on October 13, on Yom Kippur, a large crowd followed the Israeli diplomats from the synagogue to the Metropole Hotel, chanting, "Next year in Jerusalem."[132]

The two trends—the ethnicization of the Soviet state and the nationalization of ethnic Jews—kept reinforcing each other until Stalin and the new Agitprop officials made two terrifying discoveries.

First, the Jews as a Soviet nationality were now an ethnic diaspora potentially loyal to a hostile foreign state. After the creation of Israel and the launching of the Cold War, they had become analogous to the Germans, Greeks, Finns, Poles, and other "nonnative" nationalities presumed to be beholden to an external homeland and thus congenitally and irredeemably alien. The official assault on the Jews would be a belated application of the ethnic component of the Great Terror to an ethnic group that had escaped it (as an ethnic group) in 1937–38.

Second, according to the new Soviet definition of national belonging and political loyalty, the Russian Soviet intelligentsia, created and nurtured by Comrade Stalin, was not really Russian—and thus not fully Soviet. Russians of Jewish descent were masked Jews, and masked Jews were traitors twice over.

All Stalinist purges were about creeping penetration by invisible aliens—and here was a race that was both ubiquitous and camouflaged; an ethnic group that was so good at becoming invisible that it had become visible as an elite (perhaps *the* Soviet elite). Here was a nationality that did not possess its own territory (or rather, possessed one but refused to live there), a nationality that did not have its own language (or rather, had one but refused to speak it), a nationality that consisted almost entirely of intelligentsia (or rather, refused to engage in proletarian pursuits); a nationality that used pseudonyms instead of names (this seemed true not only of Old Bolsheviks and professional writers but also of most immigrants from the former Pale of Settlement: the children of Baruchs, Girshas, and Moshes had routinely changed their patronymics to Borisovich, Grigorievich, and Mikhailovich). Being Jewish became a crime: those who claimed a separate Yiddish culture were "bourgeois nationalists"; those who identified with Russian culture were "rootless cosmopolitans."

The more brutal, if relatively small-scale, campaign was waged against the first group (the public Jews). In January 1948, the best-known Soviet Yiddishist, Solomon Mikhoels, was murdered on Stalin's orders by the secret police. (The man who had lured him into the trap, a Jewish theater critic and police informer, V. I. Golubov-Potapov, was murdered with him. They were both tied up, thrown to the ground, and run over by a truck as part of the plot to make it look like a traffic accident.) Over the next two years, all Yiddish theaters and writers' organizations were closed, and most Yiddish writers were arrested. In the spring and summer of 1952, fifteen former members of the Jewish Anti-Fascist Committee were put on trial as "bourgeois nationalists." One was spared; one died in prison; and the remaining thirteen were sentenced to death (one month before the trial began) and shot on the same day (one month after the trial ended).

Most of the accused—especially the fiction writers David Bergelson, Isaak Fefer, Leiba Kvitko, and Perets Markish—were Communist true believers who had dedicated most of their lives to promoting Stalin's "socialist content" in Yiddish "national form." Such had been the official Party policy toward the formerly abused nationalities in general and the long-suffering Jewish people in particular. According to Fefer, "I wanted my people to be like all the others. . . . It seemed to me that only Stalin could correct the historic injustice committed by the Roman emperors. It seemed to me that only the Soviet government could correct this injustice by creating a Jewish nation." He was right, of course. The Soviet government had made a serious effort to make the Jews "like all the others" and had amply rewarded those who had helped lead the charge. As Fefer said at the trial, "I am the son of a poor teacher. The Soviet government made me a human being and a fairly well known poet too." And as Kvitko said a few days later, "Before the revolution, I lived the worthless life of a miserable stray dog. Since the Great October Revolution, I have lived thirty wonderful, soaring, useful years filled with happiness in my beloved homeland, where every blade of grass smiles on me."[133]

And then, for reasons they could not quite understand, the same Soviet government had reclassified the Jews from a would-be normal nationality comparable to the Ukrainians or Mordvinians to a potentially disloyal nationality similar to the Poles or Greeks. The Jewish national form had become the symptom of a hostile bourgeois content. Saying in public that your mother's name was Hannah had become a nationalist act.

Some refused to go along. As Solomon Lozovsky put it, "My mother's name was Hannah too; so what, am I supposed to be ashamed of it? What kind of strange mentality is that? Why is it considered nationalism?" And as for the attack against Yiddish, "if you write for a Yiddish newspaper, you write in Yiddish. But when Bergelson says that this constitutes nationalism, then what is on trial here is the Yiddish language itself. This defies comprehension. You can write in a Negro language if you want. It's up to you. What matters is what you write, not what language you write in."[134]

Such missionary universalism had long since stopped being the official Soviet policy, and most of the accused, especially those who had championed the idea of Jewish settlement in areas that had been vacated by the summarily deported Volga Germans and Crimean Tatars, knew it only too well. The question was whether the Jews would join the Crimean Tatars, who had been exiled to Uzbekistan, or the Uzbeks, whom the Soviet government had helped become a nation "like all the others." As Fefer explained, "I was very jealous as I watched the Uzbek art festival. . . . I had fought for Jewish institutions as hard as I could."

That had been before the Cold War, however—back when the Party had not considered all Jewish institutions to be subversive and Fefer "had not believed that resisting assimilation was a form of nationalist activity." Things were different in 1952. Fefer still "loved his own people" ("for who does not love his own people?"), regarded the Bible as "one of the greatest monuments of Jewish culture," and maintained, under hostile interrogation, that no other nation had "suffered as much as the Jews." Yet he was also a committed Party member and the designated agent provocateur whose job at the trial was to argue that the love of one's own people was nationalism, that nationalism was treason, and that all the defendants were therefore guilty as charged. Leiba Kvitko, another committed Communist and professional Yiddishist, seemed to agree:

> The . . . thing that I consider myself guilty of—and what I think I am being accused of and feel responsible for—is this. Believing Soviet Yiddish literature to be ideologically healthy and genuinely Soviet, we Yiddish writers, myself included (I may be guiltier than anyone), did not raise the question of how we could contribute to the process of assimilation. I am talking about the assimilation of the Jewish masses. By continuing to write in Yiddish, we could not help becoming a brake on the process of assimilation. Insofar as the work of Soviet writers is ideologically and politically healthy in content, it has helped to bring about the assimilation of the majority of the Jewish population. But in recent years the Yiddish language has stopped serving the masses because it has been abandoned by the masses and thus became a hindrance. When I was the head of the Yiddish Section of the Union of Soviet Writers, I did not propose that the section be closed down. Of this I am guilty. To use a language that has been abandoned by the masses, has become obsolete, and is responsible for setting us apart not only from the larger life of the Soviet Union but also from the bulk of the Jewish population, which has already become assimilated—to use such a language is, it seems to me, a particular form of nationalism.[135]

The Yiddish professionals and other self-described and state-appointed guardians of Jewish culture could be imprisoned or executed. There were very few of them and they had, it is true, set themselves apart "from the bulk of the Jewish population" (including their own children, virtually none of whom knew any Yiddish or showed any interest in Jewish culture). The principal targets of

Stalin's anti-Jewish campaign, however, were Russians of Jewish descent or, as far as the Party's Agitprop was concerned, Jews who claimed to be Russians in order to appear Soviet. The Party's relentless will to purge and its routine "personnel policy" merged to become an exercise in investigative genealogy: every Russian in high position was a potential Jew, and every Jew without exception was a potential enemy.

The campaign to cleanse the Soviet elite of ethnic Jews began as early as May 1939 when, in an apparent attempt to please Hitler, Stalin put Molotov in charge of Soviet diplomacy and ordered him to "get rid of the Jews" in the Commissariat of External Affairs. The purge gathered speed during the Nazi-Soviet alliance; became a part of government policy during the Great Patriotic War (as an expression of revamped official patriotism and a response to the new Jewish self-assertion); and turned into an avalanche in 1949, when ideological contagion became the regime's chief concern and Jews "by blood" emerged as its principal agents. Party officials responsible for the "cadres" flailed about in search of covert aliens. The closer to the core, the more rot they found.[136]

Who were the guardians of Marxism-Leninism? In 1949, "passport" Jews made up 19.8 percent of all Soviet professors of Marxism-Leninism, 25 percent of all those teaching Marxism-Leninism in the colleges of Moscow, Leningrad, Kiev, Kharkov, Rostov, Saratov, Kazan, and Sverdlovsk, and 7 out of 19 faculty members in the Dialectical and Historical Materialism Unit in the Philosophy Department of Moscow University. At the main Soviet research institute for the study of political economy (wrote the head of Agitprop to the head of the State Planning Agency), out of 51 senior researchers, there were 33 Jews, 14 Russians, and 4 others. (After the first series of firings, the new head of the reformed institute had to apologize to the Central Committee for the fact that out of 34 Academy of Sciences members, corresponding members, and "doctors of sciences" still employed by the institute, there were 20 Jews, 12 Russians, and 2 others.) In August 1949, the Red Presnia District Party Committee discovered that Jews made up 39 percent of the faculty at the Moscow Institute of Jurisprudence; and in 1950, the newly appointed director of the Institute for the Study of Law reported that he had succeeded in reducing the proportion of admitted Jewish graduate students from 50 to 8 percent. According to another Agitprop investigation, the secretariat of the editorial board of the multivolume *History of the Civil War* included 14 Jews, 8 Russians, and 6 others. Perhaps worst of all, a review of the main academic mini-Stalins (every discipline was supposed to have its own) revealed that the deans of Soviet philosophers (M. B. Mitin), economists (E. S. Varga), historians (I. I. Mints), and legal scholars (I. P. Trainin) were all ethnic Jews. (Varga had come from Budapest, the others from Russia's old Pale.) Finally—and most disconcertingly—B. I. Zbarsky, the man who had embalmed Lenin's body and was still the keeper of Communism's most sacred relics, was not only a Jew from the Pale of Settlement but also, according to the obligingly efficient secret police, a wrecker and a spy.[137]

And what about those other pillars of official ideology—Russian patriotism and high culture? A group of concerned scholars informed the Central Committee of the Party that 80 percent of the members of the academic council at the Academy of Sciences' Institute of Literature (the "Pushkin House") were Jews. (The Central Committee confirmed the report and ordered swift action.) The secretaries of the Writers' Union—A. Fadeev, K. Simonov, and A. Surkov—promised mass firings in response to the revelation that Jews made up 29.8 percent of the organization's Moscow branch. The head of Agitprop, G. F. Aleksandrov, wrote to the secretaries of the Central Committee about the "extremely grave situation" on the musical front: almost all of the leading lights at the Bolshoi ("the center and pinnacle of Russian musical culture"), the Moscow Conservatory, Moscow Philharmony, and Leningrad Conservatory were "non-Russians"—as were the music critics who praised their work and the heads of the arts sections of the central newspapers, who abetted the critics. Why was the *History of Russian Music* edited by a non-Russian? Why were there so many Jews among the directors of Moscow theaters (42 percent, according to the Central Committee's personnel data); art exhibits (40 percent); and popular music shows (39 percent)? Why did the 87 Soviet circus directors and administrators include 44 Jews, 38 Russians, and 4 Ukrainians? And what about the number one Russian patriot among journalists—the one whose mother's name was Hannah? And, speaking of journalists, who was instilling Marxism-Leninism, Russian patriotism, and high culture in the Soviet masses? *Pravda* had to be purged mercilessly, as did the government's *Izvestiya* and the army's *Krasnaia Zvezda*. The official organs of the Young Communist League and the Writers' Union were found to be dominated by Jews; the main sports newspaper was ordered (by the Central Committee's personnel boss, G. M. Malenkov) to fire 12 journalists; and at the Trade Union Council's *Trud*, the proportion of Jewish employees was first reduced to 50 percent and then, after 40 more firings, to a more acceptable 23 percent. The agency that organized the delivery of all 4,638 Soviet newspapers to retailers and subscribers around the country was run by 18 officials, 10 of whom were discovered to be Jews. The situation at the central censorship office (Glavlit) did not inspire "political confidence" for similar reasons.[138]

The more frequent the contact with the enemy, the greater the danger of infection. In whose hands—still speaking of journalists— was Soviet overseas propaganda, an area where political confidence was so hard to earn and so easy to abuse? Jews made up 23 percent of the top managers in the Telegraphic Agency of the Soviet Union (TASS), and 49 percent in the Radio-Telegraphic Agency of Ukraine (RATAU). The "national composition" of the Soviet Information Bureau was 48 percent Jews, 40 percent Russians, and 12 percent others; the Russian Section of the Foreign Literature Publishing House was 90 percent Jewish; and the official Soviet English-language newspaper, *Moscow News*, was being produced by 1 Russian, 1 Armenian, and 23 Jews.[139]

The economic base was as rotten as the ideological superstructure. Who was building Soviet cars? Forty-two Jews were arrested and thirteen executed in connection with the "Jewish nationalism" affair at the Moscow Automobile Plant. Who was designing Soviet airplanes? Sixty Jewish researchers were fired from the Zhukovsky Institute (but not S. A. Lavochkin, the creator of LA fighters, or M. L. Mil, the creator of MI helicopters). Why was Soviet tank production being entrusted to Isaak Moiseevich Zaltsman, from the shtetl Tomashpol in Podolia? Why, at the end of the Great Patriotic War, did Jews constitute one-third of all chief engineers at Soviet armaments plants? And who (stage whisper) was building the Soviet atomic bomb? And how were they connected to their kinsmen building the American atomic bomb? And what about the spies who were, in their own way, trying to connect the two atomic bombs?[140]

Aliens were everywhere: in your home, under your bed—or even in your bed. Was it a coincidence that Comrade Stalin's elder son, Yakov, was married to a Jewish woman? (She was arrested after Yakov's capture by the Germans but released soon after his death.) Or that Comrade Stalin's daughter kept falling in love with one Jew after another? (Svetlana's first love, A. Ya. Kapler, was sent into exile, and her first husband, G. I. Morozov, was asked to move out and given a new passport with the marriage entry removed.) And what about all those wives: Comrade Molotov's, Comrade Andreev's, Comrade Voroshilov's?[141]

Most frightening of all was the realization that the "vigilant Chekists" combating the forces of evil were themselves werewolves. A special secret police investigation of the secret police revealed a massive "Zionist conspiracy" and a hopeless confusion of friend and foe. Lev Shvartsman, the star interrogator who had coauthored Babel's confession, now produced his own, in which he claimed that he had belonged to a Jewish terrorist organization and had had sex with his son, his daughter, the former state security minister V. S. Abakumov, and the British ambassador. N. I. Eitingon, who had organized the murder of Trotsky (among many others), was accused of planning to murder the Soviet leaders; L. F. Raikhman, who had run the secret surveillance of the Jewish Anti-Fascist Committee, was arrested as a Jewish nationalist; Lieutenant Colonel Kopeliansky, who had interrogated the savior of the Budapest Jews, Raoul Wallenberg, was fired as a Jew; and M. I. Belkin, who had staged the Rajk trial in Hungary, confessed to having spied for the Zionists and recruited, among others, the head of the Hungarian secret police and his fellow Jew Gábor Péter. The Soviet espionage network in the United States had to be completely revamped because most of the agents (including the highly successful atomic spy Semyon Semenov, who had "controlled" both the Cohens and the Rosenbergs) were Jews. Even G. M. Mairanovsky, the head of the most secret of all secret police institutions, the Toxicology Laboratory of the Ministry of State Security ("Lab-X"), was unmasked as a Zionist spy. Lab-X specialized in producing poisons, testing them on Gulag inmates, and using them in secret assassinations (including the one of Raoul Wallenberg, according to Pavel Sudoplatov). Mairanovsky had directed Lab-X since 1937 and had personally administered some of his poisons to "enemies" singled out by Soviet leaders for quiet removal (sometimes in the form of an injection during a medical checkup). Now, after repeated beatings, he confessed to having belonged to a Jewish conspiracy within the Ministry of State Security and to having planned the murder of those same leaders on the orders of American Zionists.[142]

Mairanovsky was Stalin's tool, creature, and worst nightmare. Stalinist purges had always assumed that all departures from perfection were caused by deliberate acts; that deliberate acts were perpetrated by enemies selflessly committed to evil; that commitment to evil was endemic and institutionalized outside the Soviet Union; and that the Soviet Union contained "alien elements" who were predisposed to devil worship because of their social or national origins. In the 1930s, national origins had begun to overshadow social ones, and during World War II, Jewishness had emerged as a perfect combination of suspect tribe and suspect class. Much of the Soviet professional elite was Jewish, and a large number of Jews belonged to the Soviet professional elite. As far as Stalin and his investigators were concerned, the two groups might very well be identical—especially because no elite profession was more esoteric or more invasive than medicine, and because medicine was the most Jewish of all professions.

In traditional societies, those who communicate with spirits are both feared and revered. To ward off evil, one must enter into contact with it; the power to cure suggests the power to injure. By destroying the church's distinction between priests and magicians, the modern state had reintroduced shamans—or rather, professionals who possessed secret knowledge that could be used to either save or destroy souls, bodies, countries, and the planet Earth. Not unlike Nazi Germany, but much more coherently and consistently, the Soviet Union was a modern state with an official church. The

Party, embodied by Stalin, claimed both transcendental and political authority and encouraged a Faustian quest for limitless knowledge on the assumption that scientific truth pursued by trained professionals would coincide with the Marxist-Leninist truth upheld by "conscious" officials. Before the coming of the millennial fusion of the people with the Party and spontaneity with consciousness, however, the Soviet Union remained an uneasily dualistic society, with the Party enforcing ideological orthodoxy among the professionals on whose expertise it depended. In the 1920s, the opposition between commissars and "bourgeois specialists" was stark and asymmetrical; in the 1930s, it seemed to disappear as the new "Soviet intelligentsia" embraced both science and Party orthodoxy; in the 1940s and 1950s, it reemerged with a vengeance in response to the growing demands of the arms race and the widespread sense among war survivors that the great victory entitled them to a greater role in decision making. The more autonomy the Soviet professionals acquired, the more difficult it became to reconcile the science-based modernity they represented with the charismatic faith they were supposed to profess. Stalin's deathbed crowning as "the coryphaeus of Soviet science" was the last serious attempt to reestablish prewar conceptual seamlessness. In his capacity as linguist and economist, among other things, Stalin argued that no progress toward communism was possible without science, that "no science [could] develop and flourish without a struggle of opinions"; that no struggle of opinions could take place in the shadow of a "closed group of infallible leaders"; and that no one outside the Kremlin was capable of determining what constituted progress, science, or worthy opinions.[143]

For as long as Stalin was alive and incontestably infallible, such reasoning—and the world it held together—seemed to make sense to most members of the Soviet elite. There were three professions, however, that questioned the sacred unity of knowledge and virtue simply by performing their regularly assigned tasks. One was the secret police, which sought out corruption within the Party and thus persisted in acquiring secret knowledge that the Party had no direct access to. This was a familiar problem that came with two familiar solutions: the employment of Mercurian strangers and the repeated extermination of the bearers of autonomous knowledge. The second solution (embraced after the mid-1930s, when strangeness became suspect) proved both cheap and effective because the detective work demanded by Stalin required little special training beyond the mistaken conviction that unmasking more enemies was the best way not to become one. Few professional groups within Soviet society had as high a mortality rate or as little understanding of the nature of their work as the secret police. In 1940, the doomed architect of the Great Terror, N. I. Ezhov, had said: "I purged 14,000 Chekists. But my great guilt lies in the fact that I purged so few of them." In 1952, the doomed architect of the Jewish "affair," M. D. Riumin, wrote: "I only admit that during the investigation I *did not use extreme measures*, but after my mistake was pointed out to me, I *corrected* it."[144]

Another professional group that undermined the official orthodoxy as a matter of course were the nuclear physicists, whose success in building the bomb seemed to depend on their rejection of Engels's "dialectics of nature." Because the building of the bomb was of paramount importance, the official orthodoxy (including the newly mandated mistrust of ethnic Jews) had to be partially waived for the duration of the project. What made such suspension of belief possible was the fact that the group in question was extremely small and the affected portion of the canon relatively marginal. What made it dangerous in the long run was the implicit recognition by the Party that its authority was political and not transcendental. Few professional groups within Soviet society had as high a status or as little need for Marxism-Leninism as the atomic scientists.

Finally, there were the physicians. Under normal circumstances, their expertise did not obviously challenge the Party's monopoly on truth, but when Stalin entered his seventies and began to lose his vigor, it became clear that the life of the "great leader and teacher"—and thus the fate of world socialism—was in the hands of professionals whose claim to vital knowledge could not be checked or verified—except by other professionals. The Soviet unity of knowledge and virtue had always been tenuous: in one purge after another, experts had been unmasked as wreckers, engineers as saboteurs, spy catchers as spies, and priests as black magicians.

Doctors, who fought death for a living, had been featured as "poisoners" at the Bukharin trial of 1938 and in numerous rumors about the untimely deaths of various Soviet leaders. They were never targeted as a class, however—until Stalin confronted limits to his immortality and Jews were identified as key agents of contagion. The first court physicians to be arrested were ethnic Russians, but as the "doctors' plot" thickened, the campaign against "murderers in white robes" became fused with the assault on "Jewish nationalism." The most alien of nationalities had merged with the most lethal of professions.[145]

Stalin's attack on the Jews was similar to numerous other attempts to rid the Soviet Union of variously defined groups associated with the pre-Soviet past or the anti-Soviet present. While filling out his personnel form, Viktor Shtrum, in Vasily Grossman's *Life and Fate*, comes to Line No. 5, "nationality," and writes "Jew."

> He had no way of knowing what filling in Line No. 5 would soon mean for hundreds of thousands of people who called themselves Kalmyks, Balkars, Chechens, Crimean Tatars, Jews. . . . He did not know that . . . in a few years many people would be filling in Line No. 5 with the same feeling of doom with which, in past decades, the children of Cossack officers, noblemen, factory owners, and priests had filled in Line No. 6 ["social origin"].[146]

There were some differences too. Possibly as a consequence of Stalin's death in March 1953, the attack on the Jews was on a much less massive scale and was much less lethal than the treatment of the other ethnic groups on Grossman's list (and many others not on the list), the "national operations" of 1937–38, or the persecution of various "socially alien" categories during the Red Terror and then again in the 1930s. It was also much less consistent than the discrimination against "the children of Cossack officers, noblemen, factory owners, and priests" had been in the 1920s and early 1930s. But this was a matter of degree; what was particularly unusual about the anti-Jewish campaign of the late 1940s–early 1950s was that it combined a focus on the professional elite with a consistently ethnic and pointedly public selection criterion.[147]

The targets of the violent cleansing campaigns against "the bourgeoisie" and the "kulaks" had not thought of themselves as belonging to "bourgeois" or "kulak" communities. The victims of the antielite terror of 1937–38 had had no idea why they were being condemned. The majority of those arrested as part of Ezhov's "national operations" had not known about the existence of such operations and had had no way of separating their "cases" from those of other victims. Even the wholesale ethnic deportations, which had left no doubt about who was being targeted, had been conducted in secret and had gone almost totally unnoticed by the elite (because they had involved the shipment of mostly rural people from one borderland to another).

The anti-Jewish campaign was both public and relatively clear about its objectives. It was directed at some of the most vital and articulate elements of the Soviet state—and it contradicted some of that state's most fundamental official values. As Lina Kaminskaia, a college student, active Komsomol member, and daughter of a former employee of the Commissariat of Aviation Industry, said in 1952, "Our country's policy on the national question is incorrect. After the war, the country was hit by a wave of anti-Semitism, which is an expression of fascist ideology. . . . My point of view is the result of what I have been hearing and seeing. . . . Everything I say is based on a firm conviction. My opinion is shared by all my close friends from among the intelligentsia: doctors, engineers, lawyers, students."[148]

Kaminskaia was expelled from both the university and the Komsomol, but it does appear that her views were widely shared by members of the Soviet intelligentsia well beyond her circle of friends. As the prominent film director M. I. Romm wrote to Stalin several years earlier,

> Examining my feelings, I realized that for the past few months I have been forced to recall my Jewish origins quite frequently, even though I had never thought about them during the previous twenty-five years of Soviet rule because I was born in Irkutsk, raised in Moscow, speak

only Russian, and have always felt completely Russian. So, if even people like me are beginning to wonder, the situation in our movie industry must be very alarming indeed, especially if one remembers that we are fighting against fascism, which has anti-Semitism emblazoned on its banner.[149]

For the first time since the revolution, the ethnically Jewish members of the Soviet elite were being attacked directly and unequivocally—not because of some "alien elements" in their midst, as in 1937–38, but because they were ethnically Jewish. (My ethnically Russian father, who graduated from Moscow State University in 1949, could enroll in any graduate school he wished because his Jewish peers, a majority of the applicants, were not welcome. His "gentry origins" were no longer a factor; his "indigenous" nationality was.)

For the first time, Soviet citizens of all nations were being told that the internal enemies were not people who belonged to certain fluid social groups or elusive secret societies, but people who were certified members of a particular ancient tribe remembered for its treachery, as depicted in both the Christian tradition and the Mercurian stereotype, and closely associated with the cosmopolitan phase of the Bolshevik Revolution (which had always been seen by some Russians and Ukrainians as deliberately anti-Russian and anti-Ukrainian). The result was a rapid spread of anti-Semitic rumors, insults, leaflets, threats, and assaults culminating in the hysterical unmasking of "murderer physicians."[150]

For the first time, the Soviet state had turned on some of its loyal and privileged subjects according to a clear—and apparently non-Soviet—principle. For the first time, Hodl and her children found themselves among the aliens. For the first time, many of them began to doubt their Soviet faith—and the culpability of previous aliens. As Ester Markish put it,

Only our own grief made us realize the horror of our lives in general: not only the suffering of the Jews or the suffering of the intelligentsia, but the suffering of the whole country and all the social groups and peoples that lived in it. After the arrest of [Perets] Markish, our maid, who had lived in our house for more than fifteen years and had, in effect, become a member of our family, said to me: "You are crying now, but you did not mind when my father was being dekulakized, martyred for no reason at all, and my whole family thrown out in the street?"[151]

Even Pavel Sudoplatov, an ethnic Slav, top secret police official, and faithful Party warrior, was confused and dismayed by the attack on the Jews. As the head of the security ministry department in charge of assassinations and sabotage, he had participated in numerous political "liquidations," but the only murder he unequivocally condemns in his memoirs is the murder of Mikhoels (with which, as he points out, he—"fortunately"—had nothing to do). During his thirty-year service in the secret police, he had seen many of his comrades purged, but the only arrest he claims to have opposed was the arrest of N. I. Eitingon, one of the Soviet Union's most accomplished assassination experts (also known for his mischievous sense of irony and his ability to "recite Pushkin from memory"). One reason for Sudoplatov's scruples was the fact that this was the first purge of his friends and colleagues that had a discernible pattern which was both unmistakable and offensive to a true believer of the civil war generation. The other reason was the fact (not surprising to most true believers of the civil war generation) that some of Sudoplatov's best friends were Jews. The best of them all was his wife, Emma Kaganova, a professional agent provocateur who had spent most of her career reporting on Moscow intellectuals but had to retire as a lieutenant colonel in 1949 because of the anti-Jewish campaign. After a lifetime of moral certainty, the two found themselves betrayed by their Party and compelled—for the first time ever—to talk to their children about the emerging distinction between the state and the family, the public and the private, the "brazen anti-Semitic statements" and their mother's Semitic "nationality."[152]

The Sudoplatov household solution was to continue to regard *Pravda* (which, after all, "contained no hint of pogroms") as the whole Truth and nothing but the Truth, but also to emphasize (especially if asked by middle school teachers) that utmost vigilance was needed in the face of hostile provocations in the form of rumors. Such "grammatical fiction," as Arthur Koestler's Rubashov calls it, was still the dominant true-believer strategy. At the trial of the Jewish Anti-Fascist Committee, Ilya Vatenberg (a former Zionist, ardent Communist, Columbia Law School graduate, and secret police informer), declared that he had signed his falsified interrogation record because he and his interrogator were on the same side of the barricade.

> PRESIDING OFFICER: One must tell the truth everywhere, except when it needs to be hidden from the enemies.
> VATENBERG: There is no such thing as abstract truth. Truth is always class-based, and since truth is class-based, I thought, then maybe he was right, after all.
> PRESIDING OFFICER: But if he really was right, then why are you retracting your testimony?
> VATENBERG: Perhaps he really is right. I need to reconsider my whole life.[153]

There was another solution, however—virtually inconceivable for a high-ranking true believer during the Great Terror of 1937–38 but possible now, when some Party spokesmen seemed to have adopted the Nazi definition of the enemy (thereby making it impossible for a Vatenberg to remain within the fold no matter how thoroughly he reconsidered his whole life). This solution consisted in allowing for the possibility that Truth and the Party were two different entities; that Truth could be pursued according to the rational grammar of logic and common sense; and that if the Party did not agree with the Truth, then so much the worse for the Party. Remarkably, this approach was embraced by the highest-ranking of all the JAFC defendants, Solomon Lozovsky. The only person associated with the work of the JAFC because of his Party position and not because he had ever shown any interest in Yiddish culture, Lozovsky was a prominent Old Bolshevik who had been a member of the Party's Central Committee and the Presidium of the Comintern, head of the Communist Trade Union International, deputy foreign minister of the USSR, and, as head of the Soviet Information Bureau, the supreme chief of Soviet external propaganda. He had dutifully followed the Party line and had accepted the extermination of most of his old friends as part of the grammar of revolution, but when he was put on trial for having a mother called Hannah, he refused to go on speaking the Party language because he seems to have concluded that communicating in that language—even in the Bukharin-Vatenberg mode of confessional self-abasement—was no longer possible. He reconsidered his whole life and found it wanting—or rather, he expressed pride in his service to the cause but maintained throughout that the official case against him "contradicted truth, logic, and common sense." He might not have read a word of Yiddish "in sixty years," but he did not think that writing in Yiddish was a form of nationalism; was not ashamed of his parents; refused to accept that there was anything wrong with "three Soviet citizens writing a letter to their own government"; and insisted to the end that he, "not as a Central Committee member but as a regular Soviet citizen," had "the right to know" what he was going to be executed for. With an eloquence wasted on his hanging judges but not on his fellow defendants, who cautiously followed his lead, he described the indictment against them as issuing from "the realm of poetic calumny, if not of political inspiration," and concluded the proceedings by stating:

> I have said it all and want no special consideration. I demand either full rehabilitation or death. I have devoted my entire life to the Party's cause and do not want to be a parasite. If the court finds me guilty of anything at all, I request that the Government change my sentence to execution. But if it turns out someday that I was innocent, then I ask that I be posthumously readmitted to the Party and that the fact of my rehabilitation be announced in the newspapers.[154]

He received no special consideration. He was executed along with the others. Three years later he was rehabilitated and posthumously readmitted to the Party. It was a different Party from the one he had joined.

The great alliance between the Jewish Revolution and Communism was coming to an end as a result of the new crusade against Jewish Communists. What Hitler could not accomplish, Stalin did, and as Stalin did, so did his representatives in other places. In the fall of 1952, a large show trial was staged in Czechoslovakia. Eleven of the accused, including the general secretary of the Communist Party of Czechoslovakia, Rudolf Slánský, were identified as ethnic Jews and accused of being agents of international Zionism and American imperialism. Other Soviet dependencies had to follow suit, whether they wanted to or not. In Hungary, Romania, and Poland, a high proportion of the most sensitive positions in the Party apparatus, state administration, and especially the Agitprop, foreign service, and secret police were held by ethnic Jews, who had moved up the ranks because of their loyalty and now had to be squeezed out because of their nationality. All three regimes resembled the Soviet Union of the 1920s insofar as they combined the ruling core of the old Communist underground, which was heavily Jewish, with a large pool of upwardly mobile Jewish professionals, who were, on average, the most trustworthy among the educated and the most educated among the trustworthy. There were important differences, however. On the one hand, the experience of World War II in East-Central Europe had made Jews the only possible candidates for some sensitive positions; on the other, the creation of the new Stalinist regimes had coincided with Stalin's discovery of Jewish untrustworthiness. The predominantly Jewish "Moscow Hungarians," "Moscow Romanians," and "Moscow Poles" had been installed in power, then encouraged to promote the indigenous cadres who were to replace them, and finally thrown out as Zionists, Stalinists, or both. The Soviet Union's erstwhile representative in Romania, Ana Pauker, was ousted in 1952; Hungary's Mátyás Rákosi and Poland's Jakub Berman and Hilary Minc (among others) followed after Khrushchev's Secret Speech of 1956. In matters of "global historical importance" (to use a Stalinist cliché), Soviet satellites were not allowed to lag a whole generation behind (they were supposed to be younger brothers, not children). Jewish Communists were to be replaced by ethnically pure ones. Ultimately—and fatally for Communism—ethnically pure Communists would prove to be a contradiction in terms.[155]

Meanwhile, the United States Congress was conducting its own purge. In scale and severity it was not comparable to the Stalinist version, but the targets came from similar backgrounds and had similar convictions—except that in the Soviet Union they were persecuted as Jews, and in the United States as Communists. Both governments were aware of the connection, but both dismissed it as dangerous or irrelevant. The postwar Soviet officials probably realized that the attack on Jewish "cosmopolitanism" was, in some sense, an attack on Communist internationalism, yet they had no choice but to make the subject taboo because the newly ethnicized Soviet state continued to derive its legitimacy from the Great October Socialist Revolution. Likewise, Senator Joseph McCarthy and the members of the House Un-American Activities Committee knew perfectly well that many Communists, hostile witnesses, and Soviet spies were Jews, but chose not to transform this fact into a political "issue" because they thought of both America and its Soviet nemesis as purely ideological constructs.[156]

There were, of course, other reasons why associating Communism with Jewishness might not be a very good idea. The most pragmatic of them was the observable fact that the Jewish association with Communism was coming to an end. A high proportion of Communists and Soviet agents in the United States were still Jews, but the absolute numbers of Jewish Communists were falling steadily, and their place in the Jewish community was becoming marginal. At the Rosenberg trial, both the presiding judge and the prosecutor appointed to the case were Jews. This was the result of a concerted political effort to create a visible counterweight to the accused (who used their Jewishness in their defense), but it was also a faithful reflection of the new postwar reality. Beilke's children began to turn from Communism to Jewish nationalism at the same time and for many of the same reasons as their Soviet cousins: the Stalin-Hitler Pact, the destruction of European Jewry, the creation of Israel, and the Soviet purge of Jews from elite positions. But mostly, they turned away from Communism because they were doing so well in America. The two postwar decades saw the emergence of the Jews as the most prosperous, educated, politically influential, and professionally accomplished ethnoreligious group in the United States. As in fin de siècle Vienna and Budapest or early-Soviet Moscow and Leningrad, the children of Mercurian immigrants moved en masse into the professions that define and underwrite the modern state: law, medicine, journalism, entertainment, and higher education. Unlike their predecessors in Vienna and Budapest, they encountered little anti-Semitism; unlike their cousins in the Soviet Union, they were free to pursue both traditional Jewish vocations: learning and wealth.[157]

They moved from Brooklyn to Manhattan, from the Lower East Side to the Upper East Side, from the cities to the suburbs, from Weequahic High in Newark to Arcady Hill Road in Old Rimrock. In Philip Roth's *American Pastoral*, a "slum-reared" Jewish entrepreneur with the ruthless drive of Sholem Aleichem's Podhotzur or Mordecai Richler's Duddy Kravitz begets a "household Apollo" nicknamed "the Swede." The father is one of those "limited men with limitless energy; men quick to be friendly and quick to be fed up." The son is gentle, even-tempered, and considerate. The father is "no more than five seven or eight"; the son is "handsome as hell, big, carnal, ruddy as Johnny Appleseed himself." The father cannot stop climbing; the son marries a Gentile Miss New Jersey, settles in a dream house on Arcady Hill, and celebrates his American fulfillment on the "dereligionized ground" of "the American pastoral par excellence": Thanksgiving.[158]

The Swede's Thanksgiving dinners in Old Rimrock, New Jersey, are perfect replicas of the Gaister family dinners in the House of Government, Moscow. The more or less fictional Swede (Seymour Irving Levov) was born in 1927; the very real Inna Aronovna Gaister was two years older. Both had indomitably successful fathers (Podhotzur the businessman and Perchik the revolutionary) and preternaturally loving mothers (the self-effacing Beilke and the self-assertive Hodl). Both had happy childhoods, both had to deal with non-Jewish in-laws, and both worshiped the countries that had made dreams into reality. The upwardly mobile American Jews of the 1940s and 1950s loved America as passionately as their upwardly mobile Soviet cousins had loved the Soviet Union in the 1920s and 1930s. The Swede was as American as Inna Gaister had been Soviet: "He lived in America the way he lived inside his own skin. All the pleasures of his younger years were American pleasures, all that success and happiness had been American." And for both, the Paradise Found was the rural idyll of the newly welcoming

Apollonia: the dacha pastoral of Inna Gaister and the suburban pastoral of Swede Levov. According to Gaister's memoirs:

> In 1935 we started spending our summers at a dacha in Nikolina Gora. . . . The settlement was located in a beautiful pine forest, on a high hill above a bend in the Moscow River. It was a magnificent place, one of the finest in the Moscow area. . . . Our plot was right above the river, on a high bank. The dacha itself was a large two-story house, which my mother's brother, Veniamin, not without jealousy, used to call the "villa." It really was a villa. . . . In front of each dacha was a little wooden pier for swimming. . . . My friends and I liked spending time on the pier below the Kerzhentsev dacha. The water there was shallow and good for swimming. . . . Life at the dacha was wonderful.[159]

The dream of Babel's little boys had come true: not only were they the best at learning, but they could swim too—Hodl's children, and Chava's, of course, and now Beilke's, as well. "The Swede starred as end in football, center in basketball, and first baseman in baseball." In the early 1950s, as a successful businessman, he liked to walk home through the Elysian Fields of the "Garden State"—"past the white pasture fences he loved, the rolling hay fields he loved, the corn fields, the turnip fields, the barns, the horses, the cows, the ponds, the streams, the springs, the falls, the watercress, the scouring rushes, the meadows, the acres and acres of woods he loved with all of a new country dweller's puppy love for nature, until he reached the century-old maple trees he loved and the substantial old stone house he loved—pretending, as he went along, to throw the apple seed everywhere."[160]

This was immigration-as-transformation on the Soviet and Zionist model, complete with the acquisition of an Apollonian language, an Apollonian body, and perhaps even an Apollonian spouse (true of both Inna Gaister and Swede Levov but not in Palestine, where all Jews were supposed to become enlightened Apollonians while all non-Jewish Apollonians were fated to remain unenlightened). The head was still Mercurian, but now it was firmly attached to a first baseman's frame, suburban landscape, and the country's most important social and political institutions. The Superman cartoon had been created by two Jewish high school students in Cleveland, in 1934.[161]

Jewish American intellectuals, too, had stopped being exiled rebels in order to become salaried professors. A Russian-style prophetic intelligentsia had been transformed into a large contingent of rigorously trained intellectuals ("bourgeois experts") organized into professional corporations. By 1969, Jews (less than 3 percent of the population) made up 27 percent of all law faculties, 23 percent of medical faculties, and 22 percent of all biochemistry professors. In the seventeen most prestigious American universities, they accounted for 36 percent of law professors, 34 percent of sociologists, 28 percent of economists, 26 percent of physicists, 24 percent of political scientists, 22 percent of historians, 20 percent of philosophers, and 20 percent of mathematicians. In 1949, there was one Jewish professor on the faculty of Yale College; in 1970, 18 percent of Yale College professors were Jews. The United States began to catch up with the Soviet Union in the realm of Jewish accomplishment at the very time that the Kremlin set out to reverse the Jewish accomplishment in the Soviet Union. Within two decades, both had achieved a great deal of success.[162]

Having moved into the upper reaches of American society, most Jews adopted America's official faith. In the 1940s and 1950s, Liberalism replaced Marxism as the orthodoxy of Jewish intellectuals (with Lionel Trilling's *The Liberal Imagination* providing an early manifesto). Like their counterparts in Palestine and the prewar Soviet Union, American Jews of the 1940s and 1950s eagerly identified with their new home's first principles (themselves sharpened by the prewar Jewish search for "that society in which no racial barriers could possibly exist" and increasingly referred to as "Judeo-Christian"). But what exactly were those principles? State Liberalism separate from Christianity and tribalism was only half a faith—a set of legal rules, metaphysical assumptions, and founding fathers endowed with transcendental meaning but tenuously connected to the exigencies of kinship and personal immortality. To the (rather limited) extent that the postwar American state was, indeed, separate from Christianity and tribalism, it had developed a new conception of its own role and its citizens' welfare. It had become increasingly thera-peutic and substantially (if often unself-consciously) Freudian.[163]

All modern states have developed a capacity for "caring" pre-viously associated with families, churches, and licensed physicians. In the United States, the institutional and intellectual groundwork of the new regime was laid by native-born Progressive reformers (including the advocates of vocational guidance and mental hy-giene), but it was Freudianism, practiced and professed by upwardly mobile Jewish professionals, that provided the core vocabulary and some of the most durable concepts. By bringing Freudianism to America and by adopting it, briefly, as a salvation religion, Tevye's children made themselves more American while making America more therapeutic. As Andrew R. Heinze put it, "Through the idiom of modern psychology, Jews wrote middle-class Americans a moral prescription that, if followed, would produce a social order that was 'good for the Jews' but also propitious for other outsiders seeking integration into American society." To paraphrase Mark Shechner, the transformation of Jews into Americans required the transforma-tion of revolutionaries into convalescents.[164]

Freudianism was a doctrine born of the nineteenth-century Jew-ish Revolution. It shared Marxism's familial origins; partook of its obsession with patricide and universal evil; and replicated (on a much smaller scale) its institutional structure centered on priestly guardians of sacred texts. The salvation it promised, however, was strictly individual, always provisional, and ultimately dependent on marketable professional expertise. Freudianism aspired to being the religion of modern capitalism as much as Marxism aspired to being the religion of anticapitalism: it appeared to provide a scientific jus-tification for the liberal focus on the incorrigible individual; applied the tenets of political liberalism to the mysteries of the human soul; adapted the American Declaration of Independence to the religious search for personal redemption. The pursuit of individual happi-ness—like the maintenance of a decent society—turned out to be a matter of managing imperfection, of imposing fragile checks and balances on ineradicable internal pressures.

Freudianism's greatest contribution to American life, however, was in the form of overall psychological orientation and a number of influential formulas. Just as the "Marxism" adopted by various states and movements was a mosaic of readings and interpretations often attributed—also by way of rough approximation—to local revisionist prophets (Lenin, Mao, Kim Il Sung, Gramsci), so Freudianism was but an echo of the founder's voice, usually much clearer and more consistent than the original. (One crucial difference is that whereas the Marxist connection, however dubious, is proudly asserted, the Freudian paternity is often denied and even more often unacknowledged—mostly because it is shared with the prevailing culture and so either taken for granted or resented as not capable of providing a genealogy of resistance.)

In the United States, psychotherapy became optimistic: treatment could lead to complete healing; instincts could be channeled and organized; aggression and the death wish could be countered with affection and introspection or allowed to lead one to normalcy. Most important, after World War II and especially starting in the 1960s, most schools of psychotherapy switched from curing the ill to reassuring the unhappy and to "managing one's self to happiness and fulfillment through techniques of self-inspection . . . and a new vocabulary of the emotions" (as Nikolas Rose put it). Evil became a symptom of a curable sickness, and most sick people became victims of their psyches, childhoods, parents, nurses, and neighbors (as opposed to the "social system"). Everyone was normal, in other words, and all normal people were maladjusted (insofar as they were not permanently and unshakably self-satisfied). All happy families were dysfunctional (in the same way); all children were abused; and all grownups were repeatedly harassed and traumatized. Priests became therapists; therapists became priests; and the state, still separate from traditional organized religion, made increasingly sure that citizens' confessions were heard by licensed social workers, probation officers, marriage counselors, family therapists, and grief counselors, among many others. In the workplace, managers were to achieve greater productivity not by suppressing the irrational but by using it creatively and scientifically (with the help of special counselors); and of course the family became a relentlessly self-reflexive institution for the production—never quite successful—of psychologically well-adjusted individuals (i.e., future adults who would not have been abused as children).[165]

All these developments are far removed from Freud's psychoanalysis (as far, perhaps, as Castro's Cuba is from Marx's *Das Kapital*), but they are all consequences of the great psychological revolution, of which Freud was the most influential prophet (the way Marx was the most influential prophet of socialism and class revolution). Dostoevsky may have discovered the Underground Man, but it was Freud who diagnosed Dostoevsky, as well as Kafka, Proust, Joyce, and every one of their underground prototypes and creations (whether they liked it or not or indeed knew anything about it). He put together what Vladimir Nabokov's Pnin called a "microcosmos of communism"; he provided the language, the theodicy, and the prescription for the new world. As Philip Rieff put it in his *The Triumph of the Therapeutic*, "who, without Freud, would so well know how to live with no higher purpose than that of a durable sense of well-being? Freud has systematized our unbelief; his is the most inspiring anti-creed yet offered a post-religious culture."[166]

Freud's cause is very much alive, in other words, even if his personal cult and particular therapeutic techniques are not. Like Marxism, it succeeded as an intellectual blueprint; like Marxism, it was never a science and it failed as a religion. It failed as a religion because, like Marxism, it misunderstood the nature of immortality and did not outlive the first generation of converts.

All humans live in tribes. All traditional religions, including Judaism, are tribal religions. The world's greatest rebellions against tribalism, such as Christianity and Islam, survived by incorporating tribal allegiances, sacralizing marriage, enforcing sexual and dietary restrictions, and representing themselves as renewable nations (bodies of believers, Umma). The decline of Christianity resulted in the rise of nationalism as new old tribalism: the rights of man equaled the rights of the citizen ("de l'homme et du citoyen"); citizenship, on closer inspection, turned out to be more or less ethnically defined.

Both Marxism and Freudianism tackled modernity-as-liberalism without recognizing or even seeming to notice the vital modernity of nationalism. Both charted paths to salvation (collective or individual) that were not grounded in household devotion, marriage arrangements, or dietary taboos. Neither Marxism nor Freudianism could be inherited or passed on meaningfully through a succession of family rites (the way even Christianity, and certainly Judaism, could). Both lost out to nationalism without ever realizing that there was a war going on. In the Soviet Union, Marxism as a revolutionary faith did not outlive the revolutionaries—having mutated into a camouflaged nationalism, it finally expired along with the last high-ranking beneficiary of the Great Terror. In the United States, Freudianism as a salvation religion encompassed the life span of the World War II generation before transmogrifying into a doctrine of tribal, as well as personal, happiness and victimhood.

Both Marxism and Freudianism were produced and eagerly embraced by newly emancipated Jews, who had achieved conspicuous success at capitalism without recourse to the much needed protection of nationalism. In the Soviet Union, the Jewish members of the establishment would be thwarted by the rise of Russian nationalism. In the United States, the Jewish members of the establishment would be transformed and greatly strengthened by the rise of ethnic politics.

Freudianism became so influential in the United States because the United States, like the European Jews, was conspicuously successful at capitalism without having recourse to the much needed protection of nationalism. Or rather, the official nationalism in the United States was primarily political, not tribal, and thus in need of constant intravenous injections. Freudianism was one, briefly; subnational tribalism (often in the form of religion) was another—permanently. In the Mecca of rootless cosmopolitanism, the existence of secondary loyalties is a constituent part of the political arrangement. That is why America is the most church-going of all modern societies, and that is why American Jews, having exhausted the relatively meager resources of Marxism and Freudianism, joined the fold by becoming nationalists.

It was only when they entered American institutions, in other words, that secular American Jewish intellectuals felt compelled to become Jewish—while American Jewish traditionalists felt fully justified in having preserved their tradition. In the two decades after World War II, that tradition was primarily represented by the memory of the shtetl—a shtetl shorn of its economic function and Gentile surroundings (other than the pogroms); a shtetl comparable to everyone else's rural "old country"; a shtetl embodying the piety and community of the ancestral home; a shtetl all the more radiant for having been extinguished.

This quest for the blessed lost past and a meaningful American present was launched in 1943 by Maurice Samuel's remarkably eloquent *The World of Sholom Aleichem*—"a sort of pilgrimage among the cities and inhabitants of a world which only yesterday—as history goes—harbored the grandfathers and grandmothers of some millions of American citizens." These grandfathers and grandmothers were so many Tevyes and Goldes because Tevye and Golde were the real Abraham and Sarah of American Jews—just as Sholem Aleichem ("the common people in utterance, . . . the anonymous of Jewish self-expression") was—or should be, at any rate—their new Pentateuch. To become good Americans, Jews were to become the Chosen People again. "The study of history will never become obsolete, and a knowledge of one's grandfathers is an excellent introduction to history. Especially these grandfathers; they were a remarkable lot."[167]

The next landmark on the pilgrimage to Tevye's world was *Life Is with People*, an extremely popular anthropological "portrait of the shtetl" produced in 1952 under the auspices of Ruth Benedict's Research in Contemporary Cultures project at Columbia University. As Margaret Mead wrote in her foreword, "This book is an anthropological study of a culture which no longer exists, except in the memories, and in the partial and altered behavior of its members, now scattered over the world, rearing their children in new ways, to be Americans or Israelis, as members of collective farms in the changed lands of Eastern Europe."[168]

This was a book about Tevye written for Beilke's children—now that they were ready for it.

> This book is an attempt to bring our anthropological discipline to the task of preserving something of the form and the content, the

texture and the beauty, of the small-town life of Eastern European Jews, as it was lived before World War I, in some places up to World War II, as it still lives in the memories of those who were reared in the shtetl, and in the memories of Jews in other lands, who can remember the stories their grandparents told, the tremendous happy worrying bustle with which the holidays were prepared for, the unrelenting eagerness with which a grandfather tested his grandson for signs of intellectual worth. It lives on, more than a little, in the memories of those [like Margaret Mead herself] who, themselves without any Jewish birthright, nevertheless have at some point warmed their hands by a shtetl fire, or sharpened their wits against the many-faceted polishing stone of talmudic reasoning.[169]

Life Is with People begins with a description of the Sabbath Eve and never loses the warm glow of the festive candlelight. Babel's dark rooms with "Grandmother's yellow eyes" and Mandelstam's "suffocating" grandparents with their "black-and-yellow shawls" are transformed into Rembrandt-like golden interiors, at once remote and welcoming, or possibly into flickering reflections of Thanksgiving, "the American pastoral par excellence." Fittingly enough, one of the book's two coeditors and, according to Margaret Mead, "the crucial person in our seminar," was Mark Zborowski, "who combined in one person the living experience of shtetl culture in the Ukraine and Poland and the disciplines of history and anthropology through which to interpret his memories and readings, and the new materials which members of the project collected from interviews and written materials. For him, this book is the realization of a plan cherished for many years."[170]

Like the book itself and most of the book's readers, Mark Zborowski seemed to stand for the continuity between Tevye's Sabbath and American Thanksgiving, the shtetl home and academic nostalgia, self-conscious Jewishness and self-conscious Jewishness. He also stood for something else, however. In the 1930s, Zborowski (alias Étienne) had been a Soviet agent provocateur in France, where he had infiltrated the Trotskyite organization; become the closest collaborator of Trotsky's son, Lev Sedov; assisted in the publication of the *Bulletin of the Opposition*; was granted full access to Trotsky's European archive (parts of which were stolen shortly thereafter); maintained contacts with remaining Trotskyists in the USSR; and, in 1938, arranged for Sedov to be admitted to the small private clinic where he died under mysterious circumstances after an appendectomy. After Sedov's death, Zborowski had taken over the Russian Section of Trotsky's Fourth International. In 1941, he had immigrated to the United States, where he had embarked on an academic career while continuing his espionage work (which mostly consisted in befriending and betraying refugees from the Soviet Union).[171]

But of course the central event in the story of American Yiddish nostalgia was the staging of the Broadway musical *Fiddler on the Roof* in 1964, followed by the movie adaptation in 1971. Tevye, it turned out, was as prophetically American as he was proudly Jewish. Gone were his irrepressible loquacity, stylistic eccentricities, and quixotic schemes; gone were his loneliness, homelessness, and braggadocio. The Broadway and Hollywood Tevye is an Apollonian patriarch, "handsome as hell, big, carnal, ruddy as Johnny Appleseed himself." The Yiddishization of middle-class suburban Americans seemed to require the Americanization of everyone's Yiddish grandfather. Tevye stood for tradition, of course, but he also understood the value of progress, freedom of choice, individual rights, and the nuclear family. The home he would live in if he were a rich man is like Swede Levov's New Jersey house with lots of rooms and stairs going up and down, and the love he preaches to old Golde is the romantic love he learned from his rebellious daughters and his suburban American grandchildren. The only exercise of free choice he remains ambivalent about is marriage outside the tribe—for if everyone behaved like Chava, there would be no Jewish granddaughters for Tevye to be a Jewish grandfather to ("anyone can be a goy, but a Jew must be born one"). Even here, however, he finds a reasonable compromise by blessing the "mixed" couple without addressing them directly. Chava and her Gentile consort leave chastened, but not excommunicated.[172]

Of all the admirable things the Broadway and Hollywood Tevye does, the most admirable and most natural is his decision to emigrate to America—the same America the original Tevye despises so much, the same America that, in Sholem Aleichem's text, is a proper refuge for crooked Podhotzur and his long-suffering Beilke. Sholem Aleichem's book ends with Golde dead and Tevye "on the go":

> There is no getting around the fact that we Jews are the best and smartest people. *Mi ke'amkho yisro'eyl goy ekhod*, as the Prophet says—how can you even compare a goy and a Jew? Anyone can be a goy, but a Jew must be born one. *Ashrekho yisro'el*—it's a lucky thing I was, then, because otherwise how would I ever know what it's like to be homeless and wander all over the world without resting my head on the same pillow two nights running?[173]

Fiddler on the Roof ends with Tevye, Golde, and two of their daughters going to America. One of the daughters is little Beilke; there is no Podhotzur; the reason they are leaving is anti-Semitic persecution. This is a crucial part of the American Jewish genealogy. Sholem Aleichem's Tevye is expelled from his home by the government decree banning Jews from rural areas, but the real reason for his plight as he understands it is God's mysterious ways ("a lot of good it does to complain to God about God") and of course "today's children," who are "too smart for their own good" and only too ready to fall for all sorts of "craziness." As for the local "Amalekites," they never get around to smashing Tevye's windows. "Bring out the samovar," they say, "and let's have tea. And if you'd be kind enough to donate half a bottle of vodka to the village, we'll all drink to your health, because you're a clever Jew and a man of God, you are. . . ." In the United States of the 1960s, such an ending did not ring true. Act 1 of the musical ends with a pogrom (one that never takes place in the book); and act 2 concludes with a procession of somber families carrying their scant possessions into exile. As far as Tevye's American grandchildren were concerned, the locomotive of Jewish history had been anti-Jewish violence. According to the musical, there had been no Jewish Revolution and virtually no Russian Revolution (outside of the pogroms) in Eastern European Jewish life. The Jews had been unique in the Russian Empire but they were not—yet—unique in the United States. As Seth Wolitz put it, "the musical Tevye becomes a Jewish pilgrim, a victim of religious persecution, fleeing intolerant Europe to the land of fulfillment, America."[174]

American Jews rediscovered their Jewishness at the same time and for essentially the same reasons as their Soviet cousins. The Nazi mass murder (not yet conceptualized as the Holocaust), the Soviet purges, and the formation of Israel were all important factors (debated and remembered as such), but it was the spectacular Jewish success in the Soviet Union and the United States that provided the context and the impetus for the new allegiances. In both places, Jews had entered crucial sectors of the establishment: in the Soviet Union, the Jewishness of elite members was seen by the newly Russified state (and eventually by some Jews too) as a threat and a paradox; in the United States, it appeared to be a sign of perfect fulfillment—both for the liberal state and for the new elite members.

Meanwhile, Chava and her Sabra children, who served as remote beacons of authentic Jewishness for both Beilke and Hodl, had no particular interest in rediscovering Tevye because they had always been Jewish and because their Jewishness was of a very different type. Israel was the only postwar European state ("European" in both composition and inspiration) to have preserved the ethos of the great nationalist and socialist revolutions of the interwar period. Hitler's Germany and Mussolini's Italy had been defeated and discredited; Franco's Spain and Salazar's Portugal had discarded whatever fascist fervor they had tolerated; Atatürk's Turkey had routinized its triumph over both cosmopolitanism and popular religion; the National Party's South Africa had embarked on an administrative, not popular, revolution; and Stalin's Soviet Union had begun to represent itself as middle-aged, mature, a little weary, and perhaps ready for some material comforts and a bit of family happiness. Only Israel continued to live in the European 1930s: only Israel still belonged to the eternally young, worshiped athleticism and inarticulateness, celebrated combat and secret police, promoted hiking and scouting, despised doubt and introspection, embodied the seamless unity of the chosen, and rejected most traits traditionally associated with Jewishness. The realization of the scale and nature of the Nazi genocide merged with the Zionist pioneer tradition to produce a warrior culture of remarkable power and intensity. To an even greater extent than the nationalist and communist movements in interwar Europe, Israel was imbued with the sense of "never again," "enough is enough," "there is nothing to fear but fear itself." Nothing summarizes the spirit of victorious Zionism better than Stalin's 1931 "We do not want to be beaten" speech.

Israel of the 1950s and 1960s was not simply Apollonian and anti-Mercurian—it was Apollonian and anti-Mercurian at a time when much of the Western world, of which it considered itself a part, was moving in the opposite direction. In postwar Europe and North America, military messianism, youthful idealism, pioneer toughness, and worship of uniform were in decline, but the realization of the scale and nature of the Nazi genocide merged with a certain awkwardness over complicity or inaction to place Israel in a special category where general rules did not apply. The attempt to create a "normal" state for the Jews had resulted in the creation of a peculiar anachronistic exception (admired and ostracized as such). After two thousand years of living as Mercurians among Apollonians, Jews turned into the only Apollonians in a world of Mercurians (or rather, the only civilized Apollonians in a world of Mercurians and barbarians). They were still strangers—but this time they were welcome (to the Westerners) because they remained remote. During the quarter of a century following World War II, Israel was everyone's fantasy of youthful vigor, joyful labor, human authenticity, and just retribution. It was the only place where European Civilization seemed to possess a moral certainty, the only place where violence was truly virtuous. Apartheid South Africa, which also saw itself as the defender of a small ethnically pure tribe guided by manifest destiny, governed by democratic institutions, committed to making deserts bloom, and surrounded by unruly and prolific barbarians, was increasingly seen as an impostor and an embarrassment. Israel, which provided a home for Holocaust survivors while continuing to embody a genuine grassroots revolution by a nation brutally victimized by Europeans in Europe, was a righteous reproach to the "civilized world" and perhaps a guarantee of its future redemption.

The most important institution in Israel was the army; the most admired heroes were generals; and the most celebrated profession was paratrooper (and the most celebrated paratrooper in the 1950s was Ariel Sharon). One of the most popular books was Aleksandr Bek's Soviet war novel, *The Volokolamsk Highway* (1943–44), which describes how a fatherly Russian general, who combines utter simplicity with an innate knowledge of the "mystery of war" (very much in the tradition of Tolstoy's Kutuzov), and a young Kazakh lieutenant, with the "face of an Indian" carved out of bronze "by some very sharp instrument," transform a motley collection of patriotic men into a cohesive, invincible unit. Their main weapon is "psychology." In one of the novel's key passages, the lieutenant approaches a recent recruit who has not yet mastered the art of fighting or understood the true meaning of patriotism.

> "Do you want to return home, embrace your wife, and hug your children?"
> "This is not the time . . . We've got to fight."
> "Right, but what about after the war? Do you?"
> "Of course I do . . . Who doesn't?"
> "You don't!"
> "What do you mean?
> "Because whether or not you'll be able to go back home depends on you. It's all in your hands. Do you want to stay alive? If so, you must kill the guy who is trying to kill you."[175]

After Stalin's death, the anti-Jewish campaign fizzled out, and ethnic Jews returned to the top of the Soviet professional hierarchy. The rate at which they advanced was slower than before the war and less impressive than that of many other groups, but they remained by far the most successful and the most modern—occupationally and demographically—of all Soviet nationalities. In 1959, 95 percent of all Jews lived in cities (compared to 58 percent for the Russians); the proportion of employed college graduates among them was 11.4 percent (compared to 1.8 percent for the Russians); and the number of "scientific workers" per 10,000 people was 135 (compared to 10 for the Russians). Thirty years later, 99 percent of all Russian Jews lived in urban areas (compared to 85 percent for the Russians); the proportion of employed college graduates among them was 64 percent (compared to 15 percent for the Russians); and the number of "scientific workers" per 10,000 people was 530 (compared to 50 for the Russians).[176]

All Soviet nationalities were different, but some were much more different than others. According to the occupational "dissimilarity index" (which represents the percentage of one group that would have to change jobs in order to become occupationally identical to another group), the Jews were by far the most "dissimilar" of all major Russian nationalities on the eve of the Soviet collapse. The difference between Russians and Jews, for example, was greater than the difference between Russians and any other group in the Russian Federation (including the Chechens, the least urban of those surveyed). The top five occupations for Russians were metal-workers (7.2 percent of the total employed), motor vehicle drivers (6.7 percent), engineers (5.1 percent), tractor and combine drivers (2.4 percent), and "nonmanual workers with unspecified specialty" (2.4 percent). The top five occupations for Jews were engineers (16.3 percent), physicians (6.3 percent), scientific personnel (5.3 percent), primary and secondary schoolteachers (5.2 percent), and chief production and technical managers (3.3 percent). Jewish employment patterns were much less diverse, much less segregated by gender, and much more concentrated at the top of the status hierarchy. Of the main Jewish occupations, the most exclusive (the least represented among the Russians) were physicians, scientists, chief managerial personnel, artists and producers, and literary and press personnel.[177]

Jews remained prominent in the Soviet professional elite (and thus at the heart of the Soviet state) until the breakup of the USSR, but the special relationship between the Jews and the Soviet state had come to an end—or rather, the unique symbiosis in pursuit of world revolution had given way to a unique antagonism over two competing and incommensurate nationalisms. The Russian and

Jewish Revolutions died the way they were born—together. The postwar Soviet state began to apply its traditional affirmative action policies favoring "titular" nationalities to the Russians in the Russian Republic (mostly by engaging in covert and cautious negative action with regard to the Jews). At the same time, and partly for that very reason (as well as for the many reasons provided by Hitler, Stalin, and the founding of Israel), the Jewish members of the Soviet elite began assuming that "Jewish origins" stood for a common fate, not simply a remote past. Everyone was listening to the "call of blood"—and hearing different languages.

This development coincided with a general parting of the ways between the Party-state and the professional elite it had created. Ever since the revolution, upward mobility through education had been one of the most consistent and apparently successful policies of the Soviet regime. For a party representing consciousness amid spontaneity and urban modernity amid rural backwardness, the "enlightenment of the masses" coupled with breakneck technological modernization had been the only way to correct History's mistake (of staging the socialist revolution in a precapitalist country) and bring about both socialism-as-abundance and socialism-as-equality. Between 1928 and 1960, the number of Soviet college students had grown by 1,257 percent (from 176,600 to 2,396,100); the number of college-educated professionals by 1,422 percent (from 233,000 to 3,545,200); and the number of scientific personnel by 1,065 percent (from 30,400 in 1930 to 354,200). Most of the members of the new "Soviet intelligentsia" were beneficiaries of class-based affirmative action and—outside ethnic Russia—its various ethnic substitutes. Their healthy roots were supposed to ensure the unity of scientific knowledge and Party Truth—and, for a while, they did.[178]

After Stalin's death, however, things began to fall apart. The demise and posthumous damnation of the only infallible symbol of both Truth and Knowledge suggested the possibility of their separate existence; the Cold War on Earth and in outer space seemed to push scientific knowledge ever further from Party Truth; and the gradual reinterpretation of socialism as a generous welfare state and bountiful consumer society tended to invite unwelcome comparisons with a revamped postindustrial capitalism (which seemed better on both scores). The viability of Soviet modernity depended on the success of Soviet professionals; the success of Soviet professionals required "a struggle of opinions" (as Stalin had put it); the struggle of opinions led a growing number of Soviet professionals away from Soviet modernity. Unlike Marx's capitalists but very much like the Russian imperial state, the Communist Party had created its own grave diggers—the intelligentsia.

Like Peter the Great's new service elite, the new "Soviet intelligentsia" was created to serve the state but ended up serving its own "consciousness" (split, in various proportions, between "progress" and the "people"). The more desperately the state clung to its founding Truth and the more intransigent it became in its instrumental approach to the educated elite, the more passionate that elite became in its opposition to the state and its attachment to (true) progress and the people. For Andrei Sakharov, the father of the Soviet hydrogen bomb, the greatest Soviet champion of true (non-state) progress, and eventually the conscience of the Westernizing segment of the Soviet intelligentsia, the moment of truth came in 1955, after a successful test of his "device." According to Sakharov's memoirs, the test was followed by a banquet at the residence of Marshal Nedelin, the commander of Soviet Strategic Missile Forces.

> When we were all in place, the brandy was poured. The bodyguards stood along the wall. Nedelin nodded to me, inviting me to propose the first toast. Glass in hand, I rose, and said something like: "May all our devices explode as successfully as today's, but always over test sites and never over cities."
>
> The table fell silent, as if I had said something indecent. Nedelin grinned a bit crookedly. Then he rose, glass in hand, and said: "Let me tell a parable. An old man wearing only a shirt was praying before an icon. 'Guide me, harden me. Guide me, harden me.' His wife, who was lying on the stove, said: 'Just pray to be hard, old man, I can guide it in myself.' Let's drink to getting hard."
>
> My whole body tensed, and I think I turned pale—normally I blush. . . . The point of the story (half lewd, half blasphemous, which added to its unpleasant effect) was clear enough. We, the inventors,

scientists, engineers, and craftsmen, had created a terrible weapon, the most terrible weapon in human history; but its use would lie entirely outside our control. The people at the top of Party and military hierarchy would make the decision. I knew this already—I wasn't *that* naïve. But understanding something in an abstract way is different from feeling it with your whole being, like the reality of life and death. The ideas and emotions kindled at that moment have not diminished to this day, and they completely altered my thinking.[179]

Sakharov's thinking was shared by many of his counterparts across the ocean, but what was remarkable about the Soviet Union is that Sakharov's thinking was shared—with their whole beings— by a growing number of inventors, scientists, engineers, and craftsmen working on much less explosive devices. In theory—and often enough in practice to produce a sense of unrelieved humiliation— the Party claimed the right to make all decisions about everything—from the Bomb to whether one was worthy of a trip to Bulgaria (as Vladimir Zhirinovsky would recall in 1996). What added injury to insult was the fact that the Soviet economy of the "stagnation period" (like the economy of late imperial Russia or European colonial empires) could not expand fast enough to accommodate the professionals it kept manufacturing. At the same time, it became clear that the Soviet intellectual elite had congealed into a hereditary institution, and that the higher in the professional hierarchy one went, the more hereditary intellectuals one found. In the 1970s, 81.2 percent of the "young specialists" working in the research institutes of the Academy of Sciences were children of white-collar professionals. They knew they belonged to a cohesive social group with a lofty mission and an uncertain future. Many of them shared Sakharov's thinking.[180]

Acutely aware of this Frankensteinian dilemma, the Party reacted by reintroducing massive affirmative action programs for blue-collar workers. But because it did not reintroduce massive repression against white-collar workers, it merely added to the resentment of the entrenched cultural elite without jeopardizing its ascendance (well-protected by superior education and patronage). The result was an ever widening social gap between the Party ideologues, who continued to be recruited from newly promoted provincials of humble backgrounds, and the hereditary inventors, scientists, engineers, and craftsmen, who thought of themselves as the guardians of both professional competence and high culture. The Party hung on to its ideological rhetoric and political monopoly, but most apparatchiks tacitly recognized the primacy of the professionals insofar as they raised their own children to be professionals, not apparatchiks. The Soviet regime ended the way it had begun: with "dual power." In 1917, the standoff between the Provisional Government, which had formal authority but no power, and the Petrograd Soviet, which had power but no formal authority, had ended with the victory of the Bolsheviks, who had Knowledge and Truth. In the 1980s, the standoff between the Party apparatus, which had power and formal authority, and the intelligentsia, which had Knowledge and Truth, ended with the final defeat of the Bolsheviks, exposed as purveyors of the "Big Lie." The Party, unlike the intelligentsia, proved incapable of reproducing itself. The Soviet Union was a regime that served one generation—or rather, thanks to Stalin, one and a half. The original revolutionaries were killed off in the prime of life; their heirs moved up after the Great Terror, reached maturity during World War II, suffered a mild midlife crisis under Khrushchev (who attempted to force the whole country to relive his First-Five-Year-Plan youth), grew senile with Brezhnev, and finally breathed their last along with K. U. Chernenko, who died of emphysema in 1985.

Marshal Nedelin did not have to suffer the indignity of infirmity: he was killed during a missile test in 1960, at the age of fifty-eight. Academician Sakharov, who was almost twenty years younger, went on to become the patron saint of the anti-Soviet Westernizers and a member of the last Soviet parliament. He died in 1989, days short of finishing his draft of a new Soviet constitution and less than two years before the fall of the Soviet Union. In 1963, Stalin's daughter, Svetlana Allilueva, had written about Sakharov's generation (those born in the early 1920s): "They are the best of the best. . . . They are our future Decembrists, they are going to teach us all how to live. They are going to say their word yet—I am sure of that."[181]

She was right, of course: the innocent beneficiaries of Stalin's "happy childhood," proud veterans of the Great Patriotic War, melancholy bards of Khrushchev's "Thaw," and standard-bearers of Gorbachev's perestroika, they were the ones who transformed the new Soviet "specialists" (white-collar professionals of proletarian background) into the old Russian intelligentsia (lone guardians of Truth and Knowledge). They were, indeed, the Decembrists of the growing anti-Party sentiment, and they "woke up" the various bolsheviks and mensheviks of the "New Russia" that followed. And a great many of them were Jews.

The Jews were prominent among Soviet inventors, scientists, engineers, and craftsmen—especially at the top, among the hereditary members of the cultural elite most likely to be frustrated by the Party monopoly on decision making and the Party officials' social and cultural provincialism. But they had their own reasons to be frustrated too. Intelligentsia members ("foreigners at home") are strangers by definition. The Jewish intelligentsia members of the late Soviet period were doubly strangers because the newly ethnicized state was suspicious of them on account of their "blood," and they were suspicious of the newly ethnicized state for the same reason.

The distrust was mutual, but the relationship was asymmetrical. In pursuit of both general proportional representation and particular Jewish demotion, the post-Stalinist state continued, in a mild form, the policy of limiting Jewish access to elite colleges and prestigious professional positions. According to the Soviet sociologist V. P. Mishin, "Whereas some peoples (Ukrainians, Belorussians, Moldavians, Tatars, Uzbeks, Azerbajanis and others) are still far below the national average with regard to the development of higher education and the training of scientific cadres, certain other peoples (Armenians, Georgians, Jews) have greatly exceeded that average. . . . Therefore, the proper goal of the directed development of interethnic relations consists not only in the equalization of conditions, but also in the continued maintenance of real equality among the peoples of the USSR."[182]

The Soviet state did its best to achieve that goal. Between 1960 and 1970, the number of employed professionals with higher education increased by more than 100 percent among Ukrainians, Belorussians, Moldavians, Tatars, Uzbeks, and Azerbaijanis, and by 23 percent, among Jews. The Jews were still light-years ahead (166 "specialists" per 1,000 people, as compared to 25 for Ukrainians, 15 for Uzbeks, and 35 for the second-place Armenians), but the trend was clear and durable. In the two decades prior to 1970, the proportion of scientific personnel increased by 1,300 percent among Uzbeks and 155 percent among Jews.[183]

Most American readers will find Mishin's recommendations and Soviet practices fairly familiar and possibly understandable, but it is also true that the two institutional frameworks are not at all alike. The main structural difference between the United States and the Soviet Union was the fact that the Soviet Union was a federation of ethnoterritorial units; the main difference between the Jews and all the other nationalities on Mishin's list was the fact that the Jews did not have a unit of their own. (Birobidzhan was not taken seriously by anyone, and there is little reason to believe that any other Jewish unit on Soviet territory would have been.) The Georgians and Armenians were, like the Jews, overrepresented among white-collar professionals and hurt by Soviet affirmative action. Unlike the Jews, however, they had "their own" republics, within which their dominance was accepted as entirely legitimate by both the central state and all would-be competitors. The Jews were far from being the main victims of the Soviet nationalities policy (the Piedmont nationalities, such as the Finns and Poles, were not even included in official statistics, and some deported peoples, such as the Volga Germans and Crimean Tatars, remained in exile until the end of the Soviet period), but they were unique among the USSR's "major nationalities." It was the combination of cultural prominence with administrative irrelevance that made the position of the Jews (as a Soviet nationality) truly exceptional. They were Number One according to every measure of Soviet modernity except for the most reassuring one: a proto-nation-state complete with its own culture-producing institutions.

But there is an even more important difference between the late twentieth-century American and late Soviet strategies for dealing with ethnically defined inequality. Affirmative action always implies negative (relative to strict meritocracy) action toward those not targeted for preferential promotion. In the Soviet Union, unlike the United States, the negative action was focused and deliberate, albeit publicly unacknowledged. Some elite institutions were closed to ethnic Jews; others employed *numerus clausus*; yet others limited professional advancement, publication opportunities, or access to benefits. Wherever one found oneself on Soviet territory or in the Soviet status hierarchy, Jewish nationality was a stamp of (undeserved) social advantage, political unreliability, and tribal difference. The "passport Jew" was a universal target of official discrimination without a Soviet home to go back to, a formal punishment to appeal against, or a communal ethnolinguistic culture to hide behind.

There were no clear discriminatory procedures—just makeshift arrangements formulated in secret and applied selectively and unevenly across economic branches, academic disciplines, and administrative units. Some second-tier institutions left open to the Jews gained professional prominence for that very reason; some projects were too important to be deprived of skilled participants; some managers were well-connected enough to be able to protect their employees; and some ethnic Jews changed their names or edited their biographies. The anti-Jewish discrimination was relatively small-scale (the difference, for the most part, was between best and second-best) and not very successful (the enormous achievement gap between the Jews and everyone else was narrowing very slowly), but its secrecy, inconsistency, and concentration on elite positions made it all the more frustrating. This "negative action" was as obvious to everyone concerned as it was contrary to post-Khrushchev public rhetoric, which extolled professional meritocracy tempered ever so slightly by tactful assistance to those who lagged behind. Even more remarkably, it was accompanied by a deafening public silence about all things Jewish. Histories of Lithuanian or Belorussian cities were not supposed to name those cities' principal inhabitants; World War II museums never referred to the Jewish genocide; and when Kornei Chukovsky asked to be allowed to publish a children's Bible, he was granted permission on condition that the Jews were never mentioned (he refused the commission). The world chess champion Tigran Petrosian was an Armenian; the world chess champion Mikhail Tal was "from Riga." And in 1965, all archival documents relating to Lenin's Jewish grandfather were ordered "removed without leaving any copies." The reason behind this was no longer a fear of providing more ammunition to the counterrevolutionary identification of Bolshevism with the Jews (as had been the case in the 1920s and early 1930s); it was a fear of sacrilege. Jews were aliens; Soviet heroes who happened to be Jews were either not true heroes (Jews were not mentioned on the lists of war heroes as Jews) or not really Jews (Yakov Sverdlov, for instance, was primarily associated with a square in Moscow and a city in the Urals).[184]

Like the "emancipated" European Jews at the turn of the twentieth century, the Soviet Jews of the "stagnation period" combined unparalleled social success with indefensible disabilities and a "chimerical" nationality unprotected by state nationalism. Their response, in a familiar mode, was either principled liberalism (exemplified—or so it seemed—by the United States) or Jewish nationalism (represented—more and more forcefully—by Israel). The third—Soviet—option was no longer available. As Mikhail (formerly Marx-Engels-Liebknecht) Agursky wrote about the Soviet 1960s,

> The Jews had been converted into an estate of slaves. Could one really expect that a nation that had given the Soviet state political leaders, diplomats, generals, and top economic managers would agree to become an estate whose boldest dream would be a position as head of a lab at the Experimental Machine-Tool Research Institute or senior researcher at the Automatics and Telemechanics Institute? The Jews were oppressed and humiliated to a much greater degree than the rest of the population.[185]

On the face of it, this statement may appear patently untrue and perhaps morally questionable. Not only were some deported nationalities still in exile, some Christian denominations formally banned, and most nomadic communities forced to part with their children, but the overwhelming majority of the Soviet population was not allowed to reside in large cities (let alone work in elite research institutes), and most rural inhabitants, whatever their nationality, were not entitled to internal passports and remained, in effect, serfs of the state. But of course Agursky was not (on this occasion) writing a work of history—he was writing a memoir about the making of a rebel, and what made Jewish rebels was the perception of unrelieved humiliation. In late imperial Russia, Jews had been—according to various economic and cultural criteria— better off than many other groups, but they had become the most revolutionary of them all because they had measured themselves according to the strictest meritocracy (and not in reference to Lamaists or peasants); thought themselves capable of making it to the very top (with very good reason); and considered their disabilities completely illegitimate (based as they were on the old confessional, not the new liberal, state-building principle). In late Soviet Russia, the "Jewish problem" was at least as acute: the disabilities were milder, but the official position was less defensible (in official terms), and the degree of Jewish social achievement—and thus the danger of downward mobility—much greater. The Jews were not more oppressed and humiliated than the rest of the population, but they had, indeed, provided the Soviet state with political leaders, diplomats, generals, and top economic managers, and they were poised to provide more if the officially adopted meritocratic principle were duly enforced. Jews were not more oppressed than the rest of the population, in other words, but they felt more humiliated because of their peculiarly exalted and vulnerable position in Soviet society. Moreover, the covert official persecution encouraged open popular anti-Semitism, which seems to have thrived on a combination of the old Apollonian hostility to "disembodied heads" and a vested interest on the part of new-minted Slavic technocrats that some of their more successful competitors be removed as ethnically ineligible. Swann's nose was a dangerous attribute to have; the public statement "I am a Jew" was either a confession of guilt or a gesture of defiance.[186]

The Jewish problem was a distillation of the general intelligentsia predicament. The father of Russian socialism, Alexander Herzen, had rebelled against the tsar not because he was being oppressed as much as his serfs; rather, it was because he considered himself equal to the tsar but was being treated like a serf. The same was true of Andrei Sakharov, who considered himself superior to Mitrofan Nedelin (not to mention Leonid Brezhnev or Mikhail Gorbachev) but was still being treated like a serf. The same, mutatis mutandis, was true of the Jews—except that in the postwar Soviet Union they were not just analogous to the antiregime intelligentsia—they were, in many ways, the core of the antiregime intelligentsia. The Jews were overrepresented among those who were making the Soviet Union hard, and they were underrepresented among those who were doing the guiding (and felt even more underrepresented among the latter because they were so strongly overrepresented among the former). In the 1970s and 1980s, the gerontocratic Soviet state had trouble telling the Jews and the intelligentsia apart; a large proportion of Soviet intelligentsia members (especially in the most elite occupations in Moscow and Leningrad) considered themselves Jews; most Moscow and Leningrad Jews thought of themselves as intelligentsia members; and when someone was being beaten up in a dark alley for wearing glasses or having an upper-class accent, the insults "Jew" and "*intelligent*" were likely to be used interchangeably. In May 1964, the head of the KGB, V. Semichastnyi, reported to the Central Committee of the Party that the trial of the poet Joseph Brodsky had greatly agitated the "creative intelligentsia," and that the most active agitators came from the "creative intelligentsia of the Jewish nationality" (even though neither the trial nor the protests—nor, indeed, Brodsky's poetry—had anything to do with the "Jewish question"). In 1969, at a scholarly conference, Mikhail Agursky told two young colleagues, Yuri Gurevich and Yuri Gastev, a "semipolitical joke." After he left, "the vigilant Gurevich" asked Gastev:

> "Who was that guy? What does he mean by telling jokes like that? Do you know him?"
>
> "Yes, I do," said Gastev firmly.
>
> "Since when?"
>
> "Since this morning."
>
> "And you trust him?"

"Just look at his nose!"—said Gastev by way of concluding the polemic.[187]

Swann had come a long way. In the semipolitical jokes themselves, the Jew "Rabinovich" emerged as the ultimate symbol of the brutally oppressed but irrepressibly ironic *Homo sovieticus.* Or rather, traditional shtetl humor reemerged as the voice of the Soviet intelligentsia.

> A political instructor asks Rabinovich:
> "Who is your father?"
> "The Soviet Union."
> "Good. And who is your mother?"
> "The Communist Party."
> "Excellent. And what is your fondest wish?"
> "To become an orphan."

This joke was about all Soviets, of course, but it fit Rabinovich especially well because, in his case, the first two answers seemed just as truthful as the last one. As Victor Zaslavsky and Robert J. Brym wrote in their pioneering book about Jewish emigration from the Soviet Union, "while in the 1920s the notion emerged that the Jews were exceptionally loyal to the regime, the 1970s witnessed the emergence of another convenient myth of the Jews' intrinsic political unreliability. Both contained elements of a self-fulfilling prophecy."[188]

Of the three options available to Russian Jews—Liberalism, Zionism, and Communism—the third one was gone and the first two were illegal. This made most Moscow and Leningrad Jews "politically unreliable" and in some cases consistently oppositional. Of the three principal intelligentsia ideologies of the late Soviet period—Liberalism (Westernism), Zionism, and Russian nationalism—the first one was predominantly Jewish, the second one entirely Jewish, and the third one more or less anti-Semitic (because it celebrated unspoilt peasant Apollonianism in opposition to urban Mercurianism, which was now associated with the Jews, not Germans; and because the antipeasant Bolshevik Revolution had been Jewish to a considerable, if frequently exaggerated, degree).

The proportion—and importance—of ethnic Jews among Western-oriented liberal dissidents was very substantial. The movement's founding moments included the 1964 trial of Joseph Brodsky; the 1966 trial of Yuli Daniel (who was Jewish) and Andrei Siniavsky (who was Russian but wrote—by way of emphasizing his alienation—under a Jewish-sounding alias, Abram Terz); the documentary collection about the Daniel-Siniavsky trial, compiled by Aleksandr Ginzburg; the January 1968 "Appeal to World Public Opinion," written by Pavel Litvinov and Larisa Bogoraz; and the August 1968 demonstration on Red Square against the Soviet invasion of Czechoslovakia, staged by seven people, four of them ethnic Jews. As Lev Shternberg had said about their grandparents, the socialists, "it is as though thousands of the prophets of Israel have risen from their forgotten graves to proclaim, once again, . . . their urgent call for social justice."

Equally great was the Jewish share of academic innovators with cult followings, such as Yuri Lotman in literary criticism, Aron Gurevich in history, Petr Kapitsa and Lev Landau in physics, and Izrail Gelfand and Leonid Kantorovich in mathematics. Close relatives of Western scholarly icons (Einstein, Oppenheimer, Boas, Lévi-Strauss, Derrida, Chomsky, and the members of the Frankfurt School, among others), they were Thorstein Veblen's "disturbers of the intellectual peace" who stood out "among the vanguard, the pioneers, the uneasy guild of pathfinders and iconoclasts, in science, scholarship and institutional change and growth." Hodl's children had finally rejoined the family.[189]

Along with the West, a crucial source of models and inspiration for the Soviet Westernizers was the Russian avant-garde of the early twentieth century. Most of the original avant-garde artists had been strongly antiliberal (and in some cases aggressively Bolshevik), but their late Soviet followers interpreted their work as the ultimate expression of individual creative freedom (and thus the natural antipode, as well as victim, of socialist realism). The latter-day iconoclasts were even more heavily Jewish than their models: according to Igor Golomstock's survey of Soviet "unofficial" artists, "a figure of 50 percent would be too low rather than too high." From the

"Decembrist" generation of the Thaw artists, led by the monumental Ernst Neizvestny, to Oscar Rabin's "Lianozovo" chroniclers of Soviet dreariness, to the chief iconographers of late Soviet irony (Erik Bulatov, Ilya Kabakov, Vitaly Komar, and Aleksandr Melamid), most of the pathfinders and pioneers were ethnic Jews.[190]

Russia being Russia, however, the truest prophets had to be poets. With the Pushkin religion taken for granted and shared with the regime, the particular patron saints of the anti-Soviet intelligentsia were two women (Anna Akhmatova and Marina Tsvetaeva) and two ethnic Jews (Boris Pasternak and Osip Mandelstam). All four were worshiped as the lone guardians of Truth and Knowledge, martyred—out of impotent jealousy—by the demonic Party-state. Their only legitimate successor, anointed by Akhmatova before her death and canonized in his lifetime as the divine voice of the resurrected intelligentsia, was Joseph Brodsky, the son of a Soviet naval officer and the grandson of a Petersburg book publisher and a Pale of Settlement sewing-machine salesman.

The death of communism proved the undoing of Hodl's life. Some members of her generation who had survived into the 1960s and 1970s were still living their dream (in "Old Bolsheviks' Homes") or waiting for it to come true (in the land of "actually existing socialism"), but most seemed to agree that the dream had been a chimera. The author of one of the most influential samizdat exposés of Stalinism was Evgeny Gnedin, the onetime head of the Press Department of the People's Commissariat for External Affairs and the son of Parvus, who had formulated the theory of "permanent revolution" and persuaded the German government to let Lenin travel to Russia in April 1917. An even better-known camp memoir belonged to Evgenia Ginzburg, who, in the mid-1930s, had been the chair of the Department of the History of Leninism at the University of Kazan and the head of the Culture Department at the *Red Tataria* newspaper. The "inquisitor" who had sent her to prison was Abram Beilin, whose eyes, according to Ginzburg, "shone with a subdued, sardonic joy at the expense of his fellow creatures," and who "exercised his Talmudic subtlety in polishing up the definition of my 'crimes.' " Beilin, too, was later arrested, reduced to driving an oxcart in Kazakhstan, and finally allowed to retire to Moscow, where he was shunned by his old apparatchik friends (who had all read Ginzburg's manuscript).[191]

One of Beilin's old friends was Samuil Agursky, the erstwhile nemesis-in-chief of the Hebrew language who spent the last years of his life reading books on "ancient Jewish history." As his wife, Bunia, lay dying, she told their son, Mikhail, "I should have lived my life very differently." To which Mikhail responded, "I've always told you that you should have lived your life differently." And when Hope Ulanovskaia, the onetime child revolutionary and professional spy, arrived in Israel at the age of seventy, she met some women who had left the Pale for Palestine at about the same time she had left her native shtetl for Russia. Visiting their kibbutz, she felt "regret that she had not lived her life the way she should have" and "humility before her contemporaries who had chosen a different path." According to her daughter, she knew that "her life could have been as beautiful and productive as the life of these old kibbutzniks."[192]

Hodl's children all agreed that she had not lived her life the way she should have—and that neither, if they were old enough to have been happy in the 1930s, had they. The leather-clad bard of the civil war's "flashing bayonets," Mikhail Svetlov, metamorphosed into the much lionized sad clown of the 1960s, whose witticisms were written down and widely circulated. (The best known was: "What is a question mark? It is an exclamation point that has grown old.")

The "Komsomoler of the 1920s" and "pitiless" collectivizer, Lev Kopelev, became one of the best-known Soviet dissidents of the 1970s—as did his wife, Raisa Orlova, who had been a buoyantly happy member of the "first Soviet generation." Another member of that generation was Mikhail Gefter, a "frenzied" Komsomol inquisitor in Moscow University's History Department during the Great Terror who went on to become a leading moral philosopher of the perestroika period and president of the Russian Center for the Study of the Holocaust. Hope Ulanovskaia's daughter, Maia, spent more than five years (1951–56) in prisons and camps for belonging to a student organization called the Union of the Struggle for the Cause of the Revolution, almost all of whose members, including all three founders, were young Jews (Hodl's children). It was Maia's son (and Hope's grandson), born in 1959, who talked both of them into emigrating to Israel.[193]

One of the leaders of the Jewish emigration movement was Samuil Agursky's son Mikhail (the one who reproached his mother for having lived her life incorrectly). Among his fellow activists was David Azbel, whose uncle, Rakhmiel Vainshtein, had been Samuil Agursky's rival at the helm of the Party's Jewish Section. And among those who—in the late 1950s—had introduced the young Mikhail to modern Western art and Moscow's bohemian scene was the first Soviet abstract expressionist, Vladimir Slepian. Slepian's Jewish father had been the head of the Smolensk province secret police directorate.[194]

The conversion from Communism to anti-Communism might lead to a trenchant mea culpa (like Kopelev's or Orlova's), mild bemusement (like Ulanovskaia's), or labored obfuscation (like Gefter's). But it almost never led to a sense of collective responsibility—on anyone's part. The USSR's most celebrated achievements—the revolution, industrialization, victory over the Nazis, the welfare state—were largely (if inconsistently) represented as supranationally Soviet in inspiration and selflessly global in spirit. They were carried out in the name of a common future, and they could be cheered, furthered, and treasured by anyone who shared the dream. The same uncertainty (generosity) of both authorship and target was true of other things—the Red Terror, the Great Terror, forced labor, "dekulakization"—that were now seen by the aging regime as dubious accomplishments and by the new antiregime intelligentsia as terrible crimes.[195]

Acts of violence that are not committed by one tribe against another tribe cast a very short shadow. Unlike genocides, they produce no legitimate heirs—for either the victims or the perpetrators. "Germans" as actual or metaphoric children of the Nazis may be urged to repent and to atone; "Jews" as the actual or metaphoric children of the Holocaust may be entitled to compensation and apology. Communists (like animists, Calvinists, or any other nonethnic group) have no children other than those who choose to be adopted. The only identifiable collective descendants of the victims of Stalinist violence are nations: primarily the non-Russian peoples of the Soviet empire (including the Jews) but also, in some accounts, the Russians (as the main target of the Bolshevik war against rural backwardness and religion). The only identifiable collective descendants of the initiators and perpetrators of Stalinist violence are nations too: primarily the Russians but also, in some accounts, the Jews (as the most enthusiastic ethnically defined supporters of the Soviet state). The claim to ethnic victimhood is utterly convincing but—considering the overall scale and nature of Stalinist violence—relatively marginal; the identification of alleged victimizers appears dubious. The concept of ethnic responsibility is as inescapable (what is a "nation" if one is not responsible for the acts of one's "fathers"?) as it is morally uncertain (what is repentance or atonement if there is no priestly or divine authority to provide absolution?). It is even more uncertain—and thus easily and justifiably escapable—with regard to the legacy of Communism, which was almost as strongly committed to cosmopolitanism as it was to mass violence.

Communists might have children, in other words, but Communism did not. The children of Communists who did not wish to be Communists could go back to their tribal or cultural genealogies, however defined. For Hodl's children and grandchildren, this meant being a Jew and a member of the Russian intelligentsia (in various combinations). As Raisa Orlova wrote in her *Memoirs of Times Not Past*,

> I know so little. It's shocking how little I know. I know nothing about my roots, I know nothing about my genealogy. I don't even know my maternal grandmother's first name and patronymic, and she lived with us for a long time—she didn't die until after I was married. And now it is vital for me to find out. To see in my mind's eye the Kiev-Warsaw train that took my future parents on their wedding trip in March 1915. Their honeymoon.
>
> . . . The wheels are pounding. That coach in the Kiev-Warsaw train is moving forward, and the two happy passengers do not know what

lies ahead. I never heard the pounding of the wheels on that train before—but now I hear it more clearly all the time.[196]

What does she hear? Her parents' move to the center of both Russia and the world revolution (Gorky Street 6, next to the Kremlin) and their rise to the top of the Soviet bureaucratic and later cultural elite is a part of the Communist abomination she needs to forget if her true "roots" are to be recovered. What is left is her parents' rejection of Judaism, their prerevolutionary college education (Commercial Institute for her father, School of Dentistry for her mother), and her mother's passionate, lifelong love of Pushkin ("perhaps she had read Pushkin to my father on their honeymoon?").

In the 1960s, when Orlova was writing her memoirs, one of the most popular books among intelligentsia teenagers was Alexandra Brushtein's *The Road Leads Off into the Distance*, an autobiographical coming-of-age story about a sensitive girl from a Jewish intelligentsia family growing up in prerevolutionary Vilna. An engaging collection of literary clichés from the late nineteenth century, the book contains a warm and caring mother, a morally upright father (a doctor who divides his loyalties among his indigent patients, Pushkin, and the revolution), a silly German tutor, a faithful peasant nanny, and a rich collection of revolutionary exiles, ignorant priests, fat industrialists, book-reading proletarians, heartless *gymnasium* teachers, and fierce adolescent friendships in the face of the world's injustice. What it does not contain—in the midst of the Pale of Settlement—are Jews (except an occasional ghostly victim or "shadow of forgotten ancestors"). There is a lot of anti-Semitism (along with other forms of injustice), and there is the intelligentsia devoted to the cause of universal equality, but there are no Jews because most Jews are members of the Russian intelligentsia and most members of the Russian intelligentsia are Jews. Such was the genealogy of most of Brushtein's readers and the assumption behind Orlova's quest.[197]

There were other possible lineages, however. No, not Tevye: he was of no use to the late Soviet intellectuals, few of whom were curious about Judaism and virtually none of whom had any interest in shtetl culture or Yiddish literature (there could be no Soviet— i.e., anti-Soviet—*Life Is with People* or *Fiddler on the Roof*). As far as Hodl's children and grandchildren were concerned, the world she had come from was every bit as "frightening and suffocating" as she had always told them it was.

But Hodl was not Tevye's only daughter, and Hodl's children and grandchildren had cousins, as well as grandparents and great-grandparents. There were, after all, two clear alternatives to Communism that could also serve as alternatives to the Soviet Jews' precarious and—according to the state and the tribal Apollonians— illegitimate membership in the Russian intelligentsia. One was Beilke's America as unadulterated Liberalism, or possibly Liberalism diluted with "Protestantized" Judaism (the kind that assured tribal solidarity without requiring strict ritual compliance or even a faith in God). The other was Chava's Israel as Apollonian nationalism, or rather, Zionist Jewishness seemingly unpolluted by Tevye's language, self-reflexivity, or religion.

While young Soviet Jews were rebelling against Hodl's left radicalism and turning toward Zionism and—especially—Capitalism, young American Jews were rebelling against Beilke's Capitalism and turning toward Zionism and—especially—left radicalism. The Jewish participation in the radical student movements of the 1960s and early 1970s was comparable to the Jewish participation in Eastern European socialism and prewar American Communism. In the first half of the 1960s, Jews (5 percent of all American students) made up between 30 and 50 percent of SDS (Students for a Democratic Society) membership and more than 60 percent of its leadership; six out of eleven Steering Committee members of the Free Speech Movement at Berkeley; one-third of the Weathermen arrested by the police; 50 percent of the membership of California's Peace and Freedom Party; two-thirds of the white Freedom Riders who went to the South in 1961 to fight racial segregation; one-third to one-half of the "Mississippi Summer" volunteers of 1964 (and two of the three murdered martyrs); 45 percent of those who protested the release of students' grades to draft boards at the University of Chicago; and 90 percent of the sample of radical activists studied by Joseph Adelson at the University of Michigan. In 1970, in the wake of the invasion of Cambodia and the killing of four students at Kent State (three of whom were Jewish), 90 percent of the Jewish students attending schools at which there were demonstrations claimed to have participated. In a 1970 nationwide poll, 23 percent of all Jewish college students identified themselves as "far left" (compared to 4 percent of Protestants and 2 percent of Catholics); and a small group of radical activists studied at the University of California was found to be 83 percent Jewish. A large study of student radicalism conducted by the American Council of Education in the late 1960s found that a Jewish background was the single most important predictor of participation in protest activities.[198]

When, in 1971–73, Stanley Rothman and S. Robert Lichter surveyed 1,051 students at Boston University, Harvard University, the University of Massachusetts at Amherst, and the University of Michigan, they discovered that "53% of the radicals were of Jewish background, as were 63% of those who engaged in seven or more protests, 54% of those who led three or more protests, and 52% of those who formed three or more protest groups." Most important, they found that "the dichotomy between Jews and non-Jews provided the most parsimonious means of accounting for the many other social and psychological aspects of New Left radicalism. . . . After examining our results, we concluded that there was little point in dividing the non-Jewish category into several ethnic or denominational components, because these subgroups differed only slightly in their adherence to radical ideas. Jews, by contrast, were substantially more radical than any of the non-Jewish religious or ethnic subgroups."[199]

Among Jews, "radicalism rose substantially as religious orthodoxy declined. Reform Jews were more radical than orthodox or conservative Jews . . . , and Jews who specified no further affiliation were more radical still." By far the most radical of all were the children of "irreligious but ethnically Jewish parents," especially those from upper-middle-class professional households. The uncontested leaders on the radicalism scale were the offspring of Jewish academics. Curiously, the non-Jewish students from professional households were not significantly more radical than non-Jewish students from other occupational backgrounds. The connection between secular professionalism and political radicalism seemed to apply only to Jews.[200]

In nineteenth-century Europe, Jews had been overrepresented among revolutionaries because their extraordinary success in the modern state had not been protected by that state's legitimizing ideology, nationalism. Or rather, many young Jews had launched a patricidal revolution because their fathers seemed to combine boundless capitalism with "chimerical nationality." All modernity is about "nakedness" covered by modern nationalism. The Jews—tragically—had become emperors with no clothes.

Mid-twentieth-century America was a country of universal nakedness because America's commitment to capitalism seemed boundless and because the American nationality was, by European standards, chimerical. Once again, however, the most consistent "rootless cosmopolitans" in America were Jews. No one else was quite as secular, urban, or meritocratic as the Jews, and even those non-Jews who were as secular, urban, and meritocratic as the Jews were less patricidal because they were more patriarchal—more attached to the rituals, relatives, and conventions that make life meaningfully tribal. Of all the modern revolutions, the most uncompromising had been the Jewish one.

The Jewish American rebels of the 1960s were the only radicals who came from radical households—either because their parents were Communists or because their parents made the mistake of pursuing uncompromising Enlightenment liberalism in a country of subnational ethnic and religious allegiances. The Jewish parents were the only ones who believed in universal nakedness and raised their children accordingly. Philip Roth's Swede Levov married a Catholic Miss New Jersey, bought a house on Arcady Hill, and raised his daughter Merry to love the America of Thanksgiving and "perfect self-control." Instead, she grew up to become first a revolutionary terrorist and eventually a priestess of radical nonviolence.

As the Swede's father, the no-nonsense entrepreneur, put it, "once Jews ran away from oppression; now they run away from no-oppression." Or, as the Swede himself seems to have concluded, once Jews ran away from Jewishness; now they run away from non-Jewishness. "They raised a child who was neither Catholic nor Jew, who instead was first a stutterer, then a killer, then a Jain." Babel's and Mandelstam's little boys had had to overcome their Jewish muteness in pursuit of the "clear and pure" sounds of Apollonian speech. Merry Levov stuttered in her native English because Thanksgiving was a poor substitute for Passover. Or Pushkin. Or Communism.[201]

Merry was incurable: she was "gruesomely misbegotten." But most other Jewish radicals of the 1960s did recover in the 1970s because they found clothes appropriate to their station—a faith that was both warm and modern, messianic and perfectly compatible with Thanksgiving. They became self-conscious Jews sharing in their people's suffering and accomplishments. They became, in this broad sense, Jewish nationalists. According to Will Herberg,

> The third generation [of American Jews] felt secure in its Americanness and therefore no longer saw any reason for the attitude of rejection so characteristic of its predecessors. It therefore felt no reluctance about identifying itself as Jewish and affirming its Jewishness; on the contrary, such identification became virtually compelling since it was the only way in which the American Jew could now locate himself in the larger community. . . . As the third generation began to "remember" the religion of its ancestors, to the degree at least of affirming itself Jewish "in a religious sense," it also began to lose interest in the ideologies and "causes" which had been so characteristic of Jewish youth in earlier decades. Social radicalism virtually disappeared, and the passionate, militant Zionism espoused by groups of American Jews until 1948 became diffused into a vague, though by no means insincere, friendliness to the state of Israel.[202]

After the Six-Day War, Hodl's and Chava's children resumed their responsibility of endowing the lives of Beilke's children with meaning: the Soviet cousins, as victims, and the Israeli ones, as both victims and victors. In the 1970s, most American Jews by blood became Jews by conviction—and thus full-fledged Americans. Nostalgia for a lost world was replaced with an allegiance to living relatives; chimerical nationality was transformed into a proper ethnoreligious community; Tevye, it turned out, had had other choices besides martyrdom and Thanksgiving. Tevye, it turned out, had descendants who were at peace with themselves and at war with their oppressors. The American Jews had finally become regular American "ethnics," complete with an old country that was also a new state with a flag, an army, and a basketball team. More than that, they had become the first among American ethnics because their new old country was uniquely old, uniquely new, uniquely victorious, and uniquely victimized. And of course its very existence—and therefore the continued existence of all Jews, Soviet and American, was (it turned out) a response to an event that was the "most unique" of all events that had ever occurred. As Elie Wiesel wrote in the *New York Times* in 1978, "Auschwitz cannot be explained nor can it be visualized. Whether culmination or aberration of history, the Holocaust transcends history. . . . The dead are in possession of a secret that we, the living, are neither worthy of nor capable of recovering. . . . The Holocaust? The ultimate event, the ultimate mystery, never to be comprehended or transmitted."[203]

Jewish American Communism had flared up one last time in the Jewish Century before finally yielding to nationalism. Relatively few of the erstwhile cosmopolitans would become "neoconservative" champions of Israeli-style uncompromising belligerence and "moral clarity," but virtually everyone would join the "normal" modern nations in finding a decent cover for their nakedness. The place of ethnic Jews in America would ultimately depend on how normal or how unique Israel would become.

Meanwhile, the existence of ethnic Jews in the Soviet Union was becoming untenable. Most of those who had given up on Communism preferred American Liberalism (with or without the Jewish national content), but there were always those who looked to Palestine. The Moscow International Youth Festival of 1957, which launched the adulterous love affair between Soviet youth and all things foreign, included a much sought-after Israeli delegation; the "ideological struggle" waged by the Soviet state against alien penetration included periodic campaigns against "Zionist propaganda"; and the most influential heretical texts that tempted the Soviet intelligentsia away from Party orthodoxy included underground translations of such "Zionist realism" classics as Howard Fast's *My Glorious Brothers* and Leon Uris's *Exodus*. (Both books had the advantage of combining redemptive Jewish nationalism with militant Apollonian secularism; Fast, in particular, appeared to be a perfect icon—both Soviet and American—of a Communist ideologue and Stalin Peace Prize laureate awakened to the truth of Jewish chosenness and Soviet anti-Semitism.)[204]

The most important episode in the history of Soviet (and American) Zionism was the Six-Day War of 1967. "I sat at my dacha glued to the radio, rejoicing and celebrating," writes Mikhail Agursky. "And I was not the only one." Ester Markish, for one, "listened to the radio day and night. . . . The Jews were openly celebrating, saying to each other: 'We are advancing!' When the threat of war loomed over Israel, many Russian Jews made the unequivocal choice: 'Israel is our flesh and blood. Russia is, at best, a distant relative, and possibly a total stranger.' "[205]

The children of the most loyal of all Soviet citizens had become the most alienated of all antiregime intellectuals. Back in 1956, Mikhail Agursky's "sympathy" for Israel had not yet "reached the level of full identification." In those days, "Israel had been a small provincial country, whereas I lived in a large metropolis, a superpower on which the fate of the world depended. I had grown up near the Kremlin, at the center of the world. Like most citizens of my country, I was a great-power chauvinist."[206]

Now, almost overnight, the center of the world had shifted to where his family sympathy lay. "The Six-Day War convinced me that my platonic Zionism was becoming the real thing and that, sooner rather than later, I was fated to live in Israel. . . . From being a small provincial country, Israel had become a power one could identify with." And from provincial poor relations, the half-forgotten Israeli cousins had turned into heroes and possibly patrons. As Ester Markish put it, "the photographs of Israeli aunts, uncles, and cousins twice removed had been kept in the remotest drawers; it was better not to discuss them out loud or mention them in government questionnaires." Now, they had become "the distant fragments of our families that had survived Hitler's and Stalin's pogroms." They were strong; they were virtuous; and they were free. According to a popular Soviet joke from the late 1960s, Rabinovich is confronted by an NKVD investigator:

> "Why did you say on your questionnaire that you had no relatives overseas? We know you have a cousin living abroad."
>
> "I don't have a cousin living abroad," says Rabinovich.
>
> "And what is this?" says the investigator, showing him a letter from his Israeli cousin.
>
> "You don't understand," says Rabinovich, "my cousin lives at home. I am the one living abroad."[207]

After the Soviet invasion of Czechoslovakia in 1968, more and more Soviet intelligentsia members felt abroad at home and, as Elena Bonner would put it, "alone together." Or rather, more and more Soviet professionals were becoming Russian intelligentsia members ("foreigners at home"). And the most foreign of them all were the hereditary strangers—the Jews.

Not only were the Jews heavily concentrated at the top, targeted for discrimination (for that very reason), and seen as tribal aliens in an increasingly tribalized state—they did, unlike most of their fellow professionals, have a different Jerusalem to turn to; they did, literally or metaphorically, have cousins who were at home abroad. Returning to their Moscow apartment after receptions at the Israeli Embassy, Ester Markish and her children "felt dejected: it was as if we were leaving our homeland for a foreign land." Mikhail Agursky, Maia Ulanovskaia, and Tsafrira Meromskaia all felt the same way—and so did the Soviet state. Along with the Soviet Germans, Armenians, and Greeks, who also had prosperous foreign cousins willing to pay their ransom, the Jews were the only Soviet citizens—and virtually the only members of the Soviet professional elite—who were allowed to emigrate from the USSR. The official reason for the privilege was the existence of Israel: the Jewish "historic homeland."[208]

After the Six-Day War, the number of emigration applications shot up. The regime retaliated by stepping up its "anti-Zionist" campaign and multiplying Jewish disabilities in education and employment. The Jews responded by applying to emigrate in even greater numbers; the regime retaliated by charging a higher education tax; and so it continued until Gorbachev opened the emigration floodgates (along with so many others) in the late 1980s. As an official from the Central Committee's Propaganda Department, L. Onikov, wrote to his superiors in a secret memo dated September 30, 1974, "almost all the Jews, including those (the overwhelming majority) who have never considered leaving this country, are in a state of psychological tension, uncertainty, and nervous anxiety: 'What will happen to them tomorrow?' "[209]

The Party leaders seemed baffled. On the one hand, any desire to emigrate from Heaven was an open challenge to the true faith, and thus both a temptation to the faithful and an embarrassment before Hell. As Onikov wrote in his memo, "the fact of the departure of some Jews from the USSR is widely used in anti-Soviet propaganda as a confirmation of the old slander about a flight from 'Communist paradise.' " Moreover, he continued, "the emigration of some Jews to Israel has a negative effect on other nationalities, including some Germans, Balts, Crimean Tatars, and others, who ask: 'Why are Jews allowed to go to foreign countries, and we aren't?' " Finally, there was the much discussed question of the "brain drain" and the dynamics of great-power politics in the Middle East. As L. I. Brezhnev put it at a Politburo meeting on March 20, 1973, "not only academicians but even middle-level specialists shouldn't be allowed to leave—I don't want to upset the Arabs."[210]

On the other hand, why not get rid of the rotten apples? In March 1971, the KGB chief Yuri Andropov recommended that the screenwriter E. E. Sevela be allowed to leave the country on account of his "nationalist views" and his "low moral and professional level." In Onikov's words, the emigration of "Zionists and other nationalists," "religious fanatics," "adventurers," "self-seekers dreaming of private enterprise," and "losers hoping to get lucky," was a good thing. "The sooner such elements get out, the better." There was, of course, a disconcerting Brer-Rabbit-and-the-briar-patch element to this logic (Andropov, for one, might deny permission to emigrate for the same reasons he might grant it), but Party leaders seemed to agree that, in some cases at least, the benefit of getting rid of troublesome subjects justified the anguish of having to watch them prosper in exile.

Finally, some Party leaders were prepared to discourage the Jews from leaving by granting them some of what they wanted. But what did the Jews want? Brezhnev, the top Party leader, had a rather narrow view of the question. On March 20, 1973, he reported to the Politburo the surprising fact that the Soviet Union had a Yiddish magazine.

> And so I asked myself this question: we have a certain number of Gypsies, but surely not as many as Jews, right? And we don't have any laws against the Jews, do we? So why not give them a little theater of five hundred seats, a Jewish variety theater, which would be under our censorship, and its repertoire under our supervision. Let Aunt Sonya sing Jewish wedding songs there. I am not proposing this, I am just thinking out loud. Or how about opening a school? Some of our kids even study in England. Mzhavanadze's son is going to school in England. My own granddaughter graduated from a so-called English school. They do study the language, but the rest of the curriculum is standard. So I'm wondering: why not open a school in Moscow, and call it a Jewish one? The curriculum would be standard, but they would teach Yiddish, their national language. What's the big deal? After all, there are three and a half million of them, compared to 150,000 Gypsies.
>
> So I had this really bold idea. Of course, I'm always full of ideas. Anyway, I realize no one has proposed this before, but why not allow a Yiddish weekly? We do have some little Jewish weeklies in Birobidzhan. Not everyone will be able to read it. Some Jew, some old Abramovich will read it, but so what? It all comes from TASS anyway. . . .
> I am speaking freely because I am not raising my hand to vote yet. I'm just thinking out loud for now, and I am keeping my hands on the table, that's all.[211]

None of Brezhnev's bold ideas came to pass, but the reason he was entertaining them—and the reason the Jewish emigration ranked so high on the Politburo's agenda—was unrelenting political pressure from the United States. By the early 1970s, Beilke's

children—now one of the most politically and economically powerful communities in America—had rediscovered their Soviet cousins
and adopted them as "the distant fragments of their families that
had survived Hitler's and Stalin's pogroms." The transformation
of Socialists into Jews in the United States had coincided with the
transformation of Socialists into Jews in the Soviet Union, but
whereas in the United States it had marked the Jewish entry into the
elite, in the Soviet Union it had accompanied the growing Jewish
alienation. (Only a minority of American Jews had been Socialists,
of course, but there is little doubt that Protestantized Judaism had
supplanted Socialism as the dominant nontraditional Jewish ideology.) The poor relations of the 1930s had metamorphosed into the
rich uncles of the 1970s, and after Israel had vanquished its enemies
and begun to lose some of its luster and innocence, the exodus of
the Soviet Jewry had become—briefly—the American Jewry's most
urgent, emotional, and unifying cause. By 1974, a broad coalition
of Jewish organizations and politicians had managed to thwart the
Nixon-Kissinger "détente" designs by assuring congressional adoption of the "Jackson-Vanik amendment," which linked U.S.-Soviet
trade to Jewish emigration from the USSR. As J. J. Goldberg put
it, "Jewish activists had taken on the Nixon administration and the
Kremlin and won. Jews had proven to the world and to themselves
that they could stand up and fight for themselves. The stain of Holocaust abandonment had finally been removed."[212]

Although the Jackson-Vanik amendment (initiated and guided
through Congress by Senator Jackson's chief of staff, Richard Perle,
and Senator Ribicoff's chief of staff, Morris Amitay) referred to the
freedom of emigration in general, it was applied only to the Jews.
The exclusive right to request an exit visa resulted in ever greater
alienation: all ethnic Jews became would-be émigrés, and thus potential traitors. It also led to the creation of an ever growing group
of pseudo-Zionists and pseudo-Jews: the only way to leave the Soviet Union was to claim a desire to go to Israel. The late twentieth-
century exodus was similar to the early twentieth-century one in
that the overwhelming majority of émigrés preferred America to
Palestine; the main difference was that the only way to go to
America (or anywhere else) was by applying to go to Palestine.

The question of where to go mattered to some more than to others, but what mattered to all of Hodl's grandchildren was that they had the opportunity to leave the Soviet Union. The late twentieth-century exodus had much more to do with the perception that Hodl had chosen incorrectly than with the discovery that Chava and Beilke had chosen correctly. Everyone seemed to agree that Hodl's path—socialism—had been a tragic mistake, and that the only real question was whether to do now what Hodl should have done then: emigrate from a false paradise.

Many of them did—both before and after the Soviet state finally agreed that socialism had been a tragic mistake. Between 1968 and 1994, about 1.2 million Jews left the USSR and its successor states (at 43 percent of the total, a larger emigration than the one of which Beilke and Chava had been a part). The first wave, which reached Israel between 1968 and 1975, carried with it most of the ideological Zionists (such as Markish and Agursky) and many of Tsaytl's grandchildren from the former Pale of Settlement. The flood that followed was mostly U.S.-bound and included many of Hodl's Moscow and Leningrad grandchildren (about 90 percent of whom went to the United States). The Israeli government attempted to curb this trend, but it was only after 1988, when the overall proportion of those going to America reached 89 percent, that the United States agreed to significantly decrease immigration quotas for Soviet Jews. After the fall of the Berlin Wall in 1989, Israel opened its own consulates in the Soviet Union, closed down the notoriously porous transit point in Vienna, and ultimately succeeded in preventing the majority of the 1989–92 refugees (the largest group of all) from "dropping out" en route. By 1994, 27 percent of all Soviet Jewish émigrés from the USSR had been taken in by Beilke's grandchildren, and 62 percent by Chava's.[213]

Wherever they ended up, most of Hodl's descendants have remained faithful to the late Soviet concept of belonging. They are Jews by blood, Russians by (high) culture, and religious not at all (outside of the Pushkin cult). They are, therefore, not fully Jewish according to their American and Israeli hosts (many of whom seem as disappointed as anyone who has sheltered a long-lost relative). Indeed, they are like reverse Marranos: public Jews who practice their Gentile faith—complete with special feasts, rites, and texts—in the privacy of their homes. But this is a temporary condition, because the most important thing that all of Tevye's descendants share is the knowledge that they are all Tevye's descendants. Or rather, they all share Tevye's most important belief: "Anyone can be a goy, but a Jew must be born one." All Jews are Jews "by blood"; the rest is a matter of "absorption" (to use an Israeli term). Sooner or later, the Soviet Jewish émigrés to Israel and the United States will "recover their Jewishness" in its entirety. This does not mean going back to Tevye's religion, of course (any more than any renaissance means actual rebirth). In Israel, full recovery implies the supplanting of the Russian intelligentsia canon with the Israeli Hebrew one; in the United States, it requires the replacement of the Russian intelligentsia canon with a blend of Protestantized Judaism and Zionism. It is a high price to pay, but most of Hodl's grandchildren are willing to pay it. Because Hodl "should have lived her life differently," the life that she did live must be forgotten. As one of Hodl's daughters, Tsafrira Meromskaia, put it,

> I lived in Moscow for more than forty years. I loved it as passionately as one loves a human being. I thought I would not be able to live a single day without it. And yet I have left it forever—consciously, calmly, even joyfully, without a chance to see it again or any desire to return.
>
> I live without nostalgia, without looking back. Moscow, such as it is, is gone from my soul, and that is the best proof of the correctness of my decision.[214]

At the beginning of the twentieth century, Tevye's daughters had three promised lands to choose from. At the turn of the twenty-first, there are only two. Communism lost out to both liberalism and nationalism and then died of exhaustion.

The Russian part of the Jewish Century is over. The home of the world's largest Jewish population has become a small and remote province of Jewish life; the most Jewish of all states since the Second

Temple has disappeared from the face of the earth; the sacred center of world revolution has been transformed into the capital of yet another Apollonian nation-state. Hodl, who was once admired by her sisters for her association with Russia, world revolution, and the Soviet state, has become a family embarrassment, or possibly a ghost. Few Jewish histories seem to remember who she is: the twentieth century as they represent it includes the lives of Tsaytl, Beilke, Chava, and their descendants, as well the sudden exodus of Tevye's forgotten and apparently orphaned grandchildren from the captivity of the "Red Pharaohs."[215]

The Jewish part of Russian history is over too. It is closely associated with the fate of the Soviet experiment and is remembered or forgotten accordingly. Most Jewish nationalist accounts of Soviet history have preserved the memory of Jewish victimization at the hands of the Whites, Nazis, Ukrainian nationalists, and the postwar Soviet state, but not the memory of the Jewish Revolution against Judaism, Jewish identification with Bolshevism, and the unparalleled Jewish success within the Soviet establishment of the 1920s and 1930s. Some Russian nationalist accounts, on the other hand, equate Bolshevism with Jewishness in an effort to represent the Russian Revolution as a more or less deliberate alien assault on the Russian people and culture. As I write this, Alexander Solzhenitsyn has urged Jews to accept "moral responsibility" for those of their kinsmen who "took part in the iron Bolshevik leadership and, even more so, in the ideological guidance of a huge country down a false path." Citing the German acceptance of "moral and material" responsibility for the Holocaust and reviving Vasily Shulgin's arguments about Jewish "collective guilt" in the wake of the revolution, he calls on the Jews to "repent" for their role in the "Cheka executions, the drowning of the barges with the condemned in the White and Caspian Seas, collectivization, Ukrainian famine—in all the vile acts of the Soviet regime." Like most attempts to apply the Christian concept of individual sin to nationalist demands for inherited tribal responsibility, Solzhenitsyn's appeal envisions no ultimate absolution, no procedure for moral adjudication among competing claims, and no call on his own kinsmen to accept open-ended responsibility for the acts that any number of non-Russian peoples—or their self-appointed representatives—may consider both vile and ethnically Russian.[216] Both of these approaches—Hodl's victimhood under Stalinism and Hodl's moral responsibility for it—are quite marginal, however. Most accounts of twentieth-century Russian history are like most accounts of twentieth-century Jewish history in that they have nothing to say about Hodl. As Mikhail Agursky told his mother, she should have lived her life differently. Agursky's mother seemed to agree—and so did Hope Ulanovskaia, my grandmother, and most of their relatives and fellow countrymen. Oblivion in many languages seems to be their punishment.

The Jews who remain in the Russian Federation (230,000, or 0.16 percent of the population, according to the 2002 census, or about half as many as in 1994) face the choice of all Mercurian minorities in Apollonian nation-states. One option is assimilation, made possible not only by the adherence of most ethnic Jews to the Pushkin faith but also by the conversion of a growing number of ethnic Russians to universal Mercurianism. More and more Russian Jews (the absolute majority) marry non-Jews, strongly identify with Russia as a country, and show no interest in perpetuating their Jewishness in any sense whatever. According to a 1995 poll, 16 percent of Russia's ethnic Jews considered themselves religious: of those, 24 percent professed Judaism, 31 percent Orthodox Christianity, and the remaining 45 percent nothing in particular (beyond generic monotheism). At the same time, surveys of public opinion in the Russian Federation as a whole suggest that the majority of non-Jewish Russians have a favorable opinion of Jews and Israel, are neutral or positive about their close relatives' marrying Jews, would welcome Jews as neighbors or colleagues, and oppose discrimination in employment and college admissions. The younger the respondents, the more positive toward Jews or ethnicity-blind they tend to be. (By comparison, both traditional and recently acquired Russian hostility toward Gypsies, Muslims, and peoples of the Caucasus remains quite pronounced.) Most demographic indicators seem to point toward a continued reduction in the number of self-consciously Jewish citizens of the Russian Federation. One might call this the Iberian option: in the fifteenth and sixteenth centuries, most of the ethnic Jews who did not emigrate from Spain and Portugal went on to become ethnic Spaniards or Portuguese.[217]

The other possibility is that ethnic Jews will remain an over-achieving Mercurian minority in a predominantly Apollonian society. In a 1997 poll, a substantial majority of the respondents claimed that Jews lived better than other people (62 percent), avoided manual labor (66 percent), were well brought up and well educated (75 percent), and included in their midst a large number of talented people (80 percent). These are standard Apollonian generalizations about Mercurians (as well as Mercurian generalizations about themselves). Like many such generalizations, they are, to a considerable extent, true. Ethnic Jews are still heavily concentrated at the top of the professional and educational hierarchy (more heavily, in fact, than in the late Soviet period because discrimination against them has been discontinued, and because Tsaytl's grandchildren, who were mostly nonelite, emigrated from the Soviet Union at a higher rate than Hodl's). Moreover, after the introduction of a market economy, Jews quickly became overrepresented among private entrepreneurs, self-employed professionals, and those who claim to prefer career success to job security. Of the seven top "oligarchs" who built huge financial empires on the ruins of the Soviet Union and went on to dominate the Russian economy and media in the Yeltsin era, one (Vladimir Potanin) is the son of a high-ranking Soviet foreign-trade official; the other six (Petr Aven, Boris Berezovsky, Mikhail Fridman, Vladimir Gusinsky, Mikhail Khodorkovsky, and Alexander Smolensky) are ethnic Jews who made their fortunes out of "thin air" (as Tevye would have put it). In the long run, strong Jewish representation in certain positions may contribute to a continued group cohesion and recognition; the fact that those positions are familiar Mercurian ones may reinforce the traditional Russian-Jewish opposition and perpetuate the sense of Jewish strangeness (among both Jews and non-Jews). According to the polls, Russian Jews who think of themselves as Jewish or binational are more "achievement-oriented" than Russian Jews who think of themselves as Russians. Or, perhaps more to the point, the Russian Jews who specialize in dangerous and (according to most Russians) morally suspect occupations are naturally keener on preserving their strangeness (Jewishness). To return to an example cited in chapter 1, the Mon people of Thailand were divided into rice farmers and river traders. The farmers thought of themselves as Thai and were unsure about their Mon ancestry; the traders thought of themselves as Mon and felt strongly about not being of Thai descent. The main question for the future of Jews in Russia is not whether Jews will become farmers (as some tsars and Communists had hoped). In the age of universal Mercurianism (the Jewish Age), the main question is whether the Russians will learn how to become Jews.[218]

The other revolutionary option, "Chava's choice," has proven much more successful. In the most general sense, Zionism prevailed over Communism because nationalism everywhere prevailed over socialism. Tribalism is a universal human condition, and the family is the most fundamental and conservative of all human institutions (as well as the source of most religious and political rhetoric). All human cultures are organized around the regulation of reproduction, and reproduction—whatever the regulatory regime—requires a preference for some partners over others and the favoring of one's own children over those of others. All radical attempts to remake humankind are ultimately assaults on the family, and all of them either fail or dissimulate. For most humans most of the time, the pursuit of happiness involves pursuing the opposite sex, being fruitful, and raising children, all of which activities are forms of discrimination and inexhaustible springs of tribalism. No vision of justice-as-equality can accommodate the human family however constituted, and no human existence involving men, women, and children can abide the abolition of the distinction between kin and nonkin. Christianity, which urged human beings to love other people's children as much as their own, managed to survive by making marriage (a pledge of exclusive loyalty to one person) a religious sacrament analogous to the central institution of all tribal societies. Communism, which was Christianity's foolish, literal-minded younger brother, withered away after the first generation's idealism because it failed to incorporate the family and thus proved unable to reproduce itself. In the end, it was nationalism that triumphed decisively over both because it updated the traditional (genealogical) brand of immortality by introducing the tribal way of being modern and the modern way of being tribal. Nationalism needs no doctrine because it seems so natural. Whatever Chava's grandchildren think of her idealism and sacrifice, they have no trouble understanding her motives. Even the most disenchanted of Israelis would never ask Chava the bitterly uncomprehending questions that haunted Hodl at the end of her life: "Did you really believe *that*? How could you?"

Zionism prevailed over Communism because it delivered on its (relatively realistic) promises. The language of God has become a viable vernacular; a part of the Land of Israel has become the State of Israel; and the world's most accomplished Mercurians have been reforged into a new breed of Jewish Apollonians. Europe's strangest nationalism has succeeded in transforming a radical Jewish "self-hatred" (renunciation of Tevye) into a functioning nation-state.

It is a peculiar state, however—almost as peculiar as the doctrine that brought it into being. Self-consciously Western in the heart of "Oriental" darkness and ideologically Apollonian in the face of Western Mercurianism, it is the sole Western survivor (along with Turkey, perhaps) of the integral nationalism of interwar Europe in the postwar—and post–Cold War—world. The Israeli equivalent of such politically illegitimate concepts as "Germany for the Germans" and "Greater Serbia"—"the Jewish state"—is taken for granted both inside and outside Israel. (Historically, the great majority of European states are monoethnic entities with tribal mythologies and language-based high-culture religions too, but the post-1970s convention has been to dilute that fact with a variety of "multicultural" claims and provisions that make European states appear more like the United States.) The rhetoric of ethnic homogeneity and ethnic deportations, tabooed elsewhere in the West, is a routine element of Israeli political life. And probably no other European state can hope to avoid boycotts and sanctions while pursuing a policy of territorial expansion, wall building, settlement construction in occupied areas, use of lethal force against demonstrators, and extrajudicial killings and demolitions. It is true that no other European state is in a condition of permanent war; it is also true that no other European state can have as strong a claim on the West's moral imagination.

In the wake of the Six-Day War, many people in the postcolonial West enjoyed a vicarious identification with a country that was both European and Apollonian, small but victorious, virtuously democratic yet brash, tanned, youthful, determined, khaki-clad, seamlessly unified, and totally devoid of doubt. However, it was the rise of the Holocaust culture in the 1970s that provided the primary legitimation for Israel's continued defiance of the changing world. After the Yom Kippur War of 1973 and especially during Menachem Begin's premiership in 1977–83, the Holocaust became the central episode in Jewish and world history and a transcendental religious concept referring to an event described as incomparable, incomprehensible, and unrepresentable. Israel's raison d'être, it turned out, was not so much a repudiation of Tevye's life as retribution for Tevye's death; "not so much a negation of the Diaspora as a continuation of its fate in a new way" (as David Biale put it). Rather than representing a permanent escape from the ghetto, Israel became the ghetto's mirror image—an armed camp (Masada). Along with being the creature of Chava's rebellion, it became a mausoleum dedicated to Tsaytl's martyrdom.[219]

One reason for the wide acceptance of the new image of Israel was the substantial influence wielded by American Jews, whose Jewishness and possibly Americanness seemed to depend on Israel's continued chosenness and the Holocaust's transcendence of history. Another was the continued hostility and inflexibility of Israel's Arab neighbors and the growing Western antipathy toward both Islam and Arab nationalism. But the most important reason was the nature of the Jewish genocide itself—or rather, the character of Nazi ideology and practice. By identifying the Jews as the source of all imperfection and injustice, the Nazis formulated a simple solution to the problem of evil in the modern world. The Age of Man received an identifiable devil in human form; the Age of Nationalism attained the perfect symmetry of a fully ethnicized Hell (to go with the ethnicized Purgatory and Paradise); and the Age of Science acquired a clear moral purpose by becoming the main instrument of a violent racial apocalypse. The Nazis lost the war (to their messianic twin and nemesis, the Soviet Union) but they won the battle of concepts. Their specific program was rejected, but their worship of ethnicity and their focus on demonology were widely accepted. The most fundamental way in which World War II transformed the world was that it gave birth to a new moral absolute: the Nazis as universal evil.

By representing Satan in the cosmogony they helped create, the Nazis gave meaning and coherence to the world they hoped to destroy. For the first time since the European states began to separate themselves from the church, the Western world acquired a transcendental universal. God might be dead, but the princes of darkness—in their special dark uniforms—were there for all to see. They were human, as required by the Age of Man; they were ethnically defined, as desired by the Age of Nationalism (not in the sense of all Germans' being willing executioners, but in the sense that the Nazis' crimes were ethnic in content and the Germans as a nation were held responsible for the Nazis' crimes); and they were so methodically scientific in their brutality as to create a permanent link between the Age of Science and the nightmare of total violence. It was only a matter of time, in other words, before the central targets of Nazi violence became the world's universal victims. From being the Jewish God's Chosen People, the Jews had become the Nazis' chosen people, and by becoming the Nazis' chosen people, they became the Chosen People of the postwar Western world. The Holocaust became the measure of all crimes, and anti-Semitism became the only irredeemable form of ethnic bigotry in Western public life (no other kind of national hostility, however chronic or violent, has a special term attached to it—unless one counts "racism," which is comparable but not tribe-specific).

At the same time and for the same reason, Israel became a country to which standard rules did not apply. The Zionist attempt to create a normal European nation-state resulted in the creation of the most eccentric of all European nation-states. One consequence was substantial freedom of speech and action; the other was growing isolation. The two are connected, of course: freedom from convention is both a cause and an effect of isolation, and pariah status is as closely linked to exceptionalism as is heroism. In an act of tragic irony, the Zionist escape from strangeness has led to a new kind of strangeness. From being exemplary Mercurians among Apollonians, the Israeli Jews have become exemplary Apollonians among universal (Western) Mercurians. By representing violent retribution and undiluted ethnic nationalism in a world that claims to value neither, they have estranged themselves from the states they wanted to join. Chava's choice has proved successful in that her grandchildren are proud Jews in a Jewish state. It has proved a failure insofar as Israel is still a stranger among nations. Either way—because it has succeeded or because it has failed—the Zionist revolution is over. The original ethos of youthful athleticism, belligerence, and single-mindedness is carried on by a tired elite of old generals. Half a century after its founding, Israel bears a distant family resemblance to the Soviet Union half a century after the October Revolution. The last representatives of the first Sabra generation are still in power, but their days are numbered. Because Zionism is a form of nationalism and not socialism, Israel will not die when they do, but the new generals and civilians who come after them may choose to strike a different balance between normality and ethnic self-assertion.

Of the three options available to Tevye's daughters at the turn of the Jewish Century, the least revolutionary one proved the most successful. At the century's end, the great majority of Tevye's descendants seemed to agree that Beilke's choice had been the wisest. The choice that Tevye had despised ("where else do all the hard-luck cases go?"); the place that had attracted the least educated and the least idealistic; the Promised Land that had never promised a miracle or a permanent home (just the hope for more luck at the old game)—this was the option that ended up on top. America had virtue as well as riches, and it contained enough riches to make even Tevye a wealthy man. It represented Mercurianism in power, service nomadism without strangeness, full freedom of both wealth and learning.

The Jews are the wealthiest of all religious groups in the United States (including such traditionally prosperous denominations as the Unitarians and Episcopalians). They have the highest household incomes (72 percent higher than the national average), the highest rate of self-employment (three times as high as the national average), and the highest representation among the richest individual Americans (about 40 percent of the wealthiest forty, as reported by the *Forbes* magazine in 1982). Even the new immigrant households from the former Soviet Union begin to earn more than the national average within a few years of arrival.[220]

The Jews are the most educated of all Americans (almost all college-age Jews are in college, and the concentration of Jews in professional occupations is double that of non-Jews). They are also the best educated: the more prestigious the university as a general rule, the higher the percentage of Jewish students and professors. According to a 1970 study, 50 percent of the most influential American intellectuals (published and reviewed most widely in the top twenty intellectual journals) were Jews. Among the academic elite (identified in the same fashion), Jews made up 56 percent of those in the social sciences and 61 percent in the humanities. Of the twenty most influential American intellectuals, as ranked by other intellectuals, fifteen (75 percent) were Jews. The overall Jewish share of the American population is less than 3 percent.[221]

Wealth and learning come in due course, but Mercury's original job was that of a messenger. According to studies conducted in the 1970s and 1980s, Jews made up between one-quarter and one-third of the "media elite" (the news divisions of the three television networks and PBS, the three leading news magazines, and the four top newspapers). More than one-third of the most "influential" critics of film, literature, radio, and television were of Jewish background, as were almost half of the Hollywood producers of prime-time television shows and about two-thirds of the directors, writers, and producers of the fifty top-grossing movies between 1965 and 1982. In October 1994, *Vanity Fair* profiled twenty-three media moguls who made up what the magazine called "the new establishment": "men and women from the entertainment, communications, and computer industries, whose ambitions and influence have made America the true superpower of the Information Age." Eleven of them (48 percent) were Jews.[222]

"Establishments" and superpowers may change, but the degree of congruence between posttraditional economies and traditional Mercurian skills remains very high. The American Jews are successful in the same occupations as the European and Soviet Jews—which are, essentially, the same occupations that have always been pursued by literate Mercurians (and are being pursued in today's United States by the Lebanese Christians and Overseas Indians and Chinese, among others). "Doctors and lawyers" are both the oldest Jewish professions in Europe and the badge of middle-class accomplishment (and Jewish upward mobility) in the United States. In the mid-1980s, the concentration of Jews in elite positions and the occupational and educational gap between Jews and non-Jews were still growing.[223]

In the nation-states (or would-be nation-states) of Europe, Asia, and Africa, similar triumphs of strangers over the natives have led to discrimination and violence. But the United States—rhetorically—has no state-bearing natives and therefore no permanent strangers. What makes the United States different is that Mercurianism, including meritocracy, is the official ideology of the state; that traditional Mercurians, including the Jews, have no legal handicaps; and that nativist tribalism, including anti-Semitism, plays a relatively minor role in political life. American Jews are free to succeed because they are Americans—the way Soviet Jews of the 1920s and 1930s were free to succeed because they were Soviets. Of all the non-Jewish polities in the history of the world, the postwar United States is second only to the prewar Soviet Union in the importance of Jewish participation in the political process. Jews are strongly overrepresented in both houses of Congress (three to four times their percentage of the general population), and they are extremely prominent among political consultants, staffers, funders, and volunteers. Jews provide between one-fourth and one-half of all Democratic Party campaign funds, and, according to Ze'ev Chafets, in twenty-seven out of thirty-six senatorial races of 1986, "at least one of the candidates (and often both) had a Jewish campaign manager or finance chairman." A 1982 study of the American economic, cultural, and political elite found that most Protestants included in this category owed their rise to business and electoral politics; most Catholics, to trade union and party activism; and most Jews, to work in the media, public-interest organizations, and civil service. There is little doubt that the Jewish strategy is the most effective of the three because of its high degree of compatibility with the modern postindustrial state. Indeed, the Jewish prominence in the American political elite began to grow perceptibly in the 1970s, during the ascendance of nonprofit organizations, political foundations, regulatory agencies, new information technologies, and public-interest law firms. There was no single "Jewish interest," of course (other than the tendency to support the continued growth of those same institutions), but there was one question on which most of Beilke's grandchildren agreed and around which their considerable wealth, education, and political influence could be organized: the welfare of their overseas cousins.[224]

The American Jewish mobilization on behalf of the Soviet Jewish exodus from the USSR ended—as abruptly as it had begun—with the demise of the USSR and the emigration of all the ethnic Jews who wished to leave. The American Jewish identification with Israel proved more durable because it transformed America's ethnic Jews into the most accomplished and the most beleaguered of all American ethnics. But it was the identification of both Beilke's America and Chava's Israel with Tsaytl's martyrdom that became the true source of late twentieth-century Jewishness. In a world without God, evil and victimhood are the only absolutes. The rise of the Holocaust as a transcendental concept has led to the emergence of the Jews as the Chosen People for the new age.[225]

In the competitive world of American ethnic communities, there are two paths to success: upward mobility defined according to wealth, education, and political power, and downward mobility measured by degrees of victimhood.[226] Beilke's descendants are among the leaders on both counts: at the very top by dint of their own efforts along traditional Mercurian lines, and at the very bottom because of their association with Tsaytl, the universal victim. Once again, the majority of the world's Jews combine economic achievement with the status of a punished nation. But the world has changed: at the end of the Jewish Century, both titles are in universal demand. Economic achievement is an inescapable standard of worth, and victimhood is a common sign of virtue (especially for those who lack economic achievement). Jealousy of the Jews may remain both a fact of life and an ineradicable Jewish expectation.

But then again, it may not. The majority of the world's Jews live in a society that is Mercurian both by official faith and—increasingly—by membership, a society without acknowledged natives, a society of service nomads destined to redeem humanity. As the historian Joseph R. Levenson put it, "a Jewish style of life . . . may be more endangered when everyone eats bagels than when Jews eat hot cross buns." In 1940, the rate of outmarriage for American Jews was about 3 percent; by 1990, it had exceeded 50 percent. The American pastoral that eluded Swede Levov and his "gruesomely misbegotten" daughter may yet work for his son, Chris. Hodl's choice may still be available, for better or worse, in Beilke's America.

For better or for worse? Tevye was not sure. Why raise Jewish daughters if they were going "to break away in the end like the leaves that fall from a tree and are carried off by the wind?" But then again, "what did being a Jew or not a Jew matter? Why did God have to create both?"[227]

Notes

CHAPTER 1
MERCURY'S SANDALS: THE JEWS AND OTHER NOMADS

1. David Nemeth, "Patterns of Genesis among Peripatetics: Preliminary Notes from the Korean Archipelago," in *The Other Nomads: Peripatetic Minorities in Cross-Cultural Perspective*, ed. Aparna Rao (Cologne: Boehlau Verlag, 1987), 159–78; George de Vos and Hiroshi Wagatsuma, *Japan's Invisible Race: Caste in Culture and Personality* (Berkeley and Los Angeles: University of California Press, 1966), 20–28; Michael Bollig, "Ethnic Relations and Spatial Mobility in Africa: A Review of the Peripatetic Niche," in Rao, *The Other Nomads*, 179–228; James H. Vaughn, Jr., "Caste Systems in the Western Sudan," in *Social Stratification in Africa*, ed. Arthur Tuden and Leonard Plotnicov (New York: Free Press, 1970), 59–92; Sharon Bohn Gmelch, "Groups That Don't Want In: Gypsies and Other Artisan, Trader, and Entertainer Minorities," *Annual Review of Anthropology* 15 (1986): 307–30; Asta Olesen, "Peddling in East Afghanistan: Adaptive Strategies of the Peripatetic Sheikh Mohammadi," in Rao, *The Other Nomads*, 35–64; Hanna Rauber-Schweizer, "Trade in Far West Nepal: The Economic Adaptation of the Peripatetic Humli-Khyampa," in Rao, *The Other Nomads*, 65–88; Philip D. Curtin, *Cross-Cultural Trade in World History* (Cambridge: Cambridge University Press, 1984), 19. I follow most anthropologists in using the term "Gypsy" because not all groups usually covered by it are Romani-speakers or "Rom" in self-designation.

2. Curtin, *Cross-Cultural Trade*, 186–206; Bruce Masters, *The Origins of Western Economic Dominance in the Middle East: Mercantilism and the Islamic Economy in Aleppo, 1600–1750* (New York: New York University Press, 1988), 82–89; John A. Armstrong, "Mobilized and Proletarian Diasporas," *American Political Science Review* 70, no. 2 (June 1976): 400; John A. Armstrong, *Nations before Nationalism* (Chapel Hill: University of North Carolina Press, 1982), 210.

3. Ernest Gellner, *Nations and Nationalism* (Ithaca: Cornell University Press, 1983), 102; Dominique Casajus, "Crafts and Ceremonies: The Inadan in Tuareg Society," in Rao, *The Other Nomads*, 291–310; William Lancaster and Fidelity Lancaster, "The Function of Peripatetics in Rwala Bedouin Society," in Rao, *The Other Nomads*, 311–22; Hagop Barsoumian, "Economic Role of the Armenian Amira Class in the Ottoman Empire," *Armenian Review* 31 (March 1979): 310–16; Hillel Levine, *Economic Origins of Antisemitism: Poland and Its Jews in the Early Modern Period* (New Haven: Yale University Press, 1991), 59–73.

4. Edna Bonacich, "A Theory of Middleman Minorities," *American Sociological Review* 38, no. 5 (October 1973): 583–94; Paul Mark Axelrod, "A Social and Demographic Comparison of Parsis, Saraswat Brahmins and Jains in Bombay"

(Ph.D. diss., University of North Carolina at Chapel Hill, 1974), 26–39, 60; Charles A. Jones, *International Business in the Nineteenth Century: The Rise and Fall of a Cosmopolitan Bourgeoisie* (Brighton: Wheatsheaf, 1987), esp. 50 and 81–84; T. M. Luhrmann, *The Good Parsi: The Fate of a Colonial Elite in a Postcolonial Society* (Cambridge: Harvard University Press, 1996), 78–91; D. Stanley Eitzen, "Two Minorities: The Jews of Poland and the Chinese of the Philippines," *Jewish Journal of Sociology* 10, no. 2 (December 1968): 221–40; Daniel Chirot and Anthony Reid, eds., *Essential Outsiders: Chinese and Jews in the Modern Transformation of Southeast Asia and Central Europe* (Seattle: University of Washington Press, 1997), esp. editors' introductions; Joel Kotkin, *Tribes: How Race, Religion, and Identity Determine Success in the New Global Economy* (New York: Random House, 1993), 170–80; Thomas Sowell, *Migrations and Cultures: A World View* (New York: Basic Books, 1996); Edgar Wickberg, "Localism and the Organization of Overseas Migration in the Nineteenth Century," in *Cosmopolitan Capitalists*, ed. Gary G. Hamilton (Seattle: University of Washington Press, 1999), 35–55; Yuan-li Wu and Chun-hsi Wu, *Economic Development in Southeast Asia: The Chinese Dimension* (Stanford: Hoover Institution Press, 1980); Linda Y. C. Lim and L. A. Peter Gosling, eds., *The Chinese in Southeast Asia*, vols. 1 and 2 (Singapore: Maruzen Asia, 1983); Lynn Pan, *Sons of the Yellow Emperor: A History of the Chinese Diaspora* (Boston: Little, Brown, and Company, 1990), 23–152; Agehananda Bharati, *The Asians in East Africa: Jayhind and Ururu* (Chicago: Nelson-Hall, 1972), 11–22, 36, 42–116; Pierre L. van den Berghe, *The Ethnic Phenomenon* (New York: Praeger, 1987), 135–56; Dana April Seidenberg, *Mercantile Adventurers: The World of East African Asians, 1750–1985* (New Delhi: New Age International, 1996); Albert Hourani and Nadim Shehadi, eds., *The Lebanese in the World: A Century of Emigration* (London: Center for Lebanese Studies, 1992); William K. Crowley, "The Levantine Arabs: Diaspora in a New World," *Proceedings of the Association of American Geographers* 6 (1974): 137–42; R. Bayly Winder, "The Lebanese in West Africa," *Comparative Studies in Society and History* 4 (1961–62): 296–333; H. L. van der Laan, *The Lebanese Traders in Sierra Leone* (The Hague: Mouton, 1975).

5. Norman O. Brown, *Hermes the Thief: The Evolution of a Myth* (Madison: University of Wisconsin Press, 1947); Marcel Detienne and Jean-Pierre Vernant, *Cunning Intelligence in Greek Culture and Society* (Hassocks, Sussex: Harvester Press, 1978); Laurence Kahn, *Hermès passe ou les ambiguités de la communication* (Paris: François Maspero, 1978); W. B. Stanford, *The Ulysses Theme: A Study in Adaptability of a Traditional Hero* (Dallas: Spring Publications, 1992).

6. George Gmelch and Sharon Bohn Gmelch, "Commercial Nomadism: Occupation and Mobility among Travellers in England and Wales," in Rao, *The Other Nomads*, 134; Matt T. Salo, "The Gypsy Niche in North America: Some Ecological Perspectives on the Exploitation of Social Environments," in Rao, *The Other Nomads*, 94; Judith Okely, *The Traveller-Gypsies* (Cambridge: Cambridge University Press, 1983), 58–60; Curtin, *Cross-Cultural Trade*, 70; Clifford Geertz, *Peddlers*

and Princes: Social Change and Economic Modernization in Two Indonesian Towns (Chicago: University of Chicago Press, 1963), 43–44; Mark Zborowski and Elizabeth Herzog, eds., *Life Is with People: The Culture of the Shtetl* (New York: Schocken Books, 1952), 62; Armstrong, *Nations before Nationalism*, 42; Daniel J. Elazar, "The Jewish People as the Classic Diaspora," in *Modern Diasporas in International Politics*, ed. Gabriel Sheffer (London: Croom Helm, 1986), 215.

7. Brian L. Foster, "Ethnicity and Commerce," *American Ethnologist* 1, no. 3 (August 1974): 441. See also Cristina Blanc Szanton, "Thai and Sino-Thai in Small Town Thailand: Changing Patterns of Interethnic Relations," in Lim and Gosling, *The Chinese in Southeast Asia*, 2:99–125.

8. Benjamin Nelson, *The Idea of Usury: From Tribal Brotherhood to Universal Otherhood* (Chicago: University of Chicago Press, 1969); Max Weber, *Ancient Judaism* (Glencoe, Ill.: Free Press, 1952): 338–45; Curtin, *Cross-Cultural Trade*, 5–6; Alejandro Portes, "Economic Sociology and the Sociology of Immigration: A Conceptual Overview," in *The Economic Sociology of Immigration: Essays on Networks, Ethnicity, and Entrepreneurship*, ed. Alejandro Portes (New York: Russell Sage Foundation, 1995), 14; L. A. Peter Gosling, "Changing Chinese Identities in Southeast Asia: An Introductory Review," in Lim and Gosling, *The Chinese in Southeast Asia*, 2:4. For an excellent discussion including two quotations above (and many more), see Mark Granovetter, "The Economic Sociology of Firms and Entrepreneurs," in Portes, *The Economic Sociology of Immigration*.

9. Donald L. Horowitz, *Ethnic Groups in Conflict* (Berkeley and Los Angeles: University of California Press, 1985), 119; Casajus, "Crafts and Ceremonies," 303; de Vos and Wagatsuma, *Japan's Invisible Race*, 231; Werner Sombart, *The Jews and Modern Capitalism* (London: T. Fisher Unwin, 1913), 138; Gmelch, "Groups That Don't Want In," 322–23.

10. Joseph C. Berland, "Kanjar Social Organization," in Rao, *The Other Nomads*, 253; Gmelch, "Groups That Don't Want In," 320–21; Anne Sutherland, "The Body as a Social Symbol among the Rom," in *The Anthropology of the Body*, ed. John Blacking (London: Academic Press, 1977), 376.

11. *Taina Izrailia: "Evreiskii vopros" v russkoi religioznoi mysli kontsa XIX–pervoi poloviny XX v.v.* (St. Petersburg: Sofiia, 1993), 251. Throughout, translations from foreign-language works are mine, unless otherwise noted.

12. Yuri Slezkine, "Naturalists versus Nations: Eighteenth-Century Russian Scholars Confront Ethnic Diversity," *Representations* 47 (Summer 1994): 174, 180–82; Max Weber, *Ancient Judaism* (Glencoe, Ill.: Free Press, 1952), 351–55.

13. Vaughn, "Caste Systems," 77–79; Sutherland, "The Body," 378–80; Okely, *The Traveller-Gypsies*, 83–85; Axelrod, "A Social and Demographic Comparison," 51–54, 61–62.

14. See, esp., Sutherland, "The Body," and Luhrmann, *The Good Parsi*, 102; Max Weber, *The Sociology of Religion* (Boston: Beacon Press, 1963), 109; David Nemeth, "Gypsy Taskmasters, Gentile Slaves," in *The American Kalderas: Gypsies*

in the New World, ed. Matt T. Salo (Hackettstown, N.J.: Gypsy Lore Society, North American Chapter, 1981), 29–41.

15. For dissenting views, see Okely, *The Traveller-Gypsies,* 8–19; and Paul Wexler, "The Case for the Relexification Hypothesis in Romani," in *Relexification in Creole and Non-Creole Languages,* ed. Julia Horvath and Paul Wexler (Wiesbaden: Harrassowitz, 1997), 100–161. For a very helpful overview, see Yaron Matras, "Para-Romani Revisited," in *The Romani Element in Non-Standard Speech,* ed. Yaron Matras (Wiesbaden: Harrassowitz, 1998), 1–27.

16. For the main arguments, see, in order: (1) Sarah Grey Thomason and Terrence Kaufman, *Language Contact, Creolization, and Genetic Linguistics* (Berkeley and Los Angeles: University of California Press, 1988), 103 f.; (2) Ian F. Hancock, "The Social and Linguistic Development of Angloromani," *Working Papers in Sociolinguistics,* no. 38 (December 1977): 1–42; also Ian F. Hancock, "Is Anglo-Romanes a Creole?" *Journal of the Gypsy Lore Society* 49, nos. 1–2 (1970): 41–44; (3) Norbert Boretzky and Birgit Igla, "Romani Mixed Dialects," in *Mixed Languages: Fifteen Case Studies in Language Intertwining,* ed. Peter Bakker and Maarten Mous (Amsterdam: IFOTT, 1994), 35–68; and Norbert Boretzky, "Der Romani-Wortschatz in den Romani-Misch-Dialekten (Pararomani)," in Matras, *The Romani Element,* 97–132; (4) Peter Bakker and Maarten Mous, "Introduction," and Peter Bakker, "Michif, The Cree-French Mixed Language of the Métis Buffalo Hunters in Canada," in Bakker and Mous, *Mixed Languages,* 1–11 and 13–33; and (5) Jakob Ladefoged, "Romani Elements in Non-Standard Scandinavian Varieties," in Matras, *The Romani Element,* 133–64.

17. Olesen, "Peddling in East Afghanistan," 36; Bollig, "Ethnic Relations," 204, 214.

18. Casajus, "Crafts and Ceremonies," 308–9; Bollig, "Ethnic Relations," 214; Hancock, "The Social and Linguistic Development," 29; Anthony P. Grant, "Shelta: The Secret Language of Irish Travellers Viewed as a Mixed Language," in Bakker and Mous, *Mixed Languages,* 135–36; R. A. Stewart Macalister, *The Secret Languages of Ireland, with Special Reference to the Origin and Nature of the Shelta Language* (Cambridge: Cambridge University Press, 1937), 132.

19. Quoted in Macalister, *The Secret Languages,* 134–35.

20. Solomon A. Birnbaum, *Yiddish: A Survey and Grammar* (Manchester: Manchester University Press, 1979), 76, 106.

21. Max Weinreich, *History of the Yiddish Language* (Chicago: University of Chicago Press, 1980), 95–124.

22. Paul Wexler, *The Ashkenazic Jews: A Slavo-Turkic People in Search of a Jewish Identity* (Columbus, Ohio: Slavica, 1993), 59–60 and passim; Dell Hymes, "Introduction," in *Pidginization and Creolization of Languages,* ed. Dell Hymes (Cambridge: Cambridge University Press, 1971), 76, 77–78, 86–87 (the quotation is from 86); see also Ian F. Hancock, "Recovering Pidgin Genesis: Approaches and Problems," in *Pidgin and Creole Linguistics,* ed. Albert Valdman (Bloomington:

Indiana University Press, 1977), 277–94, esp. 289–90, and Ian F. Hancock, "Appendix: Repertory of Pidgin and Creole Languages," in ibid., 385.

23. Birnbaum, *Yiddish*, 82 and passim; Weinreich, *History of the Yiddish Language*, 29, 350–51, 599 f., and passim; Joshua A. Fishman, *Yiddish: Turning to Life* (Amsterdam: John Benjamins, 1991), 19–35, 189–201.

24. For the "mixed language" category, see Bakker, "Michif," 25–26. There is, of course, no doubt that Yiddish is a Germanic language according to the essentials of grammar and basic vocabulary; what makes it unique within the family is the history of its emergence and functioning.

25. Matras, "Para-Romani Revisited," 21; Yaron Matras, "The Romani Element in German Secret Languages," in Matras, *The Romani Element*, 193–94; Hancock, "Recovering Pidgin Genesis," 290.

26. Weinreich, *History of the Yiddish Language*, 199, 605.

27. Luhrmann, *The Good Parsi*, 47–59.

28. Horowitz, *Ethnic Groups in Conflict*, 168–69.

29. Michael J. Casimir, "In Search of Guilt: Legends on the Origin of the Peripatetic Niche," in Rao, *The Other Nomads*, 373–90; Olesen, "Peddling in East Afghanistan," 36; Okely, *The Traveller-Gypsies*, 216.

30. Lancaster and Lancaster, "The Function of Peripatetics," 319.

31. Van den Berghe, *The Ethnic Phenomenon*, 143. See also Bonacich, "A Theory of Middleman Minorities," 586.

32. On "corporate kinship," see William G. Davis, *Social Relations in a Philippine Market: Self-Interest and Subjectivity* (Berkeley and Los Angeles: University of California Press, 1973), 199–200; and Granovetter, "The Economic Sociology," 143–46.

33. Sutherland, "The Body," 377–78; Matt T. Salo, "Gypsy Ethnicity: Implications of Native Categories and Interaction for Ethnic Classification," *Ethnicity* 6 (1979): 78–79; Ignacy-Marek Kaminski, "The Dilemma of Power: Internal and External Leadership. The Gypsy-Roma of Poland," in Rao, *The Other Nomads*, 332–34.

34. Bharati, *The Asians in East Africa*, 42, 149; van den Berghe, *The Ethnic Phenomenon*, 147–53.

35. Van der Laan, *The Lebanese Traders*, 228–30, 241–44. The quotation is from 229.

36. Ivan H. Light, *Ethnic Enterprise in America: Business and Welfare among Chinese, Japanese, and Blacks* (Berkeley and Los Angeles: University of California Press, 1972), 45–61, 81–100; Linda Y. C. Lim, "Chinese Economic Activity in Southeast Asia: An Introductory Review," in Lim and Gosling, *The Chinese in Southeast Asia*, 1:5; Eitzen, "Two Minorities," 230; Pan, *Sons of the Yellow Emperor*, 111–27.

37. Granovetter, "The Economic Sociology," 143; see also Bonacich, "A Theory of Middleman Minorities," 586–87; and van den Berghe, *The Ethnic Phenomenon*, 139–44.

38. Quoted in Albert S. Lindemann, *Esau's Tears: Modern Anti-Semitism and the Rise of the Jews* (Cambridge: Cambridge University Press, 1997), 5.

39. Luhrmann, *The Good Parsi*, 50.

40. Berland, "Kanjar Social Organization," 249; Gmelch, "Groups That Don't Want In," 314; Maurice Samuel, *The World of Sholom Aleichem* (New York: Alfred A. Knopf, 1943), 131.

41. Detienne and Vernant, *Cunning Intelligence*, 47–48.

42. Berland, "Kanjar Social Organization," 249.

43. Gmelch, "Groups That Don't Want In," 314.

44. Jacob Katz, *Out of the Ghetto: The Social Background of Jewish Emancipation, 1770–1870* (Cambridge: Harvard University Press, 1973), 22.

45. Cf. Gellner, *Nations and Nationalism*, 103–9; Kotkin, *Tribes*, passim.

46. Luhrmann, *The Good Parsi*, 91–95, 119; Jamsheed K. Choksy, *Evil, Good, and Gender: Facets of the Feminine in Zoroastrian Religious History* (New York: Peter Lang, 2002), 109.

47. Dario A. Euraque, "The Arab-Jewish Economic Presence in San Pedro Sula, the Industrial Capital of Honduras: Formative Years, 1880s–1930s," in *Arab and Jewish Immigrants in Latin America: Images and Realities*, ed. Ignacio Klich and Jeffrey Lesser (London: Frank Cass, 1998), 95, 109; Clark S. Knowlton, "The Social and Spatial Mobility of the Syrian and Lebanese Community in São Paulo, Brazil," in Hourani and Shehadi, *The Lebanese in the World*, 292–93, 302–3; David Nicholls, "Lebanese of the Antilles: Haiti, Dominican Republic, Jamaica, and Trinidad," in Hourani and Shehadi, *The Lebanese in the World*, 339–60; Crowley, "The Levantine Arabs," 139; Nancie L. Gonzalez, *Dollar, Dove, and Eagle: One Hundred Years of Palestinian Migration to Honduras* (Ann Arbor: University of Michigan Press, 1992), 93–100; Amy Chua, *World on Fire: How Exporting Free Market Democracy Breeds Ethnic Hatred and Global Instability* (New York: Doubleday, 2003), 116, 149–50.

48. David Himbara, *Kenyan Capitalists, the State, and Development* (Boulder, Colo.: Lynne Rienner Publishers, 1994), 45; Kotkin, *Tribes*, 103, 205–9, 229; Sowell, *Migrations and Cultures*, 310–11, 344; Chua, *World on Fire*, 113, 157–58.

49. Chua, *World on Fire*, 3, 36–37, 43, 34–35; Bambang Harymurti, "Challenges of Change in Indonesia," *Journal of Democracy*, 10, no. 4 (1999): 9–10; Kotkin, *Tribes*, 165–200; Sowell, *Migrations and Cultures*, 175–76.

50. See, for example, Robert E. Kennedy, Jr., "The Protestant Ethic and the Parsis," *American Journal of Sociology* 68, no. 1 (July 1962): 11–20; Balwant Nevaskar, *Capitalists without Capitalism: The Jains of India and the Quakers of the West* (Westport, Conn.: Greenwood, 1971); Peter L. Berger and Hsin-Huang Michael Hsiao, eds., *In Search of an East Asian Development Model* (New Brunswick, N.J.: Transaction Books, 1988); S. Gordon Redding, "Weak Organizations and Strong Linkages: Managerial Ideology and Chinese Family Business Networks," in *Asian Business Networks*, ed. Gary G. Hamilton (Berlin: Walter de Gruyter,

1996), 27–42; Robert N. Bellah, *Tokugawa Religion: The Cultural Roots of Modern Japan* (New York: Free Press, 1985); Sombart, *The Jews and Modern Capitalism*. Max Weber, while keen on showing why only Protestant Christians could *produce* modern capitalism, strongly implies that, once launched, capitalism may find some religions (including those on our list) much more congenial than others. See his *Sociology of Religion*, chaps. 15–16, and esp. *Ancient Judaism*.

51. Sowell, *Migrations and Cultures*, 19, 375. For indirect suggestions along similar lines, see Bonacich, "A Theory of Middleman Minorities," 588; Gonzalez, *Dollar, Dove, and Eagle*, 81–92; Curtin, *Cross-Cultural Trade*, passim.

52. See, esp., Wong-Siu-lun, "Chinese Entrepreneurs and Business Trust"; S. Gordon Redding, "Weak Organizations and Strong Linkages: Managerial Ideology and Chinese Family Business Networks"; and Gary G. Hamilton, "The Organizational Foundations of Western and Chinese Commerce: A Historical and Comparative Analysis," and "The Theoretical Significance of Asian Business Networks," all in *Asian Business Networks*, ed. Gary G. Hamilton (Berlin: Walter de Gruyter, 1996), 13–26, 27–42, 43–58, and 283–98; Davis, *Social Relations in a Philippine Market*, 199–200; Granovetter, "The Economic Sociology," 143–46; van den Berghe, *The Ethnic Phenomenon*, 140–43.

53. Francis Fukuyama, *Trust: The Social Virtues and the Creation of Prosperity* (New York: Free Press, 1995), 74, 85, 97–112.

54. Ibid., passim.

55. Eitzen, "Two Minorities," 223; see also Pan, *Sons of the Yellow Emperor*, 31–34.

56. Nicholls, "Lebanese of the Antilles," 348–49; Brenda Gayle Plummer, "Race, Nationality, and Trade in the Caribbean: The Syrians in Haiti, 1903–1934," *International History Review* 3, no. 4 (October 1981): 517–39; Brenda Gayle Plummer, "Between Privilege and Opprobrium: The Arabs and Jews in Haiti," in Klich and Lesser, *Arab and Jewish Immigrants*, 88–89.

57. Van der Laan, *The Lebanese Traders*, 4–5; Winder, "The Lebanese in West Africa," 300; Anthony Reid, "Entrepreneurial Minorities, Nationalism, and the State," in Chirot and Reid, *Essential Outsiders*, 56, 69 n. 61. See also Kasian Tejapira, "Imagined Uncommunity: The *Lookjin* Middle Class and Thai Official Nationalism, " in Chirot and Reid, *Essential Outsiders*, 75–98.

58. Van den Berghe, *The Ethnic Phenomenon*, 155; Bharati, *The Asians in East Africa*, 97–98; Seidenberg, *Mercantile Adventurers*, 203–4; Chua, *World on Fire*, 114. The Amin quotation is from the *Los Angeles Times*, August 14, 1972, as quoted in Bonacich, "A Theory of Middleman Minorities," 591.

59. Pan, *Sons of the Yellow Emperor*, 213–14, 215–19; Chua, *World on Fire*, 36, 44–45; Mary F. Somers Heidhues, *Southeast Asia's Chinese Minorities* (Hawthorn, Victoria, Australia: Longman, 1974), 80–86; Garth Alexander, *Silent Invasion: The Chinese in Southeast Asia* (London: Macdonald, 1973), 130–43; Ben Kiernan, "Kampuchea's Ethnic Chinese under Pol Pot," *Journal of Contemporary Asia* 16, no. 1 (1986): 18–29; Wu and Wu, *Economic Development*, 39–40; Eitzen, "Two

Minorities," 224–25; Reid, "Entrepreneurial Minorities," 61; Harymurti, "Challenges of Change," 9–10. The final quotation is from Abidin Kusno, "Remembering/Forgetting the May Riots: Architecture, Violence, and the Making of Chinese Cultures in Post-1998 Jakarta," *Public Culture* 15 no. 1 (2003): 149.

CHAPTER 2
SWANN'S NOSE: THE JEWS AND OTHER MODERNS

1. See chapter 1, nn. 50 and 52, esp. Hamilton, "The Organizational Foundations."

2. Nelson, *The Idea of Usury.*

3. Ibid., xvi–xvii.

4. The quotation is from van den Berghe, *The Ethnic Phenomenon*, 140. See also Bonacich, "A Theory of Middleman Minorities," 589.

5. Heinrich Heine, *The Prose Writings of Heinrich Heine*, ed. Havelock Ellis (New York: Arno Press, 1973), 313.

6. Nelson, *The Idea of Usury*, xvi.

7. Hans Aarslef, *From Locke to Saussure: Essays on the Study of Language and Intellectual History* (Minneapolis: University of Minnesota Press, 1982), 281–82; Maurice Olender, *The Languages of Paradise: Race, Religion, and Philology in the Nineteenth Century* (Cambridge: Harvard University Press, 1992), 1–5; R. H. Robins, "The History of Language Classification," in *Current Trends in Linguistics*, ed. Thomas A. Sebeok, vol. 2 (The Hague: Mouton, 1973), 7–11; Slezkine, "Naturalists versus Nations," 84 and passim.

8. William Blake, *William Blake's Writings*, ed. G. E. Bentley, Jr. (Oxford: Clarendon Press, 1978), 1:318.

9. See Harold Bloom, *Shakespeare: The Invention of the Human* (New York: Riverhead, 1998).

10. Sutherland, "The Body"; John M. Efron, *Medicine and the German Jews: A History* (New Haven: Yale University Press, 2001).

11. Cf. Zygmunt Bauman, *Modernity and the Holocaust* (Ithaca: Cornell University Press, 1989).

12. The "Third Estate" quotation is from Sigmund Mayer, *Ein jüdischer Kaufmann 1831–1911: Lebenserinnerungen* (Leipzig, 1911), as quoted in Steven Beller, *Vienna and the Jews 1867–1938: A Cultural History* (Cambridge: Cambridge University Press, 1989), 110. See also 84–121.

13. David S. Landes, *The Unbound Prometheus: Technological Change and Industrial Development in Western Europe from 1750 to the Present* (Cambridge: Cambridge University Press, 1969): Landes refers to the rise of modern technology, in particular, but the metaphor seems applicable to the Modern Age as a whole; Calvin Goldscheider and Alan S. Zuckerman, *The Transformation of the Jews* (Chicago: University of Chicago Press, 1984), 89; Arthur Ruppin, *The Jews in the Modern*

World (London: Macmillan, 1934), 144–47; Ezra Mendelsohn, *The Jews of East Central Europe between the World Wars* (Bloomington: Indiana University Press, 1987), 28; Joseph Jacobs, *Jewish Contributions to Civilization: An Estimate* (Philadelphia: Jewish Publication Society in America, 1919), 239; Saul Friedländer, *Nazi Germany and the Jews: The Years of Persecution, 1933–1939* (New York: Harper Collins, 1997), 77; Donald L. Niewyk, *The Jews in Weimar Germany* (Baton Rouge: Louisiana State University Press, 1980), 15; William O. McCagg, "Jewish Wealth in Vienna, 1670–1918," in *Jews in the Hungarian Economy 1760–1945: Studies Dedicated to Moshe Carmilly-Weinberger on His Eightieth Birthday,* ed. Michael K. Silber (Jerusalem: Magnes Press, 1992), 75, 79–89; Siegmund Kaznelson, ed., *Juden im deutschen Kulturbereich* (Berlin: Jüdischer Verlag, 1959), 720–59; Niall Ferguson, *The World's Banker: The History of the House of Rothschild* (London: Weidenfeld & Nicolson, 1998), 7 and passim; Robert S. Wistrich, *Socialism and the Jews: The Dilemmas of Assimilation in Germany and Austria-Hungary* (East Brunswick, N.J.: Associated University Presses, 1982), 61, 180–81.

14. McCagg, "Jewish Wealth in Vienna," 74–91, William O. McCagg, *Jewish Nobles and Geniuses in Modern Hungary* (Boulder, Colo.: East European Quarterly, 1972), 16, 30, 42–43; Andrew C. Janos, *The Politics of Backwardness in Hungary, 1825–1945* (Princeton: Princeton University Press, 1982), 114, 225; Friedländer, *Nazi Germany and the Jews*, 80; Ruppin, *The Jews in the Modern World*, 207–11; Kaznelson, *Juden im deutschen Kulturbereich*, 760–97; Mendelsohn, *The Jews of East Central Europe*, 244–45; Jacobs, *Jewish Contributions to Civilization*, 237–46; Cecil Roth, *The Jewish Contribution to Civilization* (New York: Harper and Brothers, 1940), 278–83; György Lengyel, "Hungarian Banking and Business Leaders between the Wars: Education, Ethnicity and Career Patterns," in Silber, *Jews in the Hungarian Economy,* 230; Nathaniel Katzburg, *Hungary and the Jews: Policy and Legislation 1920–1943* (Ramat Gan: Bar-Ilan University Press, 1981), 30; W. D. Rubinstein, *The Left, the Right, and the Jews* (London: Croom Helm, 1992), 13, 27; for W. D. Rubinstein's data on Jewish participation in various economic elites, see Niall Ferguson, *The Cash Nexus: Money and Power in the Modern World, 1700–2000* (London: Allen Lane, 2001), 378; Wistrich, *Socialism and the Jews,* 59–61, 180–81; on the Rothschilds, see Ferguson, *The World's Banker,* 3, 1034–36.

15. Ruppin, *The Jews in the Modern World,* 151–53. The Heine quotation is from Jacobs, *Jewish Contributions to Civilization,* 239–40; Janos, *The Politics of Backwardness,* chap.. 3; Ferguson, *The World's Banker,* 7–11, 505–7 and passim, esp. 147 and 173; Fritz Stern, *Gold and Iron: Bismarck, Bleichröder, and the Building of the German Empire* (New York: Alfred A. Knopf, 1977); Alexander Herzen [Aleksandr Gertsen], *Byloe i dumy* (Moscow: Khudozhestvennaia literatura, 1969), 1:643–51.

16. Beller, *Vienna and the Jews,* 52–67. Efron, *Medicine and the German Jews,* 236–37. Cf. Lengyel, "Hungarian Banking and Business Leaders." Among Jewish businessmen-fathers in Hungary, the proportion of self-made men with little for-

mal secular education was much higher than among non-Jews. For overrepresentation among *gymnasium* students, see Goldscheider and Zuckerman, *The Transformation of the Jews*, 86; and Victor Karady, "Les juifs de Hongrie sous les lois antisémites," *Actes de la recherche en sciences sociales*, no. 56 (March 1985): 28.

17. Beller, *Vienna and the Jews*, 33–34; Goldscheider and Zuckerman, *The Transformation of the Jews*, 85–87; Efron, *Medicine and the German Jews*, 236; Mária M. Kovács, *Liberal Professions and Illiberal Politics: Hungary from the Habsburgs to the Holocaust* (Oxford: Oxford University Press, 1994), 18; Mendelsohn, *The Jews of East Central Europe*, 237.

18. Goldscheider and Zuckerman, *The Transformation of the Jews*, 90; Beller, *Vienna and the Jews*, 38–39; Mendelsohn, *The Jews of East Central Europe*, 27, 101. See also Kovács, *Liberal Professions*, 17–19; and Katzburg, *Hungary and the Jews*, 30–31.

19. Beller, *Vienna and the Jews*, 38–40 (the quotation is from 40); Friedländer, *Nazi Germany and the Jews*, 79–80; Niewyk, *The Jews in Weimar Germany*, 36–38; Kaznelson, *Juden im deutschen Kulturbereich*, 131–46; Wistrich, *Socialism and the Jews*, 182–83.

20. John Murray Cuddihy, *The Ordeal of Civility: Freud, Marx, Lévi-Strauss, and the Jewish Struggle with Modernity* (New York: Basic Books, 1974), 8; Milton Himmelfarb, *The Jews of Modernity* (New York: Basic Books, 1973), 23; Katz, *Out of the Ghetto*, 42–56 (the quotation is on 45), 84; Beller, *Vienna and the Jews*, 40–41; Hannah Arendt, *The Origins of Totalitarianism* (New York: Harcourt Brace Jovanovich, 1973), 59–62; Kaznelson, *Juden im deutschen Kulturbereich*, 862–914; Friedländer, *Nazi Germany and the Jews*, 79–80; Zygmunt Bauman, "Exit Visas and Entry Tickets: Paradoxes of Jewish Assimilation," *Telos* 77 (1988): 52–53; Niewyk, *The Jews in Weimar Germany*, 33–41; István Deák, *Weimar Germany's Left-Wing Intellectuals: A Political History of the Weltbühne and Its Circle* (Berkeley and Los Angeles: University of California Press, 1968), 27–28; Frederic V. Grunfeld, *Prophets without Honour: A Background to Freud, Kafka, Einstein and Their World* (New York: Holt, Rinehart and Winston, 1979), 26–29 and passim.

21. Beller, *Vienna and the Jews*, 14–32; Niewyk, *The Jews in Weimar Germany*, 33–41; Kaznelson, *Juden im deutschen Kulturbereich*, passim; McCagg, *Jewish Nobles and Geniuses*, 15–16 and passim; David Nachmansohn, *German-Jewish Pioneers in Science 1900–1933: Highlights in Atomic Physics, Chemistry, and Biochemistry* (New York: Springer-Verlag, 1979). The Gundolf quotation is from Himmelfarb, *The Jews of Modernity*, 44; see also Cuddihy, *The Ordeal of Civility*, 8. On the Rothschild myth, see Ferguson, *The World's Banker*, 11–28.

22. Houston Stewart Chamberlain, *Foundations of the Nineteenth Century*, vol. 1 (New York: John Lane, 1912), 574, 492–93, 330, 238, 232, 254, 391.

23. Jacobs, *Jewish Contributions to Civilization*, 10, 56–57.

24. Sombart, *The Jews and Modern Capitalism*, 321, 343, 209, 226–27.

25. Ibid., 237–38.

26. Matthew Arnold, *Culture and Anarchy* (Cambridge: Cambridge University Press, 1966), 129–44.

27. Friedrich Nietzsche, *Beyond Good and Evil: Prelude to a Philosophy of the Future*, sec. 195, in *Basic Writings of Nietzsche*, trans. and ed. Walter Kaufmann (New York: Modern Library, 1968), 298.

28. Ibid., sec. 11; Max Weber, *The Protestant Ethic and the Spirit of Capitalism*, trans. Talcott Parsons (London and New York: Routledge, 1995), 180–82.

29. Madison C. Peters, *Justice to the Jew: The Story of What He Has Done for the World* (New York: Trow Press, 1910), 24, 14, 29, 44, 66, 214, 207.

30. John Foster Fraser, *The Conquering Jew* (London: Cassell, 1915), 30–31, 43, 35. On Jews and rationalism, see Steven Beller's excellent " 'Pride and Prejudice' or 'Sense and Sensibility'? How Reasonable Was Anti-Semitism in Vienna, 1880–1939?" in Chirot and Reid, *Essential Outsiders*, 99–124.

31. Sombart, *The Jews and Modern Capitalism*, 254; L. B. Namier, "Introduction," in Ruppin, *The Jews in the Modern World*, xx–xxi; Fraser, *The Conquering Jew*, 213.

32. Anatole Leroy-Beaulieu, *Israël chez les nations* (Paris: Calmann Lévy, 1893), 221.

33. Chamberlain, *Foundations of the Nineteenth Century*, 1:482–83; Leroy-Beaulieu, *Israël chez les nations*, 341–42.

34. Thorstein Veblen, "The Intellectual Pre-eminence of Jews in Modern Europe," *Political Science Quarterly* 34, no. 1 (March 1919): 33–42. See also David Hollinger, "Why Are Jews Preeminent in Science and Scholarship? The Veblen Thesis Reconsidered," *Aleph* 2 (2002): 145–63.

35. A. Jussawalla, *Missing Person*, quoted in Luhrmann, *The Good Parsi*, 55.

36. Karl Marx, "On the Jewish Question," in *Early Writings* (New York: Vintage Books, 1975), 211–41; Adolf Hitler, *Mein Kampf* (Boston: Houghton Mifflin, 1962), 26–27, 59–60.

37. Weber, *The Protestant Ethic*, 182.

38. Carl E. Schorske, *Fin-de-siècle Vienna* (New York: Alfred A. Knopf, 1980), 129; Pierre Birnbaum, *The Jews of the Republic: A Political History of State Jews in France from Gambetta to Vichy* (Stanford: Stanford University Press, 1996).

39. Beller, *Vienna and the Jews*, 100–101.

40. Bauman, "Exit Visas and Entry Tickets," 52–55; Leichter quoted in Beller, *Vienna and the Jews*, 186. See also Birnbaum, *The Jews of the Republic*.

41. See Harold Bloom, *The Western Canon: The Book and School for the Ages* (New York: Harcourt Brace & Company, 1994), for a different look at the European canon.

42. Arnold, *Culture and Anarchy*, 141.

43. Ernest Gellner, *Plough, Sword and Book: The Structure of Human History* (Chicago: University of Chicago Press, 1989), 115. See also his *Nations and Nationalism*, passim.

44. P. Ia. Chaadaev, *Izbrannye sochineniia i pis'ma* (Moscow: Pravda, 1991), 27, 32. See also Peter Uwe Hohendahl, *Building a National Literature: The Case of Germany, 1830–1870* (Ithaca: Cornell University Press, 1989), esp. 140–73.

45. Osip Mandel'shtam, *Sochineniia v dvukh tomakh*, vol. 2 (Moscow: Khudozhestvennaia literatura, 1990), 14–15.

46. Grunfeld, *Prophets without Honor*, 6 ("Denk ich an Deutschland in der Nacht / Dann bin ich um den Schlaf gebracht"); Goldstein quoted in Michael Löwy, *Redemption and Utopia: Jewish Libertarian Thought in Central Europe* (Stanford: Stanford University Press, 1992), 31, and Friedländer, *Nazi Germany and the Jews*, 78; Beller, *Vienna and the Jews*, 150–51. See also Janos, *The Politics of Backwardness*, 117–18.

47. Gershom Scholem, *On Jews and Judaism in Crisis: Selected Essays* (New York: Schocken Books, 1976), 79; Beller, *Vienna and the Jews*, 151; Rosenzweig quoted in Sidney M. Bolkosky, *The Distorted Image: German Jewish Perceptions of Germans and Germany, 1918–1935* (New York: Elsevier, 1975), 16.

48. Vladimir (Zeev) Zhabotinskii, *Izbrannoe* (Jerusalem: Biblioteka Aliia, 1992), 28.

49. Ibid., 160; Goldstein quoted in Friedländer, *Nazi Germany and the Jews*, 78.

50. Bolkosky, *The Distorted Image*, 13.

51. Chaadaev, *Izbrannye sochineniia*, 28.

52. Otto Weininger, *Sex and Character* (London: William Heinemann, 1907), 308, 313.

53. Joseph Hayyim Brenner, "Self-Criticism," in *The Zionist Idea: A Historical Analysis and Reader*, ed. Arthur Hertzberg (New York: Atheneum, 1959), 307–12.

54. Weininger, *Sex and Character*, 328.

55. See "Letter to His Father" and "Selections from Diaries, 1911–1923," in *The Basic Kafka* (New York: Washington Square Books, 1979), 217, 191, 259, 261. See also Erich Heller's introduction, xviii.

56. Marcel Proust, *In Search of Lost Time*, vol. 4, *Sodom and Gomorrah*, trans. C. K. Scott Moncrieff and Terence Kilmartin, rev. D. J. Enright (London: Chatto and Windus, 1992), 16–17, 19.

57. Ibid., 104; Arendt, *The Origins of Totalitarianism*, 82.

58. All *Ulysses* quotations are from James Joyce, *Ulysses*, ed. Hans Walter Gabler with Wolfhard Steppe and Claus Melchior (New York: Vintage Books, 1986). The first number refers to chapter, the second to line.

59. The best books on Marxism and Freudianism are, respectively, Leszek Kolakowski, *Main Currents of Marxism: Its Rise, Growth, and Dissolution* (Oxford: Clarendon Press, 1978); and Ernest Gellner, *The Psychoanalytic Movement, or The Cunning of Unreason* (London: Paladin Grafton Books, 1988).

60. Gellner, *Plough, Sword and Book*, 34–35.

61. Marx, "On the Jewish Question," 236, 237, 241. See also Cuddihy, *The Ordeal of Civility*, 119–20, 152–54, and passim; and Wistrich, *Socialism and the Jews*, 25–34 and passim.

62. Dennis B. Klein, *Jewish Origins of the Psychoanalytic Movement* (New York: Praeger, 1981), 93–94.

63. Beller, *Vienna and the Jews*, 17; Niewyk, *The Jews in Weimar Germany*, 26–27; Friedländer, *Nazi Germany and the Jews*, 91–93; Kaznelson, *Juden im deutschen Kulturbereich*, 557–61; Mendelsohn, *The Jews of East Central Europe*, 95; István Deák, "Budapest and the Hungarian Revolutions of 1918–1919," *Slavonic and East European Review* 46, no. 106 (January 1968): 138–39; William O. McCagg, Jr., "Jews in Revolutions: The Hungarian Experience," *Journal of Social History*, no. 6 (Fall 1972): 78–105. The Seton-Watson quotation is from Katzburg, *Hungary and the Jews*, 35.

64. Deák, *Weimar Germany's Left-Wing Intellectuals*, 28–29. For a general discussion, including the Deák quotation, see Stanley Rothman and S. Robert Lichter, *Roots of Radicalism: Jews, Christians, and the New Left* (New York: Oxford University Press, 1982), 84–86. See also Niewyk, *The Jews in Weimar Germany*, 37–38; Kaznelson, *Juden im deutschen Kulturbereich*, 561–77, 677–86; Wistrich, *Socialism and the Jews*, 83–85 and passim.

65. Max Horkheimer and Theodor W. Adorno, *Dialectic of Enlightenment* (New York: Herder and Herder, 1927), 173, 187, 192, 197, 184; T. W. Adorno, "Prejudice in the Interview Material," in *Authoritarian Personality*, ed. Adorno et al. (New York: Harper and Brothers, 1950), 608, 618. On the Jewishness of the members of the Frankfurt School, see Martin Jay, *Dialectical Imagination: A History of the Frankfurt School and the Institute of Social Research 1923–1950* (Boston: Little, Brown, and Company, 1973), 31–36.

66. Horkheimer and Adorno, *Dialectic of Enlightenment*, 43–80, esp. 43, 50, 57, 61.

67. Ibid., 61–62.

68. Ibid., 55.

69. Ibid., 68–69.

70. Ibid., 200.

71. Janos, *The Politics of Backwardness*, 177; Andrew Janos, *East Central Europe in the Modern World: The Politics of the Borderlands from Pre- to Postcommunism* (Stanford: Stanford University Press, 2000), 150–51; Jaff Schatz, *The Generation: The Rise and Fall of the Jewish Communists of Poland* (Berkeley and Los Angeles: University of California Press, 1991), 76, 96–97; Arthur Liebman, *Jews and the Left* (New York: John Wiley and Sons, 1979), 46–66.

72. Stephen J. Whitfield, *American Space, Jewish Time* (Hamden, Conn.: Archon Books, 1988), 125; Grunfeld, *Prophets without Honor*, 153.

73. Werner Sombart, *Der proletarische Sozialismus* (Jena: Verlag von Gustav Fischer, 1924), 1:75–76, 2:298–303; Nikolai Berdiaev, *Smysl istorii. Opyt filosofii chelovecheskoi sud'by* (Paris: YMCA-PRESS, 1969), 116–17, 109.

74. Sonja Margolina, *Das Ende der Lügen: Russland und die Juden im 20. Jahrhundert* (Berlin: Siedler Verlag, 1992), 101. Cf. Isaac Deutscher, *The Non-Jewish Jew and Other Essays* (London: Oxford University Press, 1968).

75. Löwy, *Redemption and Utopia*, 136, 59–60; Lev Shternberg, "Problema evreiskoi natsional'noi psikhologii," *Evreiskaia starina* 11 (1924): 36, 44.

76. Shternberg, "Problema," 37.

77. Lazar' Kaganovich, *Pamiatnye zapiski rabochego, kommunista-bol'shevika, profsoiuznogo, partiinogo i sovetsko-gosudarstvennogo rabotnika* (Moscow: Vagrius, 1996), 41.

78. *Burnaia zhizn' Lazika Roitshvanetsa*, in I. Erenburg, *Staryi skorniak i drugie proizvedeniia* (n.p., 1983), 115.

79. Schatz, *The Generation*, 138.

80. Ibid.

81. See, esp., Lewis S. Feuer, "Generations and the Theory of Revolution," *Survey* 18, no. 3 (Summer 1972): 161–88; and Lewis S. Feuer, *The Conflict of Generations: The Character and Significance of Student Movements* (New York: Basic Books, 1969).

82. Quoted in McCagg, *Jewish Nobles and Geniuses*, 106–7.

83. McCagg, "Jews in Revolutions," 96; Rudolph L. Tőkés, *Béla Kun and the Hungarian Soviet Republic* (New York: Frederick A. Praeger, 1967), 53; György Borsányi, *The Life of a Communist Revolutionary, Béla Kun* (New York: Columbia University Press, 1993), 431; Kaganovich, *Pamiatnye zapiski*, 40.

84. Quoted in Abram Kardiner and Edward Preble, *They Studied Man* (Cleveland: World Publishing Company, 1961), 139; and Löwy, *Redemption and Utopia*, 33.

85. Schatz, *The Generation*, 57.

86. Janos, *The Politics of Backwardness*, 182; Marjorie Boulton, *Zamenhof: Creator of Esperanto* (London: Routledge and Kegan Paul, 1960), 19–20; Evgenii Gnedin, *Vykhod iz labirinta* (Moscow: Memorial, 1994), 8.

87. Arendt, *The Origins of Totalitarianism*, 40; Marx, "On the Jewish Question," 239.

88. On the German Jewish "blood and soil," see George L. Mosse, *Germans and Jews: The Right, the Left, and the Search for a "Third Force" in Pre-Nazi Germany* (New York: Howard Fertig, 1970), 77–115.

89. Samuel, *The World of Sholom Aleichem*, 6. Benjamin Harshav, *Language in Time of Revolution* (Stanford: Stanford University Press, 1993), 25–29 and passim.

CHAPTER 3
BABEL'S FIRST LOVE: THE JEWS AND THE RUSSIAN REVOLUTION

1. Hirsz Abramowicz, *Profiles of a Lost World: Memoirs of East European Jewish Life before World War II* (Detroit: Wayne State University Press, 1999), 65, 79; Robert J. Brym, *The Jewish Intelligentsia and Russian Marxism: A Sociological Study of Intellectual Radicalism and Ideological Divergence* (London: Macmillan, 1978), 30–34; Arcadius Kahan, *Essays in Jewish Social and Economic History* (Chi-

cago: University of Chicago Press, 1986), 1–69; Benjamin Nathans, *Beyond the Pale: The Jewish Encounter with Late Imperial Russia* (Berkeley and Los Angeles: University of California Press, 2002), 4, 40; Alexander Orbach, "The Development of the Russian Jewish Community, 1881–1903," in *Pogroms: Anti-Jewish Violence in Modern Russian History*, ed. John D. Klier and Shlomo Lambroza (Cambridge: Cambridge University Press, 1992), 138–40.

2. Joachim Schoenfeld, *Jewish Life in Galicia under the Austro-Hungarian Empire and in the Reborn Poland 1898–1939* (Hoboken, N.J.: KTAV Publishing House, 1985), 8.

3. Samuel, *The World of Sholom Aleichem*, 63.

4. On Khmelnytsky and the Jewish-Ukrainian contact, see Joel Raba, *Remembrance and Denial: The Fate of the Jews in the Wars of the Polish Commonwealth during the Mid–Seventeenth Century as Shown in Contemporary Writings and Historical Research* (Boulder, Colo.: East European Monographs, 1995); and Frank Sysyn, "The Jewish Massacres in the Historiography of the Khmelnytsky Uprising: A Review Article," *Journal of Ukrainian Studies* 23, no. 1 (Summer 1998): 83–89. See also Peter J. Potichnyj and Howard Aster, eds., *Ukrainian-Jewish Relations in Historical Perspective* (Edmonton: Canadian Institute of Ukrainian Studies, 1988), esp. essays by Jaroslaw Pelenski, Frank Sysyn, Israel Bartal, and George Grabowicz; and Zenon E. Kohut, "The Image of Jews in Ukraine's Intellectual Tradition: The Role of *Istoriia Rusov*," in *Cultures and Nations of Central and Eastern Europe: Essays in Honor of Roman Szporluk*, ed. Zvi Gitelman et al. (Cambridge, Mass.: Ukrainian Research Institute, 2000), 343–53. I am grateful to Frank Sysyn and Roman Koropeckyj for help with Ukrainian history questions.

5. Zborowski and Herzog, *Life Is with People*, 152.

6. Abramowicz, *Profiles of a Lost World*, 66, 345; M. S. Al'tman, "Avtobiograficheskaia proza M. S. Al'tmana," *Minuvshee* 10 (1990): 208.

7. See chap. 1. For disguised place-names, see, esp., Peter Bakker, "Notes on the Genesis of Caló and Other Iberian Para-Romani Varieties," in *Romani in Contact: The History, Structure and Sociology of a Language*, ed. Yaron Matras (Amsterdam: John Benjamins Publishing Company, 1995), 133; and Hancock, "The Social and Linguistic Development," 28.

8. Al'tman, "Avtobiograficheskaia proza," 213.

9. Schoenfeld, *Jewish Life in Galicia*, 12.

10. Ibid., 13.

11. Howard Aster and Peter J. Potichnyj, *Jewish Ukrainian Relations: Two Solitides* (Oakville, Ont.: Mosaic Press, 1983). The "painted eggs" quotation is from Feliks Roziner, *Serebrianaia tsepochka: Sem' pokolenii odnoi sem'i* (Tel Aviv: Biblioteka Aliia, 1983), 59.

12. John A. Armstrong, "Mobilized Diaspora in Tsarist Russia: The Case of the Baltic Germans," in *Soviet Nationality Policies and Practices*, ed. Jeremy R. Azrael (New York: Praeger, 1978), 63–104, esp. 69, 75, 99n. 16 (the quotations are from 88); N. V. Iukhneva, *Etnicheskii sostav i etnosotsial'naia struktura naseleniia Pe-*

terburga: vtoraia polovina XIX–nachalo XX veka (Leningrad: Nauka, 1984), 73; Ingeborg Fleischhauer, "The Germans' Role in Tsarist Russia: A Reappraisal," in *Soviet Germans: Past and Present*, ed. Ingeborg Fleischhauer and Benjamin Pinkus (London: Hurst and Company, 1986), 18. See also John A. Armstrong, "Socializing for Modernization in a Multiethnic Elite," in *Entrepreneurship in Imperial Russia and the Soviet Union*, ed. Gregory Guroff and Fred V. Carstensen (Princeton: Princeton University Press, 1983), 84–103.

13. Iukhneva, *Etnicheskii sostav*, 184, 56–79; Thomas C. Owen, *Russian Corporate Capitalism from Peter the Great to Perestroika* (Oxford: Oxford University Press, 1995), 187–88.

14. There is still not a single Russian book on "the German" in Russian culture; for a recent article, see A. V. Zhukovskaia, N. N. Mazur, and A. M. Peskov, "Nemetskie tipazhi russkoi belletristiki (konets 1820kh–nachalo 1840kh gg.)," *Novoe literaturnoe obozrenie*, no. 34 (1998): 37–54. In German, see Dieter Boden, *Die Deutschen in der russischen und der sowjetischen Literatur: Traum und Alptraum* (Munich and Vienna: Günter Olzog, 1982), and Maximiliane Müntjes, *Beiträge zum Bild des Deutschen in der russischen Literatur von Katharina bis auf Alexander II* (Meisenheim am Glan: Verlag Anton Hain, 1971). I am grateful to Daniela Rizzi for fascinating conversations on the subject.

15. See, esp., Brym, *The Jewish Intelligentsia*, 26–34; Kahan, *Essays*, 20–27; Ezra Mendelsohn, *Class Struggle in the Pale: The Formative Years of the Jewish Workers' Movement in Tsarist Russia* (Cambridge: Cambridge University Press, 1970), 1–26.

16. See Klier and Lambroza, *Pogroms*; and Hans Rogger, *Jewish Policies and Right-Wing Politics in Imperial Russia* (Berkeley and Los Angeles: University of California Press, 1986), esp. 113–75.

17. Andrew Godley, *Jewish Immigrant Entrepreneurship in New York and London 1880–1914: Enterprise and Culture* (New York: Palgrave, 2001), 71–72; for the statistics, see ibid., 68–87, and Mordechai Altshuler, *Soviet Jewry on the Eve of the Holocaust: A Social and Demographic Profile* (Jerusalem: Center for Research of East European Jewry, 1998), 9. See also Zvi Gitelman, " 'From a Northern Country': Russian and Soviet Jewish Immigration to America and Israel in Historical Perspective," in *Russian Jews on Three Continents: Migration and Resettlement*, ed. Noah Lewin-Epstein et al. (London: Frank Cass, 1997), 23.

18. Kahan, *Essays*, 29–30; Mendelsohn, *Class Struggle*, 4–5; Steven J. Zipperstein, *The Jews of Odessa: A Cultural History, 1794–1881* (Stanford: Stanford University Press, 1985), 15; Iukhneva, *Etnicheskii sostav*, 24; Nathans, *Beyond the Pale*, 91–100.

19. B. V. Anan'ich, *Bankirskie doma v Rossii 1860–1914 gg: Ocherki istorii chastnogo predprinimatel'stva* (Leningrad: Nauka, 1991), 8–13; Alfred J. Rieber, *Merchants and Entrepreneurs in Imperial Russia* (Chapel Hill: University of North Carolina Press, 1982), 57–60; Arcadius Kahan, "Notes on Jewish Entrepreneur-

ship in Tsarist Russia," in Guroff and Carstensen, *Entrepreneurship in Imperial Russia and the Soviet Union*, 107–18.

20. Anan'ich, *Bankirskie doma*, 37, 41, 72–73, 86–87, 139, and passim; Kahan, "Notes," 122–23; Brym, *The Jewish Intelligentsia*, 25; Nathans, *Beyond the Pale*, 68, 128–29; Mikhael' Beizer, *Evrei Leningrada 1917–1939: Natsional'naia zhizn' i sovetizatsiia* (Moscow; Mosty kul'tury, 1999), 15.

21. Kahan, "Notes," 111.

22. Brym, *The Jewish Intelligentsia*, 24–25 (including the Sachar quotation); Kahan, "Notes," 118; Anan'ich, *Bankirskie doma*, 73, 135–37.

23. Kahan, "Notes," 119–20; Anan'ich, *Bankirskie doma*, 49–66; Brym, *The Jewish Intelligentsia*, 24–25.

24. Anan'ich, *Bankirskie doma*, 41, 79.

25. Kahan, *Essays*, 3.

26. Robert Weinberg, "The Pogrom of 1905 in Odessa: A Case Study," in Klier and Lambroza, *Pogroms*, 252–53; Kahan, "Notes," 115–16; Owen, *Russian Corporate Capitalism*, 188; Nathans, *Beyond the Pale*, 102–3; Iukhneva, *Etnicheskii sostav*, 211–12.

27. Kahan, *Essays*, 15–22; Kahan, "Notes," 115–17. Cf. Bonacich, "A Theory of Middleman Minorities," 586–87.

28. Nathans, *Beyond the Pale*, 217–18; Zipperstein, *The Jews of Odessa*, 108, 116. The Smolenskin quotation is on 108.

29. Isaak Babel', *Sochineniia*, vol. 2 (Moscow: Khudozhestvennaia literatura, 1992), 146. My translations are based on David McDuff's in Isaac Babel, *Collected Stories* (New York: Penguin, 1994); and Walter Morison's in Isaac Babel, *The Collected Stories* (New York: Meridian, 1974).

30. Nathans, *Beyond the Pale*, 218, 224; B. N. Mironov, *Sotsial'naia istoriia Rossii perioda imperii*, vol. 1 (St. Petersburg: D. Bulanin, 1999), 31.

31. Erich Haberer, *Jews and Revolution in Nineteenth-Century Russia* (Cambridge: Cambridge University Press, 1995), 13; Nathans, *Beyond the Pale*, 102–3, 314–15, 343–44, 354, and passim; Beizer, *Evrei Leningrada*, 14.

32. Babel', *Sochineniia*, 2:171.

33. Ibid.

34. See, esp., Ruth Apter-Gabriel, ed., *Tradition and Revolution: The Jewish Renaissance in Russian Avant-Garde Art 1912–1928* (Jerusalem: Israel Museum, 1988); John E. Bowlt, "Jewish Artists and the Russian Silver Age," in *Russian Jewish Artists in a Century of Change, 1890–1990*, ed. Susan Tumarkin Goodman (Munich: Prestel, 1995), 40–52 (the Efros quotation is on 43); and Igor Golomstock, "Jews in Soviet Art," in *Jews in Soviet Culture*, ed. Jack Miller (New Brunswick, N.J.: Transaction Books, 1984), 23–30.

35. Nathans, *Beyond the Pale*, 111–12; Iukhneva, *Etnicheskii sostav*, 208–10; Lev Deich, *Za polveka* (Berlin, 1923; reprint, Cambridge: Oriental Research Partners, 1975), 11, 17–19. Henry J. Tobias, *The Jewish Bund in Russia: From Its Origins to 1905* (Stanford: Stanford University Press, 1972), 18.

36. Abramowicz, *Profiles of a Lost World*, 118–20. See also Abraham Cahan, *The Education of Abraham Cahan* (Philadelphia: Jewish Publication Society of America, 1969), 116, and Nathans, *Beyond the Pale*, 236–37.

37. Zhabotinskii, *Izbrannoe*, 28–32; Cahan, *The Education*, 79; Boulton, *Zamenhof*, 8. See also René Centassi and Henri Masson, *L'Homme qui a défié Babel: Ludwik Lejzer Zamenhof* (Paris: L'Harmattan, 2001), 16. The Mutnikovich quotation is from Tobias, *The Jewish Bund*, 12.

38. Vladimir Iokhel'son, "Dalekoe proshloe," *Byloe*, no. 13 (July 1918): 55; Mandel'shtam, *Sochineniia v dvukh tomakh*, 2:20–21; Cahan, *The Education*, 79. See also Steven Cassedy, *To the Other Shore: The Russian Jewish Intellectuals Who Came to America* (Princeton: Princeton University Press, 1997), 6–14.

39. *Deiateli SSSR i revoliutsionnogo dvizheniia Rossii: Entsiklopedicheskii slovar' Granat* (Moscow: Sovetskaia entsiklopediia, 1989), 161. Cf. Yuri Slezkine, "Lives as Tales," in *In the Shadow of Revolution: Life Stories of Russian Women from 1917 to the Second World War*, ed. Sheila Fitzpatrick and Yuri Slezkine (Princeton: Princeton University Press, 2000), 18–30. See also Cassedy, *To the Other Shore*, 25–35.

40. Babel', *Sochineniia*, vol. 1 (Moscow: Khudozhestvennaia literatura, 1991), 39.

41. Ibid., 2:153.

42. Ibid., 143.

43. S. Marshak, *V nachale zhizni* (Moscow: Sovetskii pisatel', 1961), 89–90; the Pushkin translation is from Alexander Pushkin, *Collected Narrative and Lyrical Poetry*, trans. Walter Arndt (Ann Arbor: Ardis, 1984), 358–63. Both cases are discussed, as a version of the traditional confirmation of the Jewish boy, in Efraim Sicher, *Jews in Russian Literature after the October Revolution: Writers and Artists between Hope and Apostasy* (Cambridge: Cambridge University Press, 1995), 38.

44. Babel', *Sochineniia*, 2:175–76.

45. Cahan, *The Education*, 8.

46. Babel', *Sochineniia*, 2:174–75.

47. Cahan, *The Education*, 145; *Deiateli*, 160; A. Kushnirov, *Stikhi* (Moscow: Khudozhestvennaia literatura, 1964), 54; the Pasternak and Aronson quotations are from Bowlt, "Jewish Artists," 44.

48. Marshak, *V nachale zhizni*, 243.

49. Babel', *Sochineniia*, 2:238.

50. Raisa Orlova, *Vospominaniia o neproshedshem vremeni* (Ann Arbor: Ardis, 1983), 15.

51. Mandel'shtam, *Sochineniia v dvukh tomakh*, 2:21.

52. Babel', *Sochineniia*, 1:39–41.

53. Deich, *Za polveka*, 34; Iokhel'son, "Dalekoe proshloe," 56–57; I. J. Singer, *The Brothers Ashkenazi* (New York: Atheneum, 1980), 8; L. Trotskii, *Moia zhizn': Opyt avtobiografii*, vol. 1 (Berlin: Granit, 1930), 106; Joseph Nedava, *Trotsky and*

the Jews (Philadelphia: Jewish Publication Society of America, 1971), 31; Babel', *Sochineniia*, 2:178.

54. Cahan, *The Education*, 8; *Deiateli*, 161.

55. Ronald Sanders, *The Downtown Jews: Portraits of an Immigrant Generation* (New York: Harper and Row, 1961), 310–14; Jeffrey Veidlinger, *The Moscow State Yiddish Theater: Jewish Culture on the Soviet Stage* (Bloomington: Indiana University Press, 2000), 139–46; Nataliia Vovsi-Mikhoels, *Moi otets Solomon Mikhoels: Vospominanie o zhizni i gibeli* (Moscow: Vozvrashchenie, 1997), 81–88.

56. Cahan, *The Education*, 74, 47–48; G. A. Landau, "Revoliutsionnye idei v russkoi obshchestvennosti," in *Rossiia i evrei*, ed. I. M. Bikerman et al. (Paris: YMCA Press, 1978), 108; *Deiateli*, 161, 155; Trotskii, *Moia zhizn'*, 1:219; Nedava, *Trotsky and the Jews*, 33.

57. Sholem Aleichem, *Tevye the Dairyman and the Railroad Stories*, trans. Hillel Halkin (New York: Schocken Books, 1987), 81.

58. The "spoilt for Russia" quotation is from Alexander Herzen, *My Past and Thoughts* (Berkeley and Los Angeles: University of California Press, 1982), 66.

59. L. N. Tolstoi, *Kazaki* (Moscow: Khudozhestvennaia literatura, 1967), 35, 39–40, 122.

60. S. N. Eisenstadt, *From Generation to Generation: Age Groups and Social Structure* (New York: Free Press, 1971), 44–51 and passim. Cf. Lynn Hunt, *The Family Romance of the French Revolution* (Berkeley and Los Angeles: University of California Press, 1992).

61. See, esp., Daniel Brower, *Training the Nihilists: Education and Radicalism in Tsarist Russia* (Ithaca: Cornell University Press, 1975); and Abbott Gleason, *Young Russia: The Genesis of Russian Radicalism in the 1860s* (New York: Viking Press, 1980).

62. S. Ia. Nadson, *Stikhotvoreniia* (Moscow: Sovetskaia Rossiia, 1987), 212, 234, 293; Mandelshtam, *Sochineniia*, 2:16 (cf. Osip Mandelstam, *The Prose of Osip Mandelstam*, trans. Clarence Brown [Princeton; Princeton University Press, 1965], 84). The culmination of the Jew-as-victim theme was L. Andreev, M. Gor'kii, and F. Sologub, eds., *Shchit: Literaturnyi sbornik* (Moscow: T-vo tipografii Mamontova, 1915), which was published in the wake of the mass deportations of Jews from the border areas during World War I. See also Joshua Kunitz, *Russian Literature and the Jew* (New York: Columbia University Press, 1929), 95–168. The "islands of freedom" quotation is from Brym, *The Jewish Intelligentsia*, 53.

63. *Deiateli*, 80 (ellipses in the original). The two quotations from circle veterans are from Mendelsohn, *Class Struggle*, 38.

64. Cahan, *The Education*, 145–46.

65. Mandelshtam, *Sochineniia*, 2:16. Sofia Perovskaia and Andrei Zheliabov were executed in 1881 for the assassination of Alexander II.

66. *Deiateli*, 18–19.

67. Ibid., 158. See also Haberer, *Jews and Revolution*, 151–55. I have used Haberer's translation in slightly revised form.

68. See Brym, *The Jewish Intelligentsia*; Jonathan Frankel, *Prophecy and Politics: Socialism, Nationalism, and the Russian Jews, 1862–1917* (Cambridge: Cambridge University Press, 1981); Yoav Peled, *Class and Ethnicity in the Pale: The Political Economy of Jewish Workers' Nationalism in Late Imperial Russia* (New York: St. Martin's Press, 1989); Tobias, *The Jewish Bund*. After the Bolshevik Revolution, the Bund was disbanded, along with other non-Bolshevik parties (while continuing to function on the Polish side of the new border). It never got a fair chance, in other words—but that is part of the point: the party was too closely associated with minority nationalism to be convincingly Marxist (especially given the Jewish-friendly universalist alternative), and too emphatically Marxist and extraterritorial to be convincingly nationalist.

69. Chaim Weizmann, *The Letters and Papers of Chaim Weizmann*, gen. ed. Meyer W. Weisgal, vol. 2, ser. A, November 1902–August 1903 (London: Oxford University Press, 1971), 306–7. For a discussion of the three emigrations, see Nathans, *Beyond the Pale*, 86. For the connection between political choices and "degrees of embeddedness" in Russian and Jewish environments, see Brym, *The Jewish Intelligentsia*, 44.

70. Haberer, *Jews and Revolution*, 94. The Vilna circle, led by Aron Zundelevich, consisted almost entirely of the students of the city's rabbinical seminary. See Haberer, *Jews and Revolution*, 79.

71. Ibid., 254–57, 275, 318–19; Brym, *The Jewish Intelligentsia*; 3; Nedava, *Trotsky and the Jews*, 143.

72. Tobias, *The Jewish Bund*, 76–79; I. Domal'skii, *Russkie evrei vchera i segodnia* (Jerusalem: Alia, 1975), 53; Nedava, *Trotsky and the Jews*, 144–46; Brym, *The Jewish Intelligentsia*; 73; Oleg Budnitskii, "V chuzhom piru pokhmel'e: Evrei i russkaia revoliutsiia," in *Evrei i russkaia revoliutsiia: Materialy i issledovaniia*, ed. O. V. Budnitskii (Moscow: Mosty kul'tury, 1999), 13; Beizer, *Evrei Leningrada*, 50; Iaakov Menaker, *Zagovorshchiki, ikh spodvizhniki i soobshchniki* (Jerusalem: n.p., 1990), 171, 302.

73. For class and nationality in the Russian revolutionary movement, see Ronald Grigor Suny, *The Revenge of the Past: Nationalism, Revolution, and the Collapse of the Soviet Union* (Stanford: Stanford University Press, 1993), esp. 20–83. See also B. N. Mironov, *Sotsial'naia istoriia Rossii perioda imperii*, vol. 2 (St. Petersburg: DB, 1999), 42–43.

74. Leonard Schapiro, "The Role of the Jews in the Russian Revolutionary Movement," *Slavonic and East European Review* 40 (December 1961): 153. See also Haberer, *Jews and Revolution*, 270–71 and passim.

75. Iokhel'son, "Dalekoe proshloe," 55.

76. I. O. Levin, "Evrei v revoliutsii," in *Rossiia i evrei*, 132–33.

77. F. M. Dostoevsky, "Dnevnik pisatelia za 1877 g.," in *Taina Izrailia*, 19–20. The Pobedonostsev quotation is from Rogger, *Jewish Policies*, 67.

78. Zhabotinskii, *Izbrannoe*, 52–54. See also Vl. Zhabotinskii, *Chuzhbina* (Moscow: Mosty kul'tury; Jerusalem: Gesharim, 2000), 222–23.

79. Nathans, *Beyond the Pale*, 260, 264, 348, 351.

80. See, esp., Rogger, *Jewish Policies*, 56–112.

81. On the pogroms, see, in particular, Klier and Lambroza, *Pogroms*.

82. Maksim Gor'kii, *Iz literaturnogo naslediia: Gor'kii i evreiskii vopros*, ed. Mikhail Agurskii and Margarita Shklovskaia (Jerusalem: Hebrew University of Jerusalem, 1986), 190–202.

83. Babel', *Sochineniia*, 2:142, 148, 154–56.

84. Ibid., 143–44.

85. Gor'kii, *Iz literaturnogo naslediia*, 199.

86. A. Lunacharskii, *Ob antisemitizme* (Moscow: Gosizdat, 1929), 17.

87. V. I. Lenin, "Kriticheskie zametki po natsional'nomu voprosu," in V. I. Lenin, *Voprosy natsional'noi politiki i proletarskogo internatsionalizma* (Moscow: Politizdat, 1965), 10, 13, 15; E. E. Kirillova and V. N. Shepeleva, eds., "Vy . . . rasporiadilis' molchat' . . . absoliutno," *Otechestvennye arkhivy*, no. 3 (1992): 78–79; Gor'kii, *Iz literaturnogo naslediia*, 351. For Lenin's genealogy, see O. Abramova, G. Borodulina, and T. Koloskova, *Mezhdu pravdoi i istinoi (ob istorii spekuliatsii vokrug rodosloviia V. I. Lenina* (Moscow: Gosudarstvennyi istoricheskii muzei, 1998); and M. G. Shtein, *Ul'ianovy i Leniny: Tainy rodoslovnoi i psevdonima* (St. Petersburg: VIRD, 1997).

88. Lenin, "O prave natsii na samoopredelenie," in Lenin, *Voprosy natsional'noi politiki*, 81n.

89. Gor'kii, *Iz literaturnogo naslediia*, 170–71, 113, 115, 204, 269.

90. Eric Lohr, "Enemy Alien Politics within the Russian Empire during World War I" (Ph.D. diss., Harvard University, 1999). See also Peter Gattrell, *A Whole Empire Walking: Refugees in Russia during World War I* (Bloomington: Indiana University Press, 1999); Peter Holquist, "To Count, to Extract, and to Exterminate: Population Statistics and Population Politics in Late Imperial and Soviet Russia," in *A State of Nations: Empire and Nation-Making in the Age of Lenin and Stalin*, ed. Ronald Grigor Suny and Terry Martin (New York: Oxford University Press, 2001), 111–44; Mark von Hagen, "The Great War and the Mobilization of Ethnicity in the Russian Empire," in *Post-Soviet Political Order: Conflict and State Building*, ed. Barnett R. Rubin and Jack Snyder (London and New York: Routledge, 1998), 34–57, esp. 43; and V. V. Kanishchev, *Russkii bunt—bessmyslennyi i besposhchadnyi: Pogromnoe dvizhenie v gorodakh Rossii v 1917–1918 gg.* (Tambov: TGU, 1995).

91. On Russia's "Time of Troubles," see Peter Holquist, *Making War, Forging Revolution: Russia's Continuum of Crisis, 1914–1921* (Cambridge: Harvard University Press, 2002).

92. Babel', *Sochineniia*, 2:43, 101, 70, 36.

93. Ibid., 246.

94. E. G. Bagritskii, *Stikhotvoreniia* (Leningrad: Sovetskii pisatel', 1956), 174–76.

95. On Trotsky's first school, see Trotskii, *Moia zhizn'*, 54–58.

96. Bagritskii, *Stikhotvoreniia*, 202.

97. Babel', *Sochineniia*, 2:129.

98. Al'tman, "Avtobiograficheskaia proza," 210, 214, 219.

99. Nadezhda and Maia Ulanovskie, *Istoriia odnoi sem'i* (New York: Chalidze Publications, 1982), 30.

100. Ibid., 34, 41, 36.

101. Babel', *Sochineniia*, 2:206. For Babel's interrogation, see Vitalii Shentalinskii, *Raby svobody: V literaturnykh arkhivakh KGB* (Moscow: Parus, 1995), 26–81.

102. Iosif Utkin, *Stikhi* (Moscow: Pravda, 1939), 21–22; Bagritskii, *Stikhotvoreniia*, 250–51, 259–61, 262–63.

103. See, esp., Budnitskii, "V chuzhom piru pokhmel'e"; Henry Abramson, *A Prayer for the Government: Ukrainians and Jews in Revolutionary Times, 1917–1920* (Cambridge: Ukrainian Research Institute and Center for Jewish Studies, Harvard University, 1999); Peter Kenez, "Pogroms and White Ideology in the Russian Civil War," in Klier and Lambroza, *Pogroms*, 293–313; Holquist, "To Count, to Extract, and to Exterminate."

104. Babel', *Sochineniia*, 1:127.

105. V. Shklovskii, *Sentimental'noe puteshestvie* (Moscow: Novosti, 1990), 38–39, 43, 81.

106. Beizer, *Evrei Leningrada*, 30–32, 49–51; M. Frenkin, *Russkaia armiia i revoliutsiia, 1917–1918* (Munich: Logos, 1978), 244; Menaker, *Zagovorshchiki*, 427. The leadership of the Mensheviks (the Bolsheviks' orthodox Marxist opponents) was even more heavily Jewish, but after the formation of the Red Army and the new Soviet state, most Jewish revolutionaries identified the revolution with Bolshevism.

107. Beizer, *Evrei Leningrada*, 70.

108. Ibid., 78–79; Gabriele Freitag, "Nächstes Jahr in Moskau! Die Zuwanderung von Juden in die sowjetische Metropole 1917 bis 1932" (Ph.D. diss., Johann-Wolfgang-Goethe-Universität, Frankfurt am Main, 2000), 131–36, 143; Benjamin Pinkus, *The Jews of the Soviet Union: The History of a National Minority* (Cambridge: Cambridge University Press, 1988), 77–81. The figures for the female Bolsheviks are from *Vserossiisskaia perepis' chlenov RKP. Vypusk 5. Natsional'nyi sostav chlenov partii* (Moscow, 1924), 62. I am grateful to Gabriele Freitag for drawing my attention to these data.

109. L. Krichevskii, "Evrei v apparate VChK-OGPU v 20-e gody," in Budnitskii, *Evrei i russkaia revoliutsiia*, 320–50; Schapiro, "The Role of the Jews," 165. On the Latvians, see Andrew Ezergailis, *The Latvian Impact on the Bolshevik Revolution* (Boulder, Colo.: East European Monographs, distributed by Columbia University Press, 1983).

110. A. L. Litvin, *Krasnyi i belyi terror v Rossii, 1918–1922* (Kazan: Tatarskoe gazetno-zhurnal'noe izdatel'stvo, 1995), 168–71, 79–82; N. A. Sokolov, *Ubiistvo tsarskoi sem'i* (Moscow: Soverskii pisatel', 1991, originally published in Berlin in

1925); Edvard Radzinskii, *Gospodi ... spasi i usmiri Rossiiu* (Moscow: Vagrius, 1996); S. P. Mel'gunov, *Krasnyi terror v Rossii* (New York: Brandy, 1979), 66–71.

111. The numbers are from Golomstock, "Jews in Soviet Art," 38.

112. Beizer, *Evrei Leningrada*, 70; *Gorodskie imena vchera i segodnia; Peterburgskaia toponimika* (St. Petersburg: LIK, 1997), 216.

113. Lunacharskii, *Ob antisemitizme*, 46–47. For intermarriage statistics, see Altshuler, *Soviet Jewry on the Eve of the Holocaust*, 74.

114. Sokolov, *Ubiistvo*, 134–41, 153–61, 170.

115. V. V. Shul'gin, *"Chto nam v nikh ne nravitsia ..." Ob Antisemitizme v Rossii* (Moscow: Khors, 1992), 34–35 (italics in the original).

116. Ibid., 143. Cf. Jan T. Gross, *Neighbors: The Destruction of the Jewish Community in Jedwabne, Poland* (Princeton: Princeton University Press, 2001), 132–37.

117. Shul'gin, *"Chto nam v nikh ne nravitsia"*, 71–82, 257–58.

118. Ibid., 141–42.

119. *Rossiia i evrei*, 5–8, 22, 26, 59, 117.

120. Ia. A. Bromberg, *Zapad, Rossiia i Evreistvo: Opyt peresmotra evreiskogo voprosa* (Prague: Izd. Evraziitsev, 1931), 54–55.

121. *Rossiia i evrei*, 104, 212–13; Bromberg, *Zapad, Rossiia i Evreistvo*, 188.

122. For the "historical guilt," if not of "commissars" and "Chekists" themselves, then of their children and grandchildren, see David Samoilov, *Perebiraia nashi daty* (Moscow: Vagrius, 2000) (the quotation is on 55); Vas. Grossman, *Vse techet* (Frankfurt: Posev, 1970), 153–57 (on Leva Mekler); and Margolina, *Das Ende*.

123. For the argument that national canons are "assembled from deeds that are somehow special," see Gross, *Neighbors*, 136. For a survey of post–World War II restitution claims, see Elazar Barkan, *The Guilt of Nations: Restitution and Negotiating Historical Injustices* (New York: W. W. Norton, 2000).

124. Beizer, *Evrei Leningrada*, 46.

125. Lenin, "Kriticheskie zametki," 8–9; Levin, "Evrei v revoliutsii," 131; Lev Kopelev, *I sotvoril sebe kumira* (Ann Arbor: Ardis, 1978), 67.

126. Gor'kii, *Iz literaturnogo naslediia*, 304.

127. Ibid., 307 (including the Frumkina and Trainin quotations); Trotskii, *Moia zhizn'*, 2:61–63; Nedava, *Trotsky and the Jews*, 122.

128. A. Lunacharskii, *Ob antisemitizme*, 5–6.

129. Babel', *Sochineniia*, 2:32.

130. Ibid.

131. Ibid., 124, 252.

132. Ibid., 69.

133. Ibid., 34.

134. In Mandelstam's original ("Miauknul kon', i kot zarzhal—kazak evreiu podrazhal"), the Cossack was acting like a Jew.

135. Babel', *Sochineniia*, 1:65, 127, 128, 132, 144; 2:43, 264.

136. Ibid., 2:163.

137. Perets Markish, *Izbrannoe* (Moscow: Sovetskii pisatel', 1957), 272; Ulanovskie, *Istoriia*, 9–22 and passim; Babel', *Sochineniia*, 1:127; Anatolii Rybakov, *Roman-vospominanie* (Moscow: Vagrius, 1997), 14.

138. Based on Katerina Clark's pioneering *The Soviet Novel: History as Ritual* (Chicago: University of Chicago Press, 1981).

139. A. Fadeev, *Razgrom* (Moscow: Ogiz, 1947), 49, 89, 169. Cf. A. Fadeev, *The Rout* (Moscow: Foreign Languages Publishing House, n.d.), 162.

140. Fadeev, *Razgrom*, 153, 42, 28, 6, 50.

141. Ibid., 152–54.

142. Ibid., 116, 128.

143. Iurii Libedinskii, *Izbrannye proizvedeniia*, vol. 1 (Moscow: Khudozhestvennaia literatura, 1980), 90–94, 103, 128, 145.

144. A. Tarasov-Rodionov, *Shokolad*, in *Sobachii pereulok: Detektivnye romany i povest'* (Moscow: Sovremennyi pisatel', 1993), 298–99; Vasilii Grossman, "Chetyre dnia,' in *Na evreiskie temy*, vol. 1 (Jerusalem: Biblioteka Aliia, 1985), 45, 47.

145. Bagritskii, *Stikhotvoreniia*, 91–108.

146. Fadeev, *Razgrom*, 154; Libedinskii, *Izbrannye proizvedeniia*, 1:95; M. D. Baital'skii, *Tetradi dlia vnukov*, Memorial Archive, f. 2, op. 1, d. 8, 24; for the English translation, see Mikhail Baitalsky, *Notebooks for the Grandchildren: Recollections of a Trotskyist Who Survived the Stalin Terror*, trans. Marilyn Vogt-Downey (Atlantic Highlands, N.J.: Humanities Press, 1995), 67; Grossman, "Chetyre dnia," 54; Vas. Grossman, *Vse techet* (Frankfurt: Posev, 1970), 154–55.

147. A. Arosev, *Zapiski Terentiia Zabytogo* (Berlin: Russkoe tvorchestvo, 1922), 101–2.

148. Ibid., 105.

149. Ibid., 103.

150. Bagritskii, *Stikhotvoreniia*, 167–71.

151. M. Gor'kii, L. Averbakh, S. Firin, eds., *Belomorsko-baltiiskii kanal imeni Stalina: Istoriia stroitel'stva 1931–1934* (Moscow: OGIZ, 1934).

152. This is based on Vladimir Papernyi's *Kul'tura Dva* (Moscow; NLO, 1996).

153. Ibid., 260; Arosev, *Zapiski*, 40; Il'ia Errenburg, *Zhizn' i gibel' Nikolaia Kurbova* (Moscow: Novaia Moskva, 1923), 173. For an analysis of both Arosev's *Zapiski* and Ehrenburg's *Zhizn' i gibel'*, see Mikhail Geller, *Kontsentratsionnyi mir i sovetskaia literatura* (London: Overseas Publications, 1974), 101.

154. Eduard Bagritskii, *Stikhotvoreniia i poemy* (Minsk: Nauka i tekhnika, 1983), 147–64.

155. St. Kuniaev, "Legenda i vremia," *Dvadtsat' dva*, no. 14 (September 1980): 149; Maxim D. Shrayer, *Russian Poet/Soviet Jew: The Legacy of Eduard Bagritskii* (Oxford: Rowman & Littlefield, 2000), 74, 88–90.

CHAPTER 4

HODL'S CHOICE: THE JEWS AND THREE PROMISED LANDS

1. Sholem Aleichem, *Tevye the Dairyman and the Railroad Stories*, trans. Hillel Halkin (New York: Schocken Books, 1987), 57, 69.

2. See Harshav, *Language in Time of Revolution*, 8–11.

3. Quoted in Sanders, *The Downtown Jews*, 415. See also Eli Lederhendler, *Jewish Responses to Modernity: New Voices in America and Eastern Europe* (New York: New York University Press, 1994), 121–27.

4. Bromberg, *Zapad, Rossiia i evreistvo*, 186, 190.

5. The Brenner quotation is from Ariel Hirschfeld, "Locus and Language: Hebrew Culture in Israel, 1890–1990," in *Cultures of the Jews: A New History*, ed. David Biale (New York: Schocken Books, 2002), 1019.

6. Rybakov, *Roman-vospominanie*, 13–14; Ester Markish, *Stol' dolgoe vozvrashchenie* (Tel Aviv: n.p., 1989), 25; Meromskaia-Kol'kova, *Nostal'giia? Net!* (Tel Aviv: Lim, 1988), 19–20; Roziner, *Serebrianaia tsepochka*, passim. I am grateful to Noemi Kitron for information about her father. The term "Stalin's Zion" is from Robert Weinberg, *Stalin's Forgotten Zion. Birobidzhan and the Making of a Soviet Jewish Homeland: An Illustrated History, 1928–1996* (Berkeley and Los Angeles: University of California Press, 1998).

7. Bromberg, *Zapad, Rossiia i evreistvo*, 181.

8. Author's italics. Quoted in Amos Elon, *The Israelis: Founders and Sons* (New York: Holt, Rinehart and Winston, 1971), 134–35.

9. The Ben-Gurion quotation is from Zeev Sternhell, *The Founding Myths of Israel: Nationalism, Socialism, and the Making of the Jewish State* (Princeton: Princeton University Press, 1998), 21.

10. See Elon, *The Israelis*, 116, and Oz Almog, *The Sabra: The Creation of the New Jew* (Berkeley and Los Angeles: University of California Press, 2000), 213, 238, and passim.

11. Abraham Cahan, *The Rise of David Levinsky* (New York: Harper and Row, 1966), 459.

12. Bromberg, *Zapad, Rossiia i evreistvo*, 184. See also Cassedy, *To the Other Shore*, 63–76, 109–27.

13. Alfred Kazin, *A Walker in the City* (New York: Harcourt, Brace and Company, 1951), 61–62. See also Steven J. Zipperstein, *Imagining Russian Jewry: Memory, History, Identity* (Seattle: University of Washington Press, 1999), 24–25.

14. Vladimir (Zeev) Zhabotinskii, *Piatero* (Odessa: Optimum, 2000); Walter Benjamin, *Selected Writings*, vol. 1 (Cambridge: Harvard University Press, Belknap Press, 1996), 252.

15. Roziner, *Serebrianaia tsepochka*, 189; Mikhail Agurskii, *Pepel Klaasa. Razryv* (Jerusalem: URA, 1996), 27.

16. Freitag, *Nächstes Jahr*, 44, 69–70, 83; Beizer, *Evrei Leningrada*, 81, 116, 360; Altshuler, *Soviet Jewry on the Eve of the Holocaust*, 225, 15 (the quotation is on 15).

17. Altshuler, *Soviet Jewry on the Eve of the Holocaust*, 34–35, 220, 225, 253.

18. Izi Kharik, *Mit layb un lebn* (Minsk, 1928), 19–20; see the German translation in Freitag, *Nächstes Jahr*, 6, and the Russian translation in Izi Kharik, *Stikhi i poemy* (Moscow: Sovetskii pisatel', 1958), 110.

19. Iu. Larin, *Evrei i anti-semitizm v SSSR* (Moscow and Leningrad: Gosizdat, 1929), 97–99; 121–22; Beizer, *Evrei Leningrada*, 95–99. See also Matthias Vetter, *Antisemiten und Bolschewiki. Zum Verhältnis von Sowjetsystem und Judenfeindschaft 1917–1939* (Berlin: Metropol Verlag, 1995), 98–100.

20. V. Kirshon and A. Uspenskii, "Koren'kovshchina (epizody iz p'esy)," *Molodaia gvardiia*, no. 10 (October 1926): 43. Cf. V. Kirshon and A. Uspenskii, *Konstantin Terekhin (Rzhavchina)* (Moscow: Gosizdat, 1927). Sergei Malashkin, *Luna s pravoi storony* (Riga: Literatura, 1928), 71; Boris Levin, *Iunosha* (Moscow: Sovetskii pisatel', 1987 [originally published in 1933]), 124–25, 131–32; Matvei Roizman, *Minus shest'* (Berlin: Kniga i stsena, 1931 [written in 1925–26]). For Soviet demonology in the 1920s, see Victoria E. Bonnell, *Iconography of Power: Soviet Political Posters under Lenin and Stalin* (Berkeley and Los Angeles; University of California Press, 1997), 207–11.

21. Feliks Chuev, *Molotov: Poluderzhavnyi vlastelin* (Moscow: Olma Press, 2000), 637; G. V. Kostyrchenko, *Tainaia politika Stalina: Vlast' i antisemitizm* (Moscow: Mezhdunarodnye otnosheniia, 2001), 109–10; Mikhail Shreider, *Vospominaniia chekista-operativnika*, Memorial Archive, f. 2, op. 2, d. 100, ll. 330–77. For statistical data, see A. I. Kokurin and N. V. Petrov, eds., *Lubianka: VChK-OGPU-NKVD-NKGB-MGB-MVD-KGB, 1917–1960, Spravochnik* (Moscow: Demokratiia, 1997), 12, 104; and N. V. Petrov, K. V. Skorkin, eds., *Kto rukovodil NKVD 1934–1941: Spravochnik* (Moscow; Zven'ia, 1999), 139–40, 459–60, 495.

22. V. G. Tan-Bogoraz, ed., *Evreiskoe mestechko v revoliutsii* (Moscow and Leningrad: Gosizdat, 1926), 25; E. Markish, *Stol' dolgoe vozvrashchenie*, 76–80; Baital'skii, *Tetradi dlia vnukov*, Memorial Archive, f. 2, op. 1, d. 8, l. 24, for the English translation, see Baitalsky, *Notebooks for the Grandchildren*, 67; Rybakov, *Roman-vospominanie*, 10; Agurskii, *Pepel Klaasa*, 24; Meromskaia-Kol'kova, *Nostal'giia*, 45.

23. Altshuler, *Soviet Jewry on the Eve of the Holocaust*, 104.

24. Ibid., 106–9; Beizer, *Evrei Leningrada*, 118.

25. Altshuler, *Soviet Jewry on the Eve of the Holocaust*, 118–27, 308.

26. Freitag, *Nächstes Jahr*, 114; Beizer, *Evrei Leningrada*, 88, 120.

27. Quoted in Kostyrchenko, *Tainaia politika*, 58.

28. Beizer, *Evrei Leningrada*, 121, 125; Freitag, *Nächstes Jahr*, 124.

29. Freitag, *Nächstes Jahr*, 129; Altshuler, *Soviet Jewry on the Eve of the Holocaust*, 308, 129, 313–14; Larin, *Evrei i anti-semitizm*, 109.

30. Yehoshua Yakhot, "Jews in Soviet Philosophy," in Miller, *Jews in Soviet Culture*, 216–17; *Pervyi vsesoiuznyi s"ezd sovetskikh pisatelei, 1934. Stenograficheskii otchet* (Moscow: Khudozhestvennaia literatura, 1934), 700–702; *Istoriia sovetskoi politicheskoi tsenzury: Dokumenty i kommentarii* (Moscow: Rosspen, 1997), 102; Joachim Braun, "Jews in Soviet Music,' in Miller, *Jews in Soviet Culture*, 75–86; Arkady Vaksberg, *Stalin against the Jews* (New York: Alfred A. Knopf, 1994), 69; Vadim Tepliskii, *Evrei v istorii shakhmat* (Tel Aviv: Interpresscenter, 1997), 81–85.

31. *Stroka, oborvannaia pulei: Moskovskie pisateli, pavshie na frontakh Otechestvennoi voiny* (Moscow: Moskovskii rabochii, 1976), 138–46; and the Slezkine family archive. See also *Golosa iz mira, kotorogo uzhe net: Vypuskniki istoricheskogo fakul'teta MGU 1941. V pis'makh i vospominaniiakh* (Moscow: MGU, 1995), 7. At least one-third of the MGU History Department's 1941 graduates killed in the war were Jewish.

32. Mikhail Svetlov, *Izbrannoe* (Moscow: Khudozhestvennaia literatura, 1988), 23–25, 115, 150; Aleksandr Bezymenskii, *Izbrannye proizvedeniia v dvukh tomakh*, vol. 1 (Moscow: Khudozhestvennaia literatura, 1989), 35, 53.

33. Lev Kopelev, *I sotvoril sebe kumira* (Ann Arbor: Ardis, 1978), 191–92. For the English translation (on which mine is based), see Lev Kopelev, *The Education of a True Believer*, trans. Gary Kern (New York: Harper and Row, 1978), 166.

34. Baital'skii, *Tetradi dlia vnukov*, Memorial Archive, f. 2, op. 1, d. 8, l. 49.

35. Ibid., l. 129; Svetlov, *Izbrannoe*, 72, 102.

36. Kopelev, *I sotvoril*, 257–58; Sheila Fitzpatrick, ed., *Cultural Revolution in Russia, 1928–1931* (Bloomington: Indiana University Press, 1978), esp. Fitzpatrick's "Cultural Revolution as Class War."

37. Meromskaia-Kol'kova, *Nostal'giia*, 47.

38. Orlova, *Vospominaniia*, 52–53; Inna Shikheeva-Gaister, *Semeinaia khronika vremen kul'ta lichnosti, 1925–1953* (Moscow: Nn'iudiamed, 1998), 5–6. The "House of Government" was a residential building created especially for members of the Soviet political elite.

39. Beizer, *Evrei Leningrada*, 123; Baital'skii, *Tetradi dlia vnukov*, Memorial Archive, f. 2, op. 1, d. 8, ll. 19, 50.

40. *Pravda*, June 3, 1935; Orlova, *Vospominaniia*, 75.

41. Orlova, *Vospominaniia*, 70. On the history of IFLI, see Iu. P. Sharapov, *Litsei v Sokol'nikakh* (Moscow: AIRO-XX, 1995).

42. David Samoilov, *Perebiraia nashi daty* (Moscow: Vagrius, 2000), 120, 141. The Kopelev quotation is from Sharapov, *Litsei*, 42.

43. Pavel Kogan, *Groza* (Moscow: Sovetskii pisatel', 1989), 98, 51, 120, 70, 74, 138.

44. Boris Slutskii, *Izbrannaia lirika* (Moscow: Molodaia gvardiia, 1965), 28.

45. Kopelev, *I sotvoril*, 81.

46. Samoilov, *Perebiraia*, 57–58.

47. Ibid., 55; Meromskaia-Kol'kova, *Nostal'giia*, 32–33. For the Germans and Jews as "mobilized diasporas" in Russia and the USSR, see Armstrong, "Mobilized and Prolarian Diasporas," 403–5; for pioneering work on the Jewish-Soviet elite, see Victor Zaslavsky and Robert J. Brym, *Soviet Jewish Emigration and Soviet Nationality Policy* (London: Macmillan, 1983), 82–85.

48. Meromskaia-Kol'kova, *Nostal'giia*, 50.

49. Ibid., 205; Orlova, *Vospominaniia*, 40.

50. Agurskii, *Pepel Klaasa*, 28–29.

51. Eugenia Semyonovna Ginzburg, *Journey into the Whirlwind*, trans. Paul Stevenson and Max Hayward (New York: Harcourt, Brace and World, 1967), 295. Cf. Evgeniia Ginzburg, *Krutoi marshrut*, vol. 1 (New York: Possev-USA, 1985), 300.

52. Vasily Grossman, *Life and Fate* (New York: Harper & Row, 1980), 83; Cf. Vasilii Grossman, *Zhizn' i sud'ba* (Moscow: Vagrius-Agraf, 1998), 53, 54–55, 62.

53. Gnedin, *Vykhod iz labirinta*, 84, 26.

54. Kopelev, *I sotvoril*, 129–30, 133, 150. Cf. Kopelev, *The Education*, 102–3, 106, 124.

55. V. Izmozik, "'Evreiskii vopros' v chastnoi perepiske sovetskikh grazhdan serediny 1920-kh gg.," *Vestnik Evreiskogo universiteta v Moskve*, no. 3 (7) (1994): 172, 177, 180.

56. Ibid., 167, 169, 173, 180; the Anisimov quotation is in I. L. Kyzlasova, *Istoriia otechestvennoi nauki ob iskusstve Vizantii i Drevnei Rusi, 1920–1930* (Moscow: Izdatel'stvo Akademii gornykh nauk, 2000), 238.

57. M. A. Bulgakov, *Rukopisi ne goriat* (Moscow: Shkola-press, 1996), 580–81, 584–85.

58. Quoted in Kostyrchenko, *Tainaia politika*, 106. see also N. Teptsov, "Monarkhiia pogibla, a antisemitizm ostalsia (dokumenty Informatsionnogo otdela OGPU 1920kh gg.," *Neizvestnaia Rossiia XX vek* 3 (1993): 324–58.

59. Izmozik, "Evreiskii vopros," 165–67; Kostyrchenko, *Tainaia politika*, 107–8.

60. Trotskii, *Moia zhizn'*, 2:61–63; Chuev, *Molotov*, 257; Molotov's request is in the State Archive of the Russian Federation (GARF), f. 5446, op. 82, d. 53, ll. 1–13.

61. Kirillova and Shepeleva, "Vy," 76–83; Abramova et al., *Mezhdu*, 7, 51–67.

62. V. I. Stalin, *Marksizm i natsional'nyi vopros* (Moscow: Politizdat, 1950), 163. On Soviet nationality policy, see Yuri Slezkine, "The USSR as a Communal Apartment, or How a Socialist State Promoted Ethnic Particularism," *Slavic Review* 53, no. 2 (Summer 1994): 414–52. For the most complete, archivally based treatment, see Terry Martin, *The Affirmative Action Empire: Nations and Nationalism in the Soviet Union, 1923–1939* (Ithaca: Cornell University Press, 2002).

63. On Jewish intermarriage and loss of Yiddish, see Altshuler, *Soviet Jewry on the Eve of the Holocaust*, 74–76; 91–92, 96, 268–70; Beizer, *Evrei Leningrada*, 84, 86, 128; Freitag, *Nächstes Jahr*, 102, 140, 248.

64. Larin, *Evrei i antisemitizm*, 169; the Kaganovich quotation is from Kostyrchenko, *Tainaia politika*, 113.

65. Kostyrchenko, *Tainaia politika*, 90–99, 111–22.

66. Beizer, *Evrei Leningrada*, 102–11; Kostyrchenko, *Tainaia politika*, 100–111; *Vlast' i khudozhestvennaia intelligentsiia: Dokumenty TsK RKP(b)—BKP(b), VChK-OGPU-NKVD o kul'turnoi politike, 1917–1953*, ed. Andrei Artizov and Oleg Naumov (Moscow: Demokratiia, 1999), 255–56; *Pravda*, May 24, 1935; Vaksberg, *Stalin against the Jews*, 73–77; A. Ia. Vyshinskii, *Sudebnye rechi* (Moscow: Iuridicheskoe izdatel'stvo, 1948), 232–33, 246–47, 253, 261, 277–81, 288–89.

67. V. Veshnev, ed., *Neodolennyi vrag: Sbornik khudozhestvennoi literatury protiv antisemitizma* (Moscow: Federatsiia, 1930), 14–15, 17–18.

68. Larin, *Evrei i antisemitizm*, 115, 31, 260, 262–63, 264, 265.

69. Quoted in L. Dymerskaia-Tsigelman, "Ob ideologicheskoi motivatsii razlichnykh pokolenii aktivistov evreiskogo dvizheniia v SSSR v 70-kh godakh," *Vestnik Evreiskogo universiteta v Moskve*, no. 1 (1994): 66. On anti-Semitism in the old Pale, see Amir Weiner, *Making Sense of War: The Second World War and the Fate of the Bolshevik Revolution* (Princeton: Princeton University Press, 2001), 273–74.

70. Izmozik, "Evreiskii vopros," 166; Svetlana Allilueva, *Dvadtsat' pisem k drugu* (Moscow: Zakharov, 2000), 34.

71. Kokurin and Petrov, *Lubianka*, 17–18, 105–6; Petrov and Skorkin, *Kto rukovodil NKVD*, passim; *Sistema ispravitel'no-trudovykh lagerei v SSSR, 1923–1960: Spravochnik* (Moscow: Zven'ia, 1998), 105; Pavel Sudoplatov, *Razvedka i Kreml': Zapiski nezhelatel'nogo svidetelia* (Moscow: Geia, 1997); Babel', *Sochineniia*, 1:128.

72. Meromskaia-Kol'kova, *Nostal'giia*, 43–44.

73. Shikheeva-Gaister, *Semeinaia khronika*, 28–29; the English translation (used here) is in Fitzpatrick and Slezkine, *In the Shadow of Revolution*, 378–79.

74. Ulanovskie, *Istoriia*, 93.

75. Ibid., 96, 111–12.

76. Godley, *Jewish Immigrant Entrepreneurship*, 22–23, 51–53, 56–59; Thomas Kessner, "The Selective Filter of Ethnicity: A Half Century of Immigrant Mobility," in *The Legacy of Jewish Migration: 1881 and Its Impact*, ed. David Berger (New York: Brooklyn College Press, distributed by Columbia University Press, 1983), 169–85.

77. Stephen Steinberg, *The Academic Melting Pot: Catholics and Jews in American Higher Education* (New York: McGraw Hill, 1974), 9, 13, 15.

78. Larin, *Evrei i antisemitizm*, 113; Steinberg, *The Academic Melting Pot*, 16–31; Jerome Karabel, "Status-Group Struggle, Organizational Interests, and the

Limits of Institutional Autonomy: The Transformation of Harvard, Yale, and Princeton, 1918–1940," *Theory and Society* 13, no. 1 (1984): 1–40.

79. Kessner, "The Selective Filter of Ethnicity," 177.

80. Meyer Liben, "CCNY—A Memoir," *Commentary* 40, no. 3 (September 1965): 65.

81. David A. Hollinger, *Science, Jews, and Secular Culture: Studies in Mid-Twentieth-Century American Intellectual History* (Princeton: Princeton University Press, 1996), 50; Joseph Freeman, *An American Testament: A Narrative of Rebels and Romantics* (New York: Farrar & Rinehart, 1936), 61, 246. For a broader American context and Freeman's place within it, see David A. Hollinger's "Ethnic Diversity, Cosmopolitanism, and the Emergence of American Liberal Intelligentsia," in *In the American Province: Studies in the History and Historiography of Ideas* (Baltimore: Johns Hopkins University Press, 1985), 56–73, esp. 62–64.

82. *An American Testament*, 160–61.

83. Isaac Rosenfeld, *An Age of Enormity: Life and Writing in the Forties and Fifties*, ed. Theodore Solotaroff (New York: World Publishing Company, 1962), 332–33; see also Alexander Bloom, *Prodigal Sons: The New York Intellectuals and Their World* (New York: Oxford University Press, 1986), 41.

84. Irving Howe, *Steady Work: Essays in the Politics of Democratic Radicalism, 1953–1966* (New York: Harcourt, Brace & World, 1966), 118; on the Ulanovskys' Jewish contacts, see esp. Ulanovskie, *Istoriia*, 108.

85. Bloom, *Prodigal Sons*, 48–49.

86. Isaac Babel, *The Complete Works of Isaac Babel*, ed. Nathalie Babel, trans. with notes by Peter Constantine (New York: W. W. Norton, 2002), 748. For the Russian original, see I. Babel', *Peterburg 1918*, ed. E. Sicher (Ann Arbor: Ardis, 1989), 209. Henry Roth, *Call it Sleep* (New York: Farrar, Straus and Giroux, 1991), 145.

87. Harshav, *Language in Time of Revolution*, 137, 144–45.

88. Quoted in Almog, *The Sabra*, 64–65.

89. Ibid., 56 and passim. The Ben-Gurion quotation is from Sternhell, *The Founding Myths of Israel*, 93. See also Uri Ben-Eliezer, *The Making of Israeli Militarism* (Bloomington: Indiana University Press, 1998). On the Soviet Union, see Véronique Garros, Natalia Korenevskaya, and Thomas Lahusen, eds., *Intimacy and Terror: Soviet Diaries of the 1930s* (New York: New Press, 1995); Jochen Hellbeck, ed., *Tagebuch aus Moskau, 1931–1939* (Munich: Deutscher Taschenbuch Verlag, 1996); Jochen Hellbeck, "Fashioning the Stalinist Soul: The Diary of Ivan Podlubnyi (1931–1939)," *Jahrbücher für Geschichte Osteuropas*, no. 3 (1996): 344–73; "Writing the Self in the Times of Terror: The 1937 Diary of Aleksandr Afinogenov,' in *Self and Story in Russian History*, ed. Laura Engelstein and Stephanie Sandler (Ithaca: Cornell University Press, 2000); Igal Halfin, *From Darkness to Light: Class, Consciousness, and Salvation in Revolutionary Russia* (Pittsburgh: University of Pittsburgh Press, 2000).

90. Quoted in Almog, *The Sabra*, 75.

91. J. Arch Getty and Oleg V. Naumov, eds., *The Road to Terror: Stalin and the Self-Destruction of the Bolsheviks, 1932–39* (New Haven: Yale University Press, 1999), 557–60.

92. Ibid., 561.

93. Ulanovskie, *Istoriia*, 128–29.

94. Babel', *Sochineniia*, 2:379–81.

95. Shikheeva-Gaister, *Semeinaia khronika*, 41–42; the English translation (used here) is in Fitzpatrick and Slezkine, *In the Shadow of Revolution*, 384.

96. Roziner, *Serebrianaia tsepochka*, 194.

97. Altshuler, *Soviet Jewry on the Eve of the Holocaust*, 26–27; Kostyrchenko, *Tainaia politika*, 132; Martin, *The Affirmative Action Empire*, 424–27, 432–61; Roziner, *Serebrianaia tsepochka*, 191–93; Weiner, *Making Sense of War*, 138–49.

98. Martin, *The Affirmative Action Empire*, 311–25, 337–39; Kostyrchenko, *Tainaia politika*, 132.

99. N. I. Rutberg and P. N. Pidevich, *Evrei i evreiskii vopros v literature sovetskogo perioda* (Moscow: Grant, 2000); John Bowlt, "From the Pale of Settlement to the Reconstruction of the World," in *Tradition and Revolution: The Jewish Renaissance in the Russian Avant-Garde Art 1912–1928*, ed. Ruth Apter-Gabriel (Jerusalem: Israel Museum, 1988), 43; Kostyrchenko, *Tainaia politika*, 137.

100. I. Stalin, *Works* (Moscow: Foreign Languages Publishing House, 1955), 13:40–41.

101. Artizov and Naumov, *Vlast' i khudozhestvenaia intelligentsiia*, 132–37, 333; Martin, *The Affirmative Action Empire*, 451–61; Kostyrchenko, *Tainaia politika*, 149–77; *Pravda*, February 1, 1936; *Pravda*, February 10, 1936; B. Volin, "Velikii russkii narod," *Bol'shevik*, no. 9 (1938): 32–38. See also I. Trainin, "Bratstvo narodov v sotsialisticheskom gosudarstve," *Bol'shevik*, no. 8 (1938): 32–46, and V. Kirpotin, "Russkaia kul'tura," *Bol'shevik*, no. 12 (1938): 47–63. For a comprehensive survey, see David Brandenberger, *National Bolshevism: Stalinist Mass Culture and the Formation of Modern Russian National Identity, 1931–1956* (Cambridge: Harvard University Press, 2002).

102. Kopelev, *I sotvoril*, 141, 143, 149. Cf. Kopelev, *The Education*, 114, 116, 122.

103. Slutskii, *Izbrannaia lirika*, 30.

104. Samoilov, *Perebiraia*, 188.

105. Ibid., 196, 202.

106. Ibid., 205.

107. Ibid., 204.

108. Margarita Aliger, "Tvoia pobeda," *Znamia*, no. 9 (1945): 1–28.

109. Kopelev, *I sotvoril*, 130; Martin, *The Affirmative Action Empire*, 449–51.

110. N. V. Petrov and A. B. Roginskii, " 'Pol'skaia operatsiia' NKVD 1937–1938 gg.," in *Repressii protiv poliakov i pol'skikh grazhdan* (Moscow: Zven'ia, 1997), 36.

111. Grossman, "Ukraina bez evreev," in *Na evreiskie temy*, 2:335.

112. Quoted in Nedava, *Trotsky and the Jews*, 11–12.

113. *Evreiskii antifashistskii komitet v SSSR, 1941–1948: Dokumentirovannaia istoriia* (Moscow: Mezhdunarodnye otnosheniia, 1996), 46.

114. Grossman, *Zhizn' i sud'ba*, 57, based on Grossman, *Life and Fate*, 86–87.

115. Grossman, *Zhizn' i sud'ba*, 62; Grossman, *Life and Fate*, 94. On the effect of World War II on Soviet ideology and collective identities, including Jewishness, see Weiner, *Making Sense of War*, esp. 207–8.

116. Grossman, "Ukraina bez evreev"; Weiner, *Making Sense of War*, 273–74, 191–93; the quotation is on 270.

117. Weiner, *Making Sense of War*, 209–27.

118. *Evreiskii antifashistskii*, 35–47. The translation is based on Shimon Redlich, ed., *War, Holocaust and Stalinism: A Documented Study of the Jewish Anti-Fascist Committee in the USSR* (Luxembourg: Harwood Academic Publishers, 1995), 173–83.

119. Kostyrchenko, *Tainaia politika*, 230–31; *Evreiskii antifashistskii*, 30–35, 56–61, 179.

120. Kostyrchenko, *Tainaia politika*, 236–42; *Evreiskii antifashistskii*, 184–236; Redlich, *War*, 73–93.

121. *Evreiskii antifashistskii*, 72; translation based on Redlich, *War*, 221.

122. *Evreiskii antifashistskii*, 102; cf. Redlich, *War*, 210.

123. *Evreiskii antifashistskii*, 113; cf. Redlich, *War*, 238. On universal and particular suffering in wartime Soviet Union, see Weiner, *Making Sense of War*, esp. 209–16.

124. *Evreiskii antifashistskii*, 114; cf. Redlich, *War*, 239.

125. *Evreiskii antifashistskii*, 93.

126. Ibid., 136–39; Kostyrchenko, *Tainaia politika*, 428–41.

127. Kostyrchenko, *Tainaia politika*, 429–30; Markish, *Stol' dolgoe vozvrashchenie*, 172; *Nepravednyi sud. Poslednii stalinskii rasstrel (stenogramma sudebnogo protsessa nad chlenami Evreiskogo antifashistskogo komiteta)* (Moscow: Nauka, 1994), 28.

128. *Evreiskii antifashistskii*, 284–85; cf. Redlich, *War*, 380.

129. *Evreiskii antifashistskii*, 283–87; cf. Redlich, *War*, 382–83.

130. *Evreiskii antifashistskii*, 290; Kostyrchenko, *Tainaia politika*, 405.

131. *Evreiskii antifashistskii*, 273, 294.

132. Ibid., 302; Kostyrchenko, *Tainaia politika*, 406–7, 413–14; *Sovetsko-izrail'skie otnosheniia: Sbornik dokumentov* (Moscow: Mezhdunarodnye otnosheniia, 2000), vol. 1, pt. 1, p. 400.

133. *Nepravednyi sud*, 33, 89.

134. Ibid., 147, 150.

135. Ibid., 23, 155, 30, 33, 111.

136. Kostyrchenko, *Tainaia politika*, 194–96, Chuev, *Molotov*, 332–33.

137. Kostyrchenko, *Tainaia politika*, 561–91, 598–600; G. Kostyrchenko, *V plenu u krasnogo faraona* (Moscow: Mezhdunarodnye otnosheniia, 1994), 242;

Ethan Pollock, "The Politics of Knowledge: Party Ideology and Soviet Science, 1945–1953" (Ph.D. diss., University of California, Berkeley, 2000), 400, 413.

138. Kostyrchenko, *Tainaia politika*, 243–71, 266, 521–53, 259–64; *Istoriia sovetskoi politicheskoi tsenzury*, 102.

139. Kostyrchenko, *Tainaia politika*, 533–34, 302, 329, 363.

140. Ibid., 603–26; L. L. Mininberg, *Sovetskie evrei v nauke i promyshlennosti SSSR v period Vtoroi mirovoi voiny, 1941–1945* (Moscow: Its-Garant, 1995).

141. Kostyrchenko, *Tainaia politika*, 572–88; Allilueva, *Dvadtsat' pisem*, 156–69.

142. Kostyrchenko, *Tainaia politika*, 460–61; Sudoplatov, *Razvedka i Kreml'*, 212, 255–56, 321–23, 329–35, 343–63, 464–66; Christopher Andrew and Oleg Gordievsky, *KGB: The Inside Story* (New York: Harper Perennial, 1991), 408–12, 418–19. For Soviet espionage in the United States, see John Earl Haynes and Harvey Klehr, *Venona: Decoding Soviet Espionage in America* (New Haven: Yale University Press, 1999); Allen Weinstein and Alexander Vassiliev, *The Haunted Wood: Soviet Espionage in America—the Stalin Era* (New York: Random House, 1999).

143. On Soviet dualism, see Stephen Kotkin, *Magnetic Mountain: Stalinism as Civilization* (Berkeley and Los Angeles: University of California Press, 1995), esp. 288–98; on the role of the war, see Weiner, *Making Sense of War*; on late Stalinist ideology and science, see Pollock, "Politics of Knowledge." The quotations are from I. V. Stalin, *Sochineniia* (Stanford: Hoover Instituion Press, 1967), vol. 3 (= 16), pp. 144, 146.

144. Getty and Naumov, *The Road to Terror*, 561; Kostyrchenko, *Tainaia politika*, 649 (italics in the original).

145. Kostyrchenko, *Tainaia politika*, 629–85.

146. Grossman, *Zhizn' i sud'ba*, 431.

147. According to the data collected by Gennady Kostyrchenko (unconfirmed by a detailed archival investigation because of the inaccessibility of many relevant files), the attack on "Jewish bourgeois nationalism" resulted in approximately five hundred arrests and about fifty executions. I am grateful to Professor Kostyrchenko for sharing his conclusions with me.

148. Kostyrchenko, *Tainaia politika*, 592.

149. Ibid., 264.

150. See, esp., Mordechai Altshuler, "More about Public Reaction to the Doctors' Plot," *Jews in Eastern Europe* 30, no. 2 (Fall 1996): 24–57; A. Lokshin, " 'Delo vrachei': 'Otkliki trudiashchikhsia,' " *Vestnik Evreiskogo universiteta v Moskve*, no. 1 (1994): 52–62; and Weiner, *Making Sense of War*, 290–97.

151. Markish, *Stol' dolgoe vozvrashchenie*, 69.

152. Sudoplatov, *Razvedka i Kreml'*, 41, 349–61, 470–71.

153. Ibid., 361; Kostyrchenko, *Tainaia politika*, 452; *Nepravednyi sud*, 267, 271–72.

154. *Nepravednyi sud*, 341, 142, 146–47, 150–51, 172, 176, 196, 368.

155. George Schöpflin, "Jewish Assimilation in Hungary: A Moot Point," in *Jewish Assimilation in Modern Times*, ed. Bela Vago (Boulder, Colo.: Westview Press, 1981), 80–81; Stephen Fischer-Galati, "The Radical Left and Assimilation: The Case of Romania," in Vago, *Jewish Assimilation*, 98–99; Schatz, *The Generation*, 181–85, 206–29; András Kovacs, "The Jewish Question in Contemporary Hungary," in *The Hungarian Holocaust: Forty Years After*, ed. Randolph L. Braham and Bela Vago (New York: Columbia University Press, 1985), 210–17. See also Jeffrey Herf, *East German Communists and the Jewish Question: The Case of Paul Merker* (Washington, D.C.: German Historical Institute, 1994).

156. Seymour Martin Lipset and Earl Raab, *Jews and the New American Scene* (Cambridge: Harvard University Press, 1995), 96; Hollinger, *Science, Jews, and Secular Culture*, 10.

157. Rubinstein, *The Left, the Right, and the Jews*, 57–58, 73; Peter Novick, *The Holocaust in American Life* (New York: Houghton-Mifflin, 1999), 94.

158. Philip Roth, *American Pastoral* (New York: Vintage Books, 1997), 4, 11, 318, 402.

159. Ibid., 213; Shikheeva-Gaister, *Semeinaia khronika*, 15–17; the English translation (used here) is in Fitzpatrick and Slezkine, *In the Shadow of Revolution*, 372.

160. Roth, *American Pastoral*, 3, 318.

161. See, esp., Nathan Glazer, *American Judaism* (Chicago: University of Chicago Press, 1989). On the creation of Superman, see Stephen J. Whitfield, "Declarations of Independence: American Jewish Culture in the Twentieth Century,' in Biale, *Cultures of the Jews*, 1109–10.

162. Steinberg, *The Academic Melting Pot*, 120–23; Hollinger, *Science, Jews, and Secular Culture*, 8–9.

163. On the Jewish contribution to American liberalism, see Hollinger, *In the American Province*, 66–70; the quotation is from Freeman, *An American Testament*, 246. See also Cassedy, *To the Other Shore*, 152–55; and Jacob Neusner, *American Judaism: Adventure in Modernity* (Englewood Cliffs, N.J.: Prentice-Hall, 1972), 65–68.

164. Andrew R. Heinze, "Jews and American Popular Psychology: Reconsidering the Protestant Paradigm of Popular Thought," *Journal of American History* 88, no. 3 (October 2001): 952; Mark Shechner, *After the Revolution: Studies in the Contemporary Jewish American Imagination* (Bloomington: Indiana University Press, 1987), 241. See also Nathan G. Hale, Jr., *The Rise and Crisis of Psychoanalysis in the United States: Freud and the Americans, 1917–1985* (New York: Oxford University Press, 1995); Ellen Herman, *The Romance of American Psychology: Political Culture in the Age of Experts* (Berkeley and Los Angeles: University of California Press, 1995), esp. 1–16; 238–75, and 304–15; Fuller Torrey, *Freudian Fraud: The Malignant Effect of Freud's Theory on American Thought and Culture* (New York: Harper Collins, 1992); John C. Burnham, "The Influence of Psychoanalysis upon American Culture," in *American Psychoanalysis: Origins and Devel-*

opment, ed. Jacques M. Quen and Eric T. Carlson (New York: Brunner/Mazel, 1978): 52–72; Donald H. Blocher, *The Evolution of Counseling Psychology* (New York: Springer, 2000).

165. Nikolas Rose, *Governing the Soul: The Shaping of the Private Self* (London: Free Association Books, 1999), 117 and passim, esp. 104–17, 159–60, 202, 228, 245–57; also Burnham, "The Influence," 65; and Hale, *The Rise and Crisis*, 276–99.

166. Vladimir Nabokov, *Pnin* (New York: Doubleday, 1957), 52; Jeffrey Berman, *The Talking Cure: Literary Representations of Psychoanalysis* (New York: New York University Press, 1985), 217; Torrey, *Freudian Fraud*, 201; Philip Rieff, *The Triumph of the Therapeutic: Uses of Faith after Freud* (New York: Harper and Row, 1966), 40.

167. Samuel, *The World of Sholom Aleichem*, 3, 6, 7.

168. Zborowski and Herzog, *Life Is with People*, 12.

169. Ibid., 13.

170. Ibid., 17.

171. Isaac Deutscher, *The Prophet Outcast; Trotsky 1929–1940* (London: Oxford University Press, 1977), 346–49, 366, 389–97, 405–10, 422; Andrew and Gordievsky, *KGB*, 157, 161, 165–66; Senate Subcommittee to Investigate the Administration of the Internal Security Laws of the Committee of the Judiciary, *Hearing on Scope of Soviet Activity in the United States*, 84th Cong., 2d sess., February 29, 1956, pt. 4, pp. 77–101, and February 8, 1956, pt. 1, pp. 103–36. See also ibid., 85th Cong., 1st sess., February 14 and 15, 1957, 3421–29; Haynes and Klehr, *Venona*, 252–58; Weinstein and Vassiliev, *The Haunted Wood*, 272–74.

172. Seth L. Wolitz, "The Americanization of Tevye or Boarding the Jewish 'Mayflower,' " *American Quarterly* 40, no. 4 (December 1988): 514–36.

173. Sholem Aleichem, *Tevye the Dairyman*, 130.

174. Ibid., 45, 52, 64, 130. Wolitz, "The Americanization," 516 and passim, esp. 526–27.

175. Aleksandr Bek, *Volokolamskoe shosse* (Moscow: Voenizdat, 1962), 8, 31, 94–105. For the novel's popularity (under the title *Panfilov's Men*), see Almog, *The Sabra*, 67, 128–30.

176. *Natsional'nyi sostav naseleniia SSSR (po itogam perepisi 1959 g.)* (Moscow, 1961), 14, 23; *Vysshee obrazovanie v SSSR: Statisticheskii sbornik* (Moscow: Gosstatizdat, 1961), 70; Mordechai Altshuler, *Soviet Jewry since the Second World War: Population and Social Structure* (New York: Greenwood Press, 1987), 176; Michael Paul Sacks, "Privilege and Prejudice: The Occupations of Jews in Russia in 1989," *Slavic Review* 57, no. 2 (Summer 1998): 247–66.

177. Sacks, "Privilege and Prejudice," 253–64.

178. S. V. Volkov, *Intellektual'nyi sloi v sovetskom obshchestve* (Moscow: Fond Razvitie, 1999), 30–31, 126–27. See, esp., Sheila Fitzpatrick, *Education and Social Mobility in the Soviet Union, 1921–1934* (Cambridge: Cambridge University Press,

1974), and Sheila Fitzpatrick, *The Cultural Front: Power and Culture in Revolutionary Russia* (Ithaca: Cornell University Press, 1992).

179. Andrei Sakharov, *Memoirs* (New York: Alfred A. Knopf, 1990), 194–95. For the original, see Andrei Sakharov, *Vospominaniia* (Moscow: Prava cheloveka, 1996), 1:270–71.

180. Volkov, *Intellektual'nyi sloi*, 50, 77–78, 104, 198; Zaslavsky and Brym, *Soviet Jewish Emigration*, 107.

181. Allilueva, *Dvadtsat' pisem*, 10.

182. V. P. Mishin, *Obshchestvennyi progress* (Gorky: Volgo-Viatskoe knizhnoe izdatel'stvo, 1970), 282–83; see also Altshuler, *Soviet Jewry since the Second World War*, 117; and Zaslavsky and Brym, *Soviet-Jewish Emigration*, 108.

183. Domal'skii, *Russkie evrei*, 88, 105; *Vysshee obrazovanie v SSSR* (Moscow: Gosstatizdat, 1961), 70; *Narodnoe obrazovanie, nauka, i kul'tura v SSSR* (Moscow: Statistika, 1971), 240; *Narodnoe khoziaistvo SSSR v 1970 g.* (Moscow: Statistika, 1971), 658.

184. Beizer, *Evrei Leningrada* (introduction by Nataliia Iukhneva), 7; V. Kaverin, *Epilog* (Moscow: Agraf, 1997), 46; T. I. Bondareva and Iu. B. Zhivtsov, "Iz"iatie . . . proizvesti bez ostavleniia kopii," *Otechestvennye arkhivy*, no. 3 (1992): 67; Weiner, *Making Sense of War*, 216–23.

185. Agurskii, *Pepel Klaasa*, 331.

186. On the anti-Semitism of the underemployed Soviet middle class, see and Zaslavsky and Brym, *Soviet-Jewish Emigration*, 106–7.

187. Agurskii, *Pepel Klaasa*, 337. The Semichastnyi report is in *Istoriia sovetskoi politicheskoi tsenzury*, 142–43.

188. Zaslavsky and Brym, *Soviet-Jewish Emigration*, 109.

189. Veblen, "The Intellectual Pre-eminence," 36, 39.

190. Golomstock, "Jews in Soviet Art," 53–63 (the quotation is on 63). See also Tumarkin Goodman, *Russian Jewish Artists*, esp. 35–38 and 91–93.

191. Agurskii, *Pepel Klaasa*, 57, 334; Ginzburg, *Journey into the Whirlwind*, 14–15.

192. Agurskii, *Pepel Klaasa*, 88, 407; Ulanovskie, *Istoriia odnoi sem'i*, 5.

193. Ulanovskie, *Istoriia odnoi sem'i*, 301–441, esp. 304–29 and 437–41. For the information about Mikhail Gefter's college days, I am grateful to his classmate M. S. Al'perovich, a distinguished Soviet historian. In his "Istorik v totalitarnom obshchestve (professional'no-biograficheskie zametki)," *Odissei* (1997): 251–74, Al'perovich describes the "case" of Shura Belen'kii, a student who refused to renounce his arrested father. When, during a visit to Moscow in the summer of 2001, I asked Al'perovich about the details of the case, he mentioned that the leader of those who hounded Belen'kii and demanded his expulsion from the Komsomol (and thus from the university) was M. Gefter, "a frenzied, fervent [*ogoltelyi, iaryi*] Komsomol activist, an orthodox unmasker of those who deviated from the Party line."

194. Agurskii, *Pepel Klaasa*, 219–20; 363–64. On Vainshtein, see Zvi Y. Gitel-man, *Jewish Nationality and Soviet Politics: The Jewish Sections of the CPSU, 1917–1930* (Princeton: Princeton University Press, 1972). On Slepian, see *"Drugoe iskus-stvo": Moskva 1956–76 v khronike khudozhestvennoi zhizni* (Moscow: Interbuk, 1991), 1:23–24, 54–55; 2:164.

195. When asked by a reporter whether, as a Moscow Komsomol member, he had "believed in the regime," Gefter responded in a way that would have made the Frankfurt School proud: "If one were to say yes, it would sound, if not like a direct reproach, then at the very least like an implication of something preposter-ous. Faith—in the regime? Can a prisoner believe in the bars of his cage? And if he does, is it because he is blind or because he is perversely welded to it in his soul and in his mind? Today I would call this a Kafkaesque situation. But the 'I' who comes back to me in the shape of memories of youth rejects today's words. What you call 'regime' is for him a *way of being*. A way of being that cannot help being better than the one that went before—than all those that went before. A way of being that will definitely be that way, and therefore is. An upside-down ladder: move downward, from the desired to what 'has been'! All around you are human beings, human needs and pleasures, but for you there is nothing but a prologue, or even the prologue of a prologue. Is this self-deception? Before I can agree, I will ask: Isn't there self-deception in any faith, any claim on truth (which is always unique)? If we take self-deception out of history, will there be any history left? The gap between epochs, the break between generations is equal to a lack of coinci-dence between words. Connections are to be found precisely in the realization of this lack of coincidence. Precisely there." Mikhail Gefter, *Ekho Kholokosta i russkii evreiskii vopros* (Moscow: Rossiiskaia biblioteka Kholokosta, 1995), 176.

196. Raisa Orlova, *Memoirs*, trans. Samuel Cioran (New York: Random House, 1983), 3, 7. For the original, see Orlova, *Vospominaniia*, 13, 17.

197. Aleksandra Brushtein, *Doroga ukhodit vdal'* (Moscow: Khudozhestven-naia literatura, 1965).

198. Rothman and Lichter, *Roots of Radicalism*, 81–82; Percy S. Cohen, *Jewish Radicals and Radical Jews* (London: Academic Press, 1980), 20–21; Feuer, *The Conflict of Generations*, 423; Liebman, *Jews and the Left*, 67–69.

199. Rothman and Lichter, *Roots of Radicalism*, 215–16.

200. Ibid., 216–17, 219.

201. Roth, *American Pastoral*, 255, 386.

202. Will Herberg, *Protestant, Catholic, Jew: An Essay in American Religious Sociology* (New York: Doubleday Anchor Books, 1960), 189–90. See also Glazer, *American Judaism*, 106–28; and Neusner, *American Judaism*, passim. The "grue-somely misbegotten" quotation is from Roth, *American Pastoral*, 412.

203. Elie Wiesel, "Trivializing the Holocaust: Semi-Fact and Semi-Fiction," *New York Times*, April 16, 1978, 2:1, 29. See also Novick, *The Holocaust in Ameri-can Life*, 211; and Tim Cole, *Selling the Holocaust: From Auschwitz to Schindler,*

How History Is Bought, Packaged, and Sold (New York: Routledge, 1999), 16 and passim.

204. B. Morozov, ed., *Evreiskaia emigratsiia v svete novykh dokumentov* (Tel Aviv: Ivrus, 1998), 7–43; Stefani Hoffman, "Jewish Samizdat and the Rise of Jewish National Consciousness," in *Jewish Culture and Identity in the Soviet Union*, ed. Yaacov Ro'i and Avi Becker (New York: New York University Press, 1991), 89–94.

205. Agurskii, *Pepel Klaasa*, 325–26; Markish, *Stol' dolgoe vozvrashchenie*, 338.

206. Agurskii, *Pepel Klaasa*, 243.

207. Ibid., 325–26. Markish, *Stol' dolgoe vozvrashchenie*, 339.

208. Markish, *Stol' dolgoe vozvrashchenie*, 341.

209. Morozov, *Evreiskaia emigratsiia*, 199.

210. Ibid., 199, 165–67. See also Yaacov Ro'i, "Soviet Policy towards Jewish Emigration: An Overview," in Lewin-Epstein et al., *Russian Jews on Three Continents*, 45–67.

211. Morozov, *Evreiskaia emigratsiia*, 95–96, 110, 200, 166–67.

212. J. J. Goldberg, *Jewish Power: Inside the American Jewish Establishment* (Reading, Mass.: Addison-Wesley, 1996), 174. See also 167–74.

213. Gitelman, "From a Northern Country," 25–26, 28–30; Morozov, *Evreiskaia emigratsiia*, 24; Yehuda Dominitz, "Israel's Immigration Policy and the Dropout Phenomenon," in Lewin-Epstein et al., *Russian Jews on Three Continents*, 113–27.

214. Meromskaia-Kol'kova, *Nostal'giia*, 8.

215. The term is Gennady Kostyrchenko's. See his *V plenu u krasnogo faraona* (Moscow: Mezhdunarodnye otnosheniia, 1994).

216. A. I. Solzhenitsyn, *Dvesti let vmeste*, vol. 2 (Moscow: Russkii put', 2002), 445, 468.

217. The latest 2002 census results are at http://www.gazeta.ru/2003/11/10/perepisj.shtml. See also Rozalina Ryvkina, *Evrei v postsovetskoi Rossii—kto oni? Sotsiologicheskii analiz problem sovetskogo evreistva* (Moscow: YPCC: 1996), 123–33; Lev Gudkov, "Antisemitizm v postsovetskoi Rossii," in *Neterpimost' v Rossii: starye i novye fobii*, ed. G. Vitkovskaia and A. Malashenko (Moscow: Tsentr Carnegi, 1999), 44–98; Mark Tolts, "The Interrelationship between Emigration and the Socio-Demographic Profile of Russian Jewry," in Lewin-Epstein et al., *Russian Jews on Three Continents*, 147–76; Mark Tolts, "Recent Jewish Emigration and Population Decline in Russia," *Jews in Eastern Europe* 1, no. 35 (Spring 1998): 5–24.

218. Gudkov, "Antisemitizm v postsovetskoi Rossii," 84; Ryvkina, *Evrei v postsovetskoi Rossii*, 68–78; Foster, "Ethnicity and Commerce," 441.

219. David Biale, *Power and Powerlessness in Jewish History* (New York: Schocken Books, 1986), 160. See also Novick, *The Holocaust in American Life*, 146–69; and Cole, *Selling the Holocaust*, 121–45 and passim.

220. Calvin Goldscheider, *Jewish Continuity and Change: Emerging Patterns in America* (Bloomington: Indiana University Press, 1986), 137; Kotkin, *Tribes*, 44, 55, 63, 274; Lipset and Raab, *Jews and the New American Scene*, 26; Whitfield, *American Space*, 7; Thomas Sewel, *Ethnic America: A History* (New York: Basic Books, 1981), 98.

221. Goldscheider, *Jewish Continuity and Change*, 110–18; Calvin Goldscheider, "Jobs, Education, and Careers: The Socioeconomic Transformation of American Jews," in *Changing Jewish Life: Service Delivery and Planning in the 1990s*, ed. Lawrence I. Sternberg et al. (New York: Greenwood Press, 1991), 7–8; Whitfield, *American Space*, 9; Rubinstein, *The Left, the Right, and the Jews*, 59–64; Charles Kadushin, *The American Intellectual Elite* (Boston: Little, Brown, and Company, 1974), 18–31.

222. Richard D. Alba and Gwen Moore, "Ethnicity in the American Elite," *American Sociological Review* 47, no. 3 (June 1982): 373–83; Charles E. Silberman, *A Certain People: American Jews and Their Lives Today* (New York: Summit, 1985), 152–55; Rothman and Lichter, *Roots of Radicalism*, 97–98; Goldberg, *Jewish Power*, 280, 291, 388 (the *Vanity Fair* quotation is on 280; the list of entrepreneurs is on 388); Rubinstein, *The Left, the Right, and the Jews*, 61; Whitfield, *American Space*, 133–36; Lipset and Raab, *Jews and the New American Scene*, 27.

223. Goldscheider, *Jewish Continuity and Change*, 112–14; Kotkin, *Tribes*, passim.

224. Benjamin Ginsberg, *The Fatal Embrace: Jews and the State* (Chicago: University of Chicago Press, 1993), 1, 103, 133–43; Alba and Moore, "Ethnicity in the American Elite," 377; Goldberg, *Jewish Power*, xxi; Ze'ev Chafets, *Members of the Tribe: On the Road in Jewish America* (New York: Bantam Books, 1988), 54; Stephen D. Isaacs, *Jews and American Politics* (New York: Doubleday, 1974), 1–42.

225. Novick, *The Holocaust in American Life*; Charles S. Liebman and Steven M. Cohen, *Two Worlds of Judaism: The Israeli and American Experiences* (New Haven: Yale University Press, 1990), 31–34.

226. Cuddihy, *Ordeal of Civility*, 212.

227. Joseph R. Levenson, "The Province, the Nation, and the World: The Problem of Chinese Identity," in *Approaches to Modern Chinese History*, ed. Albert Feuerwerker, Rhoads Murphey, and Mary C. Wright (Berkeley and Los Angeles: University of California Press, 1967), 278. On Jewish-American outmarriage, see *Harvard Encyclopedia of American Ethnic Groups* (Cambridge: Harvard University Press, Belknap Press, 1980), 596; and Lipset and Raab, *Jews and the New American Scene*, 72. For intermarriage in American history, see David A. Hollinger, "Amalgamation and Hypodescent: The Question of Ethnoracial Mixture in the History of the United States," *American Historical Review* 108, no. 5 (December 2003): 1363–90. The quotations are from Sholem Aleichem, *Tevye the Dairyman*, 80–81.

Index

06